The publisher gratefully acknowledges the generous support of the African American Studies Endowment Fund of the University of California Press Foundation, which was established by a major gift from the George Gund Foundation.

Incarcerating the Crisis

AMERICAN CROSSROADS

Edited by Earl Lewis, George Lipsitz, George Sánchez, Dana Takagi, Laura Briggs, and Nikhil Pal Singh

Incarcerating the Crisis

*Freedom Struggles and the Rise of the
Neoliberal State*

Jordan T. Camp

UNIVERSITY OF CALIFORNIA PRESS

University of California Press, one of the most
distinguished university presses in the United States,
enriches lives around the world by advancing scholarship
in the humanities, social sciences, and natural sciences. Its
activities are supported by the UC Press Foundation and by
philanthropic contributions from individuals and
institutions. For more information, visit www.ucpress.edu.

University of California Press
Oakland, California

Library of Congress Cataloging-in-Publication Data

Names: Camp, Jordan T., 1979- author.
  Title: Incarcerating the crisis : freedom struggles and
the rise of the neoliberal state / Jordan T. Camp.
  Description: Oakland, California : University of
California Press, [2016] | Includes bibliographical
references and index.
  Identifiers: LCCN 2015037551| ISBN 9780520281813
(cloth : alk. paper) | ISBN 0520281810 (cloth : alk.
paper) | ISBN 9780520281820 (pbk. : alk. paper) | ISBN
0520281829 (pbk. : alk. paper) | ISBN 9780520957688
(ebook) | ISBN 0520957687 (ebook)
  Subjects: LCSH: Protest movements—United States—
History. | Race riots—United States—History. | African
Americans—United States—Social conditions—
History. | Neoliberalism—Social aspects—United
States—History. | Social problems in mass
media. | Race relations in mass media. | United
States—Race relations—History.
  Classification: LCC HN57 .C33 2016 | DDC
303.48/40973—dc23
  LC record available at http://lccn.loc.gov/2015037551

Manufactured in the United States of America

25 24 23 22 21 20 19 18 17 16
10 9 8 7 6 5 4 3 2 1

In keeping with a commitment to support
environmentally responsible and sustainable printing
practices, UC Press has printed this book on Natures
Natural, a fiber that contains 30% post-consumer waste
and meets the minimum requirements of ANSI/NISO
Z39.48–1992 (R 1997) (*Permanence of Paper*).

For Christina Heatherton

The author gratefully acknowledges the permission to reprint the following song lyrics and articles: "What's Going On," words and music by Renaldo Benson, Alfred Cleveland, and Marvin Gaye, © 1970 (renewed 1998) JOBETE MUSIC CO., INC., MGIII MUSIC, NMG MUSIC, and FCG MUSIC. All rights controlled and administered by EMI APRIL MUSIC INC. on behalf of JOBETE MUSIC CO., INC., MGIII MUSIC, NMG MUSIC, and FCG MUSIC, and EMI BLACK-WOOD MUSIC INC. on behalf of STONE AGATE MUSIC (a division of JOBETE MUSIC CO., INC.). "Inner City Blues (Make Me Wanna Holler)," words and music by Marvin Gaye and James Nyx, © 1971 (renewed 1999) JOBETE MUSIC CO., INC. All rights controlled and administered by EMI APRIL MUSIC INC. All rights reserved international copyright secured used by permission. Reprinted by permission of Hal Leonard Corporation. All rights reserved international copyright secured used by permission. "If We Must Die": by Claude McKay. Courtesy of the Literary Estate for the Works of Claude McKay. Portions of chapter 2 previously appeared in Jordan T. Camp, "Challenging the Terms of Order: Representing the Detroit Rebellions, 1967–1968," *Kalfou* 2, no. 1 (2015): 161–80. Used by permission. Portions of chapter 5 appeared as Jordan T. Camp, "We Know This Place: Neoliberal Racial Regimes and the Katrina Circumstance," *American Quarterly* 61, no. 3 (2009), 693–717. Reprinted with permission by Johns Hopkins University Press. Portions of chapter 6 previously appeared as Jordan T. Camp, "Blues Geographies and the Security Turn: Interpreting the Housing Crisis in Los Angeles," *American Quarterly* 64, no. 3 (2012), 543–670. © 2012 the American Studies Association. Reprinted with permission by Johns Hopkins University Press.

Contents

Acknowledgments   *ix*

Introduction: An Old World Is Dying   *1*

1. The Explosion in Watts: The Second Reconstruction and
   the Cold War Roots of the Carceral State   *21*
2. Finally Got the News: Urban Insurgency,
   Counterinsurgency, and the Crisis of Hegemony in Detroit   *43*
3. The Sound Before the Fury: Attica, Racialized State
   Violence and the Neoliberal Turn   *68*
4. Reading the Writing on the Wall: The Los Angeles
   Uprising and the Carceral City   *98*
5. What's Going On? Moral Panics and Militarization in
   Post-Katrina New Orleans   *116*
6. Shut 'Em Down: Social Movements Confront Mass
   Homelessness and Mass Incarceration in Los Angeles   *134*

   Epilogue: The Poetry of the Future   *146*

Notes   *155*
Bibliography   *217*
Index   *255*

Acknowledgments

Incarcerating the Crisis was conceived as an intervention in the present conjuncture. In this endeavor I have been extraordinarily fortunate to learn from social movements opposing structural racism, neoliberal globalization, gentrification, and mass incarceration across the country with the support of friends and colleagues in these struggles. As this book has traveled with me across cities for many years, I apologize to everyone I have inevitably failed to name in this long-overdue thank you.

As the title of this book no doubt suggests, I owe a particular intellectual debt to the classic work of cultural studies *Policing the Crisis: Mugging, the State, and Law and Order* by Stuart Hall, Chas Critcher, Tony Jefferson, John Clarke, and Brian Roberts. Before he passed, Stuart Hall kindly agreed to meet with me, after allowing me send him a copy of the manuscript to review. His encouragement to intervene in the conjuncture has kept me writing ever since. I thank Catherine Hall for her kindness and for her help in tracking down the photo of Stuart speaking in London's Trafalgar Square that appears in the epilogue. Many thanks to Sut Jhally for putting me in touch.

Incarcerating the Crisis began as a dissertation at the University of California, Santa Barbara, with the dream-team committee of Avery Gordon, George Lipsitz, Cedric J. Robinson, and Clyde Woods. They taught me everything I know about the practice of engaged interdisciplinary scholarship. Avery's careful readings and thoughtful suggestions have been critical in formulating my interventions. I hope the book shows how much I learned from her. George always believed that the book was important and has read and commented on more drafts than almost anybody. His work and vision continue to inspire me. My conversations with Cedric about the racial regimes of U.S. capitalism gave me the confidence to develop the criticisms here without being afraid of the conclusions. I am proud to have worked with Clyde before his untimely death. Our discussions about culture, political economy, and the unfinished business of freedom struggles are reflected here. I will carry his memory forward with me into the future.

Robin D. G. Kelley's faith in this project has sustained me since the beginning. His advice, suggestions for revision, and generosity of time and spirit have transformed me and this book. I will always be grateful for the opportunity to be in dialogue with him. In his feedback, Paul Ortiz demonstrated a level of conviction, seriousness of purpose, and graciousness that I will strive my entire career to emulate. Nikhil Pal Singh read the manuscript and offered suggestions for revision that exemplify the scholarly rigor to which I aspire. Vijay Prashad pushed me to be bolder, sharper, and also more joyful in my writing. David Roediger has been an extremely generous interlocutor. The influence of his guidance should be clear throughout these pages. I owe an enormous debt to my friends and colleagues Ruth Wilson Gilmore and Craig Gilmore, who have been inspirations for almost a decade. Guided by Ruthie's brilliance, I have wrestled with Hall's injunction to think the concrete through successive levels of abstraction. I am also indebted to S. Ani Mukherji and John Munro for reading the entire manuscript and providing essential feedback.

Many people have shared their responses to my project, commenting on drafts of chapters and/or conference presentations, and provided suggestions as the book took shape. I am grateful to Sarah Banet-Weiser, Rachel Buff, Paula Chakravartty, Glen Coulthard, Angela Y. Davis, Mike Davis, Thulani Davis, Alan Eladio Gómez, Denise Ferreira da Silva, Treva Ellison, Kai M. Green, Cornelia Grabner, Gaye Theresa Johnson, Christina Hanhardt, David Harvey, Analena Hassberg, Cheryl Higashida, Rebecca N. Hill, Moon-Ho Jung, Marian Kramer, Tammy Bang Luu, Curtis Marez, Don Mitchell, Khalil Gibran Muhammad, Russell Rodríguez, Barbara Ransby,

Tasneem Siddiqui, Marvin Surkin, Daniel Widener, Emery Wright, and Craig Wilse. Adrian Cruz, Levon Chorbajian, and Charlotte Ryan offered warmth, friendship, and encouragement during my time in the Department of Sociology at the University of Massachusetts, Lowell. I am also indebted to my students at the University of California, Santa Barbara; California State University, Long Beach; the University of California, Los Angeles; the University of Massachusetts, Lowell; and Princeton University, from whom I have learned much.

In conducting the research for *Incarcerating the Crisis* I have received financial support from the University of California Humanities and Social Sciences Research Grant; the Humanities Research Institute at the University of California, Irvine; the Davis-Putter Scholarship; the Graduate Division as well as the Department of Sociology at the University of California, Santa Barbara; and the Schomburg Center for Research in Black Culture.

I was fortunate to teach in African American Studies and serve as a visiting scholar at the Institute of American Cultures and the Ralph J. Bunche Center for African American Studies at the University of California, Los Angeles, in 2012–13. I benefited from the support of Robin D. G. Kelley, Darnell Hunt, and Mark Sawyer, as well as Bunche Center staff members Veronica Benson, Jan Freeman, and Yolanda Jones. My deepest thanks to Sarah Haley. I treasured her insights as well as her kindness during my time there.

The Center for African American Studies at Princeton University in 2014–15 gave me crucial time and space to develop the book. The CAAS staff members Allison Bland, April Peters, and Dionne Worthy made my experience particularly enjoyable. Conversations with Naomi Murakawa, Eddie Glaude, Keeanga Yamahtta-Taylor, Josh Guild, Tera Hunter, Imani Perry, Kinohe Nishikawa, Courtney Bryan, Tanisha Ford, and others enhanced my thinking considerably. I am especially grateful to Naomi. She was extremely generous with her time and feedback, and in graciously organizing a manuscript workshop with herself, Nikhil Pal Singh, and Robin D. G. Kelley. It would be difficult to overstate how central their recommendations have been to the final project.

The Center for the Study of Race and Ethnicity in America (CSREA) and the Watson Institute for International and Public Affairs at Brown University have offered exceedingly generative spaces from which to think and learn. Many thanks to Tricia Rose, Anthony Bogues, Matt Guterl, Paget Henry, Catherine Lutz, Brian Meeks, Geri Augusto, Nicole Burrowes, Yalidy Matos, Adrienne Keene, participants in the CSREA fellows seminar, and staff members Caitlin Murphy and Christina Downs.

Incarcerating the Crisis is a better study because of the opportunities to present my research at the Center for Place, Culture and Politics at the City University of New York, Graduate Center; the Center for American Studies and Research at the American University of Beirut; the Department of History at the University of Wisconsin-Milwaukee; the Urbanscape Forum at the University of Rhode Island; the Institute for Humanities Research at UC Santa Cruz; the Law School at UCLA; the Cultural Studies Program at George Mason University; as well as the meetings of the American Studies Association, Association of American Geographers, American Comparative Literature Association, Critical Ethnic Studies, Historical Materialism, National Association for Chicana and Chicano Studies, Social Science History Association, and the Southern American Studies Association.

I have benefited a great deal from the labors of archivists, and would like to particularly thank Diana Lachatanere of the Schomburg Center for Research in Black Culture; Carrolyn Davis of the Walter Reuther Labor Archives at Wayne State University; Kate Donovan, Heather Mulliner, and Sarah Moazeni of the Tamiment Library at New York University; Claude Marks of the Freedom Archives in San Francisco; Yusef Omowale and Michele Welsing of the Southern California Library in Los Angeles; and Tim Noakes and Mattie Taormina of the Department of Special Collections and University Archives, Stanford University Libraries. Thanks also to staff at the following libraries: the Department of Special Collections and University Archives, W. E. B. Du Bois Library, University of Massachusetts, Amherst; the Bancroft Library, University of California, Berkeley; the UCLA Film and Television Archive; and the Brown University Library.

The alternative archive described herein was made possible through the generosity of people such as General Gordon Baker, Dennis Cunningham, Michael Deutsh, Elizabeth Fink, Paul Garon, Nancy Kurshan, Jack O'Dell, Esther Cooper Jackson, Nancy Kurshan, Sunni Patterson, Penelope Rosemont, José Ramírez, Jerome Scott, and Steve Whitman, who allowed me to interview them and also shared materials with me. I am grateful to Terrie Albano, Cinda Firestone, Peter Gessner, Builder Levy, Barbara Movius, and Ernest Savage for permissions to use images in the book, and to Shari Segel Goldberg, Ashley Hunt, and Karen Thorsen for helping me track down copyright owners. Many thanks to Paul Buhle for permission to use the graphic that appeared alongside "Black Editor: An Interview," *Radical America* 2, no. 4 (1968) as the cover image.

I would like to thank my colleagues in the School of Unlimited Learning (S.O.U.L.) collective at UC Santa Barbara, with whom some of the first formulations of my arguments were tested, in particular George Lipsitz, Clyde Woods, Tomás Avila-Carrasco, William A. Calvo-Quiros, Jonathan Gomez, Heidi Hoechst, Daniel Olmos, Steven Osuna, Russell Rodríguez, Damien Sojoyner, Barbara Tomlinson, Erica Williams, and other colleagues and friends too numerous to mention by name. Elizabeth Robinson was also an essential part of my intellectual and political training in allowing me to cohost the public affairs show *No Alibis* with her on KCSB 91.9 FM. I only hope that she and Cedric know how much they mean to me.

Conversations with Ujju Aggarwal, Eric Ares, James Braggs, Jayne Cortez, Jim Davis, Becky Dennison, General Dogon, Martín Espada, Jordan Flaherty, Diane Gamboa, Alyosha Goldstein, Shana Griffin, Gloria House, Andy Hsiao, Anjali Kamat, Cindi Katz, Peter Linebaugh, Alex Lubin, Lydia Pelot-Hobbs, Sunni Patterson, Laura Pulido, Jim Randels, Marcus Rediker, Rob Robinson, W. F. Santiago-Valles, Malcolm Suber, Kalamu ya Salaam, Eric Tang, Bill Quigley, Pete White, Ari Wohlfeiler, and Eddie Yuen made this a better and more interesting book. Many thanks to Betsy Esch for her wit and hospitality. I also thank my friend Candice Rice, who tragically passed away before I completed this study, for our conversations.

It has been a delight to work with the University of California Press and the American Crossroads Series. My editor, Niels Hooper, has been excited about the project from the outset and provided undimmed enthusiasm throughout. I am grateful to Bradley Depew and Francisco Reinking for the professional courtesies they have extended to me. Many thanks to Lindsey Westbrook for her careful copy edits and especially her patience. I would also like to thank Lisa Rivero for the index and Liza Cariaga-Lo and the Office of Institutional Diversity at Brown University for their support.

I owe a deep debt of gratitude to my father, Thomas, who has always offered his kindness, and I appreciate him to no end. Thanks to my mother, Bernay, and the rest of my family for their patience and understanding in my long absence during the writing of this book. I would also like to thank Linda Inouye for offering much-needed assistance and sweetness throughout the research and writing.

Special thanks to my comrade, colleague, best friend, and partner, Christina Heatherton, to whom this book is dedicated. There are no words to fully capture how much her love and support have meant to this book. Christina has read endless drafts, discussed its arguments, and endured my hectic and frantic way of working for the last seven years. Being the historian of social movements and advocate of social justice that she is, she gave me critical feedback that helped me tell the story with the fierce urgency that the present conjuncture demands, driven by a hope of a better future. I look forward to realizing it with her.

Introduction

An Old World Is Dying

The crisis consists precisely in the fact that the old is dying
and the new cannot be born; in this interregnum a great
variety of morbid symptoms appear.
—Antonio Gramsci, *Prison Notebooks*, 1971

An old world is dying, and a new one . . . announces that it is
ready to be born. This birth will not be easy, and many of us
are doomed to discover that we are exceedingly clumsy
midwives. No matter, so long as we accept that our responsibility is to the newborn: the acceptance of responsibility
contains the key to the necessarily evolving skill.
—James Baldwin, *No Name in the Street*, 1972

In the epilogue to his memoir *No Name in the Street* (1972), James
Baldwin explained that the old regime in the United States was dying.
Baldwin was compelled to intervene as he witnessed the most intensive
cycle of struggle in the postwar era. Large-scale protests circulated
through city streets, campuses, prisons, factories, and fields across the
country. The expanding geography of the 1960s urban insurrections
amid growing resistance to the U.S. war in Vietnam focused increased
attention on the material conditions of the poor, working class, and
people of color both at home and abroad.[1] These cycles of rebellion
articulated demands for dignity and freedom among aggrieved and
insurgent people who had been displaced and dispossessed by joblessness, housing segregation, militarism, and aggressive policing throughout the postwar era. In historical terms, the events represented an

"organic crisis" for U.S. Jim Crow capitalism, which is a deep legitimacy crisis of the regime. A keen observer of these transformations, Baldwin identified the crisis as "part of a global, historical crisis"—one that was not "likely to resolve itself soon."[2]

Baldwin's analysis echoed the insights that the Italian Marxist theorist Antonio Gramsci described in his *Prison Notebooks,* first published in English in 1971. Whereas Gramsci had grappled with the ascendancy of an "exceptional state" during his incarceration by the fascist Italian state in the 1920s and 1930s, Baldwin took stock of the morbid symptoms in U.S. political culture during the 1960s and 1970s. The freedom movement had entered a new historical conjuncture, and, as Baldwin puts it, an understanding of the specificity of the moment was the key to developing the "skills" required to intervene. As his observations suggest, there was no single vision of class struggle that had cohered among the social movements of the period, but rather fractions and missteps that come with being "clumsy midwives." The necessary *evolving skill,* he argued, was linked to the political and ideological struggle over the interpretation of the long civil rights movement.[3]

Baldwin's *No Name in the Street* depicted the dialectical process through which struggles against U.S. racial capitalism had been represented in terms of rebellion, security, and, as he described, "the forces of law and order." He wrote, "White people seem affronted by the black distrust of the white policeman, and appear astonished that a black man, woman, or child can have any reason to fear a white cop . . . for the police are honorable and the courts are just." He added that "Americans are very carefully and deliberately conditioned to believe this fantasy: by their politicians, by the news they get and the way they read it, by the movies and the television screen, and by every aspect of popular culture." With these words, Baldwin extended the critique of the relationships between racial ordering, popular culture, and U.S. policing and prisons expressed during the Second Reconstruction.[4]

Baldwin vividly articulated the importance of what the cultural theorist and radical intellectual Stuart Hall called the "politics of signification": the political struggle in ideology and expressive culture over the meaning of events and material conditions. He saw that the racist ideology of the ruling historical bloc, an alliance between dominant class forces and sectors of the subaltern strata to maintain control over the political economy, had worn thin. He keenly depicted how the grammar of racial and class formation was shifting—a transition that would cruelly shape the decades to come. In doing so he signaled a turning point in U.S. history. In this moment of hegemonic crisis, Baldwin's poetic political interventions called up an alternative archive, one that has important implications for the future of scholarship on the rise of the neoliberal state.[5]

No one could have predicted how prophetic Baldwin's analysis would remain almost a half-century later. In the last four and a half decades millions of industrial working-class jobs were lost due to capital flight and deindustrialization—transformations that have had devastating impacts on workers, particularly in industries such as auto, rubber, and steel. Unemployment rates have skyrocketed for all workers, especially Black workers.[6] Growing numbers of young poor and working people have joined the ranks of an expanding population rendered surplus by global capitalism. Structural unemployment, concentrated urban poverty, and mass homelessness have accordingly become permanent features of the political economy. Finally, in what is perhaps the most dramatic transformation marking this period, the prison populations have exploded. This book traces the fundamental changes in the social formation wrought by capital and the state's response to the organic crisis of Jim Crow capitalism. *Incarcerating the Crisis* uses a historical materialist methodology to delineate the origins and development of the neoliberal carceral state. In this way it demonstrates how the transition to neoliberalism has led to extreme polarizations of wealth, an expanding planet of slums, and the formation of the largest carceral state on the planet.[7]

The carceral population grew from two hundred thousand people in the late 1960s to more than 2.4 million people in the 2000s. Currently, one in thirty-five, or 6.9 million adults in the United States, are in jail or prison, or on parole or probation. Increased spending on incarceration has occurred alongside the reduction of expenditures for public education, transportation, health care, and public-sector employment. Prison expansion has coincided with a shift in the racial composition of prisoners from majority white to almost 70 percent people of color. The unemployed, underemployed, and never-employed Black and Latino poor have been incarcerated at disproportionate rates. With the highest rate of incarceration on the planet, the United States currently incarcerates Black people at rates higher than South Africa did before the end of apartheid.[8] All of these numbers bespeak a collision of race, class, and carceral state power without historical precedent, but certainly not without historical explanation.[9]

Incarcerating the Crisis traces the roots of today's explosive carceral crisis to a series of turning points in U.S. history, including the Watts insurrection in 1965, the Detroit rebellion in 1967, the Attica uprising in 1971, the Los Angeles revolt in 1992, and post-Katrina New Orleans in 2005. The names of the places in the study already reveal the intensity of the struggle in language over the memory and meaning of the dramatic events: Watts, Detroit, Attica, Marion, South Central, Ninth Ward. They call up images of social conflicts in sites where some of the most turbulent events in contemporary U.S. history have taken place. As such they provide a unique optic for analyzing the structure of social relations, which is otherwise difficult to observe. By reading the dominant narratives of these events against the grain we can better understand how racialization has provided the "cement" to repair ruptures in the social formation.[10]

Rather than tracing a single city, state, or national policy, this book examines critical moments in the process through which class anxieties became translated into what I call "neoliberal racial and security regimes."[11] By neoliberal racial and security regimes I mean the modalities of relationships among racialized spaces of uneven capitalist development, mass criminalization, and securitization in cities during this precise historical moment. In this way, my book provides a materialist analysis of the role of racialization in the formation of the neoliberal carceral state. Such an analysis is urgent, as this regime has become so powerful, it appears to have no history at all.[12]

This book traces the erasure of this history by foregrounding the problem of racist ideology. In particular, it explores how racialization legitimated the counterinsurgent doctrine restricting the function of the state primarily to the enforcement of order. Correspondingly, it delineates how the insurgent demands of Black freedom and labor movements for dignity, freedom, and the redistribution of social wealth have been conversely characterized as *dis*order.[13] In this way, it traces the role of domestic counterinsurgency in the hegemonic strategy of racialized crisis management. It describes the half-century-long neoliberal political project to refuse the social wage (public housing, education, health care, employment, and other essential social programs), and violently enforce consent to this refusal. It argues that this reaction to the crisis of hegemony has enabled the most dramatic expansion of prison budgets and carceral populations in U.S. and world history.[14]

Incarcerating the Crisis asks the following research questions about these dynamics: What has been the relationship between racial regimes, capitalist restructuring, and mass antiracist and class struggle? How have carceral reactions to social and economic crisis been legitimated during the neoliberal turn? How have artists, activists, and organic intellectuals connected to social movements resisted and altered dominant narratives of events? What kind of ethical and political alternatives might be possible when conceived from the perspectives articulated in the expressive culture of radical antiracist social movements? Can an alternative political force capable of dismantling the neoliberal carceral state be constructed in the current conjuncture?

Neoliberal political and economic restructuring is inconceivable outside of the context of mass antiracist and class struggles. Insurgency has served as the antithesis for the neoliberal state and the excuse for mass incarceration from its inception. I argue that the increasing geographical scale of civil rights insurgency and mass protest against Jim Crow racial regimes in the postwar period led to the expansion of mass arrest, confinement, and incarceration in the governance of U.S. capitalism. In sharp contrast to the dominant ideology—which has depicted mass criminalization as an inevitable reaction to criminality or threats to public safety and national security—the book shows that the racialization of groups deemed enemies of the U.S. state has been essential to the legitimation of neoliberal state formation. Fears and class anxieties produced by capitalist restructuring were transformed into racist consent to security, law, and order. These purportedly color-blind discourses simultaneously disavowed racism and sustained and naturalized unprecedented prison expansion during the emergence of neoliberal capitalism.[15]

To make this case, I deploy a historical materialist methodology and theoretical framework to counter the customary narration of the relationship between race and class, the carceral state, and capitalist political economy. I illustrate that the dramatic expansion of prisons in the last four decades should not be understood as merely a "deadly symbiosis" or even "the new Jim Crow." Rather I demonstrate that prison expansion in this period has been the political expression of neoliberal racial and security regimes. Such regimes, I argue, are the outgrowth of a long counterinsurgency against the Black freedom, labor, and socialist alliance that took shape in the struggle to abolish Jim Crow racial regimes.[16] I chart the move toward counterinsurgency as a strategic response to a crisis of legitimacy, wherein freedom struggles gained more significant moral and ethical legitimacy than the forces of Jim Crow capitalism. The long civil rights movement against Jim Crow racial regimes represented a crisis of legitimacy for U.S. capital and the state. The subsequent struggle for "hearts and minds" advanced a political and ideological effort to defeat the long civil rights movement. In other words, capital and the state responded to struggles from below with mass criminalization. I trace how the legitimacy for this political project was secured through common-sense conceptions and policies of payback. My book offers this periodization in order to illuminate the counterinsurgent policies at the root of the prison boom in the United States in the last forty years.[17]

Incarcerating the Crisis offers an intervention in both historical methodology and social theory. Following from Baldwin's injunction, its goal is to advance a critical historical understanding of mass criminalization in the age of neoliberalism as well as contribute to the *necessarily evolving* skill of analyzing the present moment. In foregrounding the dialectic between the long civil rights movement and the counterinsurgent response to it in my analysis, I provide a counternarrative to Loïc Wacquant's story of an inexorable path from plantation to prison.[18] After all, Wacquant does not consider "efforts to resist, divest, or divert the imprint of the penal state from below" as essential for analyzing neoliberal forms of incarceration. In his estimation, struggles from below "have been variegated if remarkably ineffectual." Indeed, he claims that the "primary targets of penalization in the post-Fordist era . . . the precarious fractions of the proletariat concentrated in the tainted districts of dereliction . . . squeezed by the urgent press of day-to-day subsistence, have little capacity or care to contest" racism and class rule. Even where resistance has occurred among the deindustrialized proletariat, in Wacquant's analysis, it has not substantively impacted neoliberal state formation. We should be wary of conclusions too easily drawn.[19]

My book criticizes the implications of Wacquant's approach, which relies on an inconsistent explanatory framework. The rejection of struggles from below in Wacquant's efforts to develop a sociology of neoliberal incarceration prevents his framework from grappling with dramatic turning points in the history of the regime, and gives credence to a dominant narrative that purports that the civil rights movement collapsed with the urban uprisings of the 1960s. He suggests that the prison boom resulted from the "retraction of the social wing and gargantuan enlargement of the penal clutch of the state in America after the peaking of the Civil Rights movement." He argues that the rise of the "penal state" has enabled the "containment and disciplinary supervision of the problem populations dwelling at the margins of the class and cultural order." He claims that contemporary *"hyper*incarceration," as he calls it, should be read as a response to what he represents as so-called "race riots," which "shook the ghettos of its big cities and marked the closing of the Civil Rights revolution."[20] His backlash narrative of carceral state formation neglects the ways in which law and order politics sought to contain freedom struggles throughout the era of Cold War racial liberalism. It also relies on a periodization of the freedom movement that has been adamantly contested.[21]

As the work of Marie Gottschalk and Naomi Murakawa shows, the making of the postwar carceral state was as much a product of civil rights struggles over policing and law and order in the 1940s and 1950s as it was a response to the prison rebellions of the 1960s and economic crisis of the 1970s. Furthermore, historians of the long civil rights movement demonstrate how declensionist narratives prevent us from understanding the long fetch of one of the most dynamic social movements in U.S. and world history. While the standard historiography and sociology of the civil rights movement begins with the Brown v. Board of Education decision in 1954 and terminates with the civil rights legislation in 1965, or the urban rebellions, antiwar activism, and Black Power insurgencies that took shape in 1967 and 1968, *Incarcerating the Crisis* takes up a longer periodization. It follows the lead of activists, artists, and scholars who trace the roots of the long civil rights movement to the radical political cultures of the 1930s. It further resists narrating the freedom agenda as resolved by identifying the new political struggles that only were emergent in the late 1960s. As such, it contributes a re-periodization of the freedom movement that takes the events of the 1960s as a kind of turning point, rather than a denouement.[22]

The premature resolution of the freedom movement has become a consistent feature of a "post-civil rights era" narrative. Forms of social protest taken up by aggrieved and insurgent communities against police violence and mass criminalization simply do not fit the dominant sociological models for analyzing social movements. As Pamela Oliver explains, this theoretical problem is due to a rigid distinction between political activity considered legitimate and forms of dissent defined as disorderly. Even those focusing on the criminalization of street protests rarely connect it to the everyday and routine policing, surveillance, and criminalization of the racialized poor. The stakes in this intellectual and political debate are urgent. As this book describes, the poor and working-class people of color have resisted the imposition of the neoliberal state from below. Their efforts have had global significance. When these protests are obscured, the state's attempts to crush radical social movements are aided and abetted. In other words, the historically specific form of racist social control coincident with the emergence of neoliberal capitalism maintains its hegemony through the misrepresentation of social protest against it.[23]

As part of an effort to contribute to these debates, this book interrogates presiding paradigms and frameworks for understanding the problem of mass incarceration, in particular the analogy of the "new Jim Crow." Michelle Alexander's work has undoubtedly elevated public consciousness and informed public debate in an unparalleled and resonant way. In making her case through the analogy of a new Jim Crow, however, she unwittingly reproduces many of the theoretical problems of her contemporaries. Alexander traces the roots of mass incarceration to the racial politics of "conservatives in the 1970s and 1980s [who] sought to appeal to the racial biases and economic vulnerabilities of poor and working-class whites through racially coded rhetoric on crime and welfare." In doing so, Alexander locates the origins of the new Jim Crow in the promotion of the drug war by Nixon- and Reagan-era conservatives, highlighting its racially disproportionate impact on African American communities in particular. Yet, Alexander concludes, "there are important differences between mass incarceration and Jim Crow." After all, she writes, "saying that mass incarceration is the new Jim Crow can leave a misimpression. . . . Each system of control has been unique—well adapted to the circumstances to its time." While the focus on the pervasive persistence of racism through mass incarceration in a purportedly color-blind post–civil rights era is a welcome and important correction, the new Jim Crow analogy falls short as a theory of the historically specific articulation of racialization and criminalization in the present moment, as Alexander herself admits.[24]

To be sure conservative politicians have legitimated the criminalization of the Black and Latino poor through a war on drugs and crime. However, this explanation only scratches the surface of the problem. As Gottschalk's research reveals, even if every single prisoner locked up for drug crimes were released, the United States would still be the largest carceral state on the planet. This book argues that the neoliberal carceral state emerged from a bipartisan consensus forged during the Cold War about the necessity of prioritizing security—a consensus that has justified the withdrawal of the social wage and created an increasingly central role for military action, national security policies, aggressive policing, and mass prison-building programs in the counter-insurgency governance of neoliberal racial capitalism. This intervention is at the core of *Incarcerating the Crisis*. It demonstrates how racial and security regimes with roots in the early Cold War and the counterinsurgency mobilizations during the age of the civil rights movement took shape in the current neoliberal moment.[25] It explores how this transformation of the state form was legitimated in response to the organic crisis of U.S. Jim Crow capitalism, a transition that represented a rupture in a "total way of life" characterized by Fordism's purportedly high wages, mass production, industrial factories, assembly lines, bureaucratized unions, and mass-based popular culture. In this way my study concurs with the general consensus in the social sciences that the crisis of Fordism in the 1970s represented a decisive turning point in the history of capitalism. At the same time it also illuminates the neglected political and ideological dimensions in theorizing how capital and the state's response to the crisis produced a new historical moment.[26]

The ascendance of neoliberal regimes of militarized policing and mass incarceration has seemingly borne a "stamp of legitimacy." In other words, the making of the carceral state has been accompanied by the production of a racist and revanchist common sense that naturalizes its functions. I am using the concept of revanchism as the geographer Neil Smith did to describe how political reaction has combined capital's restructuring of urban space with the coercive expansion of carceral state power. The concept accounts for the ways in which ongoing struggles for justice contest the terms of law and order imposed by the neoliberal state. The term—which literally means "revenge"—was originally deployed to describe the crushing of the Paris Commune in 1871. It captures the ways in which a vengeful bourgeoisie exploited populism and nationalism in order to legitimate the restoration of state power in the face of proletarian revolt. It helped mobilize a spirit of revenge against insurgents who were represented as enemies of the nation.[27]

This revanchist spirit was revived during the counterinsurgency against the long civil rights movement. "Expressed in the physical, legal and rhetorical campaigns against scapegoats, identified in terms of class, race, gender, nationality, [and] sexual preference," Smith writes, "this reaction scripts everyday life, political administration, and media representations of the contemporary U.S. city with increasing intensity." Indeed, revanchism is reproduced through the common-sense notions of race, class, gender, and sexuality underpinning neoliberalization, and through the depiction of labor, civil rights, feminist, and socialist movements as the enemies of the nation.[28] This vendetta has prevented the long civil rights movement from realizing its most radical visions. It has thwarted the class anger unleashed by capital's abandonment of the social wage in U.S. cities through moral panics about race and crime. It has done so by defining the behavior of the purported "underclass" as a source of violence and disorder, and policing and prisons as the solution to these social problems. These revanchist definitions of the situation have justified mass criminalization in the context of deepening social inequality, rising unemployment, and declining real wages. Critical to revanchism are dominant representations of the civil rights movement as the force that created the conditions for underclass criminality and violence. Tracing this common sense allows us to understand how the expansion of policing and prisons has become a taken-for-granted feature of life under neoliberal racial capitalism.[29]

The theory of revanchism offers a more robust dialectical analysis of the rise of mass incarceration than the backlash thesis. As hegemonic racial narratives wore thin amid the organic crisis of Jim Crow capitalism, common-sense narratives of security located the source of social problems in the culture and behavior of the racialized urban poor. While these narratives have been deployed in response to specific events and within concrete historical geographies, persistent patterns have emerged, ones that help us understand the role of racialization in sustaining mass criminalization in the age of neoliberal globalization.[30] As the geographer, political economist, and anti-prison activist Ruth Wilson Gilmore has shown, the formation of the neoliberal state can be read as an organized "geographical solution to political economic crisis," a crisis that had been unleashed by the shifting geography of racial capitalism. Prison expansion enabled the construction of a new state form in one of the largest economies on the planet. The prison population increased dramatically along with a disproportionate percentage of prisoners of color because, as Gilmore illustrates, global capitalism rendered the labor of deindustrialized sectors of the urban working class—disproportionately Black and Latino workers—redundant in the political economy at the very moment that radical antiracist and anticapitalist social movements were crushed. Thus, the superstructure of the neoliberal carceral state has its roots in the "antagonism between insurgents and counterinsurgents." In turn, a historically and geographically specific articulation of racism has provided the justification for the pervasive persistence of structural unemployment, militarized policing, and massive prison construction—and thus should be understood as the "production and exploitation of group-differenti-ated vulnerability to premature death."[31]

The persistent refrain of neoliberals has been to disavow the fatal link between racism, capitalist restructuring, and mass imprisonment. This dominant historical bloc has coalesced around an antistatist ideol-ogy that represents public housing, health care, transportation, environ-mental protection, job training and provision, and education as bureaucratic restrictions on the putative freedoms provided by capital-ist markets and entrepreneurism.[32] The increasingly authoritarian char-acter of the state formation has contradicted neoliberal discourses of freedom. Thus, the neoliberal state has deployed extensive coercive measures to ensure consent. "Faced with social movements that seek collective interventions," the Marxist geographer David Harvey writes, "the neoliberal state is itself forced to intervene, sometimes repressively, thus denying the very freedoms it is supposed to uphold." Indeed, I argue that the purportedly color-blind rhetoric of security, law, and order has been effective in winning consent to the neoliberal state's deployment of carceral resolutions of crises of hegemony.[33]

Incarcerating the Crisis analyzes a series of linked events to illustrate how ostensibly "exceptional" forms of racist social control have become the rule under neoliberal capitalism. It shows how the early Cold War's countersubversive demonology was rearticulated as a counterinsurgent discourse about the rule of law. This demonization of the "domestic enemy" has underpinned mass criminalization.[34] To make this case, this book takes seriously the insights of Black freedom movement intellectu-als such as W. E. B. Du Bois, Paul Robeson, Martin Luther King Jr., James Baldwin, Angela Y. Davis, and June Jordan, and deliberately draws on the alternative archive they have produced. It illustrates how these figures creatively experimented with cultural productions ranging from newspapers to magazines to music to articulate distinct counter-narratives.[35] It foregrounds the dialectical struggle between the rhetoric of counterinsurgency and the poetics of resistance to demonstrate how they challenged mass criminalization. Their interventions can help us grasp the historically and geographically specific relationships between race and class, the carceral state, and the political economy of capital-ism. Indeed, I argue, the radical political visions of the long civil rights movement have articulated a viable alternative to the grim neoliberal-ism that has depopulated, deindustrialized, and devastated U.S. cities.[36]

Incarcerating the Crisis explores how the cultural productions of the long civil rights movement have altered "metaleptic" definitions of events—that is, definitions that assume that social conflicts could not have had different outcomes. In this way, it illustrates how expressive culture has been essential to the articulation of social visions that have been incompatible with counterinsurgent solutions to crisis.[37] These works of expressive culture consistently help us better understand how authoritarian politics and austerity economics have come to be taken for granted in the neoliberal period. They provide an alternative archive of the memories, hopes, and social visions of the long civil rights era. The story of this insurgency and the wide circulation of its visions suggest that the making of the neoliberal carceral state was not inevitable, and that alternative outcomes have been and continue to be possible.[38]

RACISM, REVANCHISM, AND CARCERAL STATE FORMATION

Well, if one really wishes to know how justice is administered in a country, one does not question the policemen, the lawyers, the judges, or the protected members of the middle class. One goes to the unprotected—those, precisely, who need the law's protection most!—and listens to their testimony.

—James Baldwin, *No Name in the Street*, 1972

The prison industrial-complex is a result of the *failure* to enact abolition democracy.

—Angela Y. Davis, *Abolition Democracy*, 2011

James Baldwin actively participated in the freedom movement's efforts to undermine the legitimacy of racial regimes in the postwar period. In 1963 he published *The Fire Next Time,* predicting urban revolts in U.S. cities.[39] The uprisings in Harlem (1964), Watts (1965), Detroit (1967), and hundreds of other US. cities circulated around the country with unprecedented intensity, proving the accuracy of his prophetic prediction. Almost always the provocation was an incident of police violence, ranging from arrests to beatings to shootings. The revanchist responses to the insurgencies demonstrated the power of the counterinsurgent state's security apparatus. At the same time, they sparked political and cultural resistance as well as criticism at the grassroots. Taken together, these struggles were unmatched in intensity in U.S. history since the Civil War and Reconstruction.[40]

Sparked by the self-activity and collective struggles unleashed by the masses on the move, the urban multiracial working class organized for itself as insurgent communities of resistance in the wake of the urban uprisings of the 1960s. Between 1967 and 1973 industrial workers engaged in the most intensive cycle of strike activity in the postwar era in cities such as Detroit where race and class conflicts were being resolved by an urban multiracial working class led by the organic intellectuals in the League of Revolutionary Black Workers.[41] As the multiracial working class participated in mass direct actions on the streets and in the factories, prison revolts led by criminalized sectors of the proletariat ripped through the U.S. system, culminating in the dramatic Attica rebellion in upstate New York in 1971. Many insurgents began to emphasize multiracial class struggles, turning to writings by Black radical and socialist intellectuals such as Baldwin and Angela Y. Davis to theorize and confront the articulation between racism, capitalism, and domestic counterinsurgency.[42] The overturning of the status quo seemed like a distinct possibility. Taken together, these struggles had a significant impact on U.S. political culture creating a crisis of hegemony. Amid the events of 1968, the countersubversive ideology that had legitimated the criminalization of dissent in the early Cold War wore thin.[43]

At the very moment that antiracist and socialist critiques gripped the imaginations of radical social movements, police surveillance and incarceration increased as strategies for managing social crisis. As race and class conflicts intensified between civil rights activists and segregationists, autoworkers and factory owners, the urban poor and police, socialists and security-state bureaucrats, and prisoners and prison guards, these antagonisms were compounded by the onset of a global economic crisis in 1971 and the crash in property markets that occurred in 1973.[44] The ensuing recession of the 1970s was particularly acute in the United States, where industrial production was cut in half, the stock market crashed, and unemployment increased to numbers not experienced since the 1930s. In response to this social and economic crisis, neoliberals were able to impose their definition of events and win consent to neoliberal restructuring, resulting in a withdrawal of the social wage, and the expansion of the carceral-security apparatus. Once these events unfolded, there was no turning back.[45]

ARGUMENT AND METHODOLOGY

The crisis of the ruling class's hegemony . . . occurs either because the ruling class has failed in some major political undertaking for which it has requested, or forcibly extracted, the consent of the broad masses . . . or because huge masses . . . have passed suddenly from a state

of political passivity to a certain activity and put forward demands
which taken together, albeit not organically formulated, add up to a
revolution . . . this is precisely the crisis of hegemony, or general
crisis of the state.

—Antonio Gramsci, *Prison Notebooks,* 1971

A crisis of hegemony marks a moment of profound rupture in the
political and economic life of a society, an accumulation of contradictions. . . . Such moments signal, not necessarily a revolutionary
conjuncture nor the collapse of the state, but rather the coming of
"iron times" . . . Class domination will be exercised, in such
moments, through a modification in the *modes of hegemony* . . . and
the powerful orchestration . . . of an *authoritarian* consensus. . . .
The forms of state intervention thus become more overt and more
direct.

—Stuart Hall, Chas Critcher, Tony Jefferson, John Clarke, and
  Brian Roberts, *Policing the Crisis: Mugging, the State, and
  Law and Order,* 1978

This book's methodology owes a great deal to Antonio Gramsci's theoretical advances in his *Prison Notebooks* penned during the late 1920s
and early 1930s. As an incarcerated revolutionary intellectual, Gramsci
introduced the methodology of conjunctural analysis to distinguish
between political, economic, and ideological factors in shaping social
formations.[46] "When an historical period comes to be studied," Gramsci explained, "the great importance of the distinction becomes clear."
As he famously put it, "A crisis occurs, sometimes lasting for decades.
This exceptional duration means that incurable structural contradictions have revealed themselves." Analyzing these dramatic moments in
the history of a social formation, he argued, would illuminate "the
political forces which are struggling to conserve and defend the existing
structure." For him, "These incessant and persistent efforts (since no
social formation will ever admit that it has been superseded) form
the terrain of the 'conjunctural.' And it is upon this terrain that the
forces of opposition organise." In other words, the purpose of conjunctural analysis is to enable a concrete analysis of the world in order to
change it.[47]

Drawing upon and elaborating Gramsci's interventions, Stuart Hall
and his colleagues in Birmingham have emphasized for decades the
importance of Gramscian or conjunctural analysis of racial and class
formation. Writing amid the crisis of the 1970s, for example, Hall,
Chas Critcher, Tony Jefferson, John Clarke, and Brian Roberts's seminal
collaborative work of Marxist cultural studies, *Policing the Crisis:
Mugging, the State, and Law and Order* (1978), suggested how Gram-

sci's relevance stemmed from his confrontation with actually existing historical conditions. Taking up this insight from Gramsci, Hall and his colleagues showed how a tilt toward state authoritarianism in Britain stemmed from a "crisis of hegemony" for capital and the state in the 1960s and 1970s. The depth of the crisis made it increasingly impossible for the state to politically manage the situation "without an escalation in the use and forms of repressive state power." *Policing the Crisis* famously analyzed the role of racial ideologies in the media in legitimating authoritarian solutions to crisis. It theorized how consent to the concentration of coercive state power was won "through race." The capitalist state was sanctioned to deploy force against a racialized enemy of purported criminals and muggers through a series of "moral panics" around race, crime, and law and order. As such, race provided the "correlative of the crisis," and that is the terrain in which class anxieties were "worked through." To paraphrase the authors' famous insight, race was the modality through which class was experienced, lived, and fought out. As such, languages of race provided a "prism through which the whole conjuncture could be read symptomatically."[48]

In an interview on the thirty-fifth anniversary of the text in 2013, Hall suggested that understanding the relevance of the work in the present moment "obliges us to do a policing the crisis of now . . . to do a conjunctural analysis . . . on this moment and put race and crime at the center of it."[49] Taking up this challenge, my book provides a conjunctural analysis of the role of racialization in the formation of the neoliberal carceral state in the United States. Accordingly, the dialectic of insurgency and counterinsurgency is the centerpiece of my theoretical analysis of neoliberal state formation. I show how moral panics around race, crime, disorder, security, and law and order became the primary legitimating discourse for the expanded use of policing, prisons, and urban securitization in the state's management of social and economic crises. I argue that mass criminalization did not appear all of a sudden in the late twentieth century as liberalism waned and as the rise of the Right took hold in the 1960s, as some scholars have asserted, but rather that it took hold as part of a continuum of Cold War racial liberalism's strategy of containment in the postwar period.[50] To sustain this argument, my study begins with an examination of the dialectical struggle between the long civil rights movement and the national security state between the 1930s and the 1970s. The bulk of the book then examines the dialectics of insurgency during the neoliberal turn from the 1970s to the present. These periods constitute two distinct conjunctures, which are understood here less as moments in time and more in keeping with Hall's definition as an "accumulation of contradictions."[51]

In this way, my book demonstrates how the neoliberal state was produced within a long counterinsurgency whose historical and geographical roots stem from the early Cold War. The consolidation of the neoliberal state represented the victory in the dominant historical bloc's ideological struggle to win the battle for "hearts and minds." It produced a new revanchist common sense that saw as its historic mission the undoing of the historic gains of Black freedom, radical labor, feminist, and socialist movements between the 1930s and the 1970s.[52] In using Gramsci's category of "common sense" to understand how mass incarceration became naturalized in the U.S. political culture, I am specifying how the expansion of policing and prisons has become a taken-for-granted feature of life under capitalism in the contemporary era. Throughout the rise of neoliberalism, at the regional, national, and international scale, the geography of U.S. racial capitalism profoundly shifted. Capitalist restructuring created an accumulation of wealth and affluence for the few, on the one hand, and deepened poverty, unemployment, mass homelessness, and declining real wages for poor and working people on the other. Cuts in expenditures for social budgets and social safety nets disproportionately impacted poor and working-class people of color, who endured unemployment at Depression-era levels for decades.[53]

It was in this precise historical and geographical context that purportedly color-blind discourses of law and order, safety, and security became the key legitimating narratives for securing consent to carceral resolutions of social crises. Neoliberal nostrums of security imposed new ways of seeing events. These common-sense and purportedly color-blind narratives have provided ideological justification for the state's strategy of incarcerating the crisis. Politicians of both parties, prominent journalists, and even many social scientists have justified this strategy by articulating common-sense notions of race, class, gender, and sexuality that represent the behavior of the so-called underclass as the source of social and political problems.[54]

Incarcerating the Crisis shows how elite leaders of both major political parties have represented prisons as a legitimate site where surplus populations can be geographically disposed. It interrogates how the racist logic of carcerality is rooted in material conditions and operates through spaces of social control outside of prison itself and through the uneven development of cities and their regions.[55] It examines how neoliberal ideology has been deployed to justify security fixes in a time of ideological incoherence. It has helped render the everyday and routine militarized policing and surveillance of urban working-class communities of color as natural responses to subaltern criminality, violence, illegality, and chaos perpetuated by the "underclass." At the same time it explores how this strategy has produced its own contradictions. It has created new possibilities for radical social movements to engage in class struggles in language over the meaning of events. These social movements can articulate an alternative common sense and new counterhegemonic vision to confront the counterinsurgent ideology of the neoliberal carceral state.[56]

To trace the ideological architecture of neoliberal security regimes, I argue for the importance of what Ranajit Guha calls the "prose of counterinsurgency," and that is the state's representations of subaltern insurrections as irrational and violent acts that must be crushed to restore order and enforce the rule of law.[57] This prose occurs not only in official state documents, but more insidiously through well-circulated mass-mediated narratives in newspapers, magazines, television, film, radio, and new media. The suffering that motivates rebellions, insurrections, and uprisings against police violence and mass criminalization is often poorly translated. Even political discourses that have offered sentimental depictions of such suffering and accurate descriptions of the social conditions that produced them have often reproduced the very logic of counterinsurgency in their representations of events. Reading this range of narratives against the grain enables them to be analyzed as primary sources of evidence documenting how crises have been narrated and defined in the interest of capital and the state. After all, events framed in the rhetoric of counterinsurgency provide "an image caught in a distorting mirror." Interrogating these narratives as the prose of counterinsurgency enables the careful reader to discern that this "distortion has a logic to it," as Guha put it.[58]

The logic of counterinsurgency has traveled from the suppression of subaltern insurrections to the confinement of actually or potentially rebellious populations rendered surplus by capitalist restructuring. Consequently, this prose has justified carceral reactions to the uneven development of U.S. racial capitalism. Yet this rhetoric has rested uneasily alongside declining real wages, pervasive poverty, precarious employment, and persistent class polarization during the neoliberal turn.[59] Indeed, the prose of counterinsurgency has dramatically clashed with the definitions of events rendered vivid by what I call an "insurrection of poetic knowledges," or the alternative ways of seeing articulated in the "poetry of social movements." These insurgent poetics represent a complex struggle to counter the hegemony of dominant historical blocs and to shift the common sense of the conjuncture. They provide poetic visions of a new society emerging from the contradictions of the old. That is not to say that "the arm of criticism" can "replace the criticism of arms," since as Karl Marx famously put it; "Material force can only be overthrown by material force; but theory itself becomes a material force when it has seized the masses." As such, I explore interventions in expressive culture that have attempted to seize the imagination of the masses. They represent an alternative archive of change over time and across space. They pose bold challenges to the common-sense construction of poor urban communities of color as a dysfunctional and criminal underclass that threatens safety and security in cities. They authorize an insurgent counternarrative of these communities under siege as an urban multiracial working class—one that continues to suffer from the onslaught of neoliberalization and mass incarceration.[60]

Drawing from these alternative archives, my study illuminates how freedom struggles have provided critiques of the common sense underpinning neoliberalism. Such visions enable a fidelity to the dreams of Black freedom, radical labor, feminist, and socialist movements of the long civil rights era. They suggest that there could have been, and still could be, a different world in the making, one that includes the expansion of public expenditure for public housing, education, health care, and parks—in short, a social wage—rather than policing, prisons, and permanent warfare. Utilizing the evidence culled from these archives, I explore how demands for a social wage have enabled and can continue to enable the formation of a popular democratic alliance against neoliberalism and for redistributive justice.[61]

ORGANIZATION

Incarcerating the Crisis is organized around major turning points in U.S. history. Each chapter is concerned with analyzing a dramatic event, an alternative archive of social texts, and the politics of signification.[62] The first three chapters consider the struggle over the meaning of events in the period between the rise of the long civil rights movement in the 1930s and the crisis of hegemony during the 1970s. Chapter 1 examines the relationships between the freedom movement, the Watts insurrection, and the formation of the carceral-security apparatus during the Cold War. It explores how the counterinsurgency against the Black freedom movement created the conditions of possibility for the Watts rebellion of 1965. In turn, it suggests that these developments, alongside the rise of Ronald Reagan in California, created the political foundation upon which the neoliberal carceral state would flourish.

Chapter 2 shows how Detroit's Black Marxist autoworkers in the Dodge Revolutionary Union Movement and League of Revolutionary Black Workers as well as their community of supporters engaged in a complex struggle over the meaning of urban and labor rebellions during the crisis of hegemony between 1967 and 1973. I examine how the cultural products of this social movement provided a distinct counterpoint to dominant ideologies of race, class, gender, and sexuality in the midst of urban rebellions, the Kerner Commission report, and news coverage of uprisings and social movements. Through an analysis of the poetics of insurgency it also delineates the historical and geographical roots of the contemporary conjuncture. Chapter 3 interrogates the struggle over the meaning of the 1971 Attica prison uprising, arguing that the racist representation of the rebellion informed the depiction of New York City as synonymous with crime and urban decay during the fiscal crisis of the 1970s. While most histories of neoliberalism trace its roots to the CIA-backed military coup in Chile, I explore the relationships between the crushing of the Attica uprising and the neoliberalization of New York. I argue that neoliberals responded to the events in a spirit of revenge; a reaction that helps us understand the subsequent rise of the super-maximum-security prison during the age of Reaganism.

The last three chapters connect the high tide of neoliberalism in the 1980s, 1990s, and 2000s to the earlier buildup of carceral-security regimes during the Cold War. Chapter 4 examines the competing definitions of the Los Angeles rebellion of 1992 in the historical and geographical context of structural unemployment, concentrated poverty among the Black and Latino poor, mass homelessness, and the unprecedented expansion of policing and prisons. It argues that the rhetoric of counterinsurgency legitimated mass criminalization as a strategy of managing actual or potential social unrest in the worst economic crisis since the Great Depression. Chapter 5 focuses on struggles over the meaning of the post-Katrina New Orleans crisis. It shows how antiracist activists, authors, and artists provided distinct ways of seeing the event in the city with the highest incarceration rate of any city in the state, in the state with more prisoners than anywhere in the country, in the country with the largest carceral apparatus on the planet. It also interrogates how the crisis was seen as an opportunity to confront the racist and revanchist common sense underpinning the neoliberal state and complete the unfinished business of the long civil rights movement.

Chapter 6 interrogates the relationships between mass homelessness and mass incarceration in the wake of the global financial crisis of 2008 in Skid Row Los Angeles, an area of downtown that has the highest concentration of poverty, policing, and homelessness in the United States. It examines the connections between structures and processes of racialization, gentrification, and the policing of urban space. It also suggests lessons that we might learn from the social movements in the city that are formulating demands for civil and human rights, a social wage, and the right to the city. Finally, the epilogue explores how activists, artists, and intellectuals are currently playing prominent public roles in reclaiming a collective memory of freedom struggles—shared perceptions about the history of movements that are sparking the imagination of political struggles in the present, and articulating the poetry of the future. Their visions suggest that alternative futures have been and continue to be possible. I take the politics of historical excavation and theoretical explication seriously, attending to what Hall describes as "a set of contested, localized, conjunctural knowledges that have to be debated in a dialogic way." "But," as Hall intervened, this theoretical labor is "also a practice which always thinks about its intervention in a world in which it would make some difference, in which it would have some effect." The goal of this work is to contribute to the evolving skills in the way readers understand the world as they struggle to change it.[63]

CHAPTER 1

The Explosion in Watts

The Second Reconstruction and the Cold War Roots of the Carceral State

The explosion in Watts reminded us all that the northern ghettos are the prisons of forgotten men.
—Dr. Martin Luther King Jr., New York, September 18, 1965

In August 1965, the California Highway Patrol stopped an unemployed resident of South Central Los Angeles named Marquette Frye and proceeded to beat him. Frye's assault ignited the fury of the Black working class in Watts. Many took up burning and looting as their form of protest against this particular episode and the more general epidemic of police violence. Over the next five days the masses were on the move. The uprising—popularly known as the Watts rebellion or insurrection— occurred within days of the passage of the historic Voting Rights Act in 1965. National and international attention was drawn to the events, especially as they appeared to contradict the dominant national narrative of appeasement and racial overcoming.[1] Moved by the events, Martin Luther King Jr. was compelled to visit Los Angeles. Against the counsel of advisors who recommended that King denounce the rebellion and the conditions that produced it, King met with the participants of the then–largest urban uprising in U.S. history. In a press conference shortly after the meeting he stated that the rebellion "was a class revolt of underprivileged against privileged." While King celebrated the political victories of the freedom movement, he framed the Watts insurrection as the outcome of class anger among those who found their material conditions, despite the new legislation, unchanged.[2]

In the wake of this encounter, King and his colleagues increasingly worked to articulate alternatives to the race and class inequality they witnessed in Watts. King came to the ethical position that "something is wrong with capitalism. . . . There must be a better distribution of wealth, and maybe America must move toward a democratic socialism." This realization transformed King as he sided with working people in the struggle against racism, militarism, and poverty.[3] King thus affirmed the insurgent impulse of the urban uprisings, as he well understood the material conditions that had produced them. In his estimation, the struggle of the urban multiracial poor was the decisive factor in elevating the crisis of racism and poverty to the national political stage.[4]

King sought to rebuild an alliance between civil rights and labor movements to confront the crisis politically. As part of this effort, he located the origins of the rebellion in the automation and deindustrialization in the period. This focus resonated as the intersecting crises of racism, urban poverty, unemployment, and police violence disproportionately impacted the African American and Mexican American working class in the city. In his speeches he increasingly highlighted the social forces producing concentrated unemployment and poverty among the racialized poor. He therefore provided a critique of the changing geography of U.S. racial capitalism. He inspired a radical return in the freedom movement to materialist analysis and class questions that had been marked as outside the bounds of tolerable discourse during the Cold War.[5]

That is not to say that visions of redistribution had not been central to the freedom movement well before Watts. They had played a powerful role in connecting labor and civil rights movements for decades. Taking a long view of the civil rights movement, this chapter traces the rise of what activists, artists, and intellectuals in the Black freedom movement called the Second Reconstruction during the 1930s. It explores how they formed a popular alliance with radical labor and socialist movements against Jim Crow capitalism. It shows how they offered a materialist analysis of racialization, and critiqued policing and prisons as political expressions of the systemic inequalities of capitalism. It also explores how their critique was silenced as "subversion" during the post–World War II Red Scare amid the broader criminalization of antiracist freedom struggles. It demonstrates that this reaction created a political vacuum in which the logic of the carceral state would come to flourish.[6]

As the Cold War took hold after 1948, incarceration rates expanded. African American workers were members of the reserve army of labor. They were the last hired, first fired, and also increasingly subjected to surveillance, arrest, and incarceration. Prisons began to fill with people who were young and working class—groups who also made up the social basis for the labor and civil rights struggles of the postwar era.[7] This was particularly true in California, where the dispossessed had been forced to migrate from the South in search of waged work during World War II. Indeed, while the incarceration rate for the United States as a whole remained relatively steady in the two and half decades after the war, as the journalist Min S. Yee observed, the California prison population by contrast grew from about five thousand in 1944 to more than twenty-eight thousand by 1968. This shift coincided with a transformation in the racial demographics of the prison. The California prison population went from 68 percent white and 17 percent Black in the 1940s to 54 percent white and 28 percent Black in the 1960s, even while the percentage of Black people in California remained between 5 and 6 percent of the population throughout the period. This seemingly exceptional form of carceral control requires explanation, especially as it became the dominant strategy of racialized crisis management in the long late twentieth century.[8]

This chapter shows how carceral policies were developed in response to the most radical political and economic demands of the long civil rights movement. It argues that the national security state's attempts to silence materialist critiques of racism produced the political and ideological conditions of existence for the Watts insurrection in 1965. In turn, it suggests that the state's response to the revolt and the rise of Ronald Reagan during the late 1960s in California created the political foundation for the making of a neoliberal carceral state. By analyzing the speeches and writings of figures such as King and James Baldwin, I seek to demonstrate that the rebellion was a turning point in the history and future of freedom struggles. I argue that the Watts insurrection represented an organic crisis of Jim Crow racial regimes, one that presented the opportunity to form a broad alliance against racism, militarism, and poverty. I conclude by focusing on the dialectical struggle between the prose of counterinsurgency and the poetry of social movements over the meaning of this moment, illustrating how it marked a turning point in the development of the carceral state.[9]

THE SECOND RECONSTRUCTION

Many people thought that the radical thirties could be the Second Reconstruction. The language was certainly there: sharecropping as

the new slavery, the CIO as the new abolitionists, class struggle
between working people and capitalists as the new Civil War.

—Toni Cade Bambara, "A Second Reconstruction? 1934–
1948," in *W.E.B. Du Bois: A Biography in Four Voices*, 1995

Reconstruction presents an opportunity to study inductively the
Marxian theory of the state.

—W.E.B. Du Bois, *Black Reconstruction in America*, 1935

The Black freedom struggle in the mid-twentieth century, referred to as
the Second Reconstruction, took root in the radical 1930s. The publication of W.E.B. Du Bois's *Black Reconstruction in America* in 1935 represented a turning point in the history of the struggle against U.S. racial
capitalism. During the economic crisis of the 1930s, and amid an emergent insurgent multiracial labor movement, Du Bois devoted his scholarly
energies to a study of the race and class struggles of the post–Civil War
Reconstruction period. *Black Reconstruction in America* described how
the First Reconstruction (1868–76) represented an unusually successful
interracial working-class movement.[10] In Du Bois's explanation, Black
workers had won their own freedom by creating a "general strike" in the
fields, and in turn were guided by a vision of "abolition democracy." He
was also driven by the idea that these workers had created a multiracial
class alliance with poor whites that led to the formation of the Reconstruction government. This government opened the ballot to poor whites,
who had been denied rights due to their lack of access to property. It
abolished the whipping post, the stocks, and other forms of barbaric punishment. It pursued equal accommodation in public spaces and implemented civil rights. In short, the movement was able to transform a racial
contradiction into a class confrontation. These efforts to combine political and economic rights, Du Bois argued, represented a model for confronting Jim Crow during the global crisis of capitalism in the 1930s.[11]

Drawing on Black radical historiography, Marxist theory, and the
alternative archives of expressive culture, Du Bois claimed that Reconstruction represented one of the "most extraordinary experiments in
Marxism that the world, before the Russian Revolution, had ever seen."
He demonstrated how racial and labor regimes, centuries in the making, had worn thin in the face of democratic insurgencies among the
poor and working class in the 1860s and 1870s. These antiracist and
class struggles had created a radical rupture in the U.S. social formation. In reconfiguring the goals and capacities of the state, Black workers and their radical allies had raised the fundamental question as to
"whom this wealth was to belong to and for whose interests laborers

were to work"—a question that continued to burn at the height of the Great Depression, a period that marked the rise of the Second Reconstruction.[12] Against the advance of socialist democracy, the overthrow of the First Reconstruction gave rise to Jim Crow in the late nineteenth and early twentieth centuries. In turn, Jim Crow served as the primary instrument of social control for capital and the state, as it ensured a largely segregated labor movement on a mass scale between the 1890s and the 1930s.[13]

At the time Du Bois published *Black Reconstruction in America*, there was evidence that the racial and labor regime was fraying. With the book's publication, militant labor and civil rights activists in the radical 1930s were increasingly able to draw on a collective memory of the unfinished business of abolition democracy to press for its completion. In the decade after this signal intervention, radical Black freedom movement activists and intellectuals built a historic bloc with the multiracial Congress of Industrial Organizations (CIO) and communist and socialist organizations to confront U.S. Jim Crow capitalism. Between 1929 and 1948, five hundred thousand Black workers gained access to unionized industrial jobs, a large scale experiment in unionization for industrial workers for the first time in U.S. history. In turn, Black industrial workers and organic intellectuals provided moral and ethical leadership in the class struggles of the postwar era.[14]

In 1946 in Columbia, South Carolina, Du Bois delivered a speech on a program with Paul Robeson and Howard Fast at the meetings of the Southern Negro Youth Congress, a Communist organization based in Birmingham, Alabama (a place also known as "America's Johannesburg"). Esther Jackson introduced the lecture before an integrated audience at Benedict College in the Jim Crow South. In poetic prose, Du Bois's address "Behold the Land" predicted that the region would become an epicenter for antiracist and class struggles. Du Bois observed, "The working people of the South, white and black, must come to remember that their emancipation depends upon their mutual cooperation." The speech illuminated the ways in which Jim Crow segregation produced Black workers as a source of cheap labor power. It explored how this racial regime served to control the working class as a whole. It declared that this system of social relations reached far beyond the geographical boundaries of the U.S. South, having been exported around the planet through U.S. racial capitalism and imperialism. As part of an effort to articulate an ethical alternative to this political economy, Du Bois argued for the formation of a historical bloc made up of Black freedom, anti-imperialist, labor, and socialist movements. Such a bloc

FIGURE 1. W. E. B. Du Bois with Shirley Graham and indicted members of the Peace Information Center, Washington, DC, 1951. Courtesy the Department of Special Collections and University Archives, W. E. B. Du Bois Library, University of Massachusetts, Amherst.

would press for human rights and an augmented social wage—one that included equitable housing, education, and transportation for all workers—especially workers of color who had been excluded from the New Deal. In this, Du Bois was perhaps the most prominent radical historian and social theorist during this formative moment of the age of the civil rights movement.[15]

During this period, Du Bois observed that an ever-increasing number of poor people "stagger out of prison doors embittered, vengeful, hopeless, ruined." Of this "army of the wronged," as he called them, the proportion of Black people was "frightful." Du Bois penned these observations during his persecution for the antiwar activism he conducted with the Stockholm-based Peace Information Center. In a clear use of Red Scare tactics, he was labeled a "foreign agent" and the Soviet Union was named as the "foreign principal" by the prosecution. As a result, the senior scholar-activist of the Black freedom movement faced an extended trial in federal court in 1951 and was forced to fight for his right to pursue radical alternatives to the Jim Crow police state. It took a national and international campaign to save him from being incarcerated. The ordeal of the trial gave him some new perspective. In reflecting on the experience, he observed the ways in which criminalization migrated from the persecution of radical intellectuals to the "great mass" of the Black poor and working class.[16]

Du Bois's urgent words offered a radical challenge to the violent exclusion of "the army of the wronged" in carceral spaces.[17] They dramatize the deleterious effects of prisons as modes of social control. In his writings Du Bois sought to help audiences interpret and resist coercive methods for securing consent to U.S. hegemony. Specifically, he invited readers to consider how the national security state emerged in continuity with earlier forms of social control, and how racism, capitalism, and the state were connected in the early Cold War. In doing so, Du Bois articulated a materialist critique of the carceral apparatus during the rise of postwar U.S. globalism. His intervention reveals the relationship between consent and coercion during this distinct historical conjuncture.[18]

THE LONG CIVIL RIGHTS MOVEMENT AND COLD WAR COUNTERSUBVERSION

This bill of particulars, *We Charge Genocide*, is the documented story of the frame-up of thousands of innocent Negroes; of the attempt to stamp the brand of criminality on Negro youth; of packed lily-white juries; of the intimidation of lawyers and witnesses; of police brutality and murder, legal lynching, Ku Klux Klan and mob violence; of racist laws enforced by city, state and Federal officials and courts; of denial of the vote, Jim-Crow in employment, the ghetto system, premature death and malnutrition and preventable diseases . . . and of Jim-Crow.

—William L. Patterson, "We Charge Genocide!" *Political
    Affairs*, 1951

Like Du Bois, William L. Patterson of the Civil Rights Congress (CRC) engaged in a struggle to confront the criminalization of the Black working class. He noted that there had been a "conscious attempt to place the brand of criminality" upon the Black working class, whom he defined as victims of the Jim Crow police state. This analysis informed the CRC's effort to provide political, ethical, and moral leadership in the struggle to prevent young working-class people of color from being criminalized. The group also organized civil liberties campaigns to support imprisoned communists—both those who were card-carrying members of the Communist Party and those fellow travelers indicted by Cold War hysteria. The Los Angeles CRC was influential. It organized against the police violence experienced by African American and Mexican American working-class residents in particular. The organization worked in partnership with groups such as El Congreso del Pueblo de Habla Español and the Asociación Nacional México Americana. For working-class communities of color throughout the city, the group provided political education about the historical and material roots of racism and police violence in the political economy of capitalism during a critical moment in the history of the long civil rights movement.[19]

The CRC included the significant participation of activists from the Communist Party with branches in places such as Detroit, Oakland, Los Angeles, New Orleans, and New York. Its leadership included veterans of the Communist movement such as William L. Patterson, who had engaged in the defense of the "Scottsboro Boys" in Alabama during the early 1930s. They organized multiracial social protests challenging racism in housing and employment, as well as police brutality. The fights for jobs, unemployment relief, and public housing, and against the policing of the racialized poor, had been critical to the broader radical struggle against racial capitalism since the Great Depression.[20] The Los Angeles CRC often held its meetings at the local CIO offices. This siting was a deliberate means to link with labor in a fight against the police brutality suffered by workers of color, particularly those experiencing unemployment due to plant closures. CRC activists argued that there was a direct link between racism, unemployment, police repression, and postwar capitalist development. They gathered and presented evidence illustrating that more than one third of the Los Angeles Police Department (LAPD) was deployed to police about one mile of territory in South Central Los Angeles. By contrast, they showed that only two officers were assigned per square mile in predominantly white and wealthy West Side neighborhoods such as Hollywood, Wilshire, and the Valley. Such racial and spatial disparity informed the CRC's effort to fight the criminalization of racialized sectors of the class who, Patterson argued, "lie rotting in the prisons of American cities."[21]

The Los Angeles CRC worked in conjunction with a number of media and cultural figures, some of whom were themselves members of the local chapter, to confront the common-sense associations between race and criminality. Charlotta Bass, editor of the Los Angeles–based newspaper the *California Eagle*, played a key role in this fight over meaning and material conditions. She had become a close colleague of prominent figures on the Black Left such as Du Bois, Patterson, and Paul Robeson through her activism and journalism. Throughout the long civil rights era she was pivotal in facilitating multiracial alliances between African Americans and Mexican Americans. Bass was a board member of the CRC, and accordingly saw her mission as to connect struggles against Jim Crow capitalism with resistance to the policing of racialized space, and to advance a socialist vision of the redistribution of wealth.[22]

The insurgent counternarratives provided by Bass and other journalists in the *California Eagle* were critical for working-class communities of color in Los Angeles. This was especially true in the postwar period, which witnessed an upsurge in police violence and incarceration as unemployment increased. In Watts, a majority of Black residents reported that they had been stopped and frisked, and subjected to illegal search and seizures. Despite problems with police violence, middle-class civil rights organizations such as the National Association for the Advancement of Colored People (NAACP) generally failed to get involved in working-class confrontations with police violence, brutality, and harassment. In this context the CRC gained local acclaim for its resistance to criminalization perpetuated by the LAPD. Rather than pursuing the middle-class strategy of respectability, one that insisted that defendants be upstanding citizens and defended as such, the CRC took on unpopular cases in which people were not innocent victims. Indeed, many of the CRC's clients had been arrested for crimes they very well could have committed such as public drunkenness and vagrancy.[23]

Raising the profile of the struggle, major cultural figures, most notably the singer and actor Paul Robeson, lent their celebrity to the cause. In 1948 Robeson performed a free concert in Los Angeles to fundraise for the CRC's campaigns against racism, policing, and violations of civil rights and civil liberties.[24] Robeson had achieved the status of folk hero among many in labor and social movements for his political and cultural resistance to Jim Crow capitalism and U.S. imperialism, as well as for his ability to articulate the links between Black expressive culture and the socialist vernacular cultures of working people across the planet. His free concert in Los Angeles, along with many others like it, was organized to build solidarity in the labor, civil rights, civil liberties, socialist, and Communist movements that characterized the period. It

FIGURE 2. Paul Robeson and two women activists from a delegation present *We Charge Genocide* petition to the UN Secretariat. *Daily Worker/Daily World* Photographs Collection, Tamiment Library, New York University.

was cohosted by organizations such as the CRC and the CIO as part of this broader social movement. Taking place at the Second Baptist Church in Los Angeles, the event provided a social space to articulate radical political visions and economic demands in this dynamic social movement.[25]

The cultural and ideological struggles of the CRC were taken up alongside significant legal and policy-oriented political challenges. William Patterson submitted *We Charge Genocide* at the United Nations in Paris, which documented widespread state-sanctioned and extralegal violence deployed against Black people in the postwar period. This event was coordinated so that Robeson was able to submit the document to the United Nations in New York at the same time. Signatories included prominent figures on the antiracist Left such as Du Bois, Charlotta Bass, Alphaeus Hunton, and Jessica Mitford. In a speech he delivered in New York on November 12, 1951, at a release event for *We Charge Genocide,* William Patterson explained that the article represented the struggle against the "premature death" created by racism, state violence, and finance capital's dominance, as he described it.[26]

U.S. state officials were not sympathetic to the appeal. The report was dismissed by anticommunists—both racial liberals and conservatives—as propaganda promoted by the Communist Party. As a result of their activism the CRC was singled out for political repression by the national security state. Against their efforts to end police brutality, racist violence, segregation, and civil and human rights violations, the Subversive Activities Control Board declared the CRC a Communist front. As such, the claims of the petition were de-authorized and the United Nations was prevented from considering the petition. While Robeson had been able to translate his cultural visibility as a celebrity into organizing efforts for the Black freedom, labor, and socialist alliance, he became an outlier in an increasingly countersubversive entertainment industry. Such countersubversion was part and parcel of the postwar Red Scare.[27]

Throughout the rise of the Cold War national security state in the post-1948 period, Black radicals such as Du Bois and Robeson who promoted socialist solutions to racial and class inequality were demonized as subversives. At the national scale, the Red Scare under President Harry Truman's administration oversaw the political attack and criminalization of the antiracist Left. The national security state pursued the arrest, incarceration, and deportation of hundreds of Black radical figures such as Du Bois, Robeson, Claudia Jones, and C.L.R. James while overseeing the surveillance of artists such as Ruby Dee, Ossie Davis, Lorraine Hansberry, Canada Lee, Lena Horne, Elizabeth Catlett, and other luminaries.[28] By persecuting those who rendered vivid the articulation between race and class, the national security state demonized the social vision most able to provide viable alternatives to what would later be called "white supremacist capitalism."[29]

Indeed, racial liberals in the Truman administration who supported anticommunism attributed criminality to civil rights and created the conditions of existence for the McCarthy era. As Jessica Mitford, the journalist and former executive secretary of the East Bay CRC in Oakland, put it, "The soil for the noxious growth of McCarthyism had been well prepared by the Truman Administration, and the anti-Communist crusade was well under way before the junior senator from Wisconsin himself appeared on the scene."[30] While conservatives and liberals used languages of anticommunism to justify the expansion of the domestic security apparatus, millions of workers dispossessed by the mechanization of agricultural production were forced to migrate to industrial cities in search of waged work. Dispossession, forced migration, urbanization, and wartime increases in production in industrial cities created an increasingly working-class dynamic in the Black freedom struggle. In turn, Black working people elevated the struggle against white supremacist capitalism to new geographical scales. The movement intensified with unparalleled force and led to a situation where not even the arrest, incarceration, and deportation of radicals could stop the forward motion unleashed by the freedom movement.[31]

THE BLACK FREEDOM STRUGGLE AND THE WATTS INSURRECTION OF THE 1960S

I never intend to become adjusted to the evils of segregation and discrimination. I never intend to adjust myself to the tragic inequalities of an economic system which takes necessities from the masses to give luxuries to the classes.

—Dr. Martin Luther King Jr., Highlander Folk School,
  Monteagle, Tennessee, September 2, 1957

With its strategically located means of cultural production in Hollywood and the postwar expansion of the military-industrial complex, Southern California became an epicenter of the Cold War reaction against the Black freedom, radical labor, and socialist alliance. California countersubversives carried an organized political attack on labor and civil rights activists. They recognized that workers of color experiencing racial segregation and who were also being denied access to the social wage and means of social reproduction were sympathetic to struggles for economic justice. This countersubversive tradition extended from Southern California across the state as well as throughout the state government. Richard Nixon and Ronald Reagan in particular rose to prominence in California by carrying out domestic Cold War campaigns that practiced "anticommunism as governmentality." Efforts by civil rights organizers and the multiracial Left to resist segregation were demonized as subversive in order to win consent to political and economic policies that were antagonistic to the interests of the majority of working people. As deindustrialization began wiping out jobs in segregated neighborhoods followed by waves of foreclosures, housing became a central site of struggle. Public housing as a solution to housing shortages for the poor and people of color was promoted by progressives and the antiracist Left. These class demands were represented in countersubversive narratives as a "creeping socialism."[32]

The relationship between countersubversion and the expansion of carceral forms of social control was rendered vivid in Los Angeles throughout the reign of LAPD Chief William Parker. Depicted by the press in a positive light much like FBI Director J. Edgar Hoover, Parker was celebrated for modernizing the department. In addition to promoting a militaristic culture, Parker, a former Marine Corps officer, encouraged the racist repression of the city's African American, Asian American, and Mexican American working-class residents. Parker described this style of authoritarian policing as a front line of defense against communism. The chief was a member of the right-wing populist and white supremacist organization the John Birch Society, which actively resisted the advances of Black freedom, labor, and socialist struggles. In his various capacities working for the state and the city, Parker fanned the flames of racism and anticommunism. In so doing he helped popularize the California tradition of countersubversion among reactionary forces.[33]

Countersubversives marginalized the radical critique of racial capitalism and state violence promoted by labor and civil rights activists. They also articulated a Cold War racial discourse of security and law and order. This discourse naturalized the accumulation of wealth among middle- and ruling-class whites. White flight to the suburbs, for example, occurred alongside massive public investment in education and transportation that enabled the expansion of a white middle class. This encouraged whites to see their class interests as linked to finance capital, insurance, and real estate industries, rather than to the struggles of workers of color for better wages, working conditions, and access to public goods and services. Thus, the ideology of whiteness naturalized the uneven capitalist development of urban and suburban areas, an unevenness that led to differential wages and disastrous inequalities in wealth. As the suburbs experienced greater prosperity, areas in the city occupied by working-class people of color did not. Instead, urban renewal policies displaced and dispossessed poor African Americans, Asian Americans, and Latinos from inner-city neighborhoods. This strategy of uneven geographical development led to capital and the state's abandonment of inner cities, which eroded the economic basis of urban areas. Taken together, these policies were at the root of the "urban crisis of the 1960s."[34]

As deindustrialization, a decline in trade unionism, and the defeat of the left wing of the multiracial civil rights movement took hold, as the historian Gerald Horne demonstrates, cultural nationalist movements held increasing sway. The period witnessed the expansion of the Nation of Islam's (NOI) influence in the late 1950s and early 1960s. In turn, the

LAPD also depicted the NOI as a security threat and targeted the organization for police and state surveillance, particularly due to the efforts of Malcolm X to establish a mosque and expand their influence in the region. According to Manning Marable, "Such activities were noticed and monitored by the California Senate Fact-Finding Committee on Un-American Activities, which feared the NOI had Communist affiliations." The state purported that there was a "parallel" between the NOI and the Communist Party to justify surveillance and aggressive policing. In April 1962, LAPD officers killed seven unarmed Nation of Islam members, including the Korean War veteran Ronald Stokes, in a raid on a mosque. Stokes had his hands up when he was shot. The police raid compelled Malcolm X to address a growing trend in California where Black people were killed a rate ten times higher than whites. Between 1963 and 1965, sixty African Americans in Los Angeles were killed by the LAPD. Many of these victims were unarmed, and twenty-seven of them were shot in the back. These police killings were deemed legitimate.[35]

The policing of the urban crisis in the 1960s occurred amid a booming political economy that had been fueled by federal expenditures in the military industrial complex in California. At the same time, automation, militarization, and outsourcing were leading to a reduction in industrial jobs, which disproportionately impacted the African American working class. It was in this context that Dr. King observed, "The unemployment rate in Watts was a staggering 34 percent." These figures were akin to the situation of the U.S. working class during the Great Depression of the 1930s. Hundreds of thousands of Black working people, King noted, had "no unemployment insurance, no social security, no Medicare, no minimum wage." These conditions, King and his former advisor Jack O'Dell argued, led to the Watts uprisings. Indeed, O'Dell suggested that the event was an expression of the resentment and anger of the working class due to unemployment, police brutality, poor housing, and poverty.[36]

The explosion in Watts marked the end of the postwar period of economic growth, the decline of industrial urbanization, and the rise of permanent structural unemployment in the political economy. During this period, factories began leaving the city for suburban areas in search of reduced taxes, cheaper land, and new markets. For example, in the two years before the rebellion in 1965, at least twenty-eight factories left South Central and East Los Angeles. Dropout rates in local high schools increased. The dismantling of public transit ensured that poor people would remain trapped in increasingly deindustrialized neighborhoods in homes they largely did not own. Instead, a majority of South Central Los Angeles's housing stock was owned and operated by absentee slumlords.[37] In November 1964, Proposition 14 was passed by California voters, which undid the Rumford Fair Housing Act that had sought to restrict racial segregation in housing. This repeal of open housing was symptomatic of the pervasive and persistent white resistance to the demands of the long civil rights movement. One of the consequences of the combination of racism, militarism, and poverty was the Watts insurrection. In this age of the civil rights movement, organic intellectuals responded to the events with distinct visions of social change.[38]

THE CRISIS IN U.S. CITIES

The bombs in Vietnam explode at home. The security we profess to seek in foreign ventures we will lose in our decaying cities.

—Martin Luther King, Jr., "The Crisis in America's Cities: An
    Analysis of Social Disorder and a Plan of Action Against
    Poverty, Discrimination, and Racism in Urban America,"
    Atlanta, August 15, 1967

In the late 1960s, King was determined in this period to "break the silence" about war both at home and abroad. Significantly, he also saw how racist narratives of the crisis were gaining traction. He observed the spread of racialized discourses of internal security and law and order as symptomatic of the "madness of militarism." Such discourses purported that the militarization of urban space could serve as a viable political solution to social and economic crisis. This emerging common sense would produce incalculable damage in the decades to come. Thus, he saw that the civil rights movement was engaged in a struggle to transform the conditions as well as the common sense.[39] Broadly speaking, he extended a radical perspective articulated by figures on the Black Left such as Du Bois, Patterson, Robeson, and Bass during the postwar period. Sparked by the self-activity of the masses on the move during the insurrection and inspired by the radical turn in the civil rights movement, analysts increasingly argued that the multiracial working class in U.S. cities portended the most viable potential for social transformation in North America.[40]

At an event celebrating the one hundredth anniversary of W. E. B. Du Bois's birthday on February 23, 1968, at Carnegie Hall in New York, sponsored by *Freedomways* magazine, which was cofounded by Dr. Bu Bois, Shirley Graham Du Bois, Esther Cooper Jackson, W. Alpheus

FIGURE 3. James Baldwin and Martin Luther King Jr. at the one hundredth birthday celebration of W. E. B. Du Bois, sponsored by *Freedomways* magazine, Carnegie Hall, New York, February 23, 1968. Courtesy of Esther Cooper Jackson.

Hunton, Margaret G. Burroughs, and others. Dr. King delivered the keynote. He paid tribute to Du Bois by countering the ways in which anticommunism had deprived the Black freedom struggle of its radical leadership. He declared, "It is time to cease muting the fact that Dr. Du Bois was a genius and chose to be a communist. Our irrational obsessive anticommunism has led us into too many quagmires to be retained as if it were a mode of scientific thinking." King extended his admonition beyond the Black community. He argued that white Americans also owed a debt to Du Bois: "Dr. Du Bois gave them a gift of truth for which they should eternally be indebted to him."[41]

With the shared goal of extending this "gift of truth," King articulated an alternative narrative about the causes and consequences of urban rebellions, and reactions to them by the state apparatus. Against those quick to define the events not as motivated by racism and class exploitation, but as a problem of the behavior of militant Black power activists and poor inner-city residents, King intoned an alternative reading. He argued that racial capitalism itself was the source of social and

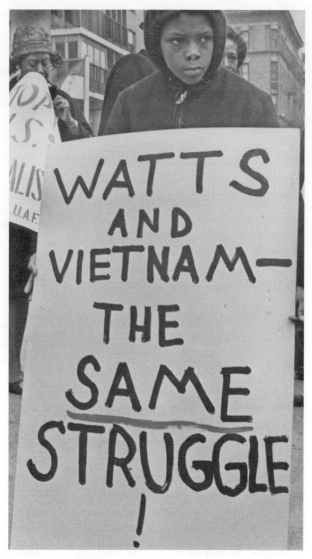

FIGURE 4. Photo by Builder Levy, *Watts and Vietnam*, Citywide Peace March to End War in Vietnam, Harlem contingent, New York, 1967. James E. Jackson and Esther Cooper Jackson Photographs Collection, Tamiment Library, New York University.

economic problems, a reading borne out by social movements emerging among the masses of people themselves.[42] In developing this analysis of the origins of the crisis in U.S. cities, King linked the national security state's counterinsurgency campaigns in Vietnam to the suppression of subaltern insurrections in Watts and Detroit. While analysts were (and continue to be) quick to describe the urban rebellions and rise of Black power in the wake of the events as markers of the collapse of the civil rights movement, he emphasized that they were rather signs of its unfinished business. King compelled social movements to see that the United States' imperialist war in Vietnam, which drew its soldiers from the poor, working class, and people of color, directed resources away from the social wage and toward the militarization of the political economy.[43]

By contrast, President Lyndon B. Johnson's statement on the Watts uprising drew a chain of equivalence between rioters and Klansmen, and revealed how a Cold War racial liberalism coalesced with racial conservatism in shaping the state's reaction to the crisis in U.S. cities. In August 1965, Johnson remarked, "A rioter with a Molotov cocktail in his hands is not fighting for civil rights any more than a Klansman with a sheet on his back and a mask on his face. They are both more or less what the law declares them: lawbreakers, destroyers of constitutional rights and liberties, and ultimately destroyers of a free America. They must be exposed and they must be dealt with." Johnson purported that equal treatment under the law required a tougher carceral response, a conclusion that revealed bipartisan consensus about authoritarian solutions to "disorder." This reaction to the events, reinforced by journalists, politicians, and cultural producers, also marked a shift from countersubversion to counterinsurgency as the hegemonic strategy of racialized crisis management. A wave of liberal social science research followed, similarly investigating the causes of the complex events deemed "civil disorders" in the psychological and sociological terms deemed within the tolerable bounds of Cold War racial discourse. United in an untidy unity against the Left, an alliance of conservatives, liberals, and nationalists denounced and even criminalized materialist analyses of race and racism that strayed from the emergent common-sense explanation.[44]

In what would be his last book, *Where Do We Go from Here: Chaos or Community?* (1968), King directly challenged the definitions of Johnson's administration as "prepared to implement measures leading to full equality but [having] waited in vain for the civil rights movement to offer the programs." King renounced the depiction of the Cold War national security state as benevolent and the freedom movement as lacking a program. He saw how this definition of the situation shifted the burden away from "the white majority" and offloaded responsibility onto "the oppressed minority." It represented the former as "withholding nothing" and the latter as "asking for nothing." "This is a fable," King explained, "not a fact." The circumstances themselves cried out for activists to carefully consider how to organize a multiracial alliance against poverty, King argued, "so that the government cannot elude our demands." He explained that organizers armed with the "knowledge of the science of social change" could study how state power actually works, and can "always finally be traced to those forces which we describe as ideological, economic and political." This analysis of the situation expressed the materialist analysis of race and class that had grown out of the Second Reconstruction.[45]

The Second Reconstruction sought the overthrow of Jim Crow and the creation of new, radically democratic institutions. In particular, it set its sights on access to the social wage programs that working-class people of color had been excluded from under Jim Crow. The passage of the Civil Rights Act (1964) and the Voting Rights Act (1965) were victories borne of an alliance between Black freedom, radical labor, and socialists rooted in the 1930s. The legal victories of the Black freedom movement to end Jim Crow segregation inspired Asian Americans, Mexican Americans, Puerto Ricans, and Native Americans to intensify their struggles against racism and for civil rights and access to public transportation, housing, education, and other essential infrastructure. Struggles for women's rights, gay rights, immigrant rights, and labor rights all benefited. The pressure of abolition democracy enabled unprecedented access and greater quality of social wage programs such as public education, hospitals, and post offices as well as expanded democracy at the point of production during the 1960s and 1970s. Just as the First Reconstruction had formed the first system of public education and inspired the labor movement for the eight-hour working day during the 1860s and 1870s, so too did the Second Reconstruction represent a dramatic turning point in the history of social movements.[46]

Yet the freedom movement only partially achieved its goals in the struggle for dignity, social justice, and freedom. Its victories, though substantial, were not enough to overturn dramatic polarizations of wealth and poverty within the United States. These material conditions obtained not just among Black communities in the Jim Crow South, but among poor and working people across the country. More than

60 percent of Black working people lived in urban industrial slums where their conditions were defined by poverty, exploitation, unemployment, inadequate education, and negligent medical care—conditions also experienced by at least fifty million poor and working people of all colors.[47] This dynamic pointed to the central contradictions of race and class in U.S. cities and regions in the postwar era. They highlighted the unfinished business of the long civil rights movement.[48]

Recognizing the "fierce urgency" of the situation, King argued for economic justice, thereby changing the terms of the debate and shifting the representation of the crisis. He increasingly called for a reallocation of public spending away from militarism and toward housing, health care, education, and jobs. By 1968 King was leading a fight for an Economic Bill of Rights for African Americans, Chicanos, Native Americans, Puerto Ricans, and poor whites. The Poor People's campaign specifically demanded a guaranteed income, low-income housing, and a jobs program in the radical tradition of the labor movement of the 1930s.[49] As he carried out this organizing, he was shunned by prominent Cold War liberals and ultimately assassinated in Memphis on April 4, 1968, "in the consciously chosen company of the poor," as the historian and civil rights activist Vincent Harding put it. Just as the freedom dreams unleashed during the First Reconstruction may have led to different outcomes but were crushed by counterrevolutionary forces, the revanchist response to the Second Reconstruction prevented the movement from fully realizing its visions.[50]

NO NAME IN THE STREET

White America remains unable to believe that black America's grievances are real; they are unable to believe this because they cannot face what this fact says about themselves and their country.

—James Baldwin, No Name in the Street, 1972

Following the assassination of King, a new wave of desperation and rebellion circulated through hundreds of U.S. cities. In response, the state deployed the largest number of federal troops since the Civil War to quell the insurrections.[51] James Baldwin was living in California during the turbulent events of 1968, where Ronald Reagan was governor. Baldwin remembered that what he "really found unspeakable about the man [Ronald Reagan] was his contempt, his brutal contempt for the poor."[52] Reagan had ridden a wave of reaction into the governor's mansion based on his promise to restore order in the wake of the Watts

rebellion of 1965. His 1966 gubernatorial campaign featured a rhetorical vengeance that appealed to a more punitive California political
economy and culture. In turn, Reagan's governor's office became a war
room for the development of revanchist solutions to social and economic crisis.[53]

In particular, Reagan set his sights on the Black Panther Party for
Self-Defense, a group formed in Oakland by Huey P. Newton and
Bobby Seale in 1966 to promote self-defense against police violence in
the wake of the Watts insurrection. Newton argued that the state's reaction to this new development within the Black freedom struggle led to
the expansion of a coercive state apparatus. Civil rights and nationalist organizations ranging from the SCLC to the Congress of Racial
Equality (CORE) to the NOI to the NAACP provided analyses of the
conditions that led to urban rebellions, including racial segregation,
unemployment, police brutality, poor health care, and unequal education. Noting that the Black Panther Party provided a socialist critique
of the material causes and consequences of the rebellions, Newton
claimed that the group was therefore targeted by the national security
state.[54]

The FBI had inaugurated its counterintelligence program (COIN-
TELPRO) in 1956 in order to crush the Communist Party. It expanded
the program in the late 1960s during the counterinsurgency against the
Black freedom struggle. Modeled on this counterinsurgency program,
police and sheriff's departments and other law enforcement agencies
repressed Black freedom movement organizations, antiwar groups that
challenged the legitimacy of the U.S. war in Vietnam, student activists,
and working-class labor organizers. They particularly labeled the Black
Panther Party as a national security threat.[55] During this period, a culture of counterinsurgency was nourished in police departments. This
counterinsurgency took a distinct shape in Los Angeles in the post-
rebellion restructuring of urban space. After Watts, LAPD police officer
Daryl Gates developed the Special Weapons and Tactics (SWAT) team.
Officers on the SWAT teams were trained in policing techniques that
had been developed during the Vietnam War. On December 8, 1969, the
Black Panther Party for Self-Defense's office on 41st and Central Avenue
was attacked by a Gates-led SWAT team, and police officials understood the attack as a domestic counterinsurgency mission.[56]

Baldwin depicted how the logic of counterinsurgency informed the
policing of the crisis: "The Panthers thus became the native Vietcong,
the ghetto became the village in which the Vietcong were hidden, and in

the ensuing search-and-destroy operations, everyone in the village became suspect."[57] With these words, Baldwin signaled how counterinsurgent ideologies in media and popular culture justified aggressive policing as a strategy of racialized crisis management. He also suggested how racialized law-and-order narratives of events obscured the counternarrative articulated in the expressive culture of the Black freedom movement. Such works not only challenged U.S. racial capitalism, they also indexed how such resistance was criminalized by the forces of law and order. They demonstrated an escalation in the use of counterinsurgent solutions to domestic social conflict that had been developed in the U.S. war in Vietnam. Such deployment of force marked a critical moment in the development of the neoliberal carceral state. Its foundation was set by the political victories of Cold Warriors, neoliberals, and counterinsurgents in California during this conjuncture.[58]

This dialectic persisted and intensified during the political and ideological struggle over the meaning of the dramatic events of 1967 and 1968. Activists, artists, and advocates connected to Black freedom, radical labor, and socialist movements attempted to complete the Second Reconstruction rooted in the 1930s. They would soon face the quandary of sustaining the freedom struggle amidst the economic crisis of the 1970s, the worst since the Great Depression.[59]

CHAPTER 2

Finally Got the News

Urban Insurgency, Counterinsurgency, and
the Crisis of Hegemony in Detroit

The actual fact of the matter is the movement of Black
workers is a class movement that is calling for a total change
in the relationship between workers and owners all together.

—John Watson in *Finally Got the News*, 1970

Money, we make it
Fore we see it you take it. . . .
Bills pile sky high
Send that boy off to die. . . .
Trigger happy policing
Panic is spreading
God knows where we're heading
Oh, make me wanna holler

—Marvin Gaye, "Inner City Blues (Make Me Wanna Holler)," from
the 1971 album *What's Going On?*

What's Going On? was Marvin Gaye's first self-composed album. The
songs fused Gaye's political concerns with the perspectives of the social
struggles being waged against racism, class exploitation, police repression, and the U.S. imperialist war in Vietnam. As Detroit's Black freedom and working-class struggles protested against racial capitalism and
for economic justice while playing bongo drums, Gaye's music drama-
tized these struggles to its own bongo drum beat.[1] In doing so, it articulated the social visions of the masses in motion.[2]

In the late 1960s Detroit was an epicenter of Black freedom, radical
labor, and student movements. In December 1968, John Watson, a

twenty-four-year-old Wayne State University student, newspaper editor, Black radical, socialist, and member of the Dodge Revolutionary Union Movement (DRUM) in Detroit traveled to Italy for an international anti-imperialist conference, where he was an invited speaker. The conference had grown out of the political struggles of students and workers in Italy and France. Watson, with overlapping membership in both the Panthers and DRUM, was an especially compelling speaker. At the conference he delivered a dynamic presentation on Black, working-class, and student struggles that had coalesced in the moment. Watson was so well received, he was invited to return in 1970 to distribute the film about the League of Revolutionary Black Workers in Detroit, *Finally Got the News,* amid a new wave of struggle in Italian factories and campuses. The film represented the League's vision of social change in the wake of the Detroit rebellion of 1967 and the May 1968 wildcat strikes in the Chrysler Corporation's Hamtramck Assembly plant, formerly known as the Dodge Main. In its depiction of struggle, the film offers an excellent point of departure for understanding the social visions articulated by the Black urban labor movement during this decisive historical moment.[3]

While much has been written about the events of 1968 in Paris, Prague, and Mexico City, less attention has been paid to the global significance of class struggles in Detroit during the period.[4] After all, as Stuart Hall, Chas Critcher, Tony Jefferson, John Clarke, and Brian Roberts observed in *Policing the Crisis,* the world revolution of 1968 was "an act of collective will, the breaks and ruptures stemming from the rapid expansion in the ideology, culture and civil structures of the new capitalism." This revolutionary moment constituted a crisis of hegemony. In Detroit, this crisis was expressed in the form of popular mobilizations against racism, capitalism, and imperialism in the industrial city.[5]

What was the relationship between the crisis of hegemony and mass antiracist and class struggle in the period? How did organic intellectuals resist and alter counterinsurgent narratives of events? What lessons do they suggest about the struggle for hegemony, even where these revolutionaries failed to achieve their goals? According to movement intellectuals and activists, the Detroit rebellion of July 1967, then the largest urban uprising in U.S. history, was essentially a working-class rebellion. The revolt was met with deadly force once state officials deployed National Guard troops, federal soldiers, and police officers to contain the insurrection. As a result, more than forty people were killed. While the events demonstrated the repressive power of the state, the rebellion also exposed the vulnerability of the auto corporations to the pressure of class struggle at the point of production. Nine months after the July rebellion in May 1968, more than four thousand workers shut down the Dodge Main auto plants that contained the lowest paying and most dangerous jobs. These events led to the formation of DRUM, the Eldon Avenue Revolutionary Movement, and the Ford Revolutionary Union Movement, which later became the League of Revolutionary Black Workers.[6]

The League represented a radical form of self-organization among Black industrial workers. Mike Hamlin, Ken Cockrel, John Watson, and General Gordon Baker were the initial members. Like many members of Detroit's African American working class, the leadership of the League's central committee had its roots in Black freedom-movement organizations such as the National Association for the Advancement of Colored People (NAACP), the Student Non-Violent Coordinating Committee, and the Congress of Racial Equality (CORE), while also sharing membership in trade unions such as the United Auto Workers (UAW). The League's organic intellectuals had honed their skills in Marxist theory through a study group on Karl Marx's *Capital* with Martin Glaberman, himself a member of a number of socialist groups in the city, including the Johnson-Forest Tendency associated with C. L. R. James, Raya Dunayevskaya, and James and Grace Lee Boggs. Glaberman had also been an organic intellectual working in the auto plants for two decades before teaching at Wayne State University. He first met young future League members such as John Watson in a class taught by the Marxist historian and sociologist George Rawick at Monteith College of Wayne State University.[7]

The League proposed a dialectical and materialist critique of material conditions in a vernacular style. It articulated a kind of radical social theory that engaged the self-activity of the working class involved in forms of social struggle such as urban rebellions and wildcat strikes—activities that had been roundly criminalized.[8] They questioned the legitimacy of capitalist hegemony and challenged the racist common sense. They presented a Marxist framework designed to explain the roots of class exploitation, poverty, and police brutality. They meshed Black working-class expressive culture with socialist visions of class struggle to contribute to the philosophy of praxis. In doing so they provided a counterpoint to dominant ideologies of race, class, gender, and sexuality in the midst of urban rebellions, the Moynihan Report, the Kerner Commission, and the televised representations of uprisings and

FIGURE 5. John Watson presents a lecture on the relationship between race and class in the United States against a backdrop of posters from the events of 1968 in a scene from the film *Finally Got the News* (1970) by Stewart Bird, Rene Lichtman, and Peter Gessner. Produced in association with the League of Revolutionary Black Workers.

social movements. They produced the radical film *Finally Got the News* as well as the newspaper *Inner City Voice* and distributed the Wayne State University paper the *South End* to provide ways of seeing how the urban uprisings in the streets and strikes in the auto factories were perceived and fought out. Their cultural productions declared that the Black working class represented the vanguard of socialist transformation. They theorized strategies and tactics relevant to the workers' struggle at the point of production in the context of an entire community fighting for liberation. They demanded an end to racism in the plants as well as in the unions and were willing to call strikes on their own behalf.[9]

The years between 1967 and 1971 saw the highest number of strikes in the postwar period, except 1946. Most of them were wildcats. These strikes represented one of the largest work stoppages in North American history, and a high tide in the history of the class struggle.[10] The League consciously drew on collective memories of what W. E. B. Du Bois called the "general strike" of 1863–65, when one million Black workers freed themselves through a general strike and sparked one of the most success-ful interracial working-class movements in U.S. history. In that period workers ruptured a racial and labor regime that had been centuries in the making, and initiated the most dramatic effort at democracy, waged *by* the poor and *for* "the working millions[,] that this world had ever seen."[11] These episodes of working-class self-emancipation in the 1860s and the 1960s were, as C. L. R. James put it, "historical events of the first importance in the history of Black people at any time and today."[12]

Black radicals and socialists in Detroit deployed cultural productions to counter dominant narratives of events, and used them to illuminate the importance of collective memory for radical social movements. They therefore provide particularly compelling examples of "*conjunc-tural interventionist* work."[13] The production of meaning through cul-tural expression was a practical activity by the most strategically located sector of the North American working class at the time. Their cultural products suggested how the rebellions in the streets and factories were part of Black freedom and radical working-class movements rather than instances of criminality and violence that betrayed the vision of the civil rights movement. In this chapter, I argue that the counterinsurgent response to the events in Detroit sustained and naturalized the state's strategy of incarcerating the crisis.[14]

THE COLD WAR AND THE CRISIS OF FORDISM IN DETROIT

The risks were great, the pressure enormous, but it was exhilarating, and the success impacted black workers not only at Chrysler but throughout the auto industry and workplaces of all types. It also brought back militancy to the working class and broke the shackles that had suppressed the class struggle during the McCarthy period.

—Mike Hamlin, foreword to *Rebel Rank and File: Labor Militancy and Revolt from Below During the Long 1970s,* 2010

Perhaps more than any other industrial city in North America, Detroit symbolized the contradictions of Fordism during the twentieth cen-tury.[15] Deployed by Antonio Gramsci, the concept of Fordism described the ways in which this mode of production created "complications, absurd positions, and moral and economic crises often tending toward catastrophe." In doing so, it sought to explain the system of mass pro-duction typified by the introduction of the assembly line by Henry Ford before World War I. Fordism was inaugurated with Ford's introduction of the five-dollar, eight-hour day for workers who passed the company's sociology exam. While workers soon discovered that this wage was a fiction, as Martin Glaberman observed, Fordism's combination of so-called high wages with an intensification of exploitation in the auto industry provided a crucial turning point in the history of capitalist development, as did Fordism's decline in the last half of the twentieth century.[16]

Ford, Chrysler, and General Motors located their headquarters and plant operations in and around Detroit. Their wealth depended on the extraction of surplus value from an industrial working class that continually struggled over the conditions of its labor. Thus, Detroit was an epicenter of class struggle. The owners of the auto plants in the city sought to consolidate their class power through the importation of uprooted migrants and the exploitation of their labor. Since World War II required higher production, the auto industry followed Henry Ford's lead in transforming assembly lines to produce military equipment such as airplanes, tanks, and vehicles for the warfare state. Indeed, the city was an epicenter of the military-industrial complex. This shift in production absorbed surpluses of capital and labor by forcing millions of dispossessed migrants to move from rural areas in the South to the war-industry city of Detroit. Fordist economics, politics, and culture fundamentally shifted the social relations of production. As part of their effort to regulate the contradictions these changes unleashed, capitalists drew on a U.S. tradition of counterinsurgency in the factories to maintain a divided proletariat by segregating different "races" into different places. This strategy of racial and spatial discipline provided a primary mechanism of social control for U.S. industrial capitalism.[17]

Black workers who had been critical in the formation of the Congress of Industrial Organizations (CIO) were at the forefront of the freedom movement to abolish Jim Crow. Since the 1930s and 1940s the Black industrial working class had engaged in struggles that gave a "moral impetus" to the efforts to complete the Second Reconstruction.[18] At the end of World War II, at least 1.25 million Black organized workers were in industrial unions. African American workers in unions provided key leadership in the movement to overturn Jim Crow and achieve full citizenship. Indeed, it was the CIO's commitment to the struggle for civil rights that earned it widespread support among workers of color. At the same time, however, the CIO failed to put Black workers in the leadership of the organization, and did not organize extensively among domestic and agricultural workers who had been excluded from the New Deal. They also agreed to a no-strike pledge during the war that undermined their organizing among Black workers in the plants. But the most decisive turning point came in the wake of the strike wave in 1945 and 1946, the largest in U.S. labor history, when the CIO expelled eleven unions led by the Left, who had "the best record in promoting antiracism and defending the civil and legal rights of workers of color."[19]

By the late 1940s anticommunism had become the primary tool of countersubversives for suppressing dissent in domestic spaces, and for legitimating the geographical expansion of U.S. capital internationally. Moral panics about communism were invoked in order to win consent to the imperatives of capital. By exaggerating communist threats to national security, these panics created a sense of crisis among working people. In turn, these security narratives provided justification for the promotion of Cold War policies. In the face of increasing militancy among Black workers, most powerfully represented by the 1945 and 1946 strike wave, this postwar red baiting was accompanied by the promotion of a pro-segregationist ideology. Such Cold War security narratives legitimated the criminalization of dissent. By demonizing groups depicted as internal enemies or agents of foreign powers, the practices and policies of countersubversion became institutionalized within a national security state, especially through President Harry S. Truman's ascent to the White House. Such moves put the security state on the path of permanent warfare. Significantly, this militarization of the political economy during the Cold War launched an age of U.S. hegemony in the world capitalist system.[20]

While the living standards of U.S. workers increased during the postwar period, these higher wages were combined with a political assault on radical organizations that undermined working-class power in the long run. Perhaps the clearest illustration of this repression was the Taft-Hartley Act of 1947, which suppressed the right of Communists to organize in the unions. In Detroit, former radical Walter Reuther opportunistically joined the Alliance of Catholic Trade Unionists and other anticommunists to solidify his power over the UAW. The rise of Reuther to the presidency of the union led to a withdrawal of support for Black leadership in trade unionism, despite his commitment to funding civil rights initiatives.[21]

During the early Cold War, Reuther forged an alliance among liberals that ultimately directed the union away from militant Black freedom struggles and toward a tacit acceptance of the segregationist politics promoted by capitalist forces in the city.[22] Trade union membership declined from 5.2 million at the end of the war to 3.7 million in 1950 as the countersubversive bloc within labor collaborated with capital and the Cold War national security state. The UAW's direction of the labor movement away from radicalism and toward Cold War racial liberalism under Reuther continued for the next two decades, a fact that suggests the ideological basis of the postwar settlement of organized labor with big capital.[23]

Capitalists in the postwar era likewise deployed anticommunist narratives to legitimate their class power. Their countersubversive ideology helped maintain and justify a racial division of labor and structured the social relations of production. Such racist practices at the point of production were combined with other federal programs and incentives toward similar ends. For example, massive federal subsidies were offered to whites to build houses in suburbs in the postwar period. In the absence of such policies, the Black poor were relegated to overcrowded housing in urban ghettos. The Black urban poor were displaced from inner-city neighborhoods as a result of urban renewal programs in Detroit. This uneven development facilitated capital's move away from investments in industrial production and toward speculative investments in office construction, luxury housing, art museums, and other real estate projects. These urban policies contributed to a distinct pattern of racial and class formation in the city, and encouraged whites to invest in their whiteness rather than in a multiracial class struggle for better wages and working conditions.[24]

At the same time, increasingly politicized confrontations between the Black poor and the almost all-white Detroit police department occurred in the context of broad-based and increasingly violent white resistance to civil rights protests. The aggressive organizing of white homeowners alongside the repressive policing and the discriminatory practices of banks and real estate brokers maintained the segregation of Detroit. This repression of struggles for access to housing, busing to integrate public schools, and other key aspects of the social wage was an essential aspect of the era. These conflicts occurred in a context where racial segregation left Black workers spatially and economically "trapped" in overcrowded neighborhoods where they endured a fatal link between poverty and police repression. They also experienced an intensification of the rate of exploitation because of the articulation between increasing rates of production and strategies of racial management.[25]

During the late 1960s Black workers became the majority of laborers in Detroit auto plants for the first time. Many of these workers were young and politicized by participating in the long civil rights movement. For example, League members John Watson and Mike Hamlin had worked with both CORE and the NAACP. Hamlin and Watson also admired the commitment to the class struggle of Communists and socialists they encountered through their speeches and organizing in the city. These young militants therefore sought to blend the Black freedom struggle's approach to antiracism with a Marxist focus on organizing the working class for fundamental social change, a commitment that ruptured the appearance of consensus under Cold War liberalism.[26] Indeed, the historical example of the League directs our attention to the central role of workers in the social movements of the 1960s.[27]

As these Black radicals took the lead in struggles for social change, unwaged Black workers once again disproportionately filled the ranks of the relative surplus population having been the last hired and first fired.[28] The auto corporations saw the changing demographics in the factory and presence of a reserve army of labor as an opportunity to increase the rate of exploitation on the shop floor through unprecedented production levels. These speed-ups also sparked increased militancy in the plants. As John Watson explained, Black workers protested vigorously against speed-ups that required them to produce at levels "previously done by three white men." In so doing they confronted a racial division of labor where more than 90 percent of the foremen, superintendents, skilled tradesmen, and skilled apprentices were white. This racist hierarchy at the point of production produced a situation where safety conditions were systematically ignored. These race and class dynamics on the shop floor were sure to produce their own negation. Black workers not only struggled for control at the point of production, but also engaged in grassroots social protests against police brutality, second-class houses, and second-class schools. In these ways they contributed to the self-organization of an entire community fighting for liberation.[29]

URBAN INSURGENCY IN DETROIT

First—let there be no mistake about it—the looting, arson, plunder and pillage which have occurred are not part of the civil rights protest. . . That is crime—and crime must be dealt with forcefully, and swiftly, and certainly.

—President Lyndon B. Johnson, address to the nation, July
    27, 1967

Political and expressive cultures were perhaps more interwoven in Detroit than in any other North American industrial city. Berry Gordy, the founder of Motown records, was a former autoworker, and many musicians came from Detroit's Black working-class neighborhoods, including Diana Ross and the Supremes, Florence Ballard, and Mary Milson. Dance halls and nightclubs provided spaces of leisure for industrial workers subjected to backbreaking labor as a workforce. On July 23, 1967, the then-largest insurrection in U.S. history began in a downtown Detroit club.[30]

The Detroit rebellion began as city residents witnessed police harassment of a homecoming party for two Black soldiers returning from service in the U.S. war in Vietnam. The party occurred at a bar called the United Community and Civil League on Twelfth Street. On July 22, the Detroit police raided a series of so-called blind pigs (after-hours clubs), with the fifth and final raid being the venue that hosted the party. Only a few blocks away from the club, twenty-seven-year-old Army veteran Danny Thomas had recently been murdered by a gang of white youths. Community members were still reeling. While harassment for after-hours drinking was a persistent practice in Detroit, the police usually forced people to disperse and arrested just a few. But that night they arrested all eighty-five people at the party.[31] It did not take long for the aggrieved people of Detroit's slums and nightclubs to resist this criminalization "on their own terms."[32]

As Dan Georgakas and Marvin Surkin show in their indispensable book *Detroit: I Do Mind Dying*, photos of the revolt documented "systematic and integrated looting" among Black and poor white working-class participants "shopping for free."[33] Yet it was described in massmediated cultural outlets such as the *New York Times* as a riot waged by "Negroes in Detroit," which they asserted created a rampage of crime, violence, and chaos. A curfew was issued to suppress the insurrection. Soon after the uprising, U.S. Attorney General Ramsey Clark was contacted by Michigan Governor George Romney in order to request federal troops be sent in to crush the rebellion. On July 27 Johnson addressed the nation as part of an effort to ensure that order would be restored. He appealed to the Insurrection Act of 1807 as the legal basis for the deployment of troops in domestic territory. Johnson's attempt to distinguish between a legitimate civil rights protest and crime while calling on the Insurrection Act should compel us to reconsider the crisis of hegemony. By defining the ghetto revolt against joblessness, police brutality, and exploitation at the point of production as a riot, the narrative of counterinsurgency endorsed the expansion of milita-rized-carceral solutions to the crisis.[34]

The prose of counterinsurgency depicted the event as an instance of crime, violence, and chaos. In fact, it purported that the revolt was not about civil rights violations or motivated by working-class grievances, but rather as an outburst of criminality. This definition of the situation provided a distorted image.[35] This distortion has had material conse-quences, ones that are particularly critical for understanding the his-torically specific and contingent relationships between racial ordering, capitalist restructuring, and the formation of the carceral state. Such narratives depicted resistance as violent, irrational, and futile expres-sions that justified violent reactions by the state apparatus to impose the rule of law and restore order. The capitalist state's expansion of coun-terinsurgency in cities can therefore be understood as a reaction to the crisis of hegemony for capital and the state represented by the overturn-ing of Jim Crow racial regimes.[36]

Counterinsurgency and uneven capitalist development had been articulated as part of U.S. political and economic policy throughout W. W. Rostow's tenure as the U.S. national security advisor under Presi-dent Johnson between 1964 and 1968. Rostow's stage theory of eco-nomic development purported that capitalist development first required security forces to impose order. In the wake of the Detroit rebellion, Rostow wrote to President Johnson: "At home your appeal is for law and order as the framework for economic and social progress. Abroad we fight in Vietnam to make aggression unprofitable . . . [to] build a future of economic and social progress." In Rostow's words, national security counterinsurgency policies had a direct impact on the policing of the urban crisis.[37]

Journalistic narratives often reproduced the state's counterinsurgent definitions of crisis. Consider for example *Newsweek*'s take on the events in the earliest hours of July 23: "The trouble burst on Detroit like a firestorm and turned the nation's fifth largest city into a theater of war. Whole streets lay ravaged by looters, whole blocks immolated by flames. Federal troops—the first sent into racial battle outside the South in a quarter of a century—occupied American streets at bayonet point."[38] Such narratives of burning and looting sought to legitimate the military occupation of domestic space. "If there is one point that has been proved repeatedly over four summers of ghetto riots," *Time* magazine suggested, "it is that when the police abandon the street, the crowd takes it over, and the crowd can swiftly become a mob. It happened in

Watts, in Boston's Roxbury district, in Newark and in blood and fire in Detroit." Magazine audiences were led to believe that the police and military merely helped restore order. The *Time* narrative continued, "Typically enough, Detroit's upheaval started with a routine police action. Seven weeks ago, in the Virginia Park section of the West Side, a 'blind pig' (after-hours club) opened for business on Twelfth Street, styling itself the 'United Community League for Civic Action.' Along with the after hours booze that it offered to minors, the 'League' served up Black-power harangues and curses against Whitey's exploitation. It was at the blind pig, on a sleazy strip of pawnshops and bars, rats and pimps, junkies and gamblers, that the agony began."[39]

Profound anxieties are represented in this narrative. Fears of urban revolt certainly shape this description, but tellingly, it is replete with moral panics over the proletarian pursuit of pleasure. Detroit's dance halls and nightclubs were targeted as sites of criminality. The *Time* and *Newsweek* narratives did not define the events as being motivated by structural racism and class exploitation, but rather as resulting from the behavior of Black power activists and poor inner-city residents. The logic of such representations suggested that proletarian bodies needed discipline by the state that was not otherwise being provided by the sheer "force of circumstance." This definition of the situation implied that the police raid of the club was as much about policing the purported immorality of Black workers as it was about preventing alcohol from being served after hours.[40]

According to General Gordon Baker, cofounder of DRUM and the League of Revolutionary Black Workers, such taken-for-granted narratives should be read against the grain, since blind pigs were "part of the culture of Detroit." Black workers engaged in these cultural practices to turn segregated places into spaces of congregation. Because of the racist allocation of shifts by management, Black workers on the infamous second and third shifts would work until as late as three in the morning while bars officially closed at two. Baker recounts how on the weekends young workers would go to the blind pigs after work to have drinks. Given the commonality of the practice, the police attack on this cherished custom was a clear insult to the working people of Detroit, all the more so since this particular blind pig was hosting a party for returning soldiers from Vietnam. Baker remembers, "To attack a blind pig was just ridiculous." This type of policing was a key factor that motivated the aggrieved and insurgent residents of Detroit's nightclubs and ghettos to risk life and limb to participate in the then-largest urban revolt in U.S. history.[41]

The revolt turned the world upside down. In an atmosphere akin to the carnivalesque, the poor and working people of Detroit directly appropriated the social wealth. Residents of the industrial slum took food from grocery stores and seized property such as electric guitars, amps, albums, and other items from the many pawnshops in the Twelfth Street neighborhood that was the epicenter of the uprising.[42] As a former resident, Baker explains, "I mean hell, everybody lived on the pawnshop. . . . And on the back of pawnshop slip it says in great big letters and it is still there today 'not responsible for fire, theft, and other unavoidable accidents.' So the pawnshops got tore open and everybody broke into the pawnshops and then it just spread." As the insurgent ghetto residents engaged in the appropriation and burning of property, fire quickly engulfed the city because, as Rawick observed, Detroit's ghettos were "fire traps," with as "bad a housing as any industrial country in the world."[43]

General Baker was one of the more than seven thousand people arrested and taken to the state prison in Ionia, Michigan, after the rebellion. "My cellblock looked like the damned assembly lines," he remembers. "People had seen the naked role of the state and they hated these goddamned police."[44] When the Detroit working class went back to the shop floor in the wake of the rebellion, Baker concludes, "they were different folks. They were not the same folks they were before the rebellion." Baker reasons that the uprising quickened the step of the working class at the point of production by sparking a new consciousness of the ability they had to alter the relations of class power.[45]

The self-activity and collective struggles of urban proletarians led to an end "for the period of the revolt of the infamous second and third shifts, because they refused to work at night."[46] The revolt also caused the "shutdown of three giants of American capitalism: Ford, Chrysler, and General Motors," as Glaberman noted. The significance of Detroit's autoworkers winning a temporary end to the infamous night shift in the factories is best understood when compared to Karl Marx's analysis of the Paris Commune. Marx celebrated the abolition of night work for bakers and, as Friedrich Engels noted, "the closing of the pawnshops, on the ground that they were a private exploitation of labour, and were in contradiction with the right of the workers to their instruments of labour and to credit."[47]

The Detroit rebellion of 1967 provides an important historical lesson: the refusal of mass criminalization by the working and wageless people of Detroit represented a crisis of hegemony.[48] While the uprising in Detroit was one of hundreds of urban rebellions during the moment, it occurred in the context of a deeply politicized and concentrated Black working-class community in Detroit's ghetto and factories. The self-activity and collective struggles of the Black working class on the move led antiracists and socialists to theorize the revolt as a point of reference for the working class movement on both sides of the Atlantic. They argued that this direct challenge to the capitalist state opened up new possibilities for antiracist, feminist, and socialist movements during the age of liberation struggles.[49]

A CRISIS OF COLD WAR RACIAL LIBERALISM

The criminals who committed these acts of violence against the people deserve to be punished—and they must be punished.

—President Lyndon B. Johnson, address to the nation, July 27, 1967

The culture of poverty that results from unemployment and family breakup generates a system of ruthless, exploitative relationships within the ghetto. Prostitution, dope addiction, and crime create an environmental "jungle" characterized by personal insecurity and tension. Children growing up under such conditions are likely participants in civil disorder.

—Report of the National Advisory Commission on Civil Disorders, 1968

Activists, grassroots artists, journalists, and intellectuals connected to Black freedom and socialist movements were not the only ones desiring an analysis of the rebellions in Detroit and other cities across the country. Indeed, the urban revolts drew increased political and scholarly attention to the themes of race, rebellion, crime, and law and order. For example, the sociologist and White House advisor Daniel Patrick Moynihan, who had earlier asserted that Black resilience strategies constituted a "tangle of pathology," weighed in: "What needs to be done is first garrison the central cities. We've got to prevent this kind of lack of authority." He went on to call for creating employment opportunities for the Black poor and for an immediate rebuilding of the burned-out areas, but he prioritized the expansion of policing and security measures.[50] At the same time, social scientists asserted that the urban rebellions were caused by "outside agitators" and unemployed, unskilled criminals. Yet as attorney and journalist Frank Donner explains, "The crowd phobias of the past, the 'riff-raff' theories, lost credibility."[51]

It was in the context of this crisis of authority that President Johnson gave a speech calling for the establishment of a commission to determine the causes of the events. He appointed Illinois governor Otto Kerner to lead the inquiry that would eventually be published as *The Report of the National Advisory Commission on Civil Disorders.* The Kerner Commission was instructed to determine the causes of the uprisings to prevent them from occurring again. Made up of representatives of political elites from industry, government, labor, police, and mainstream civil rights organizations, the commission was a critical force in the development of new strategies of crisis management. When the document was released in early 1968 with a foreword by *New York Times* columnist Tom Wicker, it was extremely well received and sold as many as two million copies of the paperback edition in the United States.[52]

Not since Gunnar Myrdal's *An American Dilemma,* published in 1944, had an analysis of race been carried out at the scale of the Kerner Commission report. It became the defining statement of liberalism on race in the postwar period. It provided a definition of the urban crisis of the 1960s that has become taken for granted. It did so through a strategic and selective presentation of its conclusions through mass-media outlets. In one of its most-often-quoted phrases, the report claimed, "Our nation is moving toward two societies, one Black, one white— separate and unequal." It famously argued that "what white Americans never understood—but what the Negro can never forget—is that white society is deeply implicated in the ghetto. White institutions created it, white institutions maintain it, and white society condones it." The Kerner Commission's conclusions were based on data primarily gathered during the Detroit rebellion, and were widely circulated in mass-media narratives.[53]

Making use of an array of statistics and qualitative interviews, the Kerner report described conditions such as unemployment, poverty, housing discrimination, income inequality, and racial perceptions to provide a causal argument to understand how to prevent rebellions labeled as civil disorders. Despite the commission's findings based on what most experts agreed was a sound assessment that white racism and poverty were the key factors shaping the urban uprisings, the report would still assert that structural and institutionalized inequality could not fully explain the causes of the rebellions. It shifted its focus from politics and economics to family structures by claiming that conditions of unemployment among Black poor people produced a "culture of poverty." The report reflected a growing common sense that a culture of poverty in the ghetto caused social problems. Its framework was rooted in the logic of the Moynihan Report, which asserted that poor Black people's family structures prevented social and economic development. To be sure, dominant ideologies of race, gender, and sexuality were crucial to the narratives employed by traditional intellectuals in analyzing the causes of the revolt. Deploying behavioral models prevalent in liberal social science at the time, the Kerner Commission shifted the structure of understanding away from long-term structural inequality to establish a causal chain from family structure to social crisis.[54]

Crucially, the report legitimated the perception that a "culture of poverty . . . generates a system of ruthless exploitative relationships within the ghetto." In doing so, it sanctified the racial liberal common sense that criminality in poor communities of color was "the pathological outcome of racial discrimination."[55] It further argued that counterintelligence units "staffed with full-time personnel should be established to gather, evaluate, analyze and disseminate information on potential as well as actual disorders. . . . It should use undercover police personnel and information." The commission recommended integrating leaders and organizations from communities of color into surveillance operations. It also argued that media should "improve coordination with police in reporting riot news through advance planning and cooperate with the police in the designation of police information centers . . . and [the] development of mutually beneficial guidelines for riot reporting."[56]

While the Kerner Commission rejected countersubversive narratives of events promoted by figures such as FBI director J. Edgar Hoover, who depicted radicals and revolutionaries as the source of uprisings, "urged broader social intelligence programs to provide a barometer of potential disturbances," according to Donner. As such, these recommendations distorted its message of race and class inequality conveyed in the two-nation thesis, and this distortion had a logic to it. It provided justification for carceral resolutions of the urban crisis. As such, the Kerner Commission's call for expanding police surveillance as a tactical response to rebellions represented a shift in the hegemonic form of racialized crisis management, one that simultaneously named racial inequality as a problem and made counterinsurgent appeals to security to secure its legitimacy.[57]

VISIONS OF THE FUTURE IN THE PRESENT

The dispossessed of this nation—the poor, both white and Negro—
live in a cruelly unjust society. They must organize a revolution
against that injustice, not against the lives of the persons who are
their fellow citizens, but against the structures through which the
society is refusing to . . . lift the load of poverty.
—Martin Luther King Jr., *The Trumpet of Conscience*, 1968

The Kerner Commission's definition of the urban crisis of the 1960s
should compel us to reconsider how it contrasted with the perspectives
of the Black freedom movement. As we saw in the previous chapter,
Martin Luther King Jr. responded to the urban rebellion of the 1960s by
challenging the structure of racism, militarism, and poverty. In his
speeches he linked the racist and imperialist war in Vietnam to the political and economic repression of the poor and working-class people of
color. As they initiated demands on the state for an end to police brutality, equal access to the social wage, and civil and human rights, Dr. King
sought to articulate the struggle for the redistribution of social wealth.[58]
In February of 1968 King visited Detroit to gain support for the Poor
People's Campaign. Then Black sanitation workers went on strike in
Memphis, and he joined them. Dr. King's tragic assassination in April
of 1968 in that city sparked new upheavals in Detroit and across the
country.[59]

Perhaps like no year since 1848, 1968 is remembered as a year of
global revolution and counterrevolution. The tumultuous events
included urban uprisings in more than two hundred cities after Dr.
King's murder, student and worker mobilizations in Paris in May, mobilizations in Mexico City among students and workers, and uprisings in
Kingston, Jamaica, after the Black Marxist historian Walter Rodney
was prevented from reentering the country. These struggles were not
unrelated. The spontaneous rebellions of the poor asserted the emergence of an aggrieved and insurgent people with specific class aims and
interests.[60]

Black freedom and radical labor struggles in Detroit gained momen-
tum following the garbage workers' strike in Memphis. In May, more
than four thousand autoworkers initiated wildcat strikes at the Dodge
Main. As part of an effort to organize the energies unleashed by the
urban rebellions into a social force at the point of production, Black
workers in DRUM established picket lines at the factory gates to shut
down the plant while marching to the rhythm of bongo drums.

The Voice Of Revolution

Inner City Voice

20¢ In Detroit

Vol. 1, No. 7   Detroit's Black Community Newspaper   APRIL 1968

AND NOW KING
WHO IS NEXT ?

On Thursday evening, April 4, 1968, while standing on the balcony of a Memphis hotel, Dr. Martin Luther King, Jr. was felled by an assasin's bullet. Within one hour's time, the news media across the country was announcing the King was murdered by a lone assasin and that no conspiracy was involved; as we go to press one week later one lone assassin is still being sought

Why no conspiracy Because even though Dr Martin Luther King Jr. was the most famous black leader in the Civil Rights Movement, in relation to America's racist, decadent society, he was just another "black nigger". We reiterate that a blackman living under the scope and influence of American society, be he Ralph Bunche, Martin Luther King, or Joe P. Jones, exists as a super-exploited subject with less rights than a common street dog. To state that there was a conspiracy involved in Dr. King's murder would in essence be like saying that it takes an elaborate plan, a meeting of minds for a "whiteman to kill a nigger". In contrast, everytime a black brother anyplace in the U.S. picks up a brick and breaks a white store owner's window, he finds himself involved in a giant conspiracy by the time he gets to court.

We cry out that not only was the assassination of Dr. King a conspiracy but it is part and parcel of the largest and most brutal conspiracies in history and that even the attitudes and prostrations the honkies have been going through, acting like they are mourning, are conspiratory. This conspiracy is part of the step by step escalation of the brutal, bestial, inhumane war of genocide being waged by the ruling white powers and their fascist machines against the Afro-American population pinned up in the confines of these 50 racist states

WHY DR. KING

Dr. King was the foremost advocate of non-violence to which we are, have been, and always will be opposed to, because it is some of the most ridiculous hogwash to ever be taugh in the history of mankind's struggle against oppression. Dr King offered no threat to the system; his intent was for black people to share equally in the exploitation and plunder of the rest of the world. King's preaching put him in the chorus of the tomming non-violent preachers along with Roy Wilkins, Whitney Young, Jr., and the likes. But King differed from the rest in the sense that he showed signs of moving independently at times. Dr. King came out in opposition to the racist war in Vietnam. He voiced his opposition long after Black revolutionaries and students had staged massive demonstrations against the brutal onslaught, but he did oppose it. Dr. King moved again to the dislike of the power structure by supporting the black workers struggle in Memphis before his d ath. Also, as far back as winter of 1.64-65, J. Edgar Hoover came out and called Dr. King "The biggest liar in the country," indicating further the uneasy trust the power structure had for him Roy Wilkins and Whitney Young have proven their positions; they will support any action whatsoever the power structure takes, be it the napalm bombing of black ghettos in American, or the shooting of black workers who are courageous enough to resist the oppression and exploitation of Chrysler, Ford, G.M. or other capitalist giants. These supertoms will stick as close to the power structure's actions as Vice President Ky of South Vietnam's puppet government is sticking to Fascist General Westmoreland's decisions on Vietnam.

Continued on pg. 2

inside

Page no.
Crusader................. 12

Defense and survival..... 18
Panthers................. 10 & 2
Capon corner............. 10
Editorial................ 9

The new address of the Inner City Voice:
8661 Grand River
Detroit, Michigan

FIGURE 6. Cover of the *Inner City Voice*, produced by the League of Revolutionary Black Workers in the wake of Martin Luther King Jr.'s assassination in 1968. Newspapers Collection, Tamiment Library, New York University.

Company officials used photography as a mode of surveillance against direct action and subsequently used the pictures as evidence to punish Black workers. Twenty-six workers, including strike leader General Baker, were fired, and other workers were forced to miss workdays. As a cultural and political tool to counter the criminalization of worker self-activity, militants formed a semi-autonomous Black worker caucus. They produced a newsletter to address the racist conditions in the plant as part of their effort to channel discontent into political organization on the shop floor. They eventually succeeded in getting the laid-off workers rehired. From the outset, the newsletter highlighted the racism of the company as well as the consistent failures of the UAW to respond to the grievances of Black workers. The newsletter similarly decried the UAW's support of the Detroit police department's brutality directed at the Black community.[61]

DRUM used cultural productions to dramatize the contradictions of life under U.S. racial capitalism and the emergent carceral state. Toward that end, they published leaflets documenting racist conditions in the plants and published the *Inner City Voice* to tap the energy unleashed by the 1967 rebellion at the point of production. John Watson also edited the Wayne State University campus paper, the *South End,* and used it to provide news and analysis about antiracist and anticapitalist struggles. These cultural productions delineated the ideas and actions of an autonomous Black workers' struggle that included demands for the elimination of racism in the union and in corporate bureaucracies as part of a coordinated Black freedom struggle for moral authority at the point of knowledge production, a better social wage, and the democratic transition to socialism. The Black students and workers in the group were able to build a federation of community-based struggles over housing, schools, police brutality, wages, and cultural dignity— forming the League to coordinate their political and cultural activity.[62]

League organizers were long-term antiracist and anticapitalist activists. They called attention to the social struggle against racial capitalism and for a new society, while their cultural productions intertwined with the heightened working-class militancy of the period. Interventions in culture seized the political imagination of many radicals, and underscored the importance of the ideological class struggle. Representing the contradictions of race and class in U.S. industrial cities, the League struggled over which definition of the dramatic events of 1968 would capture the political imagination. They engaged in a class struggle in culture to transform the common sense by articulating an antiracist and socialist vision of social transformation, a vision that attempted to neu-tralize the prose of counterinsurgency.[63]

Filmed in the context of the events of 1968, and following the rebel-lion of the previous year, *Finally Got the News* tells the dramatic story of the dialectics of insurgency in Detroit.[64] Produced, directed, and dis-tributed in association with League members such as Cockrel, Watson, and Hamlin, the film derived its title from a chant delivered during direct-action protests by Black workers and their allies, "Finally got the news / how our dues are being used." The film takes the history of Black freedom and class struggles in North America as its point of departure. As an instance of revolutionary filmmaking, it presents the cultural history of social struggles. It taps the poetic and musical practices that shape the lives of the working class in Detroit. It presents the roots of a distinct phase of political, economic, and ideological development in a popular form. Set against the background of the music of Detroit, it provides a powerful representation of the freedom dreams of labor and freedom struggles. The film draws on the aesthetic poetics of the Black radical tradition to delineate a distinct way of seeing transfor-mations in the political economy of U.S. industrial capitalism. This way of seeing was essential, as Fordism's promise of high wages and full employment was contradicted by the facts of punitive policing, precarious labor, and perilous housing in the postwar urban ghetto. In wrestling with the contradictions of race and class in the city and the factory in the way that it does in this precise historical conjunc-ture, the film offers a materialist critique of the conditions of the poor and the working class that highlights the unfinished business of the Second Reconstruction. It therefore serves as an alternative archive of this decisive historical conjuncture, a moment of rupture marked by radical social protest, economic crisis, and the restructuring of the state form.[65]

In the opening vignette, to a drumbeat, *Finally Got the News* presents a series of historical documents illustrating how the surplus value pro-duced by Black workers under slavery gave rise to American industrial capitalism. Inspired by the historical and theoretical frameworks in Karl Marx's *Capital* and W. E. B. Du Bois's *Black Reconstruction in America*, it provides a cinematic representation of how the emancipation of Black workers from slavery quickened the step of the American working class as a whole. As the intensity of the drumbeat increases, the audience is presented with scenes from the history of the class war that ultimately culminated in the formation of the CIO during the 1930s, a period when the working class created mass power of a kind unparalleled on an international scale. Emphasizing the dialectics of insurgency, these images are juxtaposed with the pervasive and persistent forms of antilabor and antiradical repression. In addition to tapping collective memories from radical labor and freedom movements in the United States, the film features shots from the Mexican revolutionary artist Diego Rivera's mural of Fordist auto production in the city. These representations of the history of the class struggle provide the context for the film's depiction of what was known among the working people of Detroit as the "great rebellion." In sharp contrast to the narratives of criminality, chaos, and illegality presented in the prose of the counterinsurgency, the film presents images of workers engaged in a struggle for dignity against the police state. While the moment of the uprising is short-lived, it is depicted as a return of working class militancy. In these ways *Finally Got the News* expresses in film the very radicalism sparked by the uprising.

In the first scene, John Watson provides a lecture on the centrality of the labor of Black workers in the building of the American industrial-capitalist empire against the backdrop of posters from the revolution of 1968. These images suggest his class-conscious and internationalist understanding of the revolutionary movements in China, Cuba, and Vietnam and their links to insurgencies in Detroit. In doing so *Finally Got the News* demonstrates the strategic role of expressive culture in connecting Black freedom and socialist internationalist movements. In presenting Watson as an organic intellectual, it connects the League to urban class struggles in cities such as Mexico City, Paris, Oakland, Havana, London, and Beijing during the events of 1968. The film then directs our attention to the specific situation facing the working class in Detroit. Through Watson it articulates a Marxist framework for audiences to understand the roots of the problems they face as workers, renters, and urban dwellers. In doing so, the film connects the Black radical tradition to Marxism.[66]

In a dramatic instance of Marxist social theory articulated in the film, radical attorney Kenneth Cockrel's dialectical and materialist analysis of finance capital lays bare the contradictions at the heart of the money-form.[67] "The man is fucking with shit in Bolivia," Cockrel declares, "He is fucking with shit in Chile. He is Kennicott. He is Anaconda. He is United Fruit. He is in mining! He's in what? He ain't never produced anything in his whole life. Investment banker. Stockbroker.

Insurance Man. He don't do nothing. We see that this whole society exists and rests upon workers and the whole mother-fucking society is controlled by this little clique which is parasitic, vulturistic, cannibalistic, and is sucking and destroying the life of workers everywhere."[68] He therefore interrogates speculative capital's movement beyond national borders to exploit cheap labor, and by doing so highlights a critical feature of the political economy of U.S. and global capitalism.[69]

Finally Got the News argues that the struggles of Black workers were linked to the fate of the proletariat as a whole. In the film's vignette entitled "The White Working-Class," Watson explains, "There is a lot of confusion amongst white people in this country, amongst white workers in this country, about who the enemy is." Based on this analysis of the situation Watson says that white workers often "end up becoming counterrevolutionary, even though they should be the most staunch revolutionaries." "Basically the reason that they're racist is because of the fact that they are afraid you know that the little bit of niche they have in society is going to be lost," Watson argues, "but ain't nobody been trying to demonstrate to them that rather than being against the Black movement and being enemies of the Black movement, that they should be in favor of the Black movement and supporters of the Black movement, because the things that the Black movement is doing inside of industry are basically in their interest. The kinds of demands and the kinds of movements, you know, which Black people are making inside of the plants are not inimical to the interests of the average white worker."[70]

This part of the film points to the difficulties of organizing within and against U.S. racial capitalism.[71] Watson notes how working-class whites were subjected to the "same contradictions of overproduction, the same contradictions of increasing production," and were aware of their class exploitation. Even so, Watson describes how their class consciousness was overtaken by cultural signifiers expressed in radio, television, and newspapers that stoked fears about street crime, Black people moving into white neighborhoods, the menace of Black sexuality, or otherwise racialized images depicting the Black working class as a threat. According to Watson, discourses associating race and crime captured the cultural and political imaginary of many white workers through extensive media coverage in venues such as the television news, magazines, and newspapers. The dominant ideologies of law and order deflected poor whites' class anger away from the ruling class and toward the Black working class, who were purported to be agents of criminality. In this way, *Finally Got the News* illustrates the ways in which racialization and criminalization were essential to securing consent to authoritarian solutions to the crisis of capital and the state.[72]

The League articulated a distinct political perspective on this dramatic turning point in postwar U.S. history. They suggested that the class anger of white workers had been redirected away from capital and the state and toward poor inner-city residents who were being defined as threats to safety and security. Spaces in cities once depicted as safe became redefined as dangerous territory that would require security measures to control the population. This emergent form of securitized urbanism was endorsed through narratives of law and order. This rhetoric legitimated the formation of the neoliberal carceral state by fanning the flames of populist anger. The terms *riot, crime,* and *law and order* became euphemisms to express multiple tensions and class anxieties. The roots of economic insecurity in shifts in the political economy were effectively displaced through narratives of law and order and the racist construction of scapegoats.[73]

Finally Got the News also suggests how the counterinsurgency unleashed in response to the struggles in the streets and factories of Detroit shaped the restructuring of urban space. Urban police squads launched counterinsurgent campaigns that systematically violated the civil liberties of aggrieved communities, who were depicted as internal enemies of the domestic security apparatus. Strategies of containment utilized by the U.S. state to crush Communist insurgencies in Vietnam were deployed by law enforcement agencies in domestic spaces. Police departments, sheriff departments, and law enforcement agencies repressed Black radicals, antiwar activists, and the Left. Their effort to crush radical social movements in the name of protecting "the people" from threats to law and order is a central factor in understanding the political foundation of the carceral state. By shifting our characterization of the conjuncture we can better understand how carceral policies have served as instruments of both racism and class rule.[74]

As Georgakas and Surkin noted, the leadership of the League saw that capital would "abandon the regions and the populations that had made them so wealthy and powerful." The League's materialist analysis of the situation was vindicated. The resulting unemployment devastated cities and hit the Black working class particularly hard. By the end of the 1970s more than 50 percent of Black industrial workers lost their jobs as a result of automation, capital flight, and deindustrialization. In the past, the local state had been a site to institutionalize victories of Black freedom and labor movements. In the aftermath of these struggles, members of the League noted how local politicians abandoned the pretense of a social wage in favor of funding law-and-order approaches.[75] Law-and-order narratives have painted a highly racialized portrait of unemployed Black workers as socially and economically inassimilable in the context of aggressive austerity measures, attacking spending on public education, health care, housing, and other essential elements of a social wage. In turn they justified increased expenditures for policing and prisons. By making state security the central issue, discourses of law and order presented the repression of surplus workers as a natural response to disorder on one hand, and denied Black insurgent workers recognition as subjects of their own history on the other.[76]

While the League's victories in its struggle for rights, resources, and recognition for Black workers represents a historical advance—and it made significant contributions to the class struggle in culture through its newspapers and films—it was not able to stop plant closures, capital flight, structural unemployment, or the expansion of policing, prisons, and permanent war. Just as the victories of the Second Reconstruction gave Black workers a new terrain from which to fight, the economic crisis of the 1970s led to increases in poverty not seen since the Great Depression. Prison populations exploded in the ensuing neoliberal turn in U.S. and global capitalism. In the current period, one in twenty-two people in the state of Michigan are in jail, in prison, or on parole or probation, which costs the state more than $7 million per year. One in sixteen people have been incarcerated on the east side of Detroit. The prisoners are disproportionately Black, poor, young males who have been rendered disposable by capital. Representations of surplus workers as menaces to social order and internal security have been pivotal in the construction of domestic enemies against which the neoliberal project of expanding police and prisons has defined itself. The dominant depiction of surplus workers as security threats has served as a justification for the expansion of the neoliberal state.[77]

Yet the story does not end quite so neatly. *Finally Got the News* is a film that very few people have seen, and *Inner City Voice* is a paper that few people outside of the antiracist Left may have read, but they survive as important sources of evidence about the historical and geographical roots of the current conjuncture. They underscore the potential to facilitate alliances between activists, artists, and authors in articulating conjunctural interventions. They relay the types of discourses and practices needed to counter the hegemony of the neoliberal carceral state. This knowledge of social contradiction serves as an important counterpoint to the security ideology that has institutionalized counterinsurgency as a modality of neoliberal governance. Seizing hold of social memories articulated in the poetics of insurgency as they flashed up briefly, the League attempted to subvert the rhetoric of counterinsurgency. Its cultural productions therefore function as powerful social forces. It shows that alternative resolutions of crisis have been possible—a historical lesson that was further demonstrated in the Attica rebellion.[78]

CHAPTER 3

The Sound Before the Fury

Attica, Racialized State Violence, and the
Neoliberal Turn

Beneath the political implications of this bloody event there is
also an anguish, which has endured in my country for almost
four hundred years. I myself have lived through too many
murders and too many assassinations to believe a word that
Nixon or Reagan or any of the other American authorities
say. . . . And I know that now that Black people have
discovered in their own minds, in their own hearts, that they
are not what they were told they were, that America is on the
verge of panic, on the verge of civil war.

—James Baldwin, speaking from Paris, 1971

Ideology is always in essence the site of a competition and a
struggle in which the sound and fury of humanity's political
and social struggles is faintly or sharply echoed.

—Louis Althusser, *For Marx*, 1965

There seems to be a little misunderstanding about why this
incident developed here at Attica. . . . The entire incident that
has erupted here at Attica is . . . [because of] the unmitigated
oppression wrought by the racist administrative network of
this prison . . . *What has happened here is but the sound*
before the fury of those who are oppressed.

—Elliot James L. D. Barkley, "The Attica Manifesto,"
    September 9, 1971

On September 9, 1971, more than twelve hundred prisoners seized hold of the maximum-security Attica state penitentiary in upstate New York. While state police recovered jurisdiction over most of the prison, the prisoners retained control of exercise yard D by holding thirty-nine prison guards and officials as hostages. As television viewers across the planet watched the dramatic events unfold, they confronted contrasting images on-screen. In state- and mass-mediated narratives of the event, the rebelling prisoners represented an unruly, violent mob. But images of the prisoners themselves told a different story. In one vibrant turning point, twenty-one-year-old leader Elliot James L.D. Barkley read the "Attica Manifesto," a document of demands prepared by the prisoners, in front of a coterie of cameras and news reporters.[1] Standing before a group of assembled Attica prisoners, Barkley declared: "We the imprisoned men of Attica Prison want an end to the injustice suffered by all prisoners, regardless of race, creed, or color. The preparation and content of this document has been constructed under the unified efforts of all races and social segments of the prison." Such representations of this organized group of multiracial insurgent prisoners contrasted sharply with the dominant depictions of them as a chaotic mob. As Jonathan Schell of the *New Yorker* put it: "Most of us were wholly unprepared for what we saw. . . . The crowd we saw on television was not a mob but a purposeful gathering. . . . We saw the men acting with dignity."[2]

Barkley had been incarcerated after being arrested for allegedly forging a $124 check in his hometown of Rochester, New York. He was politicized through a process of popular education at Attica, in a self-organized study group arranged by the prisoners that focused on Marxist theory and the history of Black freedom struggles. Even the commissioner of correctional services for New York, Russell Oswald, would later assert that "L.D. [Barkley] was no major criminal. . . . [He] was in a maximum-security institution because he was adjudged to be an instant militant." Oswald's assessment reveals how the insurgent consciousness represented by Barkley was both criminalized and contained. Militant prisoners such as Barkley forged alliances in a social science class, where they learned concepts critical for analyzing the social formation. There, they developed an understanding of the centrality of prisons as mechanisms of racist social control under U.S. capitalism. Such concrete analysis of their situation informed their class consciousness and presumably heightened the importance of their interracial solidarity.[3]

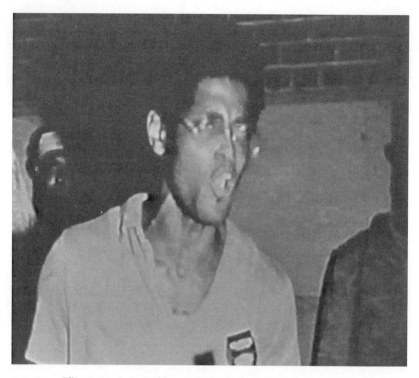

FIGURE 7. Elliot James L. D. Barkley reading prisoners' demands during a dramatic scene in the documentary film *Attica* (1974), directed by Cinda Firestone.

Black, Puerto Rican, and some poor white insurgent prisoners made history at Attica. Their revolt occurred in the context of larger cycle of rebellion that ripped through North American factories, fields, ghettos, campuses, and prisons in the period between 1965 and 1971. Visions of interracial and class solidarity had seized the political imagination of the insurgents and shaped their demands, which included amnesty, transport to a "non-imperialist country," the federalization of the prison, and a negotiating committee. Such social visions also informed their political and economic struggle for better wages, education, health care, a grievance procedure, religious and political freedom, open communication, and an end to segregation as punishment. Such demands represented an embrace of radicalism and multiracial solidarity.[4]

On the "Bloody Monday" of September 13, 1971, Barkley was one of forty-three prisoners and guards who died at the hands of the prison guards and state troopers deployed to retake the prison under orders from New York Governor Nelson Rockefeller. Rockefeller's decision (made from his estate twenty-five miles north of New York City) to send in state troopers, prison guards, and National Guardsmen to quell the revolt led to the bloodiest suppression of a prison rebellion in U.S. history. The deployment of force dealt out premature death for aggrieved and insurgent prisoners. The retaking of the prison included shootings, torture, and a systematic denial of medical care. This racist state violence was captured on camera: prisoners stripped naked, forced to lie on the ground, searched, and humiliated, actions designed to show the "price people would pay for rebellion," according to Attica attorney Elizabeth Fink. Russell Oswald and Nelson Rockefeller would have agreed on many levels with this argument, since they perceived the uprisings as the result of an alliance of revolutionary prisoners. They argued that the prisoners "forced" the state to use violence to restore order.[5] In subsequent state- and mass-mediated narratives, it was the insurgent prisoners rather than prison guards or state troopers who were represented as symbols of disorder and criminality. Walter Dunbar, the assistant corrections commissioner of New York, rationalized the violent suppression of the revolt by alleging that the insurgents had mutilated and murdered the hostages with knives. Media coverage of the event ranging from NBC News to the *New York Times* uncritically parroted these false accusations.[6]

In sharp contrast to these depictions, an autopsy report released on September 14 conducted by Dr. John Edland, the county medical examiner revealed that the hostages who were killed in the retaking of the prison died from bullet wounds, not knife wounds, as had been popularly reported. As the autopsy would corroborate, none of the prisoners had been armed. These developments revealed that the state had constructed a cover story to rationalize its deployment of lethal force to retake the prison—a counterinsurgent narrative that was reproduced in mass-mediated narratives of the event. Despite the fact that the myth about knife-wielding prisoners only lasted twenty-four hours, the narrative continued to shape the public perception of the struggle. The moral panic it generated and the subsequent specter of criminality, violence, and lawlessness once again placed security, law, and order at the center of political discourse. These narratives constructed the insurgent prisoner as the internal enemy of the state, an image that endured long after the event. To fully comprehend the material consequences of the racialization of the domestic enemy, we need to interrogate the class interests that it served.[7]

The crushing of the Attica revolt was legitimated through a revanchist common sense that took shape during a deep social and economic crisis that rocked the U.S. political economy. The mass insurgencies in prisons, factories, streets, and fields alongside rising inflation, deepening poverty, rising unemployment, and declining rates of profit led to a crisis of hegemony. The number of prison rebellions rapidly increased from five in 1968 to forty-eight in 1971, which was then the most significant legitimacy crisis for U.S. prisons in the postwar period. In response to this crisis, in particular the Attica uprising, which was at the time the largest prison rebellion in U.S. history, state officials deployed force. This counterinsurgent attack had the effect of legitimating such deployment as a main strategy to manage crisis situations. In turn, the hegemonic definition of the situation, to borrow the insights of Stuart Hall and his colleagues, "toned up and groomed the society for the extensive exercise of the repressive side of state power. It made this routinisation of control normal, natural, and thus right and inevitable." In doing so it directed attention away from more fundamental transformations of the political economy of U.S. and global capitalism.[8]

While most histories of neoliberalism trace its roots to the 1973 CIA-backed military coup in Chile, less attention has been paid to the relationships between the crushing of rebellion and the neoliberalization of New York during the 1970s. The event became a watershed moment in the formation of the carceral state, an uneven development that has been part of the neoliberal turn. It added to the spectacle of racist state violence that permeated the political and cultural landscape during the period. In May 1970, for example, National Guard soldiers shot and killed four Kent State University students, and state officials killed two students at the historically Black college Jackson State University. In keeping with the counterinsurgency against the civil rights insurgency and growing resistance to the U.S. war in Vietnam, President Richard Nixon and his strategists appealed to moral panics about security, law, and order to justify state action. Thus, Rockefeller utilized these narratives with a full understanding of their rhetorical power. In crafting the discourse in the way that he did, he gained credibility among authoritarian populists across the country. It was in this precise historical and geographical context that the Attica rebellion took on its insurgent meaning.[9]

The state's spectacular forms of violence are not hidden but rather burned into the collective memory. Through alternative archives, innovative methodologies, and radical social theories we can begin to comprehend the relationship between this turning point and the rise of the neoliberal state. By attending to the political and ideological struggle over the memory and meaning of this moment of crisis, we can begin to grasp how the historical drama was experienced and fought out. Against analysts who would ventriloquize the prose of counterinsurgency and define the event as a riot that began through an isolated period of chaos, this chapter engages directly with the insurgent consciousness articulated in the poetry of the rebellion.[10] Drawing on these alternative archives, I argue that the suppression of the Attica revolt was symptomatic of a counterinsurgency against radical social movements in the United States, and a key moment in the development of more punitive carceral policies. I conclude by suggesting that the state's response to a crisis of hegemony produced a solution—the super-maximum-security prison—that became a standard feature of neoliberal regimes of mass incarceration during the rise of Reaganism.[11]

IF WE MUST DIE

If we must die, let it not be like hogs
Hunted and penned in an inglorious spot,
While round us bark the mad and hungry dogs,
Making their mock at our accursed lot.
If we must die, O let us nobly die,
So that our precious blood may not be shed
In vain; then even the monsters we defy
Shall be constrained to honor us though dead!
O kinsmen! we must meet the common foe!
Though far outnumbered let us show us brave,
And for their thousand blows deal one death-blow!
What though before us lies the open grave?
Like men we'll face the murderous, cowardly pack,
Pressed to the wall, dying, but fighting back!

—Claude McKay, "If We Must Die," 1919

Mainstream media coverage of the Attica rebellion attempted to cover up the meaning of the event.[12] A *Time* magazine commentary from September 27, 1971, is worth quoting at length:

> Many of the self-styled revolutionaries—transferred to Attica from other prisons because of their militancy—smuggled banned books by such writers as Malcolm X and Bobby Seale into their cells, and held secret political meetings when pretending to be at chapel or engaged in intramural athletics. They passed around clandestine writings of their own; among them was a poem written by an unknown prisoner, crude but touching in its would-be heroic style.[13]

The *Time* editors purportedly did not realize that the "crude" but "touching" and "heroic" poem they quoted following this passage was none other than the seminal sonnet "If We Must Die" by the Jamaican-born Harlem Renaissance poet Claude McKay.[14]

First published in Max Eastman's magazine the *Liberator*, McKay's "If We Must Die" was widely circulated. This sonnet was a poetic expression of Black resistance during the period after the Great Migration and World War I. In McKay's words, the end of the war "was a signal for the outbreak of little wars between labor and capital and, like a plague breaking out in sore places, between colored folk and white."[15] He penned the poem during the summer of 1919. Between May and September of that year, white mobs violently attacked Black people in a series of lynchings and riots in Chicago; Charleston, South Carolina; Elaine, Arkansas; Longview, Texas; Knoxville, Tennessee; Omaha, Nebraska; and Washington, DC. Black people responded by fighting back—resistance in keeping with global movements such as the Russian Revolution of 1917. McKay explained that the poem "exploded out of me" in response to the insurgencies. He represented an emergent rebellious consciousness in the now famous words: "If we must die, O let us nobly die. . . . Pressed to the wall, dying, but fighting back!"[16]

"If We Must Die" was penned in the context of an upsurge of Black radical and proletarian struggle in the World War I period. Inspired by the Russian Revolution, which he described as "the greatest event in the history of humanity," McKay visited Russia as a member of the Harlem-based African Blood Brotherhood, and as an affiliate of the Communist Party. He was extended a hero's welcome by the Bolsheviks and met with Leon Trotsky.[17] He also participated in the Fourth Congress of the Communist International, where he presented on the "Negro Question," arguing that the Black freedom struggle was central to the world revolution—a thesis that grew from Harlem's Black radicals' interventions in the conjuncture. During the 1920s and 1930s McKay produced forms of expressive culture that combined Marxist theory with the aesthetic poetics of Black radicalism, a materialist critique that shaped the insurgent consciousness of social movements in the city for decades.[18]

The *Time* magazine editors mystified the collective memory of Black freedom and socialist struggles that had gripped the political imagination of the insurgent prisoners. Overall the magazine's representation of "If We Must Die" as "crude" but "heroic" obscured the subjectivity and advanced political consciousness represented by the rebellion.

"If we must die let it not be like hogs,
hunted and pinned in an inglorious spot,
while around us bark the mad and hungry dogs
making their mock at our accursed lot;
If we must die then let us nobly die,
so that our precious blood may not be shed in vain.
Then even the monsters we defy
shall be constrained
to honor us though dead.

We kinsmen must meet the common foe,
though far outnumbered, let us show us brave,
and for their thousand blows,
deal one death blow.
What though before us lies the open grave,
like men we'll face the murderous pack,
pressed to the wall, dying,
but fighting back."

— Claude McKay

Revolutionary Memorial Services for

George Jackson
Field Marshal, Black Panther Party

Date of Birth:
September 23, 1941

Date of Death:
August 21, 1971

FIGURE 8. Memorial service program for George Jackson. Dr. Huey P. Newton Foundation Inc. Collection. Courtesy the Department of Special Collections and University Archives, Stanford University Libraries.

That the poetry of revolt was neglected through *Time*'s representations of the Attica insurgency contradictorily underscores the centrality of collective memory in radical social movements. After all, the memory and meaning of McKay's poetics of resistance was not lost on the Black Panther Party. In fact, "If We Must Die" was printed in full on the back of George Jackson's "Revolutionary" memorial service program for his funeral on August 28, 1971, where more than one thousand people came to pay their respects.[19]

Jackson had been incarcerated at Soledad prison in California, where he was an active member of the Black Panther Party. Through his study of the Black radical tradition and Marxist theory he came to understand the function of prison as a system of racist social control under

U.S. capitalism. He also provided political education for the prisoner movement to "transform the black criminal mentality into a black revolutionary mentality." His prison letters were widely circulated and debated among the radical social movements from California to New York and beyond, and provided a vision of class struggle as a strategy for the emergent multiracial prisoners' movement. Jackson's political assassination at the hands of California prison guards in 1971 was the spark for the Attica rebellion.[20]

It was in response to Jackson's murder that the Attica prisoners organized a memorial in the mess hall to mourn his death and also to protest conditions in the prison. Their memorial protest took the political form of a silent hunger strike. As head of security of the insurgent Attica brothers, Frank "Big Black" Smith, explained, "No one picked up a spoon." The solidarity forged in this direct action foreshadowed the revolt.[21] The Attica rebellion transformed the prison space into a "revolutionary space." Contained within the prison, it was undeniably a "spatial event." Analyzing this transformation of social space enables new ways of interpreting the historical and geographical significance of the event—an insight articulated by perhaps the most influential incarcerated revolutionary intellectual of the period, Angela Y. Davis.[22]

As a leader of the Communist Party and a Marxist philosopher, Davis was uniquely able to provide a dialectical analysis of the prison space as a revolutionary space. Like Antonio Gramsci and Jackson, the experience of incarceration shaped Davis's theory of revolution in distinct ways. In the volume she edited, *If They Come in the Morning* (1971), Davis articulated the relevance of Marxist social theory for the emerging multiracial protest movement in prisons during the 1970s—which represented the largest wave of prison rebellion in U.S. history—while she herself endured incarceration. The book features contributions from figures in the movement, including Soledad brothers George Jackson, Fleeta Drumgo, and John Clutchette; Black Panther Party leaders Ericka Huggins and Huey P. Newton; and attorneys Margaret Burnham and Howard Moore. It offers a critique of what Davis and Bettina Aptheker theorized as a broader "preventive counterrevolution" against the Black freedom, student, and socialist struggles of the era.[23]

Yet, Davis's chapter in the volume, "Lessons: From Attica to Soledad," argues that the most repressive counterinsurgency tactics had been unable to contain the social consciousness of the prison move-

FIGURE 9. Lithographic portrait of Angela Y. Davis by Samuel Kamen in Edith Segal, "Letter to Angela Davis: Marin County Jail, California" (Brooklyn: Segal-Kamen, 1971). Harris Broadsides Collection, Brown University Library, Providence, Rhode Island. Courtesy Barbara Movius.

ment, which was "organically bound up with the dynamics of the liberation struggle in America and across the globe." Davis observes of the Attica insurrection, "The passions and theories of Black revolution and socialist revolution have penetrated the wall." She describes how the uprising evoked collective memories "of the Paris Commune, the liberated areas of pre-revolutionary Cuba, free territories of Mozambique." In her words the insurrection "became a pivotal factor in a dialectical inversion."[24] It turned the world upside down. The rebellion extended the prisoners' movement—which at that point was associated with the leadership of Jackson and the Black Panther Party in California's prisons—to a broader geographical scale. Its multiracial composition of insurgent prisoners extended the political strategy of building class alliances across racial lines. She concluded that the revolt revealed the extent to which the radical prisoners were engaged in the study of radical social theory. "These ideas," Davis remembers, "were developed against the backdrop of progressive revolutions transforming the globe. . . . We were part of a global revolution."[25]

It was in this context of global liberation struggles that Attica prisoners Frank Lott, Donald Noble, Peter Butler, Herbert X. Blyden, and Carl Jones-El formed the Attica Liberation Faction to

> bring about some change in the conditions of Attica. We started teaching political ideology to ourselves. We read Marx, Lenin, Trotsky, Malcolm X, Du Bois, Frederick Douglass and a lot of others. We tried a reform program on ourselves first before we started making petitions and so forth. We would hold political education classes on weekends and point out that certain conditions were taking place and the money that was being made even though we weren't getting the benefits.

This explanation suggests the changes in consciousness that can emerge through political education in Marxist theory and the history of Black freedom struggles.[26]

To be sure, the circulation of radical political theory among criminalized sectors of the Black and Latino working class was a critical factor in the praxis of the rebellion. In the wake of the New York City Tombs rebellion and the Auburn prison uprising of 1970, New York state officials had increasingly sent actual or potential militants to Attica. The state's geographical strategy of social control had been to isolate prisoners deemed troublemakers, thereby literally trapping aggrieved and insurgent people in prison space. In turn, these geographies of social control enabled radical prisoners to develop a radical political analysis of the space as a form of social control. Prisoners such as Flip Crawley explained that the uprising represented their desire to "no longer be treated as statistics, as numbers."[27] In a public declaration of a "hidden transcript," Crawley declared, "We want to be treated as human beings. . . . We *will* be treated as human beings!" Adding to the historical drama, Crawley called for what "oppressed people are advocating all over the world." He concluded by referencing "If We Must Die," proclaiming, "If we can't live as people, then *we will die like men.*" These signifying practices help us better understand the struggle over the common sense in this critical conjuncture. They also mark a critical turning point, one from which there was no turning back.[28]

FROM REBELLION TO REVANCHIST NEOLIBERALISM

We were dealing with not just an uprising over prison conditions,
over prisoners' grievances, to obtain prison reform. We were dealing
with a very sophisticated and determined coalition of revolutionaries
who were trying to exploit public sympathy to achieve their political
objectives, to trigger a chain reaction undermining authority
everywhere. This obviously was an intolerable situation . . . in terms
of preserving a democratic society dedicated to the freedom and
security of all citizens.

—Russell Oswald, *Attica: My Story*, 1972

The tragedy was brought on by the highly organized, revolutionary
tactics of militants who rejected all efforts at a peaceful settlement,
forced a confrontation, and carried out cold-blooded killings they
had threatened from the outset.

—Nelson Rockefeller, *New York Times*, September 14, 1971

Nelson Rockefeller's political ambitions led him to depict the Attica
rebellion as "an ominous world trend." In turn, the repression he
unleashed was based on a political calculation. He believed that positive
media narratives of the rebellion would reaffirm the mission of revolutionaries around the globe. A strong show of force, by contrast, would
restore the state's monopoly over legitimate violence. As such, the
intense and bloody reaction by the state was a vivid instance of the
counterinsurgency against radical social movements in the late 1960s
and early 1970s.[29]

The insurgent prisoners demanded a team of observers to come into
the prison and mediate the conflict. The members of the team included
Black Panther Party chairman Bobby Seale, Juan "Fi" Ortiz and Jose
"G.I." Paris of the Young Lords party, William Kunstler from the
Center of Constitutional Rights, the political journalist James Ingram
from the *Michigan Chronicle* out of Detroit, the publisher Clarence
Jones from the *Amsterdam News,* Assemblyman Arthur O. Eve of the
143rd District, New York, and the associate editor of the *New York
Times,* Tom Wicker, among others. Everyone on the team agreed that a
negotiation should go forward with the prisoners, eventually getting the
state to agree to twenty-eight of their demands. Yet Rockefeller would
neither bend on the crucial demand for amnesty nor come to the prison
to negotiate. The insurgents knew that their lives depended on winning
this concession. The unfolding of events would come to validate their
concerns.[30]

The repeated repressive responses to the radical demands of social
movements has produced an archive for intellectuals of the state apparatus

to study. They draw upon these materials in order to suppress revolts. The centrality of counterinsurgent narratives to these archives would be problematic to underestimate. For example, the dominant framings of the Attica events have put forth definitions of the uprising as spontaneous and irrational acts of chaos and violence.[31] Such narratives reproduce the state's narrative of events, in particular the conclusions of the McKay Commission (the New York Special Commission on Attica). State officials appointed Robert McKay, the dean of New York University School of Law, to chair the commission. Drawing extensively on the narratives of the Kerner Commission about the causes of the urban rebellions of the 1960s (explored in the previous chapter), it argued that the rebellion was "neither a long-planned revolutionary plot nor a proletarian revolution against the capitalist system." Rather, the McKay Commission argued, "Attica rebels were part of a new breed of young, more aware inmates, largely black, who came to prison full of deep feelings of alienation and hostility against the established institutions of law and government . . . and an unwillingness to accept the petty humiliations and racism that characterize prison life." The report claimed that the prison rebellion should be understood as on a continuum with the "urban ghetto disturbances of the 1960s." Indeed, it continued, "The uprising began as a spontaneous burst of violent anger and was not planned or organized in advance. . . . The highly organized inmate society in D block yard developed spontaneously, after a period of chaos."[32]

The adaptation of the Kerner thesis in the explanation of the Attica revolt helped the McKay Commission establish a legitimating narrative for the state during a crisis of hegemony. In defining the prison uprisings of the 1970s as analogous to the so-called ghetto disturbances of the 1960s—as chaotic expressions of disorder rather than as political expressions of a multiracial class struggle—the McKay Commission justified authoritarian solutions to the crisis. In particular, it recommended the intensification of counterintelligence measures to manage the threat of politicized prisoners from working-class communities of color who were entering the prison in greater numbers. Such narratives have been notable for their role in generating consent to coercion.[33]

The findings of the McKay Commission and the Kerner thesis help demonstrate how the broader management of crisis was coordinated across the state. The racialized construction of the Attica prisoners was linked to the racialized construction of cities such as Los Angeles, Detroit, and New York as synonymous with crime and urban decay. In the aftermath of Attica, New York in particular was represented as "ungovernable" by neoliberal intellectuals. As Jamie Peck convincingly argues, these neoliberals waged a "battle of ideas" against what they deemed the "bad ideas of the 1960s" amid the social and economic crisis of the 1970s. They juxtaposed their call for increased order with a denunciation of the social visions of the civil rights movement, or, as Peck puts it, a "new common sense would be developed as a dialectical alternative to the old common sense." Such neoliberal narratives depicted authoritarian solutions to crisis as necessary responses to increased violence, crime, and disorder that putatively resulted from the civil rights movement's disruption of the terms of order.[34]

It was in this context that neoliberalization took shape in New York. The dominant historical bloc reacted to the historical advance of the long civil rights struggle in what Neil Smith calls a "spirit of revenge." In both the response to the Attica rebellion and the fiscal crisis in New York, neoliberals across the state narrated crisis in a way that conflated race and class struggles with criminality, illegality, and chaos.[35] In the wake of the rebellion, politicians seized on the event as an opportunity to expand policing and prisons. The New York and national prison population started an unprecedented increase in the mid-1970s. While some analysts suggest that increased state expenditures on prisons in deindustrialized rural regions such as upstate New York have served as a form of "carceral Keynesianism," I argue by contrast that the investments in policing and prisons have served important political purposes in the neoliberal turn. The expansion of the carceral apparatus was more important as a means for cutting the social wage than a kind of Keynesian economic stimulus.[36]

As the economic crisis took hold in the mid-1970s, President Gerald Ford's administration—with Nelson Rockefeller as his vice president—responded by refusing funding to New York City. This response led to what David Harvey calls a "coup by the financial institutions against the democratically elected government of New York City . . . every bit as effective as the military coup that had earlier occurred in Chile."[37] Harvey has influentially and convincingly argued that Chile and New York were epicenters for the neoliberal turn. Yet unlike the U.S.-backed and CIA-sponsored coup in Chile, he explains that neoliberalization in the United States has been achieved less through direct force and more through winning consent to coercion. The events at Attica suggest that we neglect the role of racist state violence in producing this consent, to the detriment of our analysis of the neoliberal turn. Neoliberal state formation took shape as a cycle of revolts led by criminalized sectors of the multiracial working class ripped through U.S. cities and prisons. The moral panics about race, crime, and law and order generated by the events were seized upon by neoliberals to blame fiscal problems on the poor and people of color. They were scapegoated for the urban fiscal crisis, a racist narrative that provided the ideological justification for the deployment of policies of planned shrinkage to gut public expenditures. In turn, as Smith has shown, neoliberal public policy was defined by austerity and the slashing of the social wage such as the elimination of free tuition at the City University of New York (CUNY). The revanchist underpinning of this policy becomes particularly clear when one considers that open admissions at CUNY had only recently been implemented due to the pressure of civil rights protests, and an increasing number of working-class African Americans, Latinos, and immigrant students.[38]

Crucially it was poor people, social programs, and political advocates criticizing poverty were deemed the source of "ungovernability."[39] Neoliberal intellectuals called for deeper budget cuts and the restoration of order under the guise of fighting crime. Revanchist ideologies organized fears created by the economic crisis and transformed them into a racist and nationalist consent to mass criminalization. They depicted the consolidation of the carceral state as an effort to restore security. They were decisive for mixing moralism and desires for revenge. Indeed, state officals tapped this revanchist common sense when they argued that the source of unrest was the prison's "fiscal starvation." "Immediately after the Attica uprising," the journalist Jessica Mitford observed, "Governor Rockefeller opened up the state coffers and ordered an emergency allocation of $4 million." Three-quarters of these expenditures were deployed in the name of enhancing security at Attica through, among other things, the hiring of additional guards, the purchase of new gas masks and metal detectors, and the search for new sites for a "maxi-maxi security prison" to contain militancy.[40] The state confined prisoners to spaces of isolation as punitive and authoritarian responses to the rebellion, which for some leaders included being confined for more than twenty-three hours a day and only one hour of "solitary exercise in a small enclosure. They had lived by this routine since the uprising was ended."[41]

State officials' exploited moral panics about race and rebellion to win consent to the making of a more authoritarian carceral apparatus. For example, on January 3, 1973, Nelson Rockefeller gave his annual state of the state address. In it he argued that society must be defended: "The law-abiding people of this state have the right to expect tougher and more effective action from their elected leaders to protect them from lawlessness and crime."[42] State officials increased prison capacity to unprecedented levels in this period. The state implemented an array of infrastructural changes, including the expansion of the surveillance apparatus. Enhanced policing, prison, and urban security were depicted as the natural method of managing crisis. In a little more than a decade, the prison population increased from about 200,000 at the end of the 1960s to 420,000. Half of the prisoners were Black, and three-quarters were people of color. This expansion of the carceral state is inconceivable out of the historical, geographical, and sociological context of mass antiracist and class struggles.[43]

THE POETRY OF REVOLT

If you take these capes
Of wet sheets and broken glass
these torn hearts of meshscreens
these decorated skins of 2nd degree burns
and toilet tissue armbands
If you take these football helmets
towels and broom handle headdresses
these bullhorn mouths of mace
these spinning bullets full of navels and hostages
If you take these ornamental gifts
to the governor of shellshock
you will be rewarded
with the momentous eyes
of society's autopsy
attica

—Jayne Cortez, "National Security," in *Scarifications*, 1973

That punishment in general and the prison in particular belong to a political technology of the body is a lesson that I have learnt not so much from history as from the present. In recent years, prison revolts have occurred throughout the world. . . . They were revolts against an entire state of physical misery that is over a century old. . . . But they were also revolts against model prisons, tranquilizers, isolation, the medical or educational services. . . . In fact they were revolts, at the level of the body, against the very body of the prison.

—Michel Foucault, *Discipline and Punish: The Birth of the Prison*, 1977

Michel Foucault's first visit to a prison occurred at Attica in April 1972, just nine months after the insurrection of September 1971. This encounter had a clear impact on the development of his activism and research on prisons. Increasingly, he argued that the prison functioned as a potential site of revolutionary political struggle. In a now-famous lecture he delivered at the Collège de France on January 6, 1976, Foucault explained that what made a radical critique of the prison possible was the "insurrection of subjugated knowledges." These insurrections inspired the development of what he called genealogy, by which he meant the "coupling together of scholarly erudition and local memories, which allows us to constitute the historical knowledge of struggles and to make use of that knowledge in contemporary tactics." The Attica uprising represented a particularly powerful moment of political subjectivity for radical social movements that would ultimately demand the abolition of prisons. It should therefore compel us to reconsider the signification of the event as a site of ideological and political struggle.[44]

For example, the documentary *Attica* (1974), written and directed by Cinda Firestone, foregrounds the voices of the insurgent Black and Latino prisoners in representing the rebellion. The film depicts the relationships between race, class, and freedom struggles expressed through the event. It registers the impact of their vision on the radical political imagination. While the film does not fully interrogate how the racialization of the insurgent prisoners justified the state's monopoly over legitimate violence, it does provide access to subjugated knowledge of the event. As such, it has important implications for historical scholarship on the dramatic expansion of the carceral state in the long late twentieth century.[45]

The cultural products of social movements have provided a distinct way of understanding the counterinsurgent logic underpinning mass criminalization. Consider, for example, the poem "National Security" by the revolutionary surrealist poet and Black Arts movement icon Jayne Cortez, which gave voice to the aspirations and desires of the insurgent prisoners at Attica. In her rendering, the world needed to be turned upside down in order to provide "society's autopsy." By referencing the actual autopsy that proved that prison guard hostages were killed by representatives of the counterinsurgent state and not by the insurgent prisoners, Cortez's lyrics function as a repertoire of collective insurgent memory. The "governor of shellshock" is an indictment of Nelson Rockefeller's role in the massacre unleashed at Attica. Through Cortez's ironic use of the title "national security," she illustrates how the critique of the dominant ideology was at the core of her poetic practice. The use of the phrase "national security" troubled the ways in which it had been deployed as a justification for state violence. She articulated the revolutionary poetics of the Black radical tradition. This is clearly evidenced in other poems within the collection *Scarifications,* such as "Law and Order." This collection provides poetic images that link the racist state violence directed at the Attica insurgents with the U.S. imperialist war in Vietnam and the militarization of cities in the aftermath of the urban rebellions. Through her poetry, Cortez rehabilitated tragedy as a social form. As a Black surrealist, Cortez was committed to the "practice of poetry"—a poetry that became a social force through its links to radical political praxis.[46]

While poetry was a critical element in the struggle to capture the political imagination of the masses, jazz music achieved a distinctive popular appeal in this moment. The African American jazz saxophonist Archie Shepp's album *Attica Blues* (1972) also contributed to the ideological struggle over the meaning of the insurrection. Tracks such as "Attica Blues" and "Blues for Brother George Jackson" provided a complex intervention in the struggle over the common sense in the conjuncture. It featured poetry read by William "Beaver" Harris and political explanations provided by the civil rights attorney William Kunstler, who had been a key member of the negotiating committee. The album's insurgent critique of state violence was a political expression of Shepp's engagement with Marxist theory. Such work testifies to the power of the radical political imagination as a weapon in confronting the production of carceral landscapes. When read against the grain such poetic evidence shows that the revanchist reaction to the rebellion was not inevitable, but rather the product of a complex political and ideological struggle.[47]

THE RISE OF THE SUPERMAX

Because it caused so many deaths and involved so much property damage, because it revealed so nakedly the underlying causes of the rage that fueled it, and because for four days it was front-page news that gripped the country's attention, Attica profoundly changed the general atmosphere in which prisons were administered.

—Paul W. Keve, *Prisons and the American Conscience: A History of U.S. Federal Corrections,* 1991

One day I was unaccountably and without prior notice transferred from the maximum security prison at Marion, Illinois—one of the real hellholes of this earth, the "new Alcatraz" for "incorrigible prisoners," where I had spent most of my time in isolation.

—Leonard Peltier, *Prison Writings: My Life Is My Sun Dance,* 1999

The repression was so intense in the prisons because of the increasing numbers of political and politicized prisoners that were entering, that were filling up the jails.

—Raúl Salinas, "'We Don't Have Much Time': An Interview with Raúl Salinas," 2006

Throughout the prison revolts of the early 1970s, culminating with Attica, insurgent multiracial prisoners' movements organized themselves in order to resist the immediate violence of prison guards, indeterminate sentencing, and the harsh conditions they faced. But their concerns were not confined to the penitentiary. Their organizing efforts contributed to broader struggles for social justice. Indeed, the modern prisoners' rights movement emerged as a product of the Second Reconstruction, which inspired insurgent prisoners to organize themselves across racial lines as criminalized sectors of the multiracial working class. This social movement contested the common-sense perception of prisoners as deviants who should have no claim to civil and human rights.[48]

As the poet Raúl Salinas remembered, "The prison rebellion years were very exciting times. . . . They were some very critical highlight moments in history, and, I would think, in social movements." Salinas contended that the prisoners' rights movements of the period "weren't just challenging the state in [an] irrational, inane way, but we were very clearly outlining our arena of struggle . . . which happened to be the federal joint at that time—Leavenworth federal penitentiary, and later Marion."[49] By Marion, Salinas was referring to Marion federal penitentiary in southern Illinois, which was transformed into the first super-maximum-security prison in the United States. Purportedly unruly and insubordinate prisoners were transferred from prisons such as Attica, McNeil Island, Leavenworth, Atlanta, and Soledad to Marion. There, officials unleashed a wave of repression. Measures involved placing prisoners in the Marion control units, which were isolated segregation units known as "prisons within prisons," where they endured long-term solitary confinement for more than twenty-three hours a day. These prisoners experienced sensory deprivation, consumed their food alone in cells, and were denied access to educational, religious, or work programs. Like the prisoners at Attica, the prisoners in the Marion control units were tortured. The expansion of these control units was justified as necessary to contain the "worst of the worst."[50]

State officials made no secret of their view that the use of coercion at Marion enabled the Federal Bureau of Prisons to control and prevent unrest in prisons across the country, which in one official's words worked "because inmates fear they will be shipped to Marion." Former Roman Catholic priest and Marion warden John Clark told reporters that with the unprecedented increase in the number of people incarcerated, the prisons "should be blowing up—but that's not happening and the reason is because of Marion. . . . Guys don't want to come here, and after they've been here they don't want to come back." Clark added that while the prison was "restrictive in terms of the amount of freedom . . . the place works." The function of the Marion control unit prison was, in his estimation, "to allow the other prisons in the federal system to operate safely because we have extracted those few disruptive inmates from other penitentiaries [and] placed them in Marion where they are under fairly tight, very tight controls and restrictions."[51]

In turn, mass-mediated representations reproduced the state's depiction of the Marion control unit as "America's toughest prison."[52] As the dominant definers of the situation, the state maintained the narrative that control units were necessary to counter increased violence, which was widely circulated in the press. Prisoners transferred to Marion were depicted as troublemakers, dangerous, and "rebels who must be tightly controlled." These representations were not inconsequential. The events have had "repercussions beyond the prison. . . . Prison administrators appear to have chosen a course that favors the continual escalation of repression as a means of control." Control units became increasingly deployed as a "means of disciplining inmates deemed violent or disruptive." The narratives of illegitimate prisoner violence played a key role in securing legitimacy for and consent to coercive state violence.[53]

The Federal Bureau of Prisons officials expanded spaces of social control at the federal penitentiary in Marion to contain unruly and insubordinate prisoners.[54] First constructed in 1963 to replace Alcatraz in Northern California as the most maximum-security prison in the United States, Marion federal penitentiary was located in a rural region in southern Illinois. It was conceived as a security unit for the entire federal prison system. The region was selected due to a number of political and economic factors. The decision occurred in the context of an economic crisis and rising rates of unemployment in the region. Republican Senator Everett Dirksen promised job growth to win consent to the construction of the prison. At the same time, Keve argues, the president of the University of Illinois at Carbondale provided support through the development of an academic unit. In addition, the Fish and Wildlife Service offered the Federal Bureau of Prisons 1,200 acres of land for the prison at the wildlife refuge of Crab Orchard Lake. This surplus land enabled the surplus state capacity unleashed by the closing of Alcatraz to absorb surplus labor and surplus capital through the expansion of carceral spaces.[55]

In 1973, Marion prison warden Ralph Aron explained, "The purpose of the Marion control unit is to control revolutionary attitudes in the prison system and in the society at large." In his book *Prison Writings,* political prisoner Leonard Peltier notes how he was transferred to Marion in the early 1980s. A leading figure in the American Indian Movement, Peltier had been wrongly incarcerated following protests at the Pine Ridge Reservation in North Dakota in the 1970s. Upon arriving at Marion he participated in a cycle of social protests organized by the prisoners. In September 1980, the prisoners initiated a hunger strike. In organizing this dramatic social protest they contributed to a social struggle taking place on both sides of the Atlantic.[56] Peltier recounts: "When Bobby Sands died on May 5, 1981, millions of people from around the world joined their voices together to condemn the British government that allowed him to perish. I joined my voice to theirs. I fasted in solidarity with the Hunger Strikers for forty days during that dreadful year." In addition to hunger strikes, Marion prisoners refused to work in the prison factory. They demanded respect for Native American religious practices, and also that guards stop harassing and beating prisoners, that visiting hours be extended, and medical care and food be improved. "In January 1982," a *Mother Jones* report indicated, "the Marion administration ended the prisoners' last work strike, reported to be the longest and most peaceful in U.S. prison history, by ending the work."[57]

On October 27, 1983, the entire prison was put into a "permanent lockdown" where prisoners were confined in control units for twenty-three and half hours a day, all visitation was suspended, attorneys were denied access to the prison, and brutal repression was visited upon the prisoners. In the security narrative of events, the permanent lockdown was instituted as a response to the deaths of two guards at the hands of prisoners in the control unit on October 22, 1983. Subsequently, a prisoner was killed in the general population on October 27, 1983.[58] On October 28 the warden declared a "state of emergency" and the Federal Bureau of Prisons approved the deployment of sixty officers to help "restore order." Guards from the Special Operations Response Team at Leavenworth—a squad that referred to itself as "The A Team" after the popular TV show at the time—wearing riot gear, including helmets, visors, jumpsuits without any identification, bulletproof vests, and plastic shields, took part in the operation. This special unit carried weapons that included "three-foot clubs with steel beads on the end." Joining Marion guards, this unit went to the control unit and subjected prisoners to rectal probes under the guise of searching for weapons. As the team conducted searches of every cell in the prison and moved prisoners to other units as part of the lockdown, prisoners were assaulted, beaten, tortured, and humiliated. Later they were denied medical care. Prison officials reportedly deemed these practices necessary to protect against threats to the security and safety of prisoners and staff.[59]

Shortly after the lockdown, an inquiry into the incidents was launched. Attorneys with the Marion Prisoners' Rights Project visited the prison in early November of 1983 and conducted interviews with eighty-four prisoners. They gathered evidence showing that the 350 prisoners held at Marion were subjected to torture.[60] Their report documented brutality perpetuated by guards and the Special Operations Response Team unit that detailed prisoners being beaten, transported in leg irons, and kicked and clubbed while handcuffed and nude or barely clothed. It also documented how beatings were often accompanied by verbal taunts such as "Who runs this place?" and "Call me sir!" In addition, it demonstrated a denial of medical treatment to those who were injured as well as a refusal of showers, recreation, contact visits, warm meals, religious services, and access to the legal library.[61]

Another human rights report by Amnesty International expressed concern that the lockdown amounted to cruel and unusual punishment and violated the United Nations prohibitions against torture, which they defined as

> any act by which severe pain or suffering, whether physical or mental, is intentionally inflicted on a person for such purposes as obtaining from him or a third person information or a confession, punishing him for an act he or a third person has committed or is suspected of having committed, or intimidating or coercing him or a third person, or for any reason based on discrimination of any kind, when such pain or suffering is inflicted by or at the instigation of or with the consent or acquiescence of a public official or other person acting in an official capacity.[62]

Responding to the allegations of torture and human rights violations, the Bureau of Prisons claimed that state officials had monitored the cell moves and lockdown. It justified the deployment of control units and related practices, including confinement in windowless and badly ventilated cells, the denial of educational programs and outdoor recreation, and the use of handcuffs as disciplinary mechanisms, as necessary to protect prisoners and staff.[63]

In his book *Alcatraz: The Gangster Years*, the sociologist David Ward makes a helpful claim for understanding the material and ideological basis of the construction of the control unit or supermax prison. He argued that it "represented a rebirth of the Alcatraz model," which functioned to incarcerate prisoners who did not consent to the disciplinary mechanisms of other prisons within its particularly authoritarian confines.[64] Another article penned by Ward along with Federal Bureau of Prisons official Thomas Werlich provides such compelling evidence about the counterinsurgent logic of these units that it is worth quoting at length:

> During the 1960s, events in American society produced profound changes in both the living and working conditions in the country's prisons. . . . The rising political consciousness of their disadvantaged status by minority groups led to the division of inmate populations into warring factions based on race and ethnicity. When this conflict was combined with the growth of the drug trade, the level of violence in prisons across the country rose sharply.

Ward and Werlich represent the resulting changes in carceral practices as a "paradox of prison reform." They assert that the political challenges of the civil rights movement led to racial divisions in prison, that the primary result of struggles for civil rights had been increased violence, and that this violence prompted the transfer of unruly and insubordinate prisoners to the Marion control unit. In this way, it offers the now taken-for-granted story that the rise of super-maximum-security prisons was justified by the violent threats of gangs, rebellious prisoners, and drug dealers.[65]

Ward and Werlich suggest that their article does not represent the official views of the Federal Bureau of Prisons. At the same time, they treat the perspective of prison officials as fact and disqualify narratives of prisoners, attorneys, and social activists despite the fact that they had based their claims on evidence documenting torture and human rights violations. Ward and then director of the Federal Prison System, Norman Carlson, have retrospectively responded to legal, scholarly, and journalistic criticism of the control units.[66] They argued that the super-maximum-security prisons should be understood as a success story in prison security policies. While they acknowledge the use of "maximum coercive authority" by the state, they argue that a more effective interface with the media would have legitimated these reactions to crisis. Indeed, they concluded that it was "somewhat ironic" that officials have had to defend practices that had proven to be successful in maintaining order and enhancing state security. In doing so, they assert the legitimacy of these units despite the fact that human rights groups have shown that they constitute torture according to international law.[67]

The state's security narrative suggests that there is no single event that explains the origins of the super-maximum-security prison. Rather, the meaning of events had to be produced, circulated, and acted upon. As such, the security narrative formed the framework within which events were given meaning. The term came to stand as a symbol for a range of social conflicts, and in turn supplied the ideological justification for the expansion of control units.[68] As the cultural theorist John Sloop has convincingly argued, "The philosophy directing the Marion facility is in effect an exaggeration of the philosophy of prisons throughout the country during this period." He notes that it "becomes a magnet for discussions of the violent behavior of prisoners throughout this era." Prison guards represented prisoners "as signifiers of an inhuman form of violent behavior." In turn, Marion was increasingly "articulated as the paradigm of a secure prison and is simultaneously blamed for breeding violence." This paradigm of the secure prison suggests the contradictions of the massive expansion of incarceration under neoliberalism. Namely, the super-maximum-security prison regime has perpetuated the very thing that it purports to prevent: increased violence.[69]

It is important to recall that, as Angela Y. Davis has argued, this strategy of social control "draws on the historical conception of the panopticon. Again, black men are vastly overrepresented in these super-max prisons and control units . . . [where] the prisoners were confined to their cells for twenty-three hours a day." As such it rearticulates a strategy of permanent surveillance that first emerged during the birth of the prison. The architectural design of the panopticon featured a central guard tower above prisoners placed in solitary confinement units. These spaces of social control ensured that prisoners were unable to see each other or the prison guards in the tower. The idea was to establish centralized authority where prison guards and wardens could see all the cells, and therefore produce a landscape that made prisoners feel as though they were under permanent surveillance. It was designed as a fortification against resistance from below. Yet to understand the precise form this type of securitization has taken, we need to investigate its formation in the current conjuncture. According to Davis, "The danger of the super-max prison resides not only in the systematically brutal treatment of the prisoners confined therein but also in the way they establish standards for the treatment of all prisoners." This brutal treatment, Davis explains, is "largely a result of the racism woven into the history of the prison system in this country. The ultimate manifestation of the phenomenon can be found in the super-max prison." She concludes that its legitimacy depends on the "popular imagination viewing these populations as public enemies," a racist view that has sustained and naturalized the counterinsurgent tradition at the center of U.S. political culture and economy.[70]

REAGANISM AND REVANCHISM

In western capitalist societies, the State is undergoing considerable modification. A new form of State is currently being imposed. . . . I shall refer to this state form as *authoritarian statism* . . . namely, intensified state control over every sphere of socio-economic life *combined with* radical decline of the institutions of political democracy and with draconian and multiform curtailment of so-called "formal" liberties.

—Nicos Poulantzas, *State, Power, Socialism*, 1978

As prison populations swell to bursting, states scramble for funds to construct new control units, known by a variety of names: RHU, SMU, SHU, Supermax. Their public relations spokesmen defend such units as rural, isolated reserves for the "worst of the worst."

—Mumia Abu-Jamal, *Live from Death Row*, 1995

Writing from death row as one of the more than three thousand people who faced execution in the United States (40 percent of whom were Black), the incarcerated Black radical intellectual and political prisoner Mumia Abu-Jamal has used his writing and radio journalism to illuminate the inner connections between racism, prisons, and the militarization of the political economy.[71] His journalism functions as an ideological, ethical, and moral critique of the neoliberal carceral state. As such, these interventions can be read as part of a complex struggle to transform the carceral common sense during this conjuncture.[72]

In the chapter of his book *Live from Death Row* (1995) entitled "Human Waste Camps," Abu-Jamal describes the "Marionization" of the situation in North American prisons during the 1980s and 1990s. According to Abu-Jamal, this trend led to a context where "the barest illusion of human rehabilitation is stripped from the mission, to be replaced by dehumanization by design." His writings provide an alternative to the dominant narrative about the origins and development of the super-maximum-security prison.[73] Indeed, his work helps us to understand its roots in shifts in the political economy during the neoliberal turn. As Abu-Jamal notes, Ronald Reagan "supported a vicious war against the Black Panther Party, and the entire Black liberation movement . . . [and] sparked a deepening of the prison industrial complex that continues to ricochet across America." Reagan rode a law-and-order wave into office and promoted the militarization of the state and neoliberal economic restructuring. Abu-Jamal suggests that Reagan's "allegiance to Wall Street and his antipathy to poor and working class Americans can best be seen in his economic policies." These economic policies, Abu-Jamal proclaims, "favored the former and beggared the latter." They did so through the transfer of public wealth away from social wage programs and toward policing, prisons, and U.S. militarism. Yet the construction of this coercive apparatus was not the outcome of a simple backlash, nor was it inevitable. It required legitimation.[74]

The revanchist strategy articulated by California Governor Reagan during the 1960s and 1970s became a matter of federal public policy during his rise to power in the 1980s. During his campaign he articulated a "populist moralism" of law and order. These populist discourses appealed to simple moral codes by depicting social programs for people of color as a source of economic insecurity for whites. This race and class perception was expressed in a repudiation of civil rights and antipoverty programs.[75] The triumph of Reaganism marked the consolidation of a racial and security regime, a neoliberal regime that took shape during the Cold War counterinsurgency against the long civil rights movement. During his first public speech for his 1980 presidential campaign in Philadelphia, Mississippi, Reagan signaled his commitment to the neoliberal counterrevolution. Philadelphia had been the site of the murder of civil rights activists James Chaney, Andrew Goodman, and Michael Schwerner by Ku Klux Klan members during the Freedom Summer of 1964. Mississippi officials refused to prosecute, and in so doing solidified the state's reputation as the most racist place in the United States. Thus, when Reagan's speech used narratives of state rights it was a clear effort at solidify a revanchist common sense.[76]

Such rhetoric turned the world upside down. It sent a message to whites that their economic problems were caused by people of color winning access to the social wage during the civil rights movement. These narratives were deployed in a moment that poor and working people of all colors found themselves experiencing increased poverty due to automation, plant closures, outsourcing, and economic restructuring. These neoliberal narratives defined the behavior of the unemployed and social wage programs as the primary sources of economic insecurities. In doing so, they displaced what the civil rights activist and journalist Anne Braden would describe as the actual roots of the crisis. "The real danger today comes from the people in high places," she instructed, "from the halls of Congress to the boardrooms of our big corporations, who are telling the white people that if their taxes are eating up their paychecks, it's not because of our bloated military budget, but because of government programs that benefit black people . . . that if young whites are unemployed it's because blacks are getting all the jobs." Braden concludes that "our problem is the people in power who are creating a scapegoat mentality."[77]

In Reagan's acceptance speech at the Republican National Convention in Detroit in 1980, he declared, "I believe it is clear our federal government is overgrown and overweight. Indeed, it is time for our government to go on a diet."[78] Reagan's strategy, however, was not to reduce state power, but to redirect resources away from investments in the public sector and toward an expanded budget for the neoliberal carceral-security state. As such, narratives of security articulated during the age of Reaganism—rather than the individual statements of Ronald Reagan—provided a sense of nationalist unity in a context of capital flight, declining real wages, and the onset of a new Cold War in the early 1980s.[79]

With Reagan's election, Cold Warriors and neoliberals were able to capture state power and legitimate their class rule through appeals to security. In his first two years in the White House, Reagan doubled the FBI budget and increased the Federal Bureau of Prisons budget by 30 percent. The discourse of security was deployed as the major justification for the restructuring of the state form. Much like the U.S. state's legitimation of increased expenditures for aggressive counterinsurgency measures in Central America and apartheid South Africa in the 1980s, prison expansion domestically was presented as a legitimate reaction to security threats. Neoliberals exploited class anxieties by placing racialized images of security at the center of the popular political imagination.[80]

Since the early 1980s, prison expansion provided what Scott Christianson describes as a laboratory for "architects, builders, hardware companies, electronics firms, and other vendors who, like defense contractors, managed to pull down astronomical profits under the banner of public security." It cost the state between $30 and $75 million to construct each super-maximum-security prison. To finance this construction, the state often turned to finance capitalists such as Merrill Lynch, Goldman Sachs, and Prudential for expenditures that exceeded the amount that "most medium-sized cities spent on education, or transportation or recreation, much less the arts." This investment in prison expansion and the abandonment of the social, cultural, and economic infrastructure of cities was the product of a bipartisan consensus about prioritizing security through militarism.[81]

By the early 1980s the U.S. imprisoned 420,000 people in federal and state prisons. Over the next decade the number of prisoners would increase by more than 64 percent across the country. While the U.S. state constructed an array of new prison facilities, the political economy underwent an intense period of capitalist restructuring. Federal expenditures on corrections increased 521 percent over the next decade and a half.[82] At the end of the 1980s the United States had the highest incarceration rate of any country in the world, at 426 per hundred thousand people locked up. It contained more than one million persons in jail or in prison. About half of the prisoners were Black, less than twenty-nine years old, and working class. The majority of the prison population was and continues to be drawn from deindustrialized sectors of the urban multiracial working class. Black and Latino prisoners in particular have been disproportionately represented in control units within super-maximum-security prisons. By the early 1990s, thirty-six states adopted the use of control units. The use of solitary confinement units in the maximum-security prisons had become routine. What became known as the Marion model became the basis for the expansion of super-maximum-security prisons around the country.[83]

Pelican Bay State Prison opened in Crescent City, California, in 1989 as the state's first super-maximum-security prison. In the midst of a fiscal crisis for the state, California Republican Governor George Deukmejian legitimated the construction of this $200 million institution in the name of safety, security, and law and order.[84] Once constructed, Pelican Bay was celebrated as a model for the rest of the country. Described by state officials and major media outlets as a way to contain prisoners who were the worst of the worst, Pelican Bay represented the extension of the Marion model. It was sold as a strategy to ensure the safety and security of the public, despite the fact that the enormous costs to build such facilities led to the further erosion of public expenditures for education, hospitals, libraries, parks, and transportation.[85] Throughout Deukmejian's reign from 1983 and 1991, California embarked on an unprecedented construction of fourteen new prisons, and the prison population increased from 37,213 to 101,995. This state building project gained its legitimacy through appeals to security.[86]

While there may be nothing new in the assertion that incarceration and isolation prevent violence and contain criminality, according to Craig Haney, the super-maximum-security prison represents a new carceral form.[87] Based on his research at Pelican Bay, Haney has shown that the architecture of the supermax has distinctive features, including the "totality of the isolation," "duration of the confinement," and the use of new technologies in implementing spatial isolation. In Haney's judgment the supermax prison represents the "the most psychologically oppressive environment I've ever seen inside a correctional institution." The use of this carceral form has been legitimated through a counterinsurgent ideology that endorses torture as a response to the behavior of the worst of the worst. It naturalized the use of torture as a reaction to purported increases in violence and criminality unleashed by the civil rights movement. Prisoners are literally trapped in place through torture.[88]

Abu-Jamal provides a compelling intervention regarding the role of solitary confinement and mass incarceration in counterinsurgency:

> U.S. military authorities, politicians, and prison administrators seize on the usage of the phrase "the worst of the worst" to justify the barbarities practiced against prisoners. They use it to justify the isolation, abuse, and torture of prisoners in places like the federal lockup known as Marion Control Unit in Illinois, and in various such units in two-thirds of the states, and more recently—and infamously—at the U.S. military prisons in Guantánamo Bay, Cuba, Abu Ghraib, Iraq, and Bagram, Afghanistan.[89]

The expansion of torture abroad during the war on terror extended the practice located in domestic super-maximum-security prisons, which took the form of the control unit and was then globalized. Indeed, U.S. officials now oversee supermax prisons in Afghanistan, Iraq, and Cuba that were expanded during the war on terror. The language of antiterrorism has provided the rationale for the deployment of these prisons as part of the "endgame of globalization." Revanchist security wars have produced authoritarian political landscapes through militarization, securitization, and incarceration. Counterinsurgent security discourses both claimed to protect citizens and at the same time endorsed torture against groups deemed domestic and foreign enemies.[90]

The late twentieth century witnessed a redefinition of the meaning of security. This political transformation created what Colin Dayan describes as "a violence that goes beyond the mere logic of punishment." Carceral policy has intersected with Supreme Court decisions to articulate the legal justification for the super-maximum-security prison regime. While sensory deprivation and solitary confinement violated international human rights law as well as civil rights to due process guaranteed by the Fourteenth Amendment, the logic of supermax detention "has been extended to anyone thought to threaten national security, even to the point of extending criminal jurisdiction over foreigners in foreign countries." What began as the "'worst of the worst' has been extended to 'illegal enemy combatants,' 'security detainees,' or 'terrorists.' The future of lethal incarceration seems assured."[91]

There is a direct historical connection between the history of racist state violence, torture, and the videotaped police beating of Rodney King in Los Angeles.[92] When a jury without any Black people acquitted the white LAPD officers who brutally beat Black motorist Rodney King, it was based on the presumption that the violence was legitimate. This perceived legitimacy also shaped the dominant perception of the reactions to the revolt in April 1992. In turn, the state's response to the crisis gave rise to what the military strategist and journalist David Hackworth argued would be "the principal form of combat in the future." The reaction to the event led to the restructuring of urban space for capital accumulation. While the narrative of counterinsurgency legitimated the production of the paradigmatic carceral city, it also produced its own contradictions.[93]

CHAPTER 4

Reading the Writing on the Wall

The Los Angeles Uprising and the
Carceral City

What we saw last night and the night before in Los Angeles is
not about civil rights. It's not about the great cause of
equality that all Americans must uphold. It's not a message of
protest. It's been the brutality of a mob, pure and simple.
And let me assure you: I will use whatever force is necessary
to restore order. What is going on in L.A. must and will stop.

—President George Bush, address to the nation, May 1, 1992

In March 1991 four white Los Angeles police officers brutally beat
Black motorist Rodney King, a Dodger Stadium groundskeeper. A
nearby resident, George Holliday, captured the beating on video. Viewed
by millions of people, the film of the beating was widely interpreted as
evidence of the routine police violence in Black and Latino working-
class neighborhoods in North American cities.[1] In response to this crisis
of authority, Los Angeles Mayor Tom Bradley selected Deputy Secretary
of State and former FBI Director Warren Christopher to lead an investigation of the LAPD. The report, released in July, opened by claiming
that "the Rodney King beating stands as a landmark in the recent history of law enforcement, comparable to the Scottsboro case in 1931." It
suggested that the beating was "rightly called 'sickening' by President
Bush, and condemned by all segments of society," and provided "an
opportunity for the evaluation and reform of police procedures." It concluded that LAPD racism led to a pattern of police violence in the city
that went far beyond the specific incident. It recommended that Chief of
Police Daryl Gates retire, and that the city implement measures to
address the structural problems of racism and the excessive use of force

within the LAPD. Despite the recommendations, Gates refused to retire and retorted, "This Police Department is aggressive. We're going to use all the means at our disposal that we can bring down the crime and violence."[2]

The trial of the LAPD officers on criminal charges became a dramatic event that tested the meaning of the legal victories of the long civil rights era.[3] Adding to the unfolding drama, the venue was moved from downtown Los Angeles to elite suburban Simi Valley. In April 1992 a Simi Valley jury with no Black members acquitted Sergeant Stacey Koon, officers Laurence Powell and Theodore Briseño, and former officer Timothy Wind for the beating of Rodney King. When the acquittal was announced, hip-hop artist Chuck D of Public Enemy suggested "it was like throwing a match in a pool of gasoline." In the days that followed the verdict, tens of thousands of aggrieved and insurgent peoples took to the streets, declaring, "no justice, no peace."[4]

At the time of the verdict the Black working-class community was still reeling from the murder of fifteen-year-old Latasha Harlins by a Korean American merchant Soon Ja Du following a debate over the purchase of an orange juice in a market deli in South Central Los Angeles. Harlins had set the orange juice down and was walking out of the shop when the shopkeeper shot her in the back. The incident was captured on the store's security camera. A white judge sentenced the merchant to four hundred hours of community service and a $500 fine. The verdicts in these cases were widely perceived by inner-city residents as symptomatic of an authoritarian and racist criminal justice system.[5] Thus, mainstream commentators' surprise that the acquittal provoked large street demonstrations outside public buildings in downtown Los Angeles such as LAPD headquarters revealed a view strikingly divergent from the masses. It authorized a view of history that the critical theorist Walter Benjamin would have called untenable.[6]

The Los Angeles rebellion of 1992 was the largest uprising in U.S. urban history. As such, the dominant representations of the event should compel us to reconsider the struggle over its meaning during this precise historical and geographical moment: Southern California in the early 1990s.[7] The uprising occurred in the context of the worst economic crisis since the Great Depression. More than five hundred buildings were burned down and estimates suggest as much as $1 billion in property damage was incurred during the burning and looting that followed the initial protests downtown. As images of the events circulated through television coverage, working-class African Americans and

Latinos from the poorest neighborhoods of the city engaged in the insurrection and looted shops, many of which were owned by Korean American shopkeepers.[8]

Understanding the material basis of the conflict requires analyzing the contradictions underpinning the crisis, which, as Vijay Prashad has written, were "far removed from a simple liberal dilemma that continues to go by the name of 'black-Korean relations.'" According to Prashad, the Los Angeles revolt represented a "test case for the limits of amity within a capitalist structure that relies upon ethnicity to camouflage its power." Shifts in in the political economy produced huge increases in unemployment for workers of color. The forces of capitalist restructuring also compelled merchants and shopkeepers to aggressively market alcohol in the search of profit. But it would be incorrect to point to Korean American shopkeepers as the source of the problems of alcohol distribution and consumption. Rather, as Prashad concludes, "narcotics among the poor function, like religion, as the spirit of spiritless conditions, the opium of the people." As such, the focus on the shopkeeper in the common sense narrative of the events has obscured rather than explained the structure of social relations that gave rise of the rebellion.[9] Indeed, Eric Tang argues, "the mainstream media would offer lurid and deeply racialized accounts of looters amidst an urban crisis." The Black and Latino poor and working class were represented as symbols of lawlessness, anarchy, and deviant "thugs," "looters," "arsonists," "illegal immigrants," and "criminal threats" to the social order. These racial narratives were widely circulated in television and print media representations of the revolt. In turn, as Tang notes, Korean American merchants were depicted in dominant racial narratives as "victims of wanton black violence," a discourse that obscured the white supremacy and class hierarchies at the root of the rebellion.[10]

Political pressure was placed upon state officials by the propertied class to calm fears about the rebellion circulating throughout the city and to assure that law and order would be restored. Mayor Bradley declared of a state of emergency and a dusk-to-dawn curfew, giving officers the broad discretion to make mass arrests. As a result, the constitutional right to demonstrate in public space was restricted.[11] California Governor Pete Wilson requested that the suppression of the revolt be federalized. Even while the Justice Department announced a federal civil rights investigation about potential violations, President George Bush's address to the nation declared otherwise. In his May 1 speech, Bush stated that the events were "not about civil rights," but rather "the brutality of a mob." Appealing to the Insurrection Act of 1807 as the legal justification, Bush approved the deployment of thirteen thousand federal troops to support the LAPD and Sheriff's Department in quelling the insurrection. As Lyndon Johnson had responded to the Detroit uprising of 1967 by appealing to this exception within the law, Bush illustrated the ways in which it, in such moments, became the rule in late-twentieth-century politics.[12]

In keeping with the state's definition of the events, the rebellion was often depicted in the press as a mob riot that led to chaos and the anarchic destruction of the social order. For example, *Understanding the Riots,* published in July 1992 by the *Los Angeles Times,* depicted the uprising as the chaotic activity of looters and arsonists who expressed mob rule and the "horrors of lawlessness." Mass-mediated images and narratives were juxtaposed with photographs of armed property owners and police officers together, illustrating their common interest in crushing the revolt. They served to legitimate the militarization of the urban landscape by providing justification for the deployment of twenty thousand LAPD, California Highway Patrol, National Guard, and federal military forces.[13]

Why did the neoliberal state react to the events in the way that it did? What was the relationship between racialized representations of the revolt, the economic crisis, and the largest prison expansion in U.S. history? What is to be learned from examining the counternarratives of activists, artists, journalists, and musicians connected to antiracist social movements in Los Angeles? Opposing definitions of the event dramatically clashed in the historical and geographical context of persistent racial segregation, rising unemployment, concentrated poverty among the racialized poor, increasing social polarization, unprecedented prison expansion, and the militarization of urban space. During this period, as Ruth Wilson Gilmore has shown, Los Angeles became the city with the highest incarceration rate in globalizing California. The California prison population increased from 104,352 in 1992 to 162,064 by 1999. The number of male prisoners increased by 77 percent, and females by 108 percent nationally. These prisoners were disproportionately Black and Latino. Mass criminalization was deployed as a strategy of racialized crisis management to contain and warehouse unruly sectors of the surplus population produced by neoliberalism.[14]

According to the sociologist Janet Abu-Lughod, in this period the state's solution to urban rebellions became "reimprisoning rather than helping those most likely to participate in the riots." Following the events, the policy was essentially to "offload the 'riot-prone' populations into the carceral system or displace them into other localities."[15] Rather than addressing the problems of declining real wages, massive unemployment, homelessness, and urban poverty that gave rise to the revolt, neoliberals opted to pursue punitive paths. Politicians of both parties deepened calls for increased security through incarceration. These carceral policies reshaped the structure of urban space. Race and class anxieties found political expression in the authoritarian desires of the middle and ruling class, who not coincidentally were the dominant definers of the situation. As massive job losses rocked the California political economy and social unrest increased, prison building was promoted as a way of managing the crisis, an approach that resonated in U.S. popular and political culture.[16]

This chapter examines how struggles concealed in state- and mass-mediated discourses were experienced as a civil liberties crisis during this moment. I situate the contest over the interpretation of the uprising in the context of the connections between racialized spaces of uneven capitalist development, police, prisons, and state security forces. Specifically, the chapter shows how antiracist activists, artists, and musicians such as the poets Martín Espada and June Jordan, the muralist José Ramírez, and the left-leaning multiracial bands Ozomatli, Quetzal, and Rage Against the Machine used expressive culture to articulate critiques of racism, neoliberalism, and the prison industrial complex in the aftermath of the rebellion. These works of expressive culture hold the lessons of events in abeyance for future social movements. They document the testimony of witnesses who knew they were disqualified from testifying before they ever spoke. Therefore they provide excellent sources of evidence for elaborating the ways in which class was lived through race and gender during this decisive conjuncture. An engagement with the poetic visions of social movements, I argue, reveals the possibilities for the formation of a popular democratic alternative to the neoliberal carceral city.[17]

RACE AND CLASS STRUGGLE IN THE CARCERAL CITY

The politicians called it a riot. So did the press. But soldiers call this kind of fighting something else: insurgency, or Low Intensity Conflict (LIC), as the army's training manuals say.

—Colonel David H. Hackworth, "This Was No Riot, It Was a
  Revolt: How to Stop It Before It Grows," *Newsweek*, May
  25, 1992

The colonel and military journalist David H. Hackworth defined the Los Angeles rebellion as an "insurgency, or Low Intensity Conflict (LIC)," in keeping with the Army training manuals. The U.S. Army and Marine Corps *Counter-Insurgency Field Manual* defines counterinsurgency missions as "those military, paramilitary, political, economic, psychological, and civic actions taken by a government to defeat insurgency." According to the manual, a key to realizing this theory in practice is the struggle for legitimacy by the state apparatus. "Washington seemed to recognize this when it sent elements of the crack Seventh Infantry Division," Hackworth wrote, "the army's top LIC fighters . . . to Los Angeles along with the California National Guard. Many thinkers on warfare believe LIC will be the principal form of combat in the future." He compared the state's response to the rebellion to U.S. counterinsurgency wars around the world, arguing, "Many police officers believe that inner-city duty is similar to combat. . . . They become hardened like shock troops in an occupation zone."[18] This definition of the event should raise questions about how the narrative of counterinsurgency that widely circulated in prominent media outlets such as *Newsweek* and the *Los Angeles Times* shaped the perceptions of the event. After all, the neoliberal state's reaction to the crisis helped legitimate a new model of urban counterinsurgency.[19]

Narratives linking lawlessness, criminality, and illegality were often deployed in the press, by the police, and in official state reports in order to legitimate the neoliberal carceral state's reaction to the Los Angeles rebellion. The dominant representations of the rebellion can also be read in a negative manner as the dissent of an aggrieved and insurgent people challenging the legal codes of an authoritarian state they no longer respected. The antagonism between insurgent and counterinsurgent definitions of events was firmly rooted in the political culture.[20] The rhetoric of counterinsurgency legitimated criminalization as a political response to the rebellion, which in turn provided ideological justification for the restructuring of space and of the state form. Indeed, this rhetoric sustained the construction of the "carceral city," which, as Mike Davis argues, emerged from the "programmed hardening of the urban surface in the wake of the social polarizations of the Reagan era." The rise of the carceral city portended a demonization of the poor, people of color, immigrants, and the homeless. This mass criminalization was part of a larger restructuring of urban space that, Davis concludes, merged "urban design, architecture, and the police apparatus into a single, comprehensive security effort."[21]

Contrary to the widespread illusion of color-blindness, racism became part of the way in which economic crisis, structural unemployment, mass incarceration, and the securitization of urban space were articulated into a complex unity.[22] To be sure, a number of political, economic, ideological, and geographical factors fanned the flames of rebellion during the early 1990s, but the economic crisis was determinant *in the last instance*. As we have seen in Detroit, New York, and other U.S. cities, capitalist restructuring during the late twentieth century led to an accumulation of capital on one hand and unemployment for the working class on the other. Capital moved across borders in search of cheaper labor to exploit at the same time that neoliberal austerity policies produced a vicious increase in structural unemployment. Plant closures led to the loss of millions of industrial working-class jobs. Between 1978 and 1982 alone, the United States saw the loss of one in three industrial manufacturing jobs (at least 6.8 million), some seventy thousand of which were from Los Angeles. After 1982 the unemployment rate increased by 48 percent nationally, with Black working-class residents of neighborhoods such as South Central Los Angeles experiencing harsh consequences. At the same time, poor people of color were the targets of aggressive policing as wars on drugs and gangs were ramped up by Police Chief Daryl Gates in Operation Hammer (1987), which was experienced as a counterinsurgency against Black working-class communities in Los Angeles such as Carson, Compton, Watts, northwest Pasadena, and north Long Beach.[23]

It was in this context that Latino workers from southern Mexico and Central America were forced to migrate to the city in search of waged work as a result of multiple global processes such as the pressures of neoliberal globalization; U.S.-backed counterinsurgency campaigns in El Salvador, Guatemala, and Nicaragua; and the imposition of structural adjustment programs in their home countries by the International Monetary Fund during the 1980s.[24] Latino immigrants who could secure jobs as food-service workers, factory workers, security guards, and day laborers received wages far below the poverty level. Making up the second-largest population of Latinos outside Mexico City, Latino workers in Los Angeles experienced capitalist exploitation in multiple forms: high rents from slumlords, low wages from bosses, and exorbitant prices for goods and services from merchants. At the same time, immigrant workers from Mexico, El Salvador, and Guatemala all endured harassment from police officers, sheriffs, immigration agents, vigilante violence, and exclusion from health care, education, and housing. The U.S. capitalist state intensified policing, surveillance, and incarceration as instruments of racist social control and crisis management to contain the contradictions of neoliberal capitalism within particular spaces.[25]

During the recession of the late 1980s and early 1990s another five hundred thousand jobs were lost in Southern California, representing more than a quarter of job losses nationally.[26] In April 1992, Black people in Los Angeles experienced unemployment rates between 40 and 50 percent (forty thousand of these were teenagers) and a poverty rate of 32.9 percent. At the same time the unemployment rate dramatically increased among immigrant workers. The impacts of unemployment were compounded by political pressure to cut programs such as education, housing, and health care.[27] These measures, arguably a function of urban structural adjustment, led to growing numbers of homeless people—the overwhelming majority of whom were, and continue to be, deindustrialized workers from South Central Los Angeles—being forced downtown into Skid Row. In 1992 California ranked forty-ninth out of the fifty U.S. states in terms of providing public housing, and within which Los Angeles was the city with the largest homeless population in the country.[28]

The Los Angeles rebellion expressed the antagonistic relationships between the criminalized surplus population and the security apparatus in the carceral city. It was a revolt against a political economy where unprecedented unemployment, concentrated poverty, and mass homelessness were increasingly permanent features of everyday life in the carceral city. These intolerable social conditions motivated tens of thousands of poor and jobless residents of the city, primarily but not exclusively from poor Black and Latino communities, to participate in the insurrection.[29] As a working-class Chicana mother put it, many poor people were "trying to get something to eat for our kids." She continued, "Who knows where we're going to get food, now that everything has been destroyed? We have no choice." Similarly harsh conditions obtained in poor Black communities, where, Cynthia Hamilton explained, "basic needs are not being met by state, county, or city agencies." These interventions reflect an explosive crisis in Los Angeles well before the uprising took place.[30]

As racial and class divides deepened, the expansion of mass incarceration became a strategic reaction to the crisis. The common-sense perception of burning and looting that took hold during the insurrection legitimated the expansion of authoritarian security landscapes.[31]

The security mobilizations that followed the rebellion exploited a series of moral panics around race and crime to win consent to coercion. More than sixteen thousand arrests were made during this "state of emergency," with Black people and Latinos experiencing arrests at rates of 36 percent and 51 percent and whites at 11 percent. A third of the total arrests were for curfew violations and activities labeled "civil disturbances." Police and federal forces viewed the event as an opportunity to deport undocumented migrants (1,200 of whom were arrested during the upheaval). The emergency curfew deployed on the second day of the rebellion violated the Eighth Amendment rights of the homeless. In addition excessive bails and harsh sentences were given to people deemed looters and arsonists.[32]

The weekend after the uprising, Mayor Tom Bradley and Governor Pete Wilson contacted Peter Ueberroth—the former organizer of the 1984 Olympics in Los Angeles, Major League Baseball commissioner, and director of the Coca-Cola Company—to request that he lead a "Rebuild L.A." coalition. Ueberroth promoted an alliance between finance capital, the local state, universities, and community organizations to facilitate urban capitalist development programs following the unrest. Rebuild L.A.'s primary strategy was to attract private capital to invest in "neglected areas" of the city, by which it meant neighborhoods that experienced high poverty and unemployment rates. Within a month of the uprising, the Rebuild L.A. operations opened in a downtown office space that had been donated to the initiative. It articulated an ideology of privatization and promised that those involved in civic engagement could win the financial support of foundations and the institutional support of local universities in urban restructuring.[33] This bloc pursued its strategy of development alongside the Bush administration's Weed and Seed program to rebuild Los Angeles, a program that provided tax breaks to corporations seeking to make investments alongside dramatic increases in expenditure for policing and security to "weed out" poor people deemed the source of problems.[34]

In November 1992, Arkansas governor and Democratic Party candidate William Jefferson Clinton was elected president. Within a year of his election President Clinton supported the Violent Crime Control and Law Enforcement Act, which was signed into law in 1994. The bill included funding for one hundred thousand more police, four thousand border control officers, prison construction, and the expansion of capital punishment. The attendant increase of militarized policing, anti-immigrant hysteria, as well as Clinton's punitive elimination of welfare were all features of the revanchist 1990s.[35] With his embrace of these policies Clinton revealed the bipartisan consensus to advancing the neoliberal project that had been shored up during the age of Reaganism. Clinton promoted political strategies that deepened inequality and sharpened the influence of finance capital on governance. This financialization of the political economy led to a further evisceration of social wage programs as well as the expansion of neoliberal militarism at home and abroad.[36]

During this period, Clinton signed legislation enabling the passage of the North American Free Trade Agreement (NAFTA) on January 1, 1994. The subsequent capitalist restructuring of the U.S. and Mexican political economies led to a situation where the peso was devalued, prices in the agricultural sector drastically dropped, spending on rural development declined, and forced migration into the United States dramatically increased. Not coincidentally, the U.S. Department of Defense's Center for Low-Intensity Conflict worked with the border patrol through Operation Gatekeeper to build up hardware, border patrol agents, and training. The number of immigrants detained more than tripled during the 1990s. In turn, the criminalization of Latino migrant workers justified increased policing, arrests, and mandatory minimum sentences throughout the post-NAFTA period. The war on drugs also entailed more funding for the militarization of the U.S.-Mexico borderlands.[37]

At the same time, neoliberal ideology informed Clinton's endorsement of legislation that effectively, in his words, ended "welfare as we know it." His passage of the Personal Responsibility and Work Opportunity Act reduced the federal budget for antipoverty by $50 billion and slashed social programs such as health care. As tens of thousands of poor and working people were thrown off the welfare rolls under Clinton, the prison population exploded, increasing by seven hundred thousand prisoners during his two terms in office.[38] It was in this context that California Governor Pete Wilson oversaw the promotion of a law-and-order agenda premised on prison expansion and the repression of migrant workers. Key examples included the passage of Proposition 187, which denied undocumented workers and their children education and health care at the very moment that Southern California became an epicenter for neoliberal capital accumulation. These policies extended the neoliberal repudiation of the redistributive visions of justice of the long civil rights era and helped authorize the expansion of the carceral state.[39]

Yet the social movements that emerged in the aftermath of the Los Angeles rebellion fought to construct a polycultural alliance among the African American, Asian American, Latino, and Native American urban multiracial working class to resist the construction of the neoliberal carceral state from below. These interventions compel us to heed the visions of racial, economic, and spatial justice articulated in the expressive culture of social movements themselves.[40]

BURNING ALL ILLUSIONS TONIGHT

Fire everywhere! Across the miasma of Los Angeles the flames lift into the night and they proliferate . . . a thousand young black men whose names you never knew / whose neighborhood you squeezed into a place of helpless desolation / and whose music you despised / and whose backwards baseball caps and baggy jeans you sneered at / and whose mothers you denied assistance / and whose fathers you inducted into the Army. . . . Behold them now: revengeful, furious, defiant, and, for hours on end, at least, apparently, invincible: They just keep moving! And the fires burn! And white kids and Chicanos and Chicanas join them . . . as the graffiti proclaimed on the lone wall still standing after flames gutted an L.A. bank, "La Revolucion es la solucion."

—June Jordan, "Burning All Illusions Tonight," in *Inside the L.A. Riots: What Really Happened—and Why It Will Happen Again* (1992)

Appearing as the title of a piece of political journalism by the poet, professor, and antiracist feminist activist June Jordan, "Burning All Illusions Tonight" is a phrase that emerged from cycles of rebellion in the long late twentieth century. It can be traced to Bob Marley, who penned "Burnin' and Lootin'" while he was living and working in North America during the urban uprisings of the 1960s. The Jamaican reggae singer represented the poetic voice of aggrieved and insurgent communities during that earlier historical drama, singing: "We gonna be burnin' and a lootin' tonight / (to survive, yeah) / burnin' and a lootin' tonight / (save your babies' lives) / burning all pollution tonight / burning all illusions tonight."[41]

These lyrics articulated a popular politics during the crisis of hegemony of the 1968–73 period, which also provided the context for the state's depictions of "enemies within." Deindustrialized Black and Brown workers who engaged in a global cycle of revolt were criminalized in the prose of the counterinsurgency. By contrast, Marley's insurgent poetics called up a collective memory of anti-imperialist struggle to articulate distinct interventions in popular culture.[42] Marley's experience as a migrant worker in the United States during the 1960s shaped the social content of his cultural critique of the political and economic conditions experienced by the masses. His music spoke to the dialectics of race and class struggle caused by insecure housing, unemployment, and police harassment from Kingston to Los Angeles to London and beyond. The lyrics represented the suffering of the masses as historical phenomena that could be overcome through social struggle.[43]

Drawing on the ethical standpoints in Black expressive culture, June Jordan articulated the "moral economy" of the uprisings during her own historical moment. Consider for example her intervention that "Rodney King was denied due process of law. He was not judged by a jury of his peers! He was a young black man, not yet dead, and not yet ready, and not yet willing to die." This representation of the struggle against racism could not easily be explained away through discourses of criminality and lawlessness. Jordan expressed an insurgent poetic voice when she wrote, "Now we have Los Angeles in flames. The mode is nowhere compliant. People of color run around, or walk, without fear. We're off our knees: Heads up. Fists in the air. And fire everywhere."[44] Her poetic narrative represents a significant political intervention because it drew into razor-sharp relief the ways in which the event was regularly being signified as a "race riot" among the Black poor in South Los Angeles, a definition of the events that mischaracterized the city-wide multiracial rebellion as an ethnic or Black-Korean conflict within particular geographical boundaries.[45]

June Jordan offered an alternative way of reading the multiracial alliances, class composition, and geographical scale of the insurrection. She did so by calling upon the artistic expression of artists in the city, "as the graffiti proclaimed on the lone wall standing after flames gutted an L.A. bank, 'La Revolución es la solución.'" This writing on the wall exposed struggles for dignity concealed by racist ideologies of the mob. She argued that insurgent communities had united in a common struggle against the lawlessness of the LAPD.[46] Thus, when Jordan illuminated the writing on the wall, she was engaging in a political and ideological struggle against the dominant ideology, one that had obscured the insurgent meaning of the revolt. Among the people arrested for participating in the seizure of property and burning of symbols of domination were dispossessed migrants from Central America and southern Mexico and other immigrant workers living in Hollywood, MacArthur Park, and the eastern section of South Central.[47]

FIGURE 10. Jim Mendenhall, "Two California Highway Patrol officers stand guard near the Westside after the unrest spread beyond South Los Angeles. In the background, taggers offered their thoughts on 'the solution,'" © 1992, *Los Angeles Times*. Reprinted with permission.

The promise of poetry's role in the struggle against the neoliberal state also appears dramatically in what Martín Espada called "an *artistry* of dissent," by which he meant the combination of "poetry and politics, craft and commitment . . . the artistic imagination equal to the intensity of the experience and the quality of ideas." This artistry reclaimed an insurgent polyculturalism in order to confront the prose of counterinsurgency that, as Espada observed, demonized Black people "as aggressors. Nothing was said about African-American victims of the riots. Koreans protecting their businesses with guns were paraded by the media as evidence of African-American racism." In turn, these narratives narrowly focused on the beating of a white truck driver, thus representing "whites solely as victims of violence. Nothing was said about white rioters, or the lethal retaliation of white police." At the same time "Latinos were rendered invisible," Espada intervened, "despite the fact that nearly half of the businesses destroyed and nearly half the people arrested were Latino. The media message. The races are hopelessly polarized. Lock your doors." According to Espada, these racial narratives displaced attention from the multiracial class struggles of "*los olvidados,* the forgotten ones of that city."[48]

To understand the political significance of these polycultural struggles we need to learn to read the writing on the wall, or the ways in which artists articulated ways of seeing that were otherwise obscured by moral panics about race, violence, and crime.[49] For example, the Chicano artist and educator José Ramírez produced cultural expressions while teaching in South Central that are highly suggestive in this regard. In Ramírez's painting *Quebradita en Sur Central* (1997), he juxtaposes a popular dance among *Mexicano,* Chicano, and Latino youth, the *quebradita,* where *calavera* dancers dip at dramatic moments, with an image of a police car in flames. "It is an image from my fourth-grade classroom at Ascot Avenue Elementary looking toward downtown," Ramírez remembered. "It is an imagined scene of what it must have been like when the uprising happened. So there are people dancing in the street, a cop car burning, and an image of José Guadalupe Posada's *calaveras* dancing together." The dance style, popularized in the early 1990s, was accompanied by *banda* music and drew huge crowds of working-class immigrants and Mexican American youths to weekend club parties held throughout the city. As Ramírez depicts in his painting, couples enact the *quebradita* when male dancers dip their female partners nearly to the floor and then straighten back up quickly. The dance form requires careful timing and agility, and communication between partners so that they read each other's moves and respond. It also could be said to represent the kind of cultural cooperation and political struggle required of poor and working-class communities during the massive economic crisis of the early 1990s. Tellingly, in May 1992, when thousands of drywall workers went on strike at construction sites, picketers danced the *quebradita* at the union hall.[50]

Against a blood-red sky, Ramírez's brightly colored homes and *calavera* dancers next to a police car in flames represent the joy that emerged in the struggle against poverty, police repression, and neoliberal policies designed to punish the poor.[51] Continuing the radical tradition of Chicana/o artists and activists in the city, Ramírez made the dialectics of antiracist radicalism and state violence in Los Angeles a central aspect of his artistic expression. As working-class immigrants joined the multiracial rebellion, state officials occupied their neighborhoods and deported more than one thousand immigrant workers with impunity.[52]

In another painting entitled *Prisoners* (2007), Ramírez provides a generative way of seeing the impacts of the carceral state in this specific historical moment. The oil painting depicts eight standing figures, some

FIGURE 11. José Ramírez, *Quebradita en Sur Central*, 1997. ramirezart.com.

FIGURE 12. José Ramírez, *Prisoners*, 2007. ramirezart.com.

of whom hold Bibles, flowers, and a violin, while three others are shackled with chains around their wrists. One skeletal figure clutches a flower and stares at the viewer with hollow eyes, perhaps representing grievances of working-class communities forced to endure the mass incarceration of friends, comrades, and family members. The image also visually represents the ways in which mass incarceration is related to the everyday experiences of the Chicano and Latino working class, experiences shaped by neoliberal globalization, forced migration, criminalization, the feminization of poverty, and mass deportation. Through the painting, Ramírez helps us to understand how the carceral crisis was lived through race, class, and gender. The image also helps us to disentangle the conceptualization of the carceral moment from the tangles of teleological conceptions of history.[53] The painting is politically significant in that it shows the pressure that artists connected to social movements, as the Chicago Surrealist Group put it, can "exert to break the chains which hold the suffering under the death sentence of race and class oppression." Seizing hold of such dialectical images is particularly important for analyzing the potential for radical social transformation.[54]

Ramírez's cultural confrontation of the criminalization of working-class people of color contributed to a vibrant polycultural scene during the 1990s, one that attempted to transform racialized places of class exploitation into spaces of multiracial working-class dignity. It was in this context that bands such as Quetzal, Rage Against the Machine, and Ozomatli served as a type of "cultural front" within post–Los Angeles rebellion social movements. Their unique fusion of expressive and political culture suggested the possibility for a counterhegemonic alliance to confront the neoliberal carceral state.[55] Describing themselves as emerging from the "ashes of the Los Angeles 1992 rebellion," Quetzal has sought to represent the perspectives of movements against neoliberalism. The band's founder, Quetzal Flores, had farmworker organizer parents and was influenced by the culture of opposition he witnessed during the coming together of labor and civil rights movements in California's factories and in the fields. He was also inspired by the Zapatista uprising in Chiapas, Mexico, in 1994. Along with his partner and lead singer, Martha González, they turned to "expressive culture as an organizing platform to voice the desires, opinions, resistance to the conditions in which they found themselves," as the anthropologist Russell Rodríguez observes. They sought to represent radical social movements against neoliberalism, particularly through the practice of traditional *son jarocho* music with roots in Veracruz. The goal was to create engaged and participatory spaces modeled, as Rodríguez notes, on the band Los Lobos's performances of *son jarocho* during the civil rights protests in the Chicano movement of the 1960s and 1970s. Quetzal continued this tradition of linking popular music to social movements alongside other activist-artists such as Zach de la Rocha and Tom Morello of Rage Against the Machine.[56]

Rage Against the Machine released its self-titled debut in the wake of the Los Angeles insurrection of 1992. Tracks such as "Killing in the Name," "Township Rebellion," and "Bullet in the Head" gave voice to social critiques of the polycultural working class outraged by decades of racism, capitalist restructuring, prison expansion, and police violence. Their songs resonated as they represented the contradictions experienced by the audience. De la Rocha explains that the band sought "to bridge the gap between entertainment and activism."[57] In doing so, they often shared the stage with Ozomatli, a band that was also "a direct product of the L.A. riots" made up of members such as Wil-Dog Abers, Mairo Calire, Raúl "El Bully" Pacheco, Ulises Bella, and Cut Chemist. Tracks such as "Chota" and "The Coming War" on their self-titled debut album represented poetic protest against police violence and the prison-industrial complex.[58]

These artists contributed to what the historian Daniel Widener calls "a left-inflected sonic blending that signals the most pronounced coming together of African American and Latin American music" in generations.[59] They drew upon the appeal of popular culture to promote radical political philosophies and practices. In doing so they suggest a potential for connecting grassroots cultural expression and self-activity among urban polycultural working-class youth in street protests, dance halls, graffiti writing, and shared urban spaces with organized social movements to dismantle mass incarceration and overturn neoliberalism. These interventions in expressive culture demonstrate strategic and tactical imperatives for rejecting neoliberal multiculturalism and embracing an antiracist and "socialist polyculturalism" premised on the struggle to dismantle racist structures and redistribute social wealth.[60]

"I have learned about the histories of Native Americans and Chicanos and Asian-Americans and progressive white peoples in these United States," June Jordan wrote, "and I know that we have more in common than our genuine enemies want us to realize!" She reasoned that aggrieved and insurgent communities can unite, "in our demands for equal human rights and civil liberties," as part of a larger struggle for power. "We can gain a second Bill of Rights that will deliver at least as much money to support every African-American child as we spend on the persecution and imprisonment of young black men." She concluded that these "necessary, humane and irreversible and democratic gains cannot be won without political and moral unity centered on principle rather than identity."[61] In doing so, she pointed to cultural resources for developing a grassroots political program to confront neoliberalism.

Yet the neoliberal state's counterinsurgent reaction to the Los Angeles rebellion continues to haunt "the subsequent acts of the drama like a ghost." The security rhetoric that justified the crushing of the insurrection shaped the response to future crises of unemployment, homelessness, and the destruction of the social fabric. Like the events of 1992 in Los Angeles, so too did the restructuring of New Orleans in the wake of Hurricane Katrina in 2005 represent a turning point in the state's strategy of incarcerating the crisis.[62]

CHAPTER 5

What's Going On?

Moral Panics and Militarization in Post-Katrina New Orleans

Don't punish me with brutality
Talk to me
So you can see
What's going on

—Marvin Gaye, "What's Going On?" from the 1971 album *What's Going On?*

On August 29, 2005, Hurricane Katrina triggered one of the most dramatic unnatural disasters in U.S. history. Rather than a human rights crisis that necessitated a rescue mission, New Orleans was represented as a "war zone." The city's police department was directed to stop its rescue mission and focus on security and law and order as Black Hawk helicopters hovered over the streets.[1] Simultaneously, popular media discourses represented Black and poor survivors of the hurricane as criminals and looters. The dissemination of such messages helped sanction Louisiana Governor Kathleen Blanco's issuance of a "shoot to kill" order to National Guard soldiers fresh from Iraq in a domestic mission Blanco described as "urban warfare."[2]

Black New Orleans was depicted as being prone to violence, crime, and insurrection following Katrina. Discourses of illegality, violence, and disorder conjured an imagery of "race riots," as they have been signified in dominant narratives. Read in the context of the proliferation of such narratives following the Los Angeles revolt of 1992, it is easier to see how they have become the legitimating narratives for the buildup of the carceral state. This security narrative reflected an accumulation of anxieties about the racialized poor.[3] Accordingly, it represented the Black working class as a threat to be contained. This threat destabilized long-standing legal barriers between the military and domestic policing. The success of the neoliberal carceral-security state in defining domestic enemies in race and class terms facilitated the domestic deployment of military security forces. Appealing to the Insurrection Act of 1807 as the legal basis for the decision, President George Bush's administration deployed seventy-two thousand troops into the storm-ravaged area. Consequently, Bush's order represented the largest deployment of federal troops in a domestic situation since the Civil War.[4]

Bush's order endorsed the deployment of military measures in the city with the highest rate of incarceration of any city in the country: 1,480 per 100,000 residents. The state of Louisiana had the highest rate of incarceration in the U.S., a population that doubled between 1990 and 2010.[5] While Black residents constitute 32 percent of the population of Louisiana, they made up 72 percent of the prison population and are incarcerated at a rate almost six times higher than whites with women making up the fastest-growing sector of the prison population. The criminalized residents of New Orleans migrate between local jails, state prisons, and poor neighborhoods in the city. According to researchers in Columbia's Spatial Information Design Lab, the reaction to the crisis of Hurricane Katrina "intensified the pattern of migration that the criminal justice system had been supporting for years: large numbers of people, mainly poor and black, were displaced from the most distressed parts of the city."[6]

Criminalization facilitated racialized perceptions of the events. Despite the fact that widely circulated photographs depicted whites taking goods, the discourse of looting was mainly reserved for Black people.[7] Such representations also help explain the abandonment of the prisoners held at Orleans Parish Prison. According to Human Rights Watch, prisoners in the Orleans Parish Prison "were abandoned in their cells without food or water for days as floodwaters rose toward the ceiling." The prisoners who remained in the locked prison (almost 90 percent of whom were Black) reported seeing bodies floating in the filthy floodwaters. As the report explains: "Many of the men held at the jail had been arrested for offenses like criminal trespass, public drunkenness, or disorderly conduct. Many had not even been brought before a judge and charged, much less been convicted." Regardless of their purported crime, those abandoned to the flood waters in Orleans Parish Prison were condemned by moral panics. Such panics also ensnared New Orleans residents outside the prison. Indeed, guards from the infamous Angola State Penitentiary were brought in to securitize the city.

The Louisiana Department of Corrections sent the prison warden Burl Cain to transform a Greyhound parking lot into a cage made out of razor wire with an entrance sign: "Welcome to New Angola South."[8]

Yet mass criminalization did not go uncontested in the aftermath of Hurricane Katrina in New Orleans. While dominant representations criminalized Black and poor hurricane victims, the interventions of anti-racist activists and artists made possible a shift away from dominant perspectives and toward the poor and the working class as the "source of historical definition." The event represented what the geographer Clyde Woods called a "blues moment," one like the Great Mississippi Flood of 1927, compelled vernacular artists to intervene in the crisis with counternarratives. A focus on their interventions in popular culture allows us to assess forms of expression that have vocalized popular memories of abolition democracy in the wake of Hurricane Katrina to suggest its unfinished business. Like the blues music, poetry, and litera-ture of the 1920s and 1930s such as Bessie Smith's 1927 performance of Ma Rainey's song "Backwater Blues" or Richard Wright's short story about the flood in *Uncle Tom's Children* (1938), contemporary artists and activists have contributed to the class struggle in culture. This strug-gle reflected and constituted the structure of socio-spatial relations in the post-Katrina world.[9]

One year after the storm hit and the levees broke in New Orleans, the Dirty Dozen Brass Band released a remake of Marvin Gaye's album *What's Going On?* While Gaye's original album articulated a critique of police brutality, racism, poverty, and the U.S. imperialist war in Vietnam during the late 1960s and early 1970s, the Dirty Dozen Brass Band, with guest vocalists Chuck D, Ivan Neville, G. Love, and Guru and Bettye LaVette, offered criticism of the event of Hurricane Katrina and the criminalization of Black working-class survivors of the storm. Criticizing the interlocking and exaggerated scripts of vio-lence, looting, and crime, the album asked the question, "What's going on?"[10]

Originally released in January 1971, Marvin Gaye's *What's Going On?* was at the time perhaps the most popular soul album in the country. The soul sound articulated by Gaye, the Temptations (*Cloud Nine*, 1969), and Stevie Wonder (*Innervisions*, 1973) was a product of the expressive and political culture of the Black working class in Detroit. Gaye's album in particular registered the political concerns and perspectives of the long Black freedom movement in the context of the urban uprisings in U.S.

cities.[11] With songs such as "What's Happening Brother," "Mercy Mercy Me (The Ecology)," and "Inner City Blues (Make Me Wanna Holler)," it expressed the insurgent political critique articulated in the expressive culture of urban social movements.[12]

The Dirty Dozen Brass Band released their remake of *What's Going On?* thirty-five years later. Their reinterpretation offered an especially compelling counter to the dominant narrative of the Katrina crisis. The album threw the opposing perspectives of the contentious event into razor-sharp relief. It expressed a musical and poetic critique of conditions created by capitalist globalization, mass incarceration, and securitization in post-Katrina New Orleans. On tracks such as "Flyin' High (In the Friendly Sky)," the soul singer Bettye LaVette repeats the refrain "help me, somebody."[13] In taking old songs, lyrics, and rhythms and giving them new meaning, the Dirty Dozen Brass Band engaged in a political and cultural struggle for egalitarian social change. The songs do not propose to merely depict events. Instead, when read symptomatically, the album calls up an alternative archive that can teach us much about the socio-ideological struggle over the definition of conditions.[14]

In New Orleans, a city with a rich and unique tradition of expressive and political culture, artists, musicians, and activists drew on collective memories of past social conflicts to challenge dominant representations in the present moment. The poetry of social movements provided an alternative signification of events shaped by neoliberal economic restructuring, the withdrawal of the social wage (public education, housing, and social infrastructure such as emergency management), the militarization of racialized urban spaces, and mass incarceration.[15] To develop a critical analysis of this situation we should follow the lead of the Dirty Dozen Brass Band to think through the connections between events in Detroit in the late 1960s and New Orleans in the 2000s or, as Walter Benjamin might have us, seize hold of popular memories as they "flash up" briefly in order to "blast open the continuum of history."[16]

What are the stakes in the struggle to define the Katrina crisis? How did moral panics over race, security, and law and order justify the militarized restructuring of the city? What is to be learned by thinking from the perspective of social movements? These questions lead to another, the one asked by Marvin Gaye four decades ago, and by the Dirty Dozen Brass Band in 2006, which is now more relevant than ever: "What's going on?" Answering that question requires us to examine the ways in which the abandonment of New Orleans in the wake of the Second Reconstruction has been mediated and contested in popular and political discourse. The question represents a compelling example of the kind of counternarrative post-Katrina social movements mobilized to confront the neoliberal state. Engaging the poetic knowledge of vernacular artists enables us to better understand how neoliberal racial and security regimes perpetuate unacceptable forms of conduct.[17] It helps clarify how the poetry of social movements has been used in struggles against the mass expropriation of Black and poor people, the attempted elimination of public housing, the privatization of public education and hospitals, the criminalization of poverty and homelessness, and the exploitation of immigrant workers. At the same time it suggests the stakes in struggles to confront neoliberal narratives that have systematically obscured the historical geography and social relations that produced the conditions of possibility for the event.[18]

The Katrina crisis also represented an opportunity. It led to a public debate about race, class, and gender inequality on a scale not witnessed since the Los Angeles 1992 uprising. It revealed the nefarious effects of a more than four-decade-long withdrawal of the social wage, imposition of privatization, pervasive and persistent patterns of racial segregation, deepening social polarization, and erosion of the "means of social reproduction." As such, the crisis had a particular impact on Black working-class women that, as Barbara Ransby put it, was "fueled and framed by the rabid antipoor discourse that has cast Black single mothers as unworthy of public aid or sympathy."[19] These realities shaped by privatization, forced migration, racialization, and the feminization of poverty appear as processes for which there are no alternatives. Yet post-Katrina social movements struggled for the right to return and an augmented social wage that includes fair housing, public education, health care, employment, water, food, and transportation for the waged and unwaged. In so doing, they underscored the possibility of overcoming the neoliberal carceral state.[20]

THE KATRINA CIRCUMSTANCE

The security situation is a concern. It is a priority. . . . And there is a zero tolerance approach.

—Scott McClellan, White House Office of the Press Secretary, September 1, 2005

In the wake of Katrina, the major network news broadcasts focused attention on one of the poorest cities in the poorest region in the country—a city where, before the storm, Black people accounted for 67 percent of the city's population of 484,674.[21] Mass-mediated cultural outlets manufactured images, narratives, and imaginaries of the Black and poor as either hapless victims or the source of widespread insecurity. Poor and Black hurricane survivors abandoned by the state were represented as looters for taking items such as food, water, and other necessities. At the same time they were denied assistance by the Federal Emergency Management Agency (FEMA), whose director, Michael Brown, directed emergency aid away from devastated areas and toward security enhancement.[22]

On August 28, 2005, the day before the levees broke, New Orleans mayor Ray Nagin declared a "state of emergency." He issued an evacuation order for the city with the exception of essential personnel from the state, hospitals, and the Orleans Parish Prison—and the prisoners held there. Massive flooding overwhelmed the poorest sectors of the city.[23] Instead of determining how to best meet the basic survival needs of communities most affected by the storm, a power struggle emerged between federal politicians and those at the state level, demonstrating continuity with traditional practices of "benign neglect" of the Black poor and working class.[24]

According to the *Washington Post,* the Bush administration sought control over the National Guard soldiers and police officers then under the governor's supervision. According to one official, Bush had "clear legal authority to federalize National Guard units to quell civil disturbances under the Insurrection Act and [would] continue to try to unify the chains of command that are split among the president, the Louisiana governor, and the New Orleans mayor." Political struggles for power received precedence over rescue efforts. Left vulnerable to catastrophe by federal budget cuts and decades of city and state neglect, the poor, women, the elderly, and Black people were abandoned in neighborhoods in the floodplain most affected when the levee broke.[25]

Brigadier General Gary Jones of the Louisiana National Guard explained to Joseph Chenelly of the *Army Times* that the first objective of the military was to establish "security" in the city because "anarchy" reigned. Indeed, Chenelly characterized the deployment of troops as an effort to quell "insurgency." In an interview with ABC News, Louisiana corrections officer Melissa Murray depicted New Orleans as a "war zone." New Orleans U.S. attorney Jim Letten reported to the *Washington Post* that a temporary jail was set up for looting and, more vaguely, "other crimes." The White House's position on this specific response was unambiguous in promoting "a zero tolerance approach," and prioritizing the "security situation."[26] On September 2, President George W. Bush arrived in New Orleans, where National Guard had been deployed to purportedly bring "order to this chaotic city." The state's narrative of law and order was part of an effort to calm class anxieties and provide assurances that security would be restored.[27]

In a major conceit, the security narrative calls upon benevolence to explain the neoliberal state's efforts to prevent a purported chaotic descent into barbarism by promoting militarism. This narrative helps us to better understand that, as Amy Kaplan argued, "domestic and foreign spaces are closer than we think, and the dynamics of imperial expansion cast them into jarring proximity." The national security state requires the construction of foreign and domestic enemies. Intellectuals of the security apparatus therefore have a key role in the legitimation of securitization. Racial and class ideologies pervade these narratives. The ostensibly race-neutral language of security reinforced common-sense associations between race, crime, and chaos. Images of besieged whiteness served as justification for neoliberalization.[28]

During the neoliberal turn in New Orleans, the city was denied federal funds, much as the urban fiscal crisis in New York City. As a result, New Orleans became one of the poorest cities in the country. At the same time, its demographics changed from majority white to majority Black. By 1985 Black people experienced poverty rates at 50 percent and unemployment rates of 25 percent. Indeed, unemployment increased steadily through the last three decades of the twentieth century, as job losses in manufacturing and a decline in the centrality of the port system rocked the political economy. Concentrated poverty and unemployment became a central facet of life among the racialized poor under neoliberal capitalism. In turn, New Orleans was transformed into a carceral city well before Hurricane Katrina hit.[29]

In an unwitting demonstration of the double meaning of "coverage," news media accounts of the Katrina crisis mystified the cumulative consequences of over four decades of racism, neoliberal restructuring, prison expansion, and punitive policing. The media's reproduction of neoliberal ideologies had been essential to the conscious dismantling of the welfare state and the militarization of New Orleans just as it continues to be after the storm.[30] The Department of Homeland Security contracted the firm Blackwater to provide private security to government officials in the region. This same firm also provides security to U.S. diplomats in Iraq. Additional links between the war in Iraq and the state response in the Gulf Coast were seen in the blatant corporate profiteering. Vice President Dick Cheney's former company, Halliburton subsidiary Kellogg Brown and Root, was awarded no-bid contracts to reconstruct military bases in Mississippi and Louisiana. In contrast with official concerns over looting by poor and Black residents of New Orleans, the real danger was the sort of looting represented by the alliance of state power and private military contractors.[31]

Neoliberals viewed the events as an opportunity to advance their political project to accumulate capital through the displacement of the racialized poor.[32] Consider, for example, the work produced by Nicole Gelinas, Manhattan Institute writer and editor of its *City Journal,* in the wake of the storm. She penned a series of pieces blaming the social crisis in New Orleans on the behavior of a purported "entrenched underclass," who she asserted promoted a culture of violence, drug dealing, and drug use in public space. Gelinas claimed that the inability of the police to control the situation reflected a "deeper cultural problem." This problem purportedly grew from a culture of "political correctness" that had prevented the local state from pursuing appropriate policing policies.[33]

Gelinas celebrated the Bush administration's deployment of additional federal law enforcement and the National Guard, but argued that such military responses were insufficient. She wrote, "It's an enduring mystery why Bush hasn't used Katrina to show the world that America can rebuild a major city using bedrock conservative principles: law and order first." Indeed, she argued, the state had not been authoritarian enough before or after the storm: "The New Orleans Police Department couldn't keep order after the storm because it couldn't keep order *before* the storm."[34] To be sure, neoliberal intellectuals promoted carceral reactions to the Katrina crisis, particularly through the depiction of poor residents as criminal members of a purported underclass. They helped transform an unnatural social crisis into a neoliberal program by blaming the vulnerable as the source of their own *vulnerabilities to premature death.* At the same time they sustained, naturalized, and justified the militarization of New Orleans alongside the planned shrinkage of the public sector.[35]

The entire teaching staff (7,500 workers) of the public school system in New Orleans was fired, busting one of the most powerful unions in the city. The city's public housing residents were not allowed to return to their barely damaged apartments, which, as Cindi Katz noted, were enclosed with "chain link fences topped with barbed wire, all of their entryways covered with steel plates."[36] Landlords and state officials used the storm as a pretext for the mass expulsion of the Black working class from rental properties as part of an urban strategy of "gentrifying disaster." In 2006, Secretary of Housing Alphonso Jackson announced that thousands of public housing units would be demolished. The U.S. Department of Housing and Urban Development declared that "mixed-income units" would replace the housing. Yet activists in the city argued that this rhetoric legitimated the privatization of public housing. Grassroots organizations such as Community Labor United claimed that the withdrawal of funding for public housing occurred while "federal relief funds are funneled into rebuilding casinos, hotels, chemical plants, and the wealthy white districts in New Orleans."[37]

Despite the language about affordable housing promoted by developers, local elites such as those representing the Small Business Association also participated in the redlining of Black neighborhoods by rejecting loan applications by African Americans. Joseph Canizaro, who had the support of the Republican Party, finance capital, and Democratic Mayor Nagin's office, said to a *New York Times* reporter, "I think we have a clean sheet to start again. And with that clean sheet we have some very big opportunities." He and his class promoted the gentrification of the city, which facilitated the accumulation of capital through the dispossession of poor and Black residents and the exploitation of immigrant labor.[38]

While no-bid contracts were being disproportionately awarded to corporations such as Halliburton, contractors advertised for reconstruction jobs in Latino neighborhoods across the Southwest while denying local African Americans employment in the construction industry. In turn, as Clyde Woods argues, while immigrant workers were falsely promised secure work in New Orleans, "A dangerous script emerged that framed immigrants as job stealing mobs," he wrote, "rather than as desperate workers who arrived in a city defined by a long history of racially discriminatory employment practices." Capitalists deployed racial narratives to deflect attention away from the exploitation of immigrant workers by transnational corporations and the exclusion of many local African American workers from jobs. "In just six months after Hurricane Katrina," the labor leader Saket Soni observed, "the last twenty-five years of U.S. history played out in microcosm: the complete displacement of an African American population; the obliteration of their jobs; and the entrance on to the scene of an immigrant workforce, one group excluded, the other exploited. Both were pitted by public policy against each other." The Bush administration promoted policies that excluded African Americans from work, at the same time as National Guard and immigration agents were deployed to deport immigrant workers "when they demanded wages."[39]

In 2008, Bush met with Mexican President Felipe Calderón and Canadian Prime Minister Stephen Harper for a trilateral summit in New Orleans, the last of four meetings to discuss the passage of the Security and Prosperity Package, which included a $1.4 billion Mérida initiative to fund increases in military and police actions modeled after Plan Colombia and the war on drugs. The package was a plan to increase expenditure for expanding security measures and bolstering free-trade agreements.[40] Bush stated in a press conference with Calderón and Harper:

> New Orleans is one of America's really top cities, and they—the people of New Orleans—appreciate the help you gave them right after Hurricane Katrina. And so I want to thank you very much for that. New Orleans has always been a crossroads for our continent, and today there's no better place for our nations to look forward to a bright future, and that's what we're here to do.[41]

Bush's claim that New Orleans provided an opportune space for elites to envision the future of free trade and security was a cruel but brutally honest vision of austerity economics and authoritarian politics that the North American ruling class promotes worldwide. In a nefarious extension of neoliberal agendas, the security discourse provided justification for the punitive response to contradictions of race and class in New Orleans. In this way, the subordination of New Orleans to the hemispheric security interests of racial capitalism is linked to a revanchist regime of police and prisons that targets the poor and people of color. The results have been egregious for too many poor and working-class people of color, who are locked away in prisons and jails, on probation or parole, or serving as military labor, police, prison guards, border security, or workers in weapons production or in other forms of "security" work.[42]

As late as 2008 the National Guard continued to patrol the streets of New Orleans. A report by National Public Radio's JJ Sutherland stated: "The Guard's mission is to prevent looting and provide . . . law and order." According to the report, soldiers worked twelve-hour shifts patrolling the streets by foot and in military police vehicles. They did not make arrests, but detained people until the New Orleans police arrived.[43] In his column "This Land," the *New York Times* journalist Dan Barry wrote: "Three years after Hurricane Katrina New Orleans still needs the military to help keep some semblance of order in certain neighborhoods." Barry provides several examples to support his narrative about the legitimacy of the military presence, including a driver "suspected of being high," yet "in the ensuing search and questioning, they learn that she is on her way to work as an exotic dancer. No drugs in her purse, Specialist Sylvia says. 'Only stripping supplies and condoms.'" This story concludes with a narrative that reflects a moral panic and *anticipatory criminalization*: "Long past midnight the Crown Vic prowls the palpable absence in the Lower Ninth Ward. The beam of the sergeant's flashlight skitters across a collapsed storefront, a restored home bearing a No Trespassing sign, an abandoned house bearing an old spray-painted X. It settles there upon a man, sitting alone in the consuming pitch, waiting for something." In these ways, he sets a scene that renders the militarized policing of Black poor communities a reasonable and rational technique for ensuring order. In the last analysis, this neoliberal security narrative suggests that the predominantly Black Ninth Ward is a place of drugs, prostitution, excess, and disorder that requires regulation by the carceral apparatus. While ideologies of security legitimated this social control strategy, other social and political futures are possible.[44]

WE KNOW THIS PLACE

We have reached an important historical moment when people who had refused to see before were finally made to see . . . that we have a billionaire ruling class that does not give one damn about poor, unemployed, underemployed Black people and working-class white people. This is a fact of life. And this is a fact that we revolutionary and progressive people cannot miss out on taking advantage of in this historical moment to drive home to people that this is not the type of society that you really want to live in. This is not the type of society that you bought into. This is not the type of society that you want for your children.

—Malcolm Suber, cofounder, People's Hurricane Relief Fund,
   2007

And we know this place,
for we have seen more times than we'd like to imagine
bloated cadavers floating through waters of a city gone
   savage,
foraging the land for what can be salvaged.
But what can be saved when all is lost?
It happened in August, twenty-nine days in.
We are now five days out of the only place
we knew to call house and home.
Few things are certain:
one, we have no food;
two, there are more bodies lying at the roadside
than hot plates being distributed
or first aid being administered
or recognition as a citizen.
Fourteenth Amendment, X, refugee, check.
And we know this place.
It's ever-changing yet forever the same:
Money and power and greed, the game.
—Sunni Patterson, "We Know This Place," 2005

Because the explanations for the abandonment of New Orleans in the wake of Katrina are often filtered through mass-mediated discourses of security, the ways of seeing articulated in the expressive culture of social movements in the region require further elaboration. Artists, activists, and intellectuals often provide interventions in culture that can be drawn upon in pressing for social change. They have shown how the redistributive-justice agenda of New Orleans has become a global imperative. Prominent among these is the poet and popular educator Sunni Patterson. In sharp contrast to the racialized discourses of looting and chaos that helped implement, explain, and legitimate mass incarceration and securitization in New Orleans, Patterson brings us into a different scene by articulating poetic knowledge of social contradictions through her spoken-word art.[45] Patterson conceived the poem "We Know This Place" as an ethical agreement with enslaved ancestors to continue the struggle for dignity, justice, and full equality for the dispossessed in North America. Penned in the context of one of the most emblematic moments of social crisis in contemporary U.S. history, the poem invokes a collective memory of the Black freedom struggle: "For we have glanced more times than we'd like to share / into eyes that stare with nothing there / behind

FIGURE 13. Cover of Sunni Patterson's spoken-word album *Porch Prophesies* (New Orleans, 2006).

them but an unfulfilled wish / and an unconscious yearning for life." The image of the slave ship is particularly resonant, Patterson remembers, "because of the water . . . the boats, and how we were treated." In her words, the people demonized as actual or potential looters are instead represented as oppressed people struggling for freedom.[46]

Patterson had lived most of her life in New Orleans's Ninth Ward and the community of Algiers before being one of the 250,000 people (most of them Black) displaced after the storm. She and her family were forced to migrate to Houston, where she lived for a year before returning to the city. There is a creative link between her art and the place she grew up: "I know and understand the type of beat . . . they want to hear . . . and it is a beat I like too because I come from these same streets." Her poetry calls up an alternative archive of popular memory inside communities. It expresses a social vision that is particularly important for analyzing the struggle over the definition of the event.[47]

Patterson's poem illuminates the abuse of the civil rights won during the long Black freedom struggle. Specifically, the invocation "Fourteenth Amendment, X, refugee, check" refers to the emancipation struggle after the Civil War to create abolition democracy through the

Fourteenth Amendment. It also references the counterrevolution of property that gave rise to Jim Crow capitalism. In doing so it provides audiences with an imagery of the place rooted in the collective memory of antiracist social movements.[48] This historical knowledge was powerfully expressed in Patterson's vernacular art, but also through the circulation of her poetics in multiple venues, including *Democracy Now!* broadcasts, HBO's *Def Poetry Jam*, club and poetry gatherings, as well as colleges and university readings. In 2006 Patterson was an emcee for a historic event organized by more than a hundred groups to commemorate the year of struggle for the right to return and reconstruct the city in which Community Labor United and the People's Hurricane Relief Fund (PHRF) played key roles. Longtime community organizer and PHRF cofounder Malcolm Suber had led the local fight against police repression for decades, and helped to ensure that the organization was a vehicle to represent the interests of working people. He led a fight for the right to return, reclaim public housing, enforce rent control, and expand social wage programs such as education, hospitals, and unionized public-sector jobs. These labor and community struggles suggested that the moment represented the possibility for a direct confrontation with neoliberal urbanism. The march of thousands of Katrina survivors from across the country began where the levees broke in the Lower Ninth Ward and ended in a demonstration on the first anniversary of the storm in Congo Square, a symbolic epicenter for self-active resistance, freedom dreams, and African American expressive culture.[49]

At the U.S. Social Forum held in Atlanta in 2007, Patterson instructed her audience about the unfinished business of abolition democracy. She called up the memory of freedom struggles to legitimate social justice movements in the present. Long before the rise of the global justice movement in the late twentieth century, abolitionists in the city had created transnational alliances with revolutionaries to attack racial capitalism.[50] As the historian Moon-Ho Jung powerfully observes, New Orleans is a place that experienced the circulation of revolutionary currents across the Atlantic world as stories of "Jacobin uprisings in Paris and Saint Domingue . . . ignited kindred hopes (and fires) in the streets of New Orleans and among a motley crew of Louisiana's working peoples." Knowledge of what C. L. R. James described in his *Black Jacobins* (1938) as the first "successful slave revolt in history" convinced this motley crew to elevate their struggles for freedom to new geographical scales.[51]

Patterson's poetry helps us understand the importance of the collective memory of past revolutionary struggles for social movements in the current conjuncture. It provides a powerful counternarrative to the neo-liberal state's construction of poor and Black communities as "domestic enemies." It expresses the poetic knowledge of the Black freedom movement. There are dramatic images in the poetry that show the historical—in other words, not natural—basis of racial and class inequality. They show that the poor and working people of New Orleans have been here before, and that the descendants of humans who were treated as if they were property know all too well the costs of elevating property rights over human rights. As her poem explains:

> . . . death rests comfortably beside us. . . .
> The silent cries of the keepers are louder
> than the booms that come from the guns
> they use to occupy the space.[52]

Patterson's words denaturalize the imagined link between place and race, revealing its roots in the production of militarized space.[53]

> And we know this place.
> It's decked in all its array and splendor,
> golden streets with good intentions
> capture our attention, gadgets and inventions
> pesticide the food supply, flu-like symptoms,
> diabetic condition, a cancer in the system,
> held on hold, it's a pistol to the temple.[54]

Read against the brutal restriction of spatial mobility through mass incarceration and the securitization of urban space, Patterson's poetry suggests that these conditions were inevitable.

She taps collective memories to articulate new languages and subjectivities, claiming a "spatial entitlement," meaning, the ability to circulate in "sonic waves" voices of struggle and dignity.[55] Consider, for example, her poem "We Made It":

> So I'm from a stock
> that pitch cocktail bombs and hand grenades.
> We pour cayenne pepper around the perimeter of the building
> to keep the police dogs at bay.
> I'm like the Panther Party
> in the Desire Housing Projects in New Orleans.[56]

The Katrina tragedy occurred thirty-five years after the Louisiana chapter of the Black Panther Party's office was fired upon by the New Orleans police department across from the infamously overcrowded Desire Projects. The hurricane struck nearly four decades after Malcolm X's assassination in New York. It landed on shore a half-century after Emmett Till's murder in Mississippi. Such themes of premature death can never be far away from the social memory and lived experiences of the Black working class.[57] In historical terms, Patterson's reclamation of the collective memory of Black freedom struggles shows how the subject of violence is manipulated in the popular imaginary:

> I'm telling you, death ain't always good.
> It will leave you fending for water and food.
> It will riddle up your body in the Audubon Ballroom
> They'll El-Hajj Malik el-Shabazz you,
> crown you king, then dethrone you in a Lorraine Hotel.
> They'll disfigure your body to where folks can't tell
> if you Emmett Till or not,
> tell the mama, "Keep that casket open,
> let all the world see it ain't just burning in Mississippi."
> Hell, it's hot wherever you be,
> from the rooftop to the cell block.
> step on up to the auction block,
> and bend over,
> touch your toes,
> show your teeth,
> lift her titties,
> examine his balls,
> now, this damn near sounds like a hip-hop song,
> but it's slavery at its peak,
> it's a circus for all the freaks.[58]

The poem evokes collective memories of racist violence in U.S. political culture to situate the meaning of Katrina. It symbolizes an articulation between race, class, gender, sexuality, and class processes. Yet Patterson also articulates the uncanny ability of aggrieved communities "to look death right in the face and say we made it, we made it, we made it, we made it."[59]

In addition to her role as a politically engaged artist, Patterson worked as a public school teacher in the Students at the Center program cofounded by the teacher and labor organizer Jim Randels and the Black arts movement poet and activist Kalamu ya Salaam. This program grew out of the tradition of the Radical Reconstruction's use of public schools in the struggle for freedom. This program is critical in a context where the public education system is, as ya Salaam puts it, a "direct feeder for the . . . labor needed for the tourist-oriented economy . . . [and,] for those not fortunate enough to work in a hotel[,] . . .

the penitentiary."[60] To counter this trajectory, the Students at the Center program facilitates the production of expressive culture and the study of the history of social movements. It provides students with materials that explore how youth have played central roles in freedom struggles.

Kalamu ya Salaam intervenes that the task is to link critical social theory with African American vernacular expressions in order to articulate a philosophy of praxis: "There is no substitute for face-to-face organizing around the needs of specific communities. . . . It is critical that this struggle be a dynamic of praxis . . . a constant evaluation and realignment of thought and practice." His intervention could not be more resonant about the urgent tasks ahead.[61] It underscores the importance of studying African American history to reconstruct popular democracy in the present. The social memory forged in the civil rights era can inform contemporary struggles confronting the crisis of mass incarceration.[62]

The grassroots philosophy of social change articulated by the freedom movement represented a vision of popular democracy for the masses of ordinary working people. It focused on the development of the people's capacity for self-governance, promoted mass-based mobilizations by tapping the perspectives in vernacular culture and argued that people's movements draw their energy from the enhanced dignity gained by participation in the culture of freedom struggles. Black working-class civil rights leaders in New Orleans such as Jerome Smith, Rudy Lombard, and Oretha Castle linked directly with the struggles of the Black poor through their activism and social protest. Yet in doing so they realized that the legalistic victories of the postwar civil rights movement against Jim Crow were not enough to challenge the class character of racial inequality.[63]

The historic mission of social movements in post-Katrina New Orleans has been to take up the unfinished business of the freedom movement in overcoming racism, militarism, and poverty. Artists, activists, and protesters have demanded the right to return, reclaim the public sector, and implement a more just future for the 250,000 survivors displaced to places such as Texas, Florida, Georgia, and Washington, DC. This exclusion has occurred in a context where the many suffer from a class war on the poor, and where racialization has been deployed as a justification. It suggests the ethical imperatives of supporting the freedom dreams and collective struggles of aggrieved Katrina communities. The stakes of this struggle have to do with combating the ways in which the revanchist restructuring of New Orleans has served as a model for neoliberal urbanism across the planet.[64]

As the New Orleans–based Black feminist activist and researcher Shana Griffin put it, "The ways in which . . . punitive neoliberal social policies evolved before and after Katrina is a story worth telling." "Yet," she warns, "the stories by themselves and the many policy recommendations rarely speak on our disposability in the current social order. You need to understand this to comprehend political conflicts in the city." To combat the construction of poor people as disposable in the political economy, public intellectuals such as Griffin have revealed the necessity for an augmented social wage. Since the social wage is based on political and economic resources produced by labor, radical social movements can organize themselves to transform them into "life-enhancing use[s]." This framework shakes loose common-sense notions of structure and agency through recognition of ordinary people's collective capacity to "*make* power" and "shake the ground."[65]

The poetry of social movements suggests the possibility of crafting an alternative future out of the present. It illuminates the ability of working-class communities to, as Woods put it, "push their historic development agenda forward, ever forward."[66] On this score, Patterson's poetics not only function as a critique of neoliberal racial regimes, but also reveal a vision of freedom:

> I swear, we know this place, because we have vowed before never again to return, but here we are, back in the desert, dry mouth and thirsting for waters from Heaven. But come, come, children, rally around, and maybe together we can make a sound that will shake the trees or *rattle the ground*, make strong our knees, we's freedom bound.[67]

CHAPTER 6

Shut 'Em Down

Social Movements Confront Mass
Homelessness and Mass Incarceration
in Los Angeles

This day of action will promote the human right to housing
and reinforce the hip hop community's responsibility to social
justice causes.

—Chuck D, Operation Skid Row music festival, Los Angeles,
    January 2012

On a cordoned-off block stretching between Fifth and Sixth Streets and
Gladys in downtown Los Angeles, which on most days houses a soup
kitchen, a vacant lot, and a single-room-occupancy hotel, Chuck D and
Public Enemy performed for free at the Operation Skid Row music festival. The festival, which took place on January 15, 2012, the weekend
of Dr. Martin Luther King Jr.'s birthday, was co-organized by Chuck D
and the Los Angeles Community Action Network (LA CAN), a housing
and human rights organization. More than fifteen hundred people
crammed the street to listen to Public Enemy as well as the music of
famed LA hip-hop performers such as Freestyle Fellowship, Medusa,
Kid Frost, Yo-Yo, and Egyptian Lover, and artists from the neighborhood such as the Skid Row Playas. In the face of threats from the Los
Angeles Police Department to shut the festival down, Public Enemy
opened with one of their signature songs of defiance, "Shut 'Em Down."[1]
They did so before an audience of Skid Row residents and community
organizers; members of social movement organizations such as the Bus
Riders Union, Critical Resistance, Food Not Bombs, and INCITE!
Women of Color Against Violence; and fans from across the city. This
effort to connect hip-hop with the struggle for human rights was

FIGURE 14. Chuck D and Public Enemy performing at the Operation Skid Row music festival, Los Angeles, January 15, 2012. Image by Ernest R. Savage III, www. asavagecity.com.

significant for its timing and location. During the fifth year of the worst economic crisis since the Great Depression, this festival highlighted the material conditions in Skid Row—an area in downtown Los Angeles where Black people constitute 75 percent of the population, and where there is the highest concentration of poverty, policing, and homelessness in the United States. More than just a day of entertainment, the Operation Skid Row musical festival helped circulate a critique of the crisis through expressive culture.[2]

Artists and activists connected to social movements in Los Angeles have taken up a dramatic fight over the meaning of the crisis by calling for the human right to housing in Los Angeles, the "First World capital of homelessness." The Operation Skid Row festival was one manifestation of this effort.[3] It illuminated the material conditions experienced by the racialized poor, and how they have resisted them. Indeed, Operation Skid Row confronted the truth of the crisis, as Stuart Hall observed, "The social formation can no longer be reproduced on the basis of the preexisting system of social relations." This effort to highlight material conditions in downtown Los Angeles during the present crisis of global capitalism shows how expressive culture has provided distinct counternarratives of the crisis.[4]

Public Enemy's performance of songs such as "Shut 'Em Down" at Operation Skid Row did not simply reflect the crisis, but called attention to it and, in doing so, attempted to confront it.[5] The performance enabled grassroots social movements working on homelessness and poverty to circulate their critique at a different geographical scale. The politics of scale are crucial for the poor, evicted, and homeless residents of Skid Row. There are more homeless people in Los Angeles than in any other city in the country, affecting between sixty and one hundred thousand people. The state's response to the crisis has been to contain poor and homeless people within particular geographical boundaries. Revanchist policing strategies trap Black, Brown, and poor people in space in order to protect the interests of capital and the state. Such traps on Skid Row include the mass arrest (under the guise of public safety) of residents for activities such as loitering, jaywalking, public urination, and public drunkenness, and the mass eviction of residents from single-room-occupancy hotels in the name of reclaiming downtown through condo and loft conversions for high-end real estate development. This strategy of "accumulation by dispossession" has been sustained and justified by racial narratives. Such narratives purport that poor people of color are individually responsible for their own loss of wealth, a consequence of their attitudes, behaviors, and cultures of ineptitude.[6]

Under such logic poor people suffering from homelessness were not to be assisted through public services and employment; rather, city officials have promoted revanchist strategies of crisis management.[7] Since 2006 Los Angeles city officials have pursued a "broken windows" strategy of policing they called the Safer Cities Initiative (SCI). Developed by the Manhattan Institute and implemented at the local scale by then Mayor Antonio Villaraigosa and Chief William Bratton, SCI represented an update on the revanchist policies that Bratton helped usher in with then–New York Mayor Rudolph Giuliani in the 1990s. Bratton assumed control of the LAPD in 2002. By 2003 he implemented broken windows policing in Skid Row. With the ideological and political support of the Manhattan Institute and the criminologist George Kelling of Rutgers (who was paid at least $500,000 in consulting fees), the LAPD unleashed an unprecedented deployment of police power in less than one square mile of the Central City area, which became a laboratory for applying new policing and security technologies. This political project has required ideological legitimation. The broken windows metaphor is revealing, since, as Fred Moten observes, broken windows are not repaired—they are replaced—much as Black, Brown, and poor people are literally removed from space. The metaphor also highlights the fact that this policing strategy has a revenge-driven logic. It represents the homeless, poor, and housing-rights activists as enemies of the neoliberal state. In doing so, it has been part of an ideological and political campaign to legitimate Los Angeles's own version of incarcerating the crisis.[8]

This chapter asks and answers the following questions about these dynamics: What was the relationship between structures and processes of racialization, gentrification, and the policing of urban space in the aftermath of the global financial crisis of 2008? How have the dominant representations of the crisis provoked resistance and criticism at the grassroots? How have grassroots activists and artists confronted the parallel crises of mass homelessness and mass incarceration? What kinds of alternatives to criminalization are made possible when conceived from the perspective of the social movement for the human right to housing? Drawing inspiration from the struggle for the human right to housing, I make four principal arguments. First, the racial and spatial dynamics of the global financial crisis in 2008 underscore the need to theorize its historical and geographical origins in cities such as Los Angeles. I illustrate how contemporary housing policies have been deployed in response to shifts in the political economy in the wake of the twentieth-century Black freedom struggle.[9] I suggest how they have ensured a racially and spatially differentiated organization of the landscape in U.S. cities.[10]

Second, while there are different methodological approaches to tracing the roots of this crisis, I argue that it is crucial to analyze it as a conjuncture. Conjunctural analysis helps to grasp its relationship to the neoliberal turn in U.S. and global capitalism. It will help us periodize the shifting relationships between capital, the state, and social movements. Through a concrete analysis of the struggle for housing rights, we can better understand alternatives to the neoliberal settlement, which has justified the privatization of public housing, education, and health care and the rise of mass incarceration in globalizing California. It suggests that consent to this settlement has been secured through purportedly color-blind narratives.[11] Next, I show how these narratives have been deployed to naturalize this transformation of the political economy as inevitable. This line of argument enables us to understand how the crisis came to be represented in terms of security. It can also help us assess how racist ideologies have reinforced the logic of the current political settlement.[12] They have endorsed the withdrawal of the social wage at precisely the moment when the military, prisons, and policing have become central to the political economy of the U.S. empire.[13]

Finally, remaining attentive to the structural underpinnings of the current conjuncture, this chapter examines the perspective of events articulated in the expressive culture of social movements in Los Angeles.[14] It argues that contemporary struggles represent a continuity of campaigns waged by the long civil rights movement to contest racial capitalism's organization of space. These grassroots activists and artists show that the resolution of crisis by racialization, mass criminalization, and neoliberalization is not inevitable. The chapter proceeds in three parts: it looks at dominant depictions of the current crisis, then turns to the historical confrontation in Los Angeles between housing struggles and emergent securitization, and concludes with a consideration of what we might learn from Los Angeles about the prospects for alternative futures.[15]

NARRATING THE CRISIS

The national wave of home foreclosures, many concentrated in lower-income and minority neighborhoods, has created a strong temptation to find the villains responsible. . . . When we round up all the culprits, we shouldn't ignore the regulators and affordable-housing advocates who pushed lenders to make loans in low-income neighborhoods for reasons other than the only one that makes sense: likely repayment.

—Howard Husock, "Housing Goals We Can't Afford," *New York Times*, December 10, 2008

Poor communities of color in Los Angeles have been particularly affected by the "subprime mortgage crisis," as it has come to be signified in mass-mediated discourse. These communities were targeted for predatory and faulty subprime loans, and later represented as the primary culprits of the crisis. As people of color had experienced systematic racial exclusion in access to home loans because of historical practices of redlining, they were also increasingly given access to faulty subprime loans. These processes occurred as capital deepened its strategies of financialization. Before the foreclosure crisis took hold as a national phenomenon, Black people lost between $71 and $93 billion dollars in assets because of subprime loans between 2000 and 2008, while Latinos lost between $76 and $98 billion.[16] The crisis only compounded a reliance on credit by the poor and people of color. As mortgage rates increased while real wages went into decline and unemployment rates skyrocketed, it became increasingly difficult for people to make their payments. A wave of foreclosures followed, leading to what

United for a Fair Economy describes as "the greatest loss of wealth to people of color in modern U.S. history."[17]

The subprime mortgage crisis led to the collapse of several Wall Street banks, which in turn had the effect of spreading the crisis worldwide from its historical and geographical roots in U.S. urban spaces. While the ramifications of the financial crisis have been global, Southern California has been an "epicenter."[18] By 2010 California experienced more foreclosures than any other place in the country, with a half-million cases. At the national scale more than half of the foreclosures were experienced by African Americans and Latinos, a rate two to three times higher than for whites. It also created a spike in homelessness.[19]

The history and ongoing practices of racial segregation and policing in Southern California have concentrated the deleterious consequences of the capitalist crisis in and through the "racialization of space and spatialization of race."[20] Racial segregation has trapped poor people of color in spaces that have been targeted by finance capital for predatory lending of subprime loans. This spatial apartheid exists alongside other parasitic finance institutions, which exploit the poor and people of color through high-interest-rate loans. Taken together, such practices can be read as capital's efforts to trap people in space in order to extract wealth. Finance capitalists and their deputies have exploited the geography of poverty and spatial apartheid. In doing so, they have widened the "racial wealth gap." At the same time, mass evictions have been deployed as a solution to the foreclosure crisis in the very segregated neighborhoods that had been targeted for subprime loans. The same lenders who peddled subprime loans accumulated capital by displacing and dispossessing poor people of color.[21]

Yet in narrating the housing crisis, commentators such as the vice president of the Manhattan Institute, Howard Husock, represented the poor, people of color, housing activists, and state regulation of finance capital as the "culprits" of the crisis: "One cannot say with any certainty whether the more important cause of the current housing crisis was affordable-housing mandates or the actions of investment banks and ratings agencies." Husock simultaneously asserted that denying loans to people "based on the race of the residents or other factors unrelated to their ability to repay loans is clearly wrong," and suggests that there is no longer a need for state regulation of finance capital. In this way, he appeals to the fantasy of a raceless meritocracy where loans can be made the "old-fashioned way, on the merits of individual households."[22] Such narratives made well-established appeals to color-blindness by defining the problem as "risky borrowers" rather than risky financialization practices that created the crisis. In turn, they have functioned to displace class anxieties created through the uneven development of racial capitalism.[23]

Neoliberal think tanks such as the Manhattan Institute—which are closely aligned with the mayor, the police department, and finance capital in Los Angeles—have engaged in an ideological struggle to legitimate their revanchist solutions to the crisis.[24] As rationalizers of securitized urbanism, such think tanks—which also include the American Enterprise Institute, the Cato Institute, and the Heritage Foundation—have narrated the housing crisis in alignment with their effort to advocate for policy that restructures space in the interest of capital. The state's response to the crisis—bailing out the bankers who caused the problem rather than implementing concrete housing and jobs programs to meet the needs of the poor and the working class—suggests the extent to which neoliberal think tanks and finance capital have shaped federal policies.[25]

To understand the race and class underpinnings of the post-2008 economic crisis, we also need a long historical view of how dominant geographical interests have shaped the "security turn." The intellectuals of the neoliberal state apparatus have consistently deployed incarceration and securitization to repair ruptures in the social formation.[26] The most persistent ruptures have been created by the urban multiracial working class themselves: from the Watts insurrection (1965) to the Los Angeles rebellion (1992) to the persistent struggles waged on Skid Row in the current crisis. In each event, surplus workers have been at the center of political struggles over public space and access to wealth. They have promoted visions of social change that clash with the vision of those who seek law and order, security, and social control.[27]

Neoliberal security ideology has endorsed austerity economics and authoritarian politics.[28] As we have seen, the Black and Latino poor make up a majority of the carceral population. According to David Wagner and Pete White, the Black poor are also disproportionately represented in the U.S. homeless population, at between 40 and 56 percent. At the same time, Latinos are between 12 and 15 percent, Asian Americans are between 1 and 3 percent, Native Americans are between 3 and 4 percent, and poor whites are between 32 and 39 percent of the homeless population at the national level. Yet neoliberal racial ideologies have redirected attention away from the multiraciality of poverty, homelessness, and incarceration. They have shifted attention away from the declining material conditions for the working class in general, and, in so doing, rationalized the "new racial capitalism."[29] They have sought to prevent multiracial class alliances by scapegoating the poor, people of color, LGBTQI communities, immigrant workers, and radical organizers (which are not mutually exclusive categories) as the source of the problems they endure. Thinking conjuncturally, however, we can begin to discern the structure of social relations that are otherwise difficult to observe. The current crisis can also enable a fidelity to the unfinished business of freedom struggles from the long twentieth century.[30]

THE EPICENTER OF THE CRISIS

We dared to rise up, dared to struggle, and dared to put this country
on notice about the inequality.

—Bilal Ali, Black Panther and LA CAN housing organizer in
  *Freedom Now! Struggles for the Human Right to Housing
  in Los Angeles and Beyond*, 2012

In the aftermath of Ronald Reagan's election as president, there was a pervasive and persistent assault on federal funding for affordable housing. Activists and policy analysts have shown that contemporary mass homelessness emerged as a result. At the same time, city officials passed laws criminalizing homelessness and poverty. In turn, Skid Row in downtown Los Angeles became an "open-air prison" for people deemed disposable. As Laura Pulido's research demonstrates, the production of this securitized space has been shaped by the "geography of past racial regimes."[31]

Since the late 1970s and early 1980s the Los Angeles City Council has promoted the "containment" of homelessness on Skid Row as a way to trap Black and poor people in space.[32] Deindustrialized Black workers from South Central L.A. were forced to migrate to Skid Row as part of a survival strategy to gain food, shelter, and other basic necessities because there was a concentration of social services in this section of the city. According to the legal scholar Gary Blasi, Skid Row went from being 67 percent white and 21 percent Black in the 1970s to majority Black by the end of the 1980s. During the 1990s California ranked forty-ninth out of fifty states in terms of providing public housing. Currently Skid Row has the highest concentration of homeless people in the city and the most concentrated poverty in the United States. By analyzing the mass criminalization of the poor and disproportionately Black low-income residents and homeless people in the capital of homelessness, we can gain clarity on the dynamics of racialization, gentrification, incarceration, and capital accumulation during the continuation of a "cold war on the streets of Downtown."[33]

The gentrification of downtown Los Angeles has been accompanied by mass criminalization. These political, economic, ideological, and geographical processes need to be theorized in their totality. In an alliance with finance capital, the neoliberal state has provided police presence downtown to facilitate the production of new condos and lofts. Aggressive policing and surveillance has been deployed to criminalize resistance to these uneven developments. Real estate speculators and developers transformed single-room-occupancy hotels that were rented for about $500 a month into condos and lofts that rent for between $2,000 and $5,000 a month. As housing and land prices rose, state officials, local real estate developers, and journalists appealed to moral panics about race, crime, and law and order to justify the restructuring of the space in the interest of capital and the state. In transforming the landscape by constructing art museums, coffee shops, restaurants, dog grooming services, and other amenities for gentrifiers and owners, the city has made gentrification a centerpiece of its efforts to compete with other cities in attracting capital. Policing has been central to this urban strategy of capitalist development. Homeless residents and civil rights activists downtown are persistently subject to arrest as a result. The LAPD and the Manhattan Institute have engaged in an ideological campaign to justify neoliberal forms of aggressive policing rather than social spending as a strategy of managing the crises of mass homelessness and poverty.[34]

Consider for example an article that appeared in the Manhattan Institute's *City Journal*. Penned by LAPD Chief Charlie Beck along with Bratton and the coauthor of the broken windows theory, Kelling, the article argues that the Safer Cities Initiative represents a significant effort "to reduce crime, lawlessness, and disorder." In turn, Beck, Bratton, and Kelling assert that the problem they seek to solve has been "lawlessness" rather than "homelessness."[35] Yet such "lawlessness" can be read in an inverse and negative procedure as the dissent of homeless and housing activists challenging systematic human rights abuses in the revanchist city. This policing strategy combines vengeful security politics with the elite desire for reclaiming space from aggrieved communities. Revanchism provides the ideological underpinning for the strategy. Skid Row residents—the homeless, low-income renters, the evicted, the unemployed; in short, the surplus population—have endured increasing authoritarianism because of these revenge-driven policing and security policies. This intensified securitization has included the installation of security cameras on Skid Row, which as Richard Winton of the *Los Angeles Times* observes, makes "the downtown area the most heavily monitored part of the city." In promoting an image of L.A. as safe for gentrifiers, the local state has enacted a strategy of regulating public space through extensive policing and surveillance. Read in this context, the mayor's office depicts the police as protecting the homeless when poor and homeless residents actually need protection from the police. Indeed, as Alex Vitale has suggested, we need to ask whether or not the goal of the policy was to "reduce crime and homelessness or instead to remove a large concentration of poor people forcibly from Skid Row in hopes of encouraging the subsequent gentrification of the area." This is particularly important in a context where "a major effort to gentrify the Skid Row area has been underway for several years." At the very moment that developers have sought to invest in the area the city's policy has been to cycle poor and homeless people "through the criminal justice system" or force them to move "into other poor areas with already inadequate social services."[36]

In 2010, Deborah Burton, a Skid Row resident and organizer with LA CAN, traveled to Geneva to deliver a statement to the United Nations Universal Periodic Review about the human rights abuses represented by mass homelessness in Los Angeles. She explained that "Instead of providing the solution to homelessness—which is housing— Los Angeles and other cities choose to use the police to harass, move, and incarcerate homeless people. . . . Black people by far are the most impacted by homelessness." "My organization," Burton declared, "LA CAN, works in partnership with dozens of other organizations built and led by impacted residents. We are building power. We will make progress. We can win. But the task is huge and we will need the international communities to join us in pressuring the U.S. government." Burton's intervention underscores the importance of the ideological and political struggle over the meaning of the policing of the crisis. As the historian Rhonda Williams argues, focusing on the critiques of neoliberal governance articulated by African American working-class women activists helps us to understand "a key element of poor women's political movement ideology." Much as the long civil rights movement worked to overcome geographical boundaries by making their appeals in terms of human rights, so too have public housing residents, low-income renters,

single-room-occupancy tenants, and members of the disproportionately
Black homeless and marginally housed population claimed the human
right to housing to circulate their struggles in different cities around the
country and the planet. The demand for the human right to housing and
access to the social wage represents a confrontation with the racial
regime of U.S. capitalism.[37]

As the cofounder and codirector of LA CAN Pete White explains,
"We believe that one thing that encourages safety is housing. Housing
for all. We believe that safe spaces, green spaces, parks, educational
opportunities, [and] occupational opportunities . . . define what safety
would feel like to us." He adds, "There's $100 million, $87 million of
which went to policing, that could have gone to solutions that encour-
age safety in a whole different way." LA CAN has exposed racism as a
central contradiction in the state form. By organizing based on a democratic platform of civil and human rights, the organization has articulated a social vision that shows how antiracism is in the interest of the
urban multiracial working class as a whole. Implementing their program would require the abolition of homelessness, the production of
public housing, full employment, and an end to the Safer Cities Initiative. This would mean access to and redirection of a surplus budget of
more than $87 million spent annually on policing. This would require a
shift in the urban political economy away from militarism and toward
a social wage that would entail radical social transformations.[38]

Through their political campaigns, direct-action protests, and community meetings as well as their newspaper *Community Connection* and
innovative use of new media such as blogs, documentary filmmaking,
and Facebook, LA CAN documents and challenges the pervasive and
persistent criminalization experienced by homeless and poor residents.
As part of a regional alliance, the Western Regional Advocacy Project
(WRAP), LA CAN codirector Becky Dennison explains they have "really
expanded the bandwidth of the opposition to the criminalization of
homelessness. In four or five different states, we had four substantive
homeless Bills of Rights moving." By organizing directly with the poor
at multiple scales—local, regional, national, and international—in a
struggle for survival, they have generated antisystemic protest. This
organizing demonstrates in practice that the demand for the human right
to housing is part of a broader struggle for a better social wage. LA CAN
and their allies in organizations around the city and state, including the
Community Rights Campaign, Californians United for a Responsible
Budget, the Youth Justice Coalition, the Stop LAPD Spying Coalition,

the Labor Community Strategy Center, and Critical Resistance Los Angeles, are engaged in a dynamic struggle against criminalization and for racial and economic justice in the neoliberal city.[39]

Drawing on the social vision of the long civil rights movement, LA CAN has organized Black, Brown, poor, and homeless people downtown to contest criminalization and press for economic human rights, a social wage, and the right to the city. For example, in 2009 the United Nations Special Rapporteur on Adequate Housing, Raquel Rolnik, visited Los Angeles (cohosted locally by LA CAN) and other U.S. cities to assess the housing crisis. She found that the "subprime mortgage crisis has widened an already large gap between the supply of and demand for affordable housing. The economic crisis which followed has led to increased unemployment and an even greater need for affordable housing."[40] She concluded that gentrification and the foreclosure crisis have been the leading causes of the spike in homelessness. Accordingly, renters and homeowners alike have been affected. Poor people who lost their housing are increasingly forced into homelessness. The neoliberal state has responded to this increase by "producing anarchy in the name of order." Perhaps this is nowhere more evident than downtown L.A.[41]

Social movement organizations, including LA CAN and WRAP, have underscored the importance of confronting this crisis politically. According to WRAP Organizing Director Paul Boden, "Local 'anti-homeless' police enforcement campaigns, separate court systems, property confiscations and the closing of public spaces—these are in the forefront of today's civil rights battles." This intervention compels us to reckon with the unfinished business of the long civil rights movement in confronting mass homelessness and mass incarceration. To do so, we need to listen to activists who are demanding "house keys, not hand cuffs." They suggest that another city is not only possible but a burning necessity.[42]

Epilogue

The Poetry of the Future

The social revolution . . . cannot take its poetry from the past
but only from the future.

—Karl Marx, *The Eighteenth Brumaire of Louis Bonaparte*, 1852

Only poets, since they must excavate and recreate history,
have ever learned anything from it.

—James Baldwin, *No Name in the Street*, 1972

This book explores how elites have cynically exploited common-sense
notions about race and crime in order to win consent to the undoing of
the advances of the long civil rights movement and the construction of
the neoliberal carceral state. It also examines struggles to transform the
common sense and shift popular consciousness. In doing so it follows
James Baldwin's lead in turning to poetry as a source of "evidence of
things not seen," the alternative archive articulated in the expressive
culture of freedom struggles. Baldwin was able to draw his poetry from
the future.[1] As he saw it, this process required that poets bear "witness
to a possibility which we will not live to see, but we have to bring . . .
out." For him, these visions of the future rely on the knowledge of
"what we know human beings have been and can become, and that is
so subversive that it is called poetry."[2]

While the poetry of social movements is rarely seriously considered
in debates about alternatives to neoliberalism, its significance for understanding the present moment cannot be overstated. In providing a perspective on events that dramatically clashes with the prose of counterinsurgency, this poetry has important implications for scholarship

examining the relationship between neoliberal restructuring, mass crim-inalization, and the history of the long civil rights movement.[3] Four and a half decades after Baldwin penned his intervention, we find ourselves in a historical moment defined by unprecedented expansion of the carceral apparatus. These conditions point to unfinished agendas of freedom struggles in the present conjuncture.[4]

Amid the economic crash of 2007 and 2008, the Black feminist and socialist intellectual Angela Y. Davis argued that the project of abolition democracy that took root in the 1930s had "not been fully accom-plished." Identified by W. E. B. Du Bois in *Black Reconstruction in America* (1935), the vision of abolition democracy, Davis explains, insists upon "socialist rather than capitalist conceptions of democracy." A socialist conception of democracy includes not only the political right to vote and participate in elections but also the economic right to public housing, education, health care, employment, and transit. In elaborat-ing this socialist theory of democracy, she represents the stakes in strug-gles over the memory of the long civil rights movement in the current conjuncture.[5] For Davis, common-sense notions of the post–civil rights era have misconstrued the meaning of freedom struggles during the current age of neoliberalism. She argues that the "civil rights movement had to be declared dead in order for its legacies to be celebrated by the dominant culture," thus belying its forestalled agendas. Contesting the dominance of prisons and policing in the political economy presents an opportunity to complete its unfinished business. "In thinking specifi-cally about the abolition of prisons using the approach of abolition democracy," Davis explains, "we would propose the creation of an array of social institutions that would begin to solve the social problems that set people on the track to prison." In other words, the concept of abolition democracy enables us to see the roots of the new society in struggles over the common sense in the current conjuncture.[6]

POLICING THE CRISIS TODAY

In November 2014 Davis delivered the keynote address, "Policing the Crisis Today," at a conference held at Goldsmiths College in London dedicated to engaging and discussing the work of Stuart Hall in the wake of his passing. Her lecture reflected on the ways in which the thirty-fifth-anniversary edition of Stuart Hall, Chas Critcher, Tony Jefferson, John Clarke, and Brian Roberts's *Policing the Crisis* "resonated with the widely reported events in Ferguson, Missouri." Indeed, the publication of the new edition occurred amidst an urgent public debate about race and policing. The police killing of Michael Brown in Ferguson on August 9, 2014, led protestors to hit the streets across the country, declaring "Hands Up, Don't Shoot" and "Black Lives Matter." At the time of Davis's address and at the time of this writing, the United States has been witnessing a crisis of hegemony for U.S. policing and prisons on a scale unprecedented since the urban insurrections and prison rebellions of the 1960s and 1970s.[7] This crisis, as Davis's comments suggest, represents a moment of rupture more favorable for critically theorizing the role of racialization in maintaining the coercive hegemony of the carceral state.[8]

As Davis illuminates, and as this book also argues, *Policing the Crisis* provides readers with methodological skills to conduct their own conjunctural analysis of the moment. This means placing moral panics around race and crime at the center of the analysis, as Hall instructed. Such a methodology provides key tools for assessing how coercive authority has been articulated through race to produce consent to the current hegemonic "settlement."[9] Racialization is a key structural feature of neoliberal capitalism. It legitimates the use of policing, prisons, and permanent war as inevitable features of the political economy. As has been the case with every other turning point in U.S. history analyzed in this study, race has come to provide the terrain in which class anxieties generated by a crisis of hegemony are "worked through."[10]

As Hall argued, conjunctural analysis helps us "develop a practice which is theoretically informed." It, he argued, "establishes the *open horizon* of Marxist theorizing." It helps clarify how the organic intellectuals of social movements can articulate a philosophy of praxis. The methodology of conjunctural analysis, as I have attempted to show, illustrates the strategic role that expressive culture plays in struggles for hegemony. This book foregrounds the ongoing struggle in language and ideology over the memory and meaning of dramatic moments to help us better understand the "synchronization of the race and class aspects of the crisis." We need to take this challenge seriously and develop an informed political response to the current crisis of hegemony.[11]

The fundamental ethical and political challenge of the conjuncture is to confront the counterinsurgent tradition at the center of U.S. political economy and culture. As I have argued, the conditions of existence for the rise of the neoliberal carceral state were laid by the coercion unleashed by the security apparatus during the rise of Cold War racial liberalism.[12] Far from creating an opening for the long civil rights movement, the Red Scare—which detained Du Bois, deported Claudia Jones, destroyed Paul

FIGURE 15. Stuart Hall speaking in Trafalgar Square, central London circa 1960. Courtesy the Stuart Hall Foundation.

Robeson's career, red-baited Martin Luther King Jr., and damaged the lives of a whole generations of antiracist activists on the Left—led to a disavowal of materialist analyses of racism and class struggle in exchange for concessions from the state apparatus. This anticommunist settlement undermined the materialist analysis of racism and state violence articulated by the most radical voices in freedom struggles and created a political vacuum in which the neoliberal carceral state would flourish.[13]

The political task in this conjuncture requires, in the "first instance," the construction of a broad popular alliance for a social wage and against racism, mass incarceration, and neoliberal austerity measures. Indeed, activists, artists, and authors connected to social movements in the present policing crisis argue that this moment represents the opportunity to create a democratic advance in a larger struggle to dismantle the neoliberal carceral state.[14] It is upon this terrain that, as Antonio Gramsci would have it, the *forces of opposition organize.*[15]

THE FUTURE OF SOCIAL MOVEMENTS

As I see it, history moves from one conjuncture to another rather than being an evolutionary flow. And what drives it forward is usually a crisis. . . . Crises are moments of potential change, but the nature of their resolution is not given.

—Stuart Hall, "Interpreting the Crisis," in *Soundings,* 2010

In my life
I've had all kinds of blues—
The kind you have in winter
When there's holes in your shoes
I had the broken-hearted
And the down home blues,
I had the worried mind
And the money trouble too . . .
Just when we thought that we paid all our dues
In comes the system with some brand new blues

—Cyril Neville, "Brand New Blues," from the album *Brand New Blues*, 2009

In the title track of his album *Brand New Blues*, the New Orleans musician, longtime member of the Neville Brothers, and percussionist for the Meters, Cyril Neville, sang "Somebody listen . . . just when we thought we paid all our dues / in comes the system with some brand new blues." The song blends blues, funk, and soul to provide a poetic critique of conditions in New Orleans in the wake of Hurricane Katrina. Other songs on the album provide cultural criticism of material conditions: "Spending my money like it wasn't funny, every last dime, oh what a crime." The resonant lyrics also represent the ways in which the poor and working class have experienced the contradictions of race and class in the aftermath of the global and domestic crisis of 2008.[16] As some journalists and social scientists declared the so-called "end of neoliberalism," Neville presented the perspective of the "brand new blues"—a way of seeing that resonates with working-class audiences who continue to experience the crippling effects of neoliberalization, mass incarceration, and the criminalization of homelessness and poverty.[17]

These brand new blues also represent the unfinished business of freedom struggles: "I wonder how they could make like it is all over / make me want to rise up for justice / make me want rise up for freedom."[18] By drawing on the collective memory of the long civil rights movement, Neville articulates the moral economy and social visions of aggrieved and insurgent people. As such, his poetic intervention can help us comprehend how the current conjuncture is the product of political struggles that could have had different resolutions. It also offers resources for imagining the transition out of neoliberalism. As struggles for social justice continue to be met with racist and revanchist neoliberal political projects bent on restoring class power, Neville's brand new blues are critical for the development of an alternative common sense.[19]

From the labor-based civil rights insurgencies in the 1930s, 1940s, and 1950s, to the insurrections in the streets and factories of Watts and

Detroit in the 1960s, to the prison uprisings in California, New York, and Illinois in the 1970s and 1980s, to the Los Angeles rebellion in the 1990s, to the battle of post-Katrina New Orleans and protests against mass homelessness and mass incarceration in Skid Row, Los Angeles, in the 2000s, to the struggles in Ferguson, New York, Chicago, and Baltimore in 2014 and 2015, this book has sought to show that the struggle for freedom and dignity is not out of reach; rather, it is unfinished business. The revanchist efforts to roll back the victories of the long civil rights era have once again put antiracist struggles at the center of popular democratic movements.[20] Analyzing the freedom dreams of antiracist social movements of the past is essential for democratic struggles to confront policing and prisons in the present, sparking possibilities of abolitionist futures. Antiracist activists, artists, journalists, filmmakers, musicians, and scholars in organizations across the country have directed our attention to the work that remains in order to achieve abolition democracy. They argue for a vision of safety and security that entails a shift of resources away from mass incarceration and the securitization of cities, and toward the construction of a social wage. They have shown that the possibility for a counterhegemonic alliance is represented in the cultural and political battles being waged to resist common-sense notions of race, class, gender, and sexuality that legitimate mass criminalization.[21]

A struggle over the definition of the crisis of U.S. policing and prisons is therefore critical for developing an alternative common sense, an alternative vision of the future, and a new counterhegemonic project. Social movement organizations ranging from Hands Up United and Organization for Black Struggle in Ferguson, We Charge Genocide and the Black Youth Project 100 in Chicago, the Red Nation in Albuquerque, Dignity and Power Now! and the Los Angeles Community Action Network in Los Angeles, Critical Resistance in Oakland, Communities United for Police Reform and the Immigrant Defense Project in New York, and the #BlackLivesMatter movement are engaged in resistance to criminalization and other political expressions of neoliberal racial capitalism.[22] These movements are seeking to end police violence, overturn mass incarceration, and abolish broken windows and zero-tolerance policing. As #BlackLivesMatter cofounder Patrisse Cullors argues, they are reclaiming the "idea of public safety . . . calling on us to talk about public safety as access to jobs, access to healthy food, and access to shelter, in other words, having a framework that is about the community's response to social ills instead of a police response to social ills."[23]

Like the insurrections that exploded in Watts in 1965, in Detroit in 1967, in Attica in 1971, and in Los Angeles in 1992, the conditions that led people to protest in places such as Ferguson, New York, Chicago, and Baltimore in 2014 and 2015 have been about more than just specific incidents of police violence. The cycle of rebellion is the result of the cumulative and accumulating consequences of the racism, militarism, imperialism, and poverty that people have been experiencing for decades.[24] Social movements are tapping collective memories of the past to legitimate grassroots social change in the present. They are reclaiming materialist analyses of racism deemed outside the bounds of tolerable discourse since the Cold War counterinsurgency against the Black freedom, radical labor, and socialist alliance. In doing so, these social movements directly challenge the legitimacy of the neoliberal state. The struggle for a social wage for the poor, people of color, prisoners, immigrants, and the polycultural working class is not simply about enabling integration into the U.S. nation state. Rather, the history of freedom struggles traced here suggests that the demand for an expanded social wage provides a basis for building new alliances against racism, militarism, and poverty.[25]

This struggle will no doubt continue to be met with a combination of coercion and concessions. That is why, as Tony Jefferson recently suggested, *Policing the Crisis*'s approach to conjunctural analysis can be used as a method to distinguish the strategic options in confronting the neoliberal state, which "has revolved the old crisis, but coercively and without proper consent." This method enables analyses that go beyond the idea that the present moment is simply old wine in new bottles, or the product of a kind of "permanent, unchanging shape of reactionary ideas." As Hall suggested, "one has to fasten one's mind . . . 'violently' onto things as they are" to develop the "struggle to command the common sense . . . in order to educate and transform it."[26] The work to transform the common sense requires engaging directly with struggles in U.S. cities against policing and prisons. These struggles have a revolutionary democratic thrust that represents the cutting edge of social movements.[27]

The outcome of contemporary social struggles will be the product of political and ideological conflicts whose resolutions are not determined in advance. The victory of the project of abolition democracy will require winning people over to the antiracist idea of a social wage, and firing the political imagination about the possibility of overcoming neoliberalism. It will also depend on the strength of the alliance between labor and social movements to confront neoliberal austerity measures, polarizations of wealth, mass incarceration, and the securitization of cities. The fight for a social wage democratizes social movements in general. As Hall famously put it, "There are no guarantees that socialist ideas will and must prevail over other ideas." It requires an ongoing freedom project of political organization and popular education to transform the popular consciousness in order to produce a condition where the masses of ordinary people's "imaginations have been fired by the possibility of an alternative way of making life with other people." A vision of a different way of living does not just emerge; it "has to be made, constructed and struggled over." In that sense, I believe Hall teaches us about how we might speak to the current movement to end mass incarceration and "challenge the neoliberal victory" in a language of socialist democracy. "This is a moment for challenging," Hall wrote, "not adapting to, neoliberalism's new reality." While there are no guarantees that these struggles will be victorious, the conjuncture is ripe to make, as he says, "a leap." At this decisive moment, "nothing less will do."[28]

Notes

INTRODUCTION

1. James Baldwin, *No Name in the Street* (New York: Random House, 1972), 196; Vincent Harding, *The Other American Revolution* (Los Angeles: Center for Afro-American Studies, University of California, Los Angeles, and the Institute for the Black World, 1980), 177–200; Jack O'Dell, *Climbin' Jacob's Ladder: The Black Freedom Movement Writings of Jack O'Dell*, ed. Nikhil Pal Singh (Berkeley: University of California Press, 2010), 150–53. I am using the concept of cycle of struggle in keeping with the approach to history from below in Peter Linebaugh and Marcus Rediker, *The Many-Headed Hydra: Sailors, Slaves, Commoners, and the Hidden History of the Revolutionary Atlantic* (Boston: Beacon Press, 2001), 239.

2. On the dialectics of insurgency and counterinsurgency in the period, see Robin D. G. Kelley, "'Slangin' Rocks . . . Palestinian Style,' Dispatches from the Occupied Zones of North America," in *Police Brutality*, ed. Jill Nelson (New York: W. W. Norton and Company, 2000), 40–47. On the transformation of global capitalism in response to the crisis of U.S. hegemony during the 1960s and 1970s, see Giovanni Arrighi, *Adam Smith in Beijing: Lineages of the Twenty-First Century* (New York: Verso, 2007), 155, 161. On the relationship between Black freedom struggles and the crisis of U.S. hegemony, see Rod Bush, *We Are Not What We Seem: Black Nationalism and Class Struggle in the American Century* (New York: New York University Press, 2000), 193–213. My analysis of the connections between discourses of criminality and the organic crisis of Jim Crow capitalism follows the lead of the following works: Stuart Hall, "Great Moving Right Show," *Marxism Today* (1979): 14–20; John Solomos, Bob Findlay, Simon Jones, and Paul Gilroy, "The Organic Crisis of British Capitalism and Race: The Experience of the Seventies," in *The Empire Strikes Back: Race and Racism in 70s Britain* (1982; reprint, London: Routledge,

1994), 9–46; Paul Gilroy, "*There Ain't No Black in the Union Jack*": *The Cultural Politics of Race and Nation* (Chicago: University of Chicago Press, 1991). For an analysis that draws on Hall's Gramscian framework to theorize the "organic crisis of South Africa's racial capitalism," see John S. Saul and Stephen Gelb, *The Crisis in South Africa: Class Defense, Class Revolution* (New York: Monthly Review Press, 1981), 3–6, 9–44. The idea of "Jim Crow capitalism" is from Robin D. G. Kelley; see Jordan T. Camp, "Black Radicalism, Marxism, and Collective Memory: An Interview with Robin D. G. Kelley," *American Quarterly* 65, no. 1 (2013): 230. On the rise of "racial capitalism," see Cedric J. Robinson, *Black Marxism: The Making of the Black Radical Tradition* (1983; reprint, Chapel Hill: University of North Carolina Press, 2000). The quotes from James Baldwin come from *No Name in the Street*, 161, 196.

3. Antonio Gramsci, *Selections from the Prison Notebooks* (New York: International Publishers, 1971), 276. On the morbid symptoms in U.S. political culture in this period, see Robert Justin Goldstein, *Political Repression in Modern America: From 1870 to the Present* (New York: Schenkman Publishing, 1978), 429; Scott Christianson, *With Liberty for Some: 500 Years of Imprisonment in America* (Boston: Northeastern University Press, 1998), 253. On the "long civil rights movement," see Jacquelyn Dowd Hall, "The Long Civil Rights Movement and the Political Uses of the Past," *Journal of American History* 91, no. 4 (March 2005): 1233–1263; Nikhil Pal Singh, *Black Is a Country: Race and the Unfinished Struggle for Democracy* (Cambridge, MA: Harvard University Press, 2004), 6–9, 50, 69.

4. James Baldwin, *No Name in the Street,* 159–160. For a seminal conceptualization of the postwar freedom struggle as the Second Reconstruction, see Manning Marable, *Race, Reform, and Rebellion: The Second Reconstruction and Beyond in Black America, 1945–2006* (1984; reprint, Jackson: University of Mississippi Press, 2007).

5. For the argument about the "politics of signification," see Stuart Hall, "Encoding/Decoding," in *Culture, Media, Language,* ed. Stuart Hall, Dorothy Hobson, Andrew Lowe, and Paul Willis (1980; reprint, New York: Routledge, 1996), 138. On the class struggle in popular culture, see Stuart Hall, "Notes on Deconstructing 'The Popular,'" in *People's History and Socialist Theory,* ed. Raphael Samuel (London: Routledge and Kegan Paul Ltd., 1981), 227–40. For original analyses of the struggle in expressive culture over the definitions of material conditions, see Dick Hebdige, *Subculture: The Meaning of Style* (1979; reprint, New York: Routledge, 1989); Hazel V. Carby, *Cultures in Babylon: Black Britain and African America* (New York: Verso, 1999); Daniel Widener, *Black Arts West: Culture and Struggle in Postwar Los Angeles* (Durham, NC: Duke University Press, 2010). On the shifting dynamics of racial formation in the era, see for example Michael Omi and Howard Winant, *Racial Formation in the United States: From the 1960s to the 1990s* (New York: Routledge, 1994); Daniel Martinez HoSang, Oneka LaBennet, and Laura Pulido, eds., *Racial Formation in the Twenty-First Century* (Berkeley: University of California Press, 2012). For an inspired analysis of Baldwin's poetic political critiques, see David Roediger, *Towards the Abolition of Whiteness* (1994; reprint, New York: Verso, 2000), 3, 13. On the criminalization of the freedom movement's

resistance to the Jim Crow racial order in the name of law and order, see Naomi Murakawa, "The Origins of the Carceral Crisis: Racial Order as 'Law and Order' in Postwar American Politics," in *Race and American Political Development*, ed. Joseph Lowndes, Julie Novkov, and Dorian T. Warren (New York: Routledge, 2008), 234–55.

6. Robert Brenner, "The Political Economy of Rank-and-File Rebellion," in *Rebel Rank and File: Labor Militancy and Revolt from Below During the Long 1970s*, ed. Aaron Brenner, Robert Brenner, and Cal Winslow (New York: Verso, 2010), 38; Robin D. G. Kelley, *Into the Fire: African Americans Since 1970* (New York: Oxford University Press, 1996), 42.

7. Mazher Ali et al., *State of the Dream 2011: Austerity for Whom?* (Boston: United for a Fair Economy, 2011), 7; Michael Denning, "Wageless Life," *New Left Review* 66 (November–December 2010): 81; Gillian Hart, *Rethinking the South African Crisis: Nationalism, Populism, and Hegemony* (Athens: University of Georgia Press, 2014), 156, 229; Mike Davis, *A Planet of Slums* (New York: Verso, 2006); Mike Davis, "Hell Factories in the Field: A Prison Industrial Complex," *The Nation,* February 20, 1995, 229–34; Angela Y. Davis, "Race and Criminalization: Black Americans and the Punishment Industry," in *The Angela Y. Davis Reader,* ed. Joy James (Malden, MA: Blackwell, 1998), 66; Avery F. Gordon, "Globalism and the Prison Industrial Complex: An Interview with Angela Davis," *Race and Class* 40, nos. 2–3 (1999): 145–57; Ruth Wilson Gilmore, "Globalisation and U.S. Prison Growth: From Military Keynesianism to Post-Keynesianism Militarism," *Race and Class* 40, nos. 2–3 (October 1998–March 1999): 174; Christian Parenti, *Lockdown America: Police and Prisons in the Age of Crisis* (New York: Verso, 2000).

8. Marc Mauer, *Race to Incarcerate* (New York: New Press, 2006); Marie Gottschalk, *The Prison and the Gallows: The Politics of Mass Incarceration in America* (New York: Cambridge University Press, 2006), 170; Lauren E. Glaze and Danielle Kaeble, "Correctional Populations in the United States, 2013," Bureau of Justice Statistics, December 19, 2014, www.bjs.gov; Patrick A. Langan, "Race of Prisoners Admitted to State and Federal Institutions, 1926–86," *Bureau of Justice Statistics* (Washington, DC: U.S. Department of Justice, May 1991); John M. Sloop, *The Cultural Prison: Discourse, Prisoners, and Punishment* (Tuscaloosa: University of Alabama Press, 1996), 205; Pew Center on the States, *One in 31: The Long Reach of American Corrections* (Washington, DC: Pew Charitable Trusts, March 2009); Roy Walmsley, *World Prison Population List* (London: Kings College International Centre for Prison Studies, 2007), http://www.prisonstudies.org/research-publications?shs_term_node_tid _depth=27.

9. This methodological approach is informed by Alexander Saxton's *The Rise and Fall of the White Republic: Class Politics and Mass Culture in Nineteenth Century America* (1990; reprint, New York: Verso, 2003), 13–17.

10. Neil Smith, *The New Urban Frontier: Gentrification and the Revanchist City* (New York: Routledge, 1996), 8; Gerald Horne, *Fire This Time: The Watts Uprising and the 1960s* (New York: Da Capo Press, 1997), 41; Stuart Hall et al., *Policing the Crisis: Mugging, the State, and Law and Order* (London: MacMillan, 1978), 65, 217; Ruth Wilson Gilmore and Craig Gilmore, "Restating

the Obvious," in *Indefensible Space: The Architecture of the National Security State*, ed. Michael Sorkin (New York: Routledge, 2007), 144–45.

11. My analytic debt to Cedric J. Robinson for this conceptualization of racial regimes would be difficult to overstate. See Cedric J. Robinson, *Forgeries of Memory and Meaning: Blacks and the Regimes of Race in American Theatre and Film Before World War II* (Chapel Hill: University of North Carolina Press, 2007), xii. On the role of racism in naturalizing political and economic antagonisms, see Wahneema Lubiano, introduction to *The House that Race Built*, ed. Wahneema Lubiano (New York: Vintage Books, 1998), vii. On the ways in which anxieties produced by capitalist restructuring have been redirected, see Cindi Katz, "Childhood as Spectacle: Relays of Anxiety and the Reconfiguration of the Child," *Cultural Geographies* 15 (2008): 15–17.

12. This framework owes a great deal to the following texts in particular: Stuart Hall et al., *Policing the Crisis*; Stuart Hall, *The Hard Road to Renewal: Thatcherism and the Crisis of the Left* (New York: Verso, 1988); Mike Davis, *City of Quartz: Excavating the Future in Los Angeles* (1990; reprint, New York: Verso, 2006); Peter Linebaugh, *The London Hanged: Crime and Civil Society in the Eighteenth Century* (2003; reprint, London: Verso, 2006); Robin D. G. Kelley, *Race Rebels: Culture, Politics, and the Black Working Class* (New York: New Press, 1994), 183–209; Ruth Wilson Gilmore, *Golden Gulag: Prisons, Surplus, Crisis, and Opposition in Globalizing California* (Berkeley: University of California Press, 2007); Angela Y. Davis, *Abolition Democracy: Beyond Empire, Prisons, and Torture* (New York: Seven Stories Press, 2005); Paul Gilroy, "Police and Thieves," in *The Empire Strikes Back*. I have sharpened my analysis of neoliberal racial and security regimes in dialogue with: David Harvey, *A Brief History of Neoliberalism* (New York: Oxford University Press, 2005); Michel Foucault, *Security, Territory, Population: Lectures at the Collège de France, 1977–78*, ed. Michel Senellart, trans. Graham Burchell (New York: Palgrave MacMillan, 2007), 10–23, 30–43; David Theo Goldberg, *The Threat of Race: Reflections on Racial Neoliberalism* (Malden, MA: Blackwell, 2009), 99; Neil Smith and Deborah Cowen, "Martial Law in the Streets of Toronto: G20 Security and State Violence," *Human Geography* 3, no. 3 (2010): 37–39; Robin D. G. Kelley's introduction to Angela Y. Davis, *The Meaning of Freedom* (San Francisco: City Lights Press, 2012), 11.

13. Stuart Hall, "The Problem of Ideology: Marxism Without Guarantees," *Journal of Communications Inquiry* 10, no. 28 (1986): 29; Stuart Hall, "Variants of Liberalism," in *Politics and Ideology*, ed. James Donald and Stuart Hall (Philadelphia: Open University Press, 1986), 42. On the role of racial criminalization in managing surplus labor in cities during the rise of industrialization in early-twentieth-century U.S. urban history, see Khalil Gibran Muhammad, *The Condemnation of Blackness: Race, Crime, and the Making of Modern Urban America* (Cambridge, MA: Harvard University Press, 2010). For the insight that insurgent movements themselves have been represented as the source of disorder, see Ruth Wilson Gilmore, "Globalisation and U.S. Prison Growth," 175–76. On the long Black freedom struggle for a redistribution of wealth, see Clyde A. Woods, *Development Arrested: The Blues and Plantation Power in the Mississippi Delta* (New York: Verso, 1998), 192–200. On the

ways in the "racialization of the enemy" has been central to the use of confinement and mass incarceration in counterinsurgencies, see Laleh Khalili, *Time in
the Shadows: Confinement in Counterinsurgencies* (Stanford, CA: Stanford
University Press, 2013), 4–5, 7, 173, 211.

14. On the origins and development of strategies of racial management in
the legitimation of capitalist class power, see David Roediger and Elizabeth
Esch, *The Production of Difference: Race and the Management of Labor in U.S.
History* (New York: Oxford University Press, 2012). For the argument regarding the centrality of struggles for the social wage in the civil rights era and
its withdrawal during the making of the neoliberal state, see Vijay Prashad,
"Second-Hand Dreams," *Social Analysis* 49, no. 2 (2005): 191–98. On struggles for redistributive justice in terms of a social wage, see Gillian Hart, *Rework-
ing Apartheid Legacies: Global Competition, Gender and Social Wages in
South Africa, 1980–2000* (Geneva: United Nations Research Institute for Social
Development, 2002).

15. On the history of race, counterinsurgency, and the formation of U.S.
"domestic" and "foreign" policy, see Moon-Ho Jung, "Seditous Subjects: Race,
State Violence, and the U.S. Empire," *Journal of Asian American Studies* 14, no.
2 (June 2011): 224. See also Jodi Melamed, *Represent and Destroy: Rationalizing Violence in the New Racial Capitalism* (Minneapolis: University of Minnesota Press, 2011), 42.

16. Michelle Alexander, *The New Jim Crow: Mass Incarceration in the Age
of Colorblindness* (New York: The New Press, 2010); Loïc Wacquant, "Deadly
Symbiosis: When Ghetto and Prison Meet and Mesh," *Punishment and Society*
3, no. 1 (2001): 95–134. On the roots of the long civil rights movement in the
radical 1930s and the persistence of resistance to it in the domestic Cold War,
see Nikhil Pal Singh, *Black Is a Country*, 3, 6, 8–9, 13, 214, and Jacquelyn
Dowd Hall, "The Long Civil Rights Movement and the Political Uses of the
Past," 1235–1239, 1248–1250. My argument about the counterinsurgency
against the freedom movement follows the lead of the following works: Manning Marable, *Race, Reform, and Rebellion*, 13–39, 149–163; Clyde Woods,
"'Sittin' on Top of the World': The Challenges of Blues and Hip Hop Geography," in *Black Geographies and the Politics of Place*, ed. Katherine McKittrick
and Clyde Woods (Cambridge, MA: South End Press, 2007), 47–48; Jodi Melamed, *Represent and Destroy*, 32. On the authoritarianism at the heart of neoliberalism, see David Harvey, *Spaces of Global Capitalism: Towards a Theory
of Uneven Geographical Development* (New York: Verso, 2006), 27.

17. Laleh Khalili, *Time in the Shadows*, 66. For an account of Reagan's
policy of rollback as political payback, first in California and then at the
national and global scale, see Gerald Horne, *Fire This Time*, 282; Mahmood
Mamdani, *Good Muslim, Bad Muslim: America, the Cold War, and the Roots
of Terror* (New York: Doubleday, 2004), 95, 124. This Cold War context
has been well situated in Nikhil Pal Singh, "Cold War Redux: On the 'New
Totalitarianism,'" *Radical History Review* 85 (Winter 2003): 171–81, and
Nikhil Pal Singh, "'Learn Your Horn,'" in *Climbin' Jacob's Ladder*, 57. Perhaps
the most original and generative analysis of revanchism at the urban scale
remains Neil Smith, "Giuliani Time: The Revanchist 1990s," *Social Text* 57

(Winter 1998): 14. The impacts of this revanchist policy and common sense at the national scale are presented clearly and powerfully in H. Bruce Franklin, "The American Prison in the Culture Wars" (Washington, DC: Modern Language Association Convention, 2000), http://andromeda.rutgers.edu/~hbf/priscult.html.

18. Loïc Wacquant, "From Slavery to Mass Incarceration: Rethinking the Race Question in the U.S.," *New Left Review* 13 (January–February 2002): 41–60.

19. Loïc Wacquant, *Punishing the Poor: The Neoliberal Government of Social Insecurity* (Durham, NC: Duke University Press, 2009), xix, 310.

20. Ibid., xviii, xix, xx, 41.

21. On the limits of the backlash thesis, see Naomi Murakawa, *The First Civil Right: How Liberals Built Prison America* (New York: Oxford University Press, 2014), 7–8; Nikhil Pal Singh, *Black Is a Country*, 5–9; Daniel Martinez HoSang, *Racial Propositions: Ballot Initiatives and the Making of Postwar California* (Berkeley: University of California Press, 2010), 16–19.

22. Marie Gottschalk, *Caught: The Prison State and the Lockdown of American Politics* (Princeton, NJ: Princeton University Press, 2015), 13–14; Naomi Murakawa, *The First Civil Right*, 3–4, 29, 49. On the "long fetch of history," see George Lipsitz, *Footsteps in the Dark: The Hidden Histories of Popular Music* (Minneapolis: University of Minnesota Press, 2007), vii–viii. For a vital demonstration of the stakes in intellectual and political debates about the periodization of the freedom movement, see Jacquelyn Dowd Hall, "The Long Civil Rights Movement and the Political Uses of the Past," 1254–1261. On the historical, geographical, and sociological significance of the events of 1968, see Giovanni Arrighi, Terence K. Hopkins, and Immanuel Wallerstein, *Antisystemic Movements* (London and New York: Verso, 1989); Michael Denning, *Culture in the Age of Three Worlds* (New York: Verso, 2005), 41–44; Ruth Wilson Gilmore, *Golden Gulag*, 25–26; Nikhil Pal Singh, "The Black Panthers and the 'Undeveloped Country of the Left,'" in *The Black Panther Party Reconsidered*, ed. Charles E. Jones (Baltimore: Black Classic Press, 1998), 57–105.

23. Robin D. G. Kelley, "Thug Nation: On State Violence and Disposability," in *Policing the Planet: Why the Policing Crisis Led to Black Lives Matter*, ed. Jordan T. Camp and Christina Heatherton (New York: Verso, 2016); Pamela Oliver, "Repression and Crime Control: Why Social Movement Scholars Should Pay Attention to Mass Incarceration as a Form of Repression," *Mobilization: The International Quarterly* 13, no. 1 (2008): 9; Frances Fox Piven and Richard A. Cloward, *Poor People's Movements: Why They Succeed, How They Fail* (New York: Vintage Books, 1979); George Lipsitz, *A Life in the Struggle: Ivory Perry and the Culture of Opposition* (Philadelphia: Temple University Press, 1995); Robin D. G. Kelley, *Race Rebels*; Elizabeth Hinton, "'A War Within Our Own Boundaries': Lyndon Johnson's Great Society and the Rise of the Carceral State," *Journal of American History* 102, no. 1 (June 2015): 102–3.

24. Michelle Alexander, *The New Jim Crow*, 185–86, 195, 15; Marie Murakawa, *The First Civil Right*, 2, 211 note 5; Adolph Reed Jr., "Marx, Race, and Neoliberalism," *New Labor Forum* 22, no. 1 (2013): 53.

25. George Lipsitz, *American Studies in a Moment of Danger* (Minneapolis: University of Minnesota Press, 2001), 24; Lisa Duggan, *The Twilight of*

Equality? Neoliberalism, Cultural Politics, and the Attack on Democracy (Boston: Beacon, 2003); Nikhil Pal Singh, "'Learn Your Horn,'" 9; Marie Gottschalk, *Caught*, 5, 261–62. For a suggestive analysis of prisons as "instances of imperial spaces and projects," see Moon-Kie Jung and Yaejoon Kwon, "Theorizing the U.S. Racial State: Sociology Since Racial Formation," *Sociology Compass* 7, no. 11 (2013): 936.

26. See for example David Harvey, *The Condition of Postmodernity: An Inquiry Into the Origins of Cultural Change* (Malden, MA: Blackwell, 1990); Amin Ash, ed., *Post-Fordism: A Reader* (Malden, MA: Blackwell, 1994); Michael Hardt and Antonio Negri, *Empire* (Cambridge, MA: Harvard University Press, 2000); Leslie Sklair, *Globalization: Capitalism and Its Alternatives* (New York: Oxford University Press, 2002); William I. Robinson, *A Theory of Global Capitalism: Production, Class, and State in a Transnational World* (Baltimore: Johns Hopkins University Press, 2004); Giovanni Arrighi, *The Long Twentieth Century: Money, Power, and the Origins of Our Times* (New York: Verso, 2010). For one of the most compelling accounts of the political crisis of the state in the period, see Nicos Poulantzas, *The Poulantzas Reader: Marxism, Law, and the State* (New York: Verso, 2008), 294–95.

27. The idea of a "stamp of legitimacy" is from Stuart Hall, "Encoding/Decoding," 127. For the fullest elaboration of the concept of revanchism, see Neil Smith, *The New Urban Frontier*, 222; Don Mitchell, *The Right to the City: Social Justice and the Fight for Public Space* (New York: Guilford, 2003), 15–16, 164. On the vendetta against the Paris Commune, see Karl Marx, *The Civil War in France: The Paris Commune* (New York: International Publishers, 1988), 54. On the centrality of struggles in language over common sense in the current conjuncture, see Gillian Hart, "Gramsci, Geography, and the Languages of Populism," in *Gramsci: Space, Nature, Politics*, ed. Michael Ekers, Gillian Hart, Stefan Kipler, and Alex Loftus (Malden, MA: Wiley-Blackwell: 2013), 301. On the stakes in the construction of a "theoretical apparatus" in order to "eschew the demagogy of the 'palpitating fact', of 'common sense,' and the 'illusions of the evident,'" see Nicos Poulantzas, "The Capitalist State: A Reply to Miliband and Laclau," in *The Poulantzas Reader*, 272–73.

28. Neil Smith, *The New Urban Frontier*, 220, 222; Neil Smith, "Giuliani Time," 10; Neil Smith, "Revanchist Planet," *The Urban Reinventors* 3, no. 9 (2009): 13–14.

29. Neil Smith, *The New Urban Frontier*, 75–89; George Lipsitz, "In an Avalanche Every Snowflake Pleads Not Guilty: The Collateral Consequences of Mass Incarceration and Impediments to Women's Fair Housing Rights," *UCLA Law Review* 59, no. 6 (2012): 1753; Stuart Hall et al., *Policing the Crisis*, 221; Robin D. G. Kelley, "Playing for Keeps: Pleasure and Profit on the Postindustrial Playground," in *The House That Race Built*, 198–99; Daniel Widener, *Black Arts West*, 250–82; Paul Gilroy and Joe Simm, "Law, Order and the State of the Left," *Capital and Class* 25 (1985): 15–55; Stuart Hall, *The Hard Road to Renewal*, 188; Robin D. G. Kelley, *Yo' Mama's Disfunktional! Fighting the Culture Wars in Urban America* (Boston: Beacon Press, 1997), 8–11; Martha K. Huggins, *Political Policing: The United States and Latin America* (Durham, NC: Duke University Press, 1998).

30. Barbara Ransby, "The Black Poor and the Politics of Expendability," in *A New Introduction to Poverty: The Role of Race, Power, and Politics*, ed. Louis Kushnick and James Jennings (New York: New York University Press, 1999), 321–30; Frank Donner, *Protectors of Privilege: Red Squads and Policing in Urban America* (Berkeley: University of California Press, 1990).

31. Ruth Wilson Gilmore, *Golden Gulag*, 28, 113, 243, 247.

32. Stuart Hall, *The Hard Road to Renewal*, 123–60; Jimmie L. Reeves and Richard Campbell, *Cracked Coverage: Television News, the Anti-Cocaine Crusade, and the Reagan Legacy* (Durham, NC: Duke University Press, 1994), 73; James Donald and Stuart Hall, eds., *Politics and Ideology*; Mike Davis, *Prisoners of the American Dream* (New York: Verso, 1986); Lisa McGirr, *Suburban Warriors: The Origins of the New American Right* (Princeton, NJ: Princeton University Press, 2001); Ian F. Haney López, "Post-Racial Racism: Racial Stratification and Mass Incarceration in the Age of Obama," *California Law Review* 98, no. 3 (June 2010): 1023, 1031.

33. Stuart Hall, *The Hard Road to Renewal*, 134; David Harvey, *A Brief History of Neoliberalism*, 64, 77; George Lipsitz, *The Possessive Investment in Whiteness: How White People Profit from Identity Politics* (Philadelphia: Temple University Press, 2006), 99.

34. On the "countersubversive tradition" and its strategy of demonizing groups it deems enemies, see Michael Rogin, *Ronald Reagan, the Movie, and Other Episodes of Political Demonology* (Berkeley: University of California Press, 1987), xiii–xix, 3, 8, 10, 44, 64–80. For an analysis of the institutionalization of countersubversion in the postwar period, see George Lipsitz, *Rainbow at Midnight: Labor and Culture in the 1940s* (1981; reprint, Urbana and Chicago: University of Illinois Press, 1994), 188–90. On the expansion of policing in counterinsurgencies, see Martha K. Huggins, *Political Policing: The United States and Latin America* (Durham, NC: Duke University Press, 1998), 2–3.

35. Cedric J. Robinson, *Black Marxism*; Gerald Home, *Black and Red: W. E. B. Du Bois and the Afro-American Response to the Cold War, 1944–1963* (Albany: State University of New York, 1986); Robin D. G. Kelley, *Hammer and Hoe: Alabama Communists During the Great Depression* (Chapel Hill: University of North Carolina Press, 1990); Robin D. G. Kelley, *Freedom Dreams: The Black Radical Imagination* (Boston: Beacon Press, 2002); David R. Roediger, "Accounting for the Wages of Whiteness: U.S. Marxism and the Critical History of Race," in *Wages of Whiteness and Racist Symbolic Capital*, ed. Wulf D. Hund, Jeremy Krikler, and David Roediger (Berlin: Lit Verlag, 2010), 9–36; Tricia Rose, *Black Noise: Rap Music and Black Culture in Contemporary America* (Hanover, NH: Wesleyan University Press, 1994), 102; Robin D. G. Kelley, *Race Rebels*, 183–209; George Lipsitz, *Footsteps in the Dark*, 158, 159, 164; Stuart Hall, *The Hard Road to Renewal*, 130; Paul Gilroy, *"There Ain't No Black in the Union Jack,"* 225.

36. Michael Denning, *Culture in the Age of Three Worlds*, 37. On the role of ideology and culture in radical social movements, see Robin D. G. Kelley, "Comrades, Praise Gawd for Lenin and Them!": Ideology and Culture Among Black Communists in Alabama, 1930–1935," *Science and Society* 52, no. 1

(Spring 1988): 61. For an exemplary analysis of the period, see Mike Davis, *Prisoners of the American Dream*. This emphasis on historical and geographical specificity has been informed by debates about race and class forged in the struggle to dismantle the apartheid state. See Stuart Hall, "Race, Articulation and Societies Structured in Dominance," in *Sociological Theories: Race and Colonialism* (Paris: UNESCO, 1980), 305–45; Harold Wolpe, *Race, Class, and the Apartheid State* (Trenton, NJ: Africa World Press, 1990), 2–3, 50, 58, 76; Gillian Hart, *Rethinking the South African Crisis*, 7, 12, 141, 159.

37. For the argument about challenges to "metaleptic definitions" in expressive culture, see Kristin Ross, *The Emergence of Social Space: Rimbaud and the Paris Commune* (1988; reprint, New York: Verso, 2008), 10–11. On the class struggle in expressive culture, see for example Daniel Widener, *Black Arts West*, 6–8; Jordan T. Camp, "An Interview with Robin D. G. Kelley," 224–25. Joy James makes an important case for foregrounding "insurgent knowledge" in analyzing the political purposes of prisons in the United States; see Joy James, ed., *Warfare in the American Homeland: Policing and Prison in a Penal Democracy* (Durham, NC: Duke University Press, 2007), xii.

38. Susan George, "How to Win the War of Ideas," *Dissent* (Summer 1997): 48; Nikhil Pal Singh, "'Learn Your Horn,'" 57; Marie Gottschalk, *The Prison and the Gallows: The Politics of Mass Incarceration in America* (New York: Cambridge University Press, 2006), 195; Stuart Hall, *The Hard Road to Renewal*, 130.

39. George P. Rawick, *Listening to Revolt: The Selected Writings of George P. Rawick*, ed. David Roediger (Chicago: Charles H. Kerr Publishing, 2010), 25; James Baldwin, *The Fire Next Time* (New York: Dial Press, 1963).

40. Robin D. G. Kelley, Kelley, "'Slangin' Rocks . . . Palestinian Style,'" 39; Nikhil Pal Singh, *Black Is a Country*, 192–93; Ruth Wilson Gilmore, "Globalisation and U.S. Prison Growth," 175.

41. Manning Marable, *Race, Reform and Rebellion*, 102–3; Ambalavaner Sivanandan, *Communities of Resistance: Writings on Black Struggles for Socialism* (New York: Verso, 1990); Robert H. Mast, ed., *Detroit Lives* (Philadelphia: Temple University Press, 1994), xiii.

42. Marie Gottschalk, *The Prison and the Gallows*, 179.

43. John Clarke, "Still Policing the Crisis?" *Crime, Media, Culture* 41, no. 1 (2008): 125–26; Angela Davis and Bettina Aptheker, eds., *If They Come in the Morning: Voices of Resistance* (New York: Third Press, 1971); Ambalavaner Sivanandan, *Communities of Resistance*.

44. Stuart Hall et al., *Policing the Crisis*, 223; James O'Connor, *The Fiscal Crisis of the State* (New York: St. Martin's Press, 1973), 163; Mike Davis, *Prisoners of the American Dream*, 209–10.

45. David McNally, *Global Slump: The Economics and Politics of Crisis and Resistance* (Oakland, CA: PM Press, 2010), 31; Jamie Peck, "Liberating the City: Between New York and New Orleans," *Urban Geography* 27, no. 8 (2006): 681–713; Robin D G. Kelley, *Into the Fire*, 42; Mazher Ali et al., *State of the Dream 2011*, 7.

46. Stuart Hall and Doreen Massey, "Interpreting the Crisis," *Soundings: A Journal of Politics and Culture* 44 (Spring 2010): 57–71; Doreen Massey,

"The Political Struggle Ahead," *Soundings* 44 (Spring 2010): 15. On the theoretical practice of "incarcerated revolutionary intellectuals" in the elaboration of the philosophy of freedom, see Kelley's foreword to *The Meaning of Freedom,* 9.

47. Antonio Gramsci, *Selections from the Prison Notebooks,* 178.

48. Stuart Hall, "Gramsci and Us," *Marxism Today* (June 1987): 16–21; Stuart Hall et al., *Policing the Crisis,* 333, 306–23, 347, 394; Stuart Hall and Les Back, "In Conversation: At Home and Not at Home," *Cultural Studies* 23, no. 4 (July 2009): 681. The category "moral panic" was deployed by Stanley Cohen to explain how social phenomena defined as a threat to the social order are represented in stereotypical discourses by media and control agencies. Stanley Cohen, *Folk Devils and Moral Panics* (1972; reprint, New York: Routledge, 2002). While this conceptualization has been highly influential, my use of the term requires the further materialist specification developed by Hall and his colleagues that moral panics have been symptomatic of how political-economic crises have been "experienced" and "fought out." See Stuart Hall et al., *Policing the Crisis,* 221, and Karl Marx, "From Population, Crime and Pauperism," *New York Tribune* (1859), http://www.marxists.org/archive/marx /works/1859/09/16.htm. The Stuart Hall quote is from his conversation with Bill Schwartz, "Living with Difference," *Soundings* 37 (2007): 149.

49. "An interview with Stuart Hall (interviewed by Sut Jhally)," London, August 30, 2012, http://www.mediaed.org/stuarthall/.

50. Heather Ann Thompson, "Why Mass Incarceration Matters: Rethinking Crisis, Decline, and Transformation in Postwar American History," *Journal of American History* 97, no. 3 (2010): 705, 706, 716, 726, 727, 734.

51. Stuart Hall, *The Hard Road to Renewal,* 130.

52. Neil Smith, *The New Urban Frontier,* 75–89; George Lipsitz, "In an Avalanche Every Snowflake Pleads Not Guilty," 1753; Giovanni Arrighi, *Adam Smith in Beijing,* 8–9; George Lipsitz, *Rainbow at Midnight,* 343; Stuart Hall and Martin Jacques, eds. *The Politics of Thatcherism* (London: Lawrence and Wishart, 1983), 10–11; John Munro, "Imperial Anticommunism and the African American Freedom Movement in the Early Cold War," *History Workshop Journal* 79, no. 1 (2015): 52–75.

53. Antonio Gramsci, *Selections from the Prison Notebooks,* 323–343; Hazel V. Carby, *Cultures in Babylon,* 23; Edward Soja et al., "Urban Restructuring: An Analysis of Social and Spatial Change in Los Angeles," *Economic Geography* 59, no. 2 (April 1983): 195–230; Melvin L. Oliver et al., "Anatomy of a Rebellion: A Political-Economic Analysis," in *Reading Rodney King/Reading Urban Uprising,* ed. Robert Gooding-Williams (New York: Routledge, 1993), 122; Mazher Ali et al., *State of the Dream 2011,* 1–36.

54. Michael Rogin, *Ronald Reagan, the Movie, and Other Episodes of Political Demonology,* 77; Jimmie L. Reeves and Richard Campbell, *Cracked Coverage,* 85–90; Gillian Hart, *Disabling Globalization: Places of Power in Post-Apartheid South Africa* (Berkeley: University of California Press, 2002), 29.

55. Hazel V. Carby, *Cultures in Babylon,* 96, 102; Kimberlé Crenshaw and Gary Peller, "Reel Time/Real Justice," in *Reading Rodney King/Reading Urban Uprising,* 57; Gillian Hart, *Disabling Globalization,* 37; Roderick Fergu-

son, *Aberrations in Black: Toward a Queer of Color Critique* (Minneapolis: University of Minnesota Press, 2004), 4; David Roediger and Elizabeth Esch, *The Production of Difference*, 8; Gillian Hart, "Gramsci, Geography, and the Languages of Populism," 312; Henri Lefebvre, *The Production of Space* (Malden, MA: Blackwell, 1991).

56. David Harvey, *Rebel Cities: From the Right to the City to the Urban Revolution* (New York: Verso, 2012), 15; Mike Davis, *City of Quartz*, 223–316; Neil Smith, *The New Urban Frontier*, 15.

57. Ranajit Guha, "The Prose of Counter-Insurgency," in *Selected Subaltern Studies*, ed. Ranajit Guha and Gayatri Chakravorty Spivak (New York: Oxford University Press, 1988), 45–86.

58. Ranajit Guha, *Elementary Aspects of Peasant Insurgency in Colonial India* (Durham, NC: Duke University Press, 1999), 333. On the methodological advances for the dialectical study of insurgency elaborated in the historiography of Black radical and subaltern struggles, see Brent Hayes Edwards, "The 'Autonomy' of Black Radicalism," *Social Text* 19, vol. 2 (Summer 2001): 1–13.

59. Don Mitchell, "State Intervention in Landscape Production: The Wheatland Riot and the California Commission of Immigration and Housing," *Antipode* 25, no. 2 (1993): 91–113; Ruth Wilson Gilmore, *Golden Gulag*, 13–21; Walter Rodney, *How Europe Underdeveloped Africa* (1972; reprint, Washington, DC: Howard University, 1982); Manning Marable, *How Capitalism Underdeveloped Black America* (1983; reprint, Cambridge, MA: South End Press, 2000); Neil Smith, *Uneven Development: Nature, Capital, and the Production of Space* (Athens: University of Georgia Press, 2008); David R. Roediger, *How Race Survived U.S. History: From Settlement and Slavery to the Obama Phenomenon* (New York: Verso, 2008), x–xvi, 169–230.

60. The phrase "insurrection of poetic knowledge" represents my effort to wrestle with the original and generative work of the historians Michel Foucault and Robin D. G. Kelley and to produce a new synthesis. See Michel Foucault, *Society Must Be Defended: Lectures at the Collège de France, 1975–76*, trans. David Macey (New York: Picador, 2003), 8–9; Robin D. G. Kelley, *Freedom Dreams*, 9–10, 189; Robin D. G. Kelley, *Race Rebels*, 207. For the origin of the concept of "poetic knowledge," see Aimé Césaire, "Poetry and Knowledge," in *Refusal of the Shadow: Surrealism and the Caribbean*, ed. and trans. Michael Richardson and Krzysztof Fijalkowski (London: Verso, 1996), 134–46; Karl Marx, "Contribution to the Critique of Hegel's *Philosophy of Right*: Introduction," in *The Marx-Engels Reader*, 2nd ed., ed. Robert C. Tucker (New York: W. W. Norton & Company, 1978), 60. On the visions of social change promoted by the urban multiracial working class as distinct from the hegemonic social scientific discourse of a disfunktional and bad-behaving underclass, see Robin D. G. Kelley, *Yo' Mama's Disfunktional!*, 125–58.

61. Susan George, "How to Win the War of Ideas," *Dissent* (Summer 1997), 48; Nikhil Pal Singh, "'Learn Your Horn,'" 57; Marie Gottschalk, *The Prison and the Gallows*, 195; Gillian Hart, *Rethinking the South African Crisis*, 20.

62. The tripartite organization of my chapters has benefited from Eric Lott, *Love and Theft: Blackface Minstrelsy and the American Working Class* (New York: Oxford University Press, 1993), 8–9.

63. George Lipsitz, *A Life in the Struggle*, 18, 228; Stuart Hall, "Cultural Studies and Its Theoretical Legacies," in *Cultural Studies,* ed. Lawrence Grossberg, Cary Nelson, and Paul Treichler (New York: Routledge, 1992), 286.

CHAPTER 1: THE EXPLOSION IN WATTS

1. Vincent Harding, *The Other American Revolution* (Los Angeles and Atlanta: Center for Afro-American Studies, University of California, and Institute of the Black World, 1980), 183; Gerald Horne, *Fire This Time: The Watts Uprising and the 1960s* (New York: Da Capo Press, 1997), 45–97; Mike Davis, *City of Quartz: Excavating the Future in Los Angeles* (1990; reprint, New York: Verso, 2006), 297.

2. Martin Luther King Jr. quoted in David J. Garrow, *Bearing the Cross: Martin Luther King, Jr., and the Southern Christian Leadership Conference* (New York: HarperCollins, 1986), 440.

3. Martin Luther King Jr. quoted in Vincent Harding, introduction to Martin Luther King Jr., *Where Do We Go from Here: Chaos or Community?* (1968; reprint, Boston: Beacon, 2010), xi; Martin Luther King Jr., "A Time to Break the Silence," in *A Testament of Hope: The Essential Writings and Speeches of Martin Luther King* (New York: HarperCollins, 1986), 242; Cornel West, ed., *The Radical King* (Boston: Beacon Press, 2015), xiii.

4. On the historical context and material conditions that gave rise to the Watts revolt, see Gerald Horne, *Fire This Time*; Johnny Otis, *Listen to the Lambs* (Minneapolis: University of Minnesota Press, 2009); George Lipsitz, foreword to *Listen to the Lambs*, xii–xxxiv.

5. Gordon K. Mantler, *Power to the Poor: Black-Brown Coalition and the Fight for Economic Justice, 1960–1974* (Chapel Hill: University of North Carolina Press, 2013), 48; Martin Luther King Jr., *All Labor Has Dignity*, ed. Michael Honey (Boston: Beacon Press, 2012), 39, 41, 26.

6. Gordon K. Mantler, *Power to the Poor,* 22–23; Naomi Murakawa, *The First Civil Right: How Liberals Built Prison America* (New York: Oxford University Press, 2014), 23; Gerald Horne; *Fire This Time*, 5, 7, 10–11, 15–16.

7. Marie Gottschalk, *The Prison and the Gallows: The Politics of Mass Incarceration in America* (New York: Cambridge University Press, 2006), 170.

8. Scott Christianson, *With Liberty for Some: 500 Years of Imprisonment in America* (Boston: Northeastern University Press, 1998), 253; Min S. Yee, *The Melancholy History of Soledad Prison* (New York: Harper's Magazine Press, 1973), 5–6; Rebecca N. Hill, *Men, Mobs, and Law: Anti-Lynching and Labor Defense in U.S. Radical History* (Durham, NC: Duke University Press, 2009), 267; California Department of Corrections, "California Prisoners: Summary Statistics of Felon Prisoners and Parolees" (Sacramento: Human Relations Agency, 1969): 4–5, http://www.cdcr.ca.gov/reports_research/offender_information_services_branch/Annual/CalPris/CALPRISd1969.pdf. Nationally, the incarceration rates remained relatively stable for the half-century before 1973, then grew exponentially in the final decades of the twentieth century. See Naomi Murakawa, *The First Civil Right,* 5–7.

9. Gordon K. Mantler, *Power to the Poor*, 22–23; Manning Marable, *Race, Reform, and Rebellion: The Second Reconstruction and Beyond in Black America, 1945–2006* (Jackson: University of Mississippi Press, 2007), 25, 31; Penny M. Von Eschen, *Race Against Empire: Black Americans and Anticolonialism* (Ithaca, NY: Cornell University Press, 1997), 186–87; Barbara Ransby, *Ella Baker and the Black Freedom Movement: A Radical Democratic Vision* (Chapel Hill: University of North Carolina Press 2003), 3–6, 362–64, 371–72; Mary Helen Washington, *The Other Blacklist: The African American Literary and Cultural Left of the 1950s* (New York: Columbia University Press, 2014), 11. See Gerald Horne, *Fire This Time*, 3–22.

10. W.E.B. Du Bois, *Black Reconstruction in America: An Essay Toward a History of the Part Which Black Folk Played in the Attempt to Reconstruct Democracy in America, 1860–1880* (1935; reprint, New York: The Free Press, 1962), 383; David Levering Lewis, *W.E.B. Du Bois: The Fight for Equality and the American Century* (New York: Henry Holt and Company, 2000), 349–87.

11. George Lipsitz, "Abolition Democracy and Global Justice," *Comparative American Studies* 2, no. 3 (2004): 273; A. Sivanandan, *A Different Hunger: Writings on Black Resistance* (1982; reprint, London: Pluto Press, 1991), 124; Eric Foner, "Time for a Third Reconstruction," *Nation* 256, no. 4 (February 1, 1993): 117–20.

12. W.E.B. Du Bois, *Black Reconstruction in America*, 621–22, 590–91, 727, 358, 591; George Lipsitz, "Abolition Democracy and Global Justice," 271–86; Cedric Robinson, *Forgeries of Memory and Meaning: Blacks and the Regimes of Race in American Theatre and Film Before World War II* (Chapel Hill: University of North Carolina Press, 2007), xiii; Nikhil Pal Singh, *Black Is a Country: Race and the Unfinished Struggle for Democracy* (Cambridge, MA: Harvard University Press, 2004), 68.

13. W.E.B. Du Bois, *Black Reconstruction in America*, 580–635; David Roediger, *The Wages of Whiteness: Race and the Making of the American Working Class* (1991; reprint, New York: Verso, 2007); Cedric Robinson, *Forgeries of Memory and Meaning*, 201; George P. Rawick, *Listening to Revolt: The Selected Writings of George P. Rawick*, ed. David Roediger (Chicago: Charles H. Kerr Publishing, 2010).

14. W.E.B. Du Bois, *Black Reconstruction in America*, 381; George Lipsitz, *American Studies in a Moment of Danger* (Minneapolis: University of Minnesota Press, 2001), 23, 47–49, 65–68, 73. On the "age of the CIO" see Michael Denning, *The Cultural Front: The Laboring of American Culture in the Twentieth Century* (New York: Verso, 1996). On the ways in which African American and working-class struggles for democracy before the age of the CIO shaped the modern civil rights movement, see Paul Ortiz, *Emancipation Betrayed: The Hidden History of Black Organizing and White Violence in Florida from Reconstruction to the Bloody Election of 1920* (Berkeley: University of California Press, 2005), xv-xix.

15. Jacquelyn Dowd Hall, "The Long Civil Rights Movement and the Political Uses of the Past," *Journal of American History* 91, no. 4 (March 2005): 1243–46; David R. Roediger, *How Race Survived U.S. History: From Settlement and Slavery to the Obama Phenomenon* (New York: Verso, 2008), 176;

Levering Lewis, *W. E. B. Du Bois*, 524; Nikhil Pal Singh, *Black Is a Country*, 97; Nikhil Pal Singh, "'Learn Your Horn,'" in *Climbin' Jacob's Ladder: The Black Freedom Movement Writings of Jack O'Dell*, ed. Nikhil Pal Singh (Berkeley: University of California Press, 2010), 25; Jonathan Birnbaum and Clarence Taylor, "Introduction: The Modern Civil Rights Movement," in *Civil Rights Since 1787: A Reader on the Black Struggle* (New York: New York University Press, 2000), 328; Michael Honey, introduction to *All Labor Has Dignity*, xxii–xxiii; Naomi Murakawa, *The First Civil Right*, 3. On the age of the civil rights movement, see George Lipsitz, *American Studies in a Moment of Danger*, 24, 48–49; Jodi Melamed, *Represent and Destroy: Rationalizing Violence in the New Racial Capitalism* (Minneapolis: University of Minnesota Press, 2011), 72.

16. W. E. B. Du Bois, *Autobiography of W. E. B. Du Bois: A Soliloquy on Viewing My Life from the Last Decade of Its First Century* (New York: International Publishers, 1968), 390; Philip S. Foner, ed., *Paul Robeson Speaks* (New York: Citadel Press, 1978), 558–59; Manning Marable, *Race, Reform, and Rebellion*, 26–27; Rachel Buff, "The Deportation Terror," *American Quarterly* 60, no. 3 (September 2008): 529; Ellen Schrecker, "Immigration and Internal Security: Political Deportations During the McCarthy Era," *Science and Society* 60, no. 4 (Winter 1996–97): 393–426; David R. Roediger, *How Race Survived U.S. History*. The term "warfare-welfare" was introduced in James O'Connor, *The Fiscal Crisis of the State* (New York: St. Martin's Press, 1973). On the relationship between globalism, the warfare-welfare state, and the expansion of U.S. hegemony in the post–World War II era, see Giovanni Arrighi, *Adam Smith in Beijing: Lineages of the Twenty-First Century* (New York: Verso, 2007), 149–74.

17. W. E. B. Du Bois, *Autobiography of W. E. B. Du Bois*, 390. Julian Bond takes up and extends Du Bois's intervention about the politics of incarceration during the early Cold War to struggles to free Angela Davis and political prisoners in California during the 1960s specifically. See Julian Bond, foreword to *If They Come in the Morning: Voices of Resistance*, ed. Angela Y. Davis (New York: Signet, 1971), xi–xii.

18. Jodi Melamed, "W. E. B. Du Bois's UnAmerican End," *African American Review* 40, no. 3 (Fall 2006): 533–50; Neil Smith, *American Empire: Roosevelt's Geographer and the Prelude to Globalization* (Berkeley: University of California Press, 2003); Naomi Murakawa, "The Origins of the Carceral Crisis: Racial Order as 'Law and Order' in Postwar American Politics," in *Race and American Political Development*, ed. Joseph Lowndes, Julie Novkov, and Dorian T. Warren (New York: Routledge, 2008), 234–55; Nikhil Pal Singh, "Racial Formation in an Age of Permanent War," in *Racial Formation in the Twenty-First Century*, ed. Daniel Martinez HoSang, Oneka LaBennett, and Laura Pulido (Berkeley: University of California Press, 2012), 278, 284; Rebecca N. Hill, *Men, Mobs, and Law*, 273; Eric Porter, *The Problem of the Future World: W. E. B. Du Bois and the Race Concept at Midcentury* (Durham, NC: Duke University Press, 2010). On postwar Black freedom, anticolonial, labor, and Communist movements in the early Cold War, see John Munro, "The Anticolonial Front: Cold War Imperialism and the Struggle Against Global White

Supremacy, 1945–1960" (PhD diss., University of California, Santa Barbara, 2009).

19. William L. Patterson, "Prison Figures Show 'Brand of Criminality' Placed on Negroes," *Freedom* (May 1953); Gerald Horne, *Black Revolutionary: William Patterson and the Globalization of the African American Freedom Struggle* (Chicago: University of Illinois Press, 2013), 100; Josh Sides, "'You Understand My Condition': The Civil Rights Congress in the Los Angeles African-American Community, 1946–1952," *Pacific Historical Review* 67, no. 2 (1998): 235; Eric S. McDuffie, "Black and Red: Black Liberation, the Cold War, and the Horne Thesis," *Journal of African American History* 96, no. 2 (2011): 239; Gordon K. Mantler, *Power to the Poor*, 24.

20. Gerald Horne, *A Communist Front? The Civil Rights Congress, 1946–1956* (Rutherford, NJ: Fairleigh Dickinson University Press, 1988); Josh Sides, "'You Understand My Condition,'" 233–57; Nikhil Pal Singh, *Black Is a Country*, 252 note 23; Christina Heatherton, "Relief and Revolution: Southern California Struggles Against Unemployment, 1930–1933," in *Rising Tides of Color: Race, State Violence, and Radical Movements Across the Pacific*, ed. Moon Ho-Jung (Seattle: University of Washington Press, 2014), 159–87.

21. Josh Sides, "You Understand My Condition," 240, 241, 243; "Local Police Brutality: Is the Police Department Above the Law?" pamphlet (Los Angeles: Civil Rights Congress, undated).

22. Gaye Theresa Johnson, *Spaces of Conflict, Sounds of Solidarity: Music, Race, and Spatial Entitlement in Los Angeles* (Berkeley: University of California Press, 2013), 12; Regina Freer, "L.A. Race Woman: Charlotta Bass and the Complexities of Black Political Development in Los Angeles," *American Quarterly* 56, no. 3 (2004): 624, 626; Gordon K. Mantler, *Power to the Poor*, 22–23.

23. Josh Sides, "'You Understand My Condition,'" 238–40, 245; Angela Y. Davis, *Are Prisons Obsolete?* (New York: Seven Stories Press, 2003), 113.

24. Gerald Horne, *A Communist Front*, 333.

25. Jack O'Dell, *Climbin' Jacob's Ladder*, 202; Martha Biondi, *To Stand and Fight: The Struggle for Civil Rights in Postwar New York City* (Cambridge, MA: Harvard University Press, 2003), 175; letter from Samuel Berland of the CIO, Alice Walsh of the AFL, and William Bidner of the Civil Rights Congress, February 16, 1948; Freedomways, ed., *Paul Robeson: The Great Forerunner* (New York: International Publishers, 1998).

26. Civil Rights Congress, *We Charge Genocide: The Historic Petition to the United Nations for Relief from a Crime of the United States Government Against the Negro People* (1951; reprint, New York: International Publishers, 1971); William L. Patterson, *The Man Who Cried Genocide: An Autobiography* (New York: International Publishers, 1971), 169–208; Gerald Horne, *Fire This Time*, 8–9; Gerald Horne, "Civil Rights Congress," in *Encyclopedia of the American Left*, ed. Mari Jo Buhle, Paul Buhle, and Dan Georgakas (New York: Oxford University Press, 1988), 135; "U.S. Accused in U.N. of Negro Genocide," *New York Times*, December 18, 1951, 13; Martha Biondi, *To Stand and Fight*, 156, 200; Cedric J. Robinson, *Black Movements in America* (New York: Routledge, 1997), 137; William L. Patterson, "'We Charge Genocide!'" *Political Affairs* 30, no. 12 (1951): 43–44.

27. Naomi Murakawa, *The First Civil Right,* 57; W. E. B. Du Bois, *The Autobiography of W. E. B. Du Bois,* 361–95; Martha Biondi, *To Stand and Fight,* 153; Penny M. Von Eschen, *Race Against Empire,* 187; Angela Y. Davis, *Abolition Democracy: Beyond Empire, Prisons, and Torture* (New York: Seven Stories Press, 2005), 43–45, 89; Shana L. Redmond, *Anthem: Movement Cultures and the Sound of Solidarity in the African Diaspora* (New York: New York University Press, 2014), 122–39.

28. Manning Marable, *Race, Reform, and Rebellion,* 102; Robin D. G. Kelley, *Hammer and Hoe: Alabama Communists During the Great Depression* (Chapel Hill: University of North Carolina Press, 1990), 227, 181, 226; Claudia Jones, "An End to the Neglect of the Problems of the Negro Woman," *Political Affairs* 28, no. 6 (1949): 63–65; Mary Helen Washington, "Alice Childress, Lorraine Hansberry, and Claudia Jones: Black Women Write the Popular Front," in *Left of the Color Line: Race, Radicalism, and Twentieth-Century Literature of the United States* (Chapel Hill: University of North Carolina Press, 2003), 194–98; Mary Helen Washington, *The Other Blacklist,* 11; Rebecca Hill, "Fosterites and Feminists, or 1950s Ultra-Leftists and the Invention of AmeriKKKa," *New Left Review* 1, no. 228 (1998): 69, 73–74; Robin D. G. Kelley, *Freedom Dreams: The Black Radical Imagination* (Boston: Beacon Press, 2002), 54–55; Dayo F. Gore, *Radicalism at the Crossroads: African American Women Activists in the Cold War* (New York: New York University Press, 2011), 7–9.

29. David R. Roediger, *How Race Survived U.S. History,* 194. The formulation "white supremacist capitalism" is from Vijay Prashad, *Everybody Was Kung Fu Fighting: Afro-Asian Connections and the Myth of Cultural Purity* (Boston: Beacon Press, 2001), 115.

30. Jessica Mitford, *A Fine Old Conflict* (New York: Vintage Books, 1978), 112.

31. Robert Korstad and Nelson Lichtenstein, "Opportunities Found and Lost: Labor, Radicals, and the Early Civil Rights Movement," *Journal of American History* 75, no. 3 (1988): 786–811; Nikhil Pal Singh, *Black Is a Country,* 5–8; Robin D. G. Kelley, *Freedom Dreams,* 59.

32. Gerald Horne, *Fire This Time,* 367 note 4; Daniel Widener, *Black Arts West: Culture and Struggle in Postwar Los Angeles* (Durham, NC: Duke University Press, 2010), 54; Don Parson, *Making a Better World: Public Housing, the Red Scare, and the Direction of Modern Los Angeles* (Minneapolis: University of Minnesota Press, 2005); Nikhil Pal Singh, "'Learn Your Horn,'" 21.

33. Naomi Murakawa, "Origins of Carceral Crisis," in *Race and American Political Development,* ed. Joseph Lowndes, Julie Novkov, and Dorian T. Warren (New York: Routledge, 2008), 234–55; Michael Rogin, *Ronald Reagan, the Movie, and Other Episodes of Political Demonology* (Berkeley: University of California Press, 1987), xiii. See also Frank Donner, *Protectors of Privilege: Red Squads and Policing in Urban America* (Berkeley and Los Angeles: University of California Press, 1990), 246–47, 248; Daniel Widener, *Black Arts West,* 60–62.

34. Jodi Melamed, *Represent and Destroy,* 54; Gerald Horne, *Fire This Time,* 7–8, 47, 222–23, 249–50; Tim Sullivan, Maz Ali, Carlos Perez de Alejo, Brian Miller, and Nicole Márin Baena, *A Long Way From Home: Housing, Asset Policy and the Racial Wealth Divide* (Boston: United for a Fair Economy, 2013): 6;

George Lipsitz, *The Possessive Investment in Whiteness: How White People Profit from Identity Politics* (Philadelphia: Temple University Press, 2006), 6–7, 12; Daniel Martinez HoSang, *Racial Propositions: Ballot Initiatives and the Making of Postwar California* (Berkeley: University of California Press, 2010), 81, 68; Don Parson, *Making a Better World*, 198; David Harvey, *Rebel Cities: From the Right to the City to the Urban Revolution* (New York: Verso, 2012), 9.

35. Gerald Horne, *Fire This Time*, 7; Paul Takagi, "A Garrison State in 'Democratic' Society," *Social Justice* (2014): 122–23; Josh Sides, *L.A. City Limits: African American Los Angeles from the Great Depression to the Present* (Berkeley: University of California Press, 2003), 173–74; Manning Marable, "Malcolm X," *New York Times*, April 1, 2011, http://www.nytimes.com /2011/04/02/books/excerpt-malcolm-x-by-manning-marable.html?_r=0; Peniel E. Joseph, *Waiting 'Til the Midnight Hour: A Narrative History of Black Power* (New York: Owl Books, 2006), 52, 63–64; Joe Domanick, *To Protect and Serve: The LAPD's Century of War in the City of Dreams* (New York: Pocket Books, 1994), 176; Robin D. G. Kelley, "Watts: Remember What They Built, Not What They Burned," *Los Angeles Times*, August 11, 2015, http://www.latimes.com /opinion/op-ed/la-oe-0811-kelley-watts-civil-society-20150811-story.html.

36. Josh Sides, *L.A. City Limits*, 175; Gerald Horne, *Fire This Time*, 248; Martin Luther King Jr., *All Labor Has Dignity*, 105, 117; Jack O'Dell, *Climbin' Jacob's Ladder*, 150–52.

37. Edward W. Soja, "Poles Apart: Urban Restructuring in New York and Los Angeles," in *Dual City: Restructuring New York*, ed. Jon H. Mollenkopf and Manuel Castells (New York: Russell Sage Foundation, 1991), 361–62; Josh Sides, *L.A. City Limits*, 179–80.

38. Daniel Martinez HoSang, *Racial Propositions*, 53, 87; Friedrich Engels, *The Housing Question* (1954; reprint, Moscow: Progress Publishers, 1979); Gerald Horne, *Fire This Time*, 219; Mike Davis, "In L.A., Burning All Illusions," *The Nation*, June 1, 1992, 745; Mike Davis, *City of Quartz*, 126.

39. Martin Luther King Jr., "A Time to Break the Silence," 231–44; David J. Garrow, *The FBI and Martin Luther King, Jr.: From Solo to Memphis* (New York: W. W. Norton, 1981), 214.

40. Mike Davis, *Prisoners of the American Dream* (New York: Verso, 1986), 273, 312; John Munro, "Continuities in the Freedom Movement: Jack O'Dell in the Early Cold War," in *Jack O'Dell: The Fierce Urgency of Now* (New York: Center for the Study of Working Class Life, 2005), 3–11; Ian Rocksborough-Smith, "'Filling the Gap': Intergenerational Black Radicalism and the Popular Front Ideals of *Freedomways* Magazine's Early Years (1961–1965)," *Afro-Americans in New York Life and History* 31, no. 1 (January 2007): 7–42.

41. Dr. Martin Luther King Jr., "Honoring Dr. Du Bois, No. 2, 1968," in *Freedomways Reader: Prophets in Their Own Country*, ed. Esther Cooper Jackson (Boulder, CO: Westview Press, 2000), 37.

42. Vincent Harding, introduction to Martin Luther King Jr., *Where Do We Go from Here*, xiv; Martin Luther King Jr., *A Testament of Hope*, 315.

43. Martin Luther King Jr., "The Crisis in America's Cities: An Analysis of Social Disorder and a Plan of Action Against Poverty, Discrimination, and Racism in Urban America," presented at the Southern Christian Leadership

Conference, Atlanta, August 15, 1967, http://www.thekingcenter.org/archive/document/crisis-americas-cities; Alyosha Goldstein, *Poverty in Common: The Politics of Community Action During the American Century* (Durham, NC: Duke University Press, 2012), 137.

44. Naomi Murakawa, *The First Civil Right*, 78–79; Lyndon B. Johnson, "Statement on Watts Riots," August 21, 1965, http://www.historycentral.com/documents/LBJwatts.html.

45. Martin Luther King Jr., *Where Do We Go From Here*, 143, 145, 146.

46. Vijay Prashad, "Second-Hand Dreams," *Social Analysis* 49, no. 2 (2005): 191–98. On the significance of the victories of the Black freedom struggle for the multiracial working class as a whole, see Paul Ortiz, "Ocoee, Florida: Remembering 'The Single Bloodiest Day in Modern U.S. Political History,'" *Institute for Southern Studies* (May 14, 2010), http://www.southernstudies.org/2010/05/ocoee-florida-remembering-the-single-bloodiest-day-in-modern-us-political-history.html.

47. George P. Rawick, *Listening to Revolt*, 2–3.

48. George P. Rawick, *From Sundown to Sunup: The Making of the Black Community* (Westport, VT: Greenwood Publishing, 1972), 150–59; Russell Rickford, "'Socialism from Below': A Black Scholar's Marxist Genealogy," *Souls: A Critical Journal of Black Politics, Culture, and Society* 13, no. 4 (2011): 377; Robin D.G. Kelley, "Labor Against Empire, at Home and Abroad," keynote address, Race and Labor Matters, CUNY Graduate Center, December 5, 2003, http://arts.muohio.edu/cce/papers/labor_v_empire.pdf; Nikhil Pal Singh, "'Learn Your Horn,'" 48.

49. Martin Luther King Jr., "A Time to Break the Silence," 243; Gordon K. Mantler, *Power to the Poor*.

50. Nikhil Pal Singh, *Black Is a Country*, 6, 8, 13, 214; Vincent Harding, introduction to Martin Luther King Jr., *Where Do We Go from Here*, xiv.

51. Nikhil Pal Singh, "'Learn Your Horn,'" 5.

52. James Baldwin, *The Price of the Ticket: Collected Nonfiction, 1948–1985* (New York: St. Martin's Press, 1985), 672.

53. Gerald Horne, *Fire This Time*, 16, 301; Marie Gottschalk, *The Prison and the Gallows*, 197, 214; Richard Walker, "California Rages Against the Dying of the Light," *New Left Review*, no. 209 (1995): 52; Gerald Horne, *Fire This Time*, 16–17.

54. Huey P. Newton, *War Against the Panthers: A Study of Repression in America* (New York: Harlem River Press, 2000), 27.

55. Noam Chomsky, introduction to Nelson Blackstock, *Cointelpro: The FBI's Secret War on Political Freedom* (New York: Pathfinder Press, 1988), 9–12; Cedric J. Robinson, *Black Movements in America*, 151–52; Mike Davis, *City of Quartz*, 298.

56. Gerald Horne, *Fire This Time*, 165; Frank Donner, *Protectors of Privilege*, 421 note 47, 277; Christian Parenti, *Lockdown America: Police and Prisons in the Age of Crisis* (1999; reprint, New York: Verso, 2000), 133; Ward Churchill and Jim Vander Wall, *Agents of Repression: The FBI's Secret Wars Against the Black Panther Party and the American Indian Movement* (Boston: South End Press, 1990); Daniel Widener, *Black Arts West*, 150–51.

57. James Baldwin, *No Name in the Street* (New York: Random House, 1972), 158–59, 167.

58. Ibid., 129, 174–75, 176; Naomi Murakawa, "The Origins of the Carceral Crisis," 250–53; Richard Walker, "California Rages Against the Dying of Light," 69–72.

59. Nikhil Pal Singh, *Black Is a Country*, 8; Marie Gottschalk, *The Prison and the Gallows*, 114; Michael Denning, *Culture in the Age of Three Worlds* (New York: Verso, 2004), 230; Giovanni Arrighi, Terence K. Hopkins, and Immanuel Wallerstein, *Antisystemic Movements* (New York: Verso, 1989), 65, 109.

CHAPTER 2: FINALLY GOT THE NEWS

1. Dan Georgakas and Marvin Surkin, *Detroit: I Do Mind Dying* (Cambridge, MA: South End Press, 1998), 115; Grace Lee Boggs, *Living for Change: An Autobiography* (Minneapolis: University of Minnesota Press, 1998), 158; David Ritz, *Divided Soul: The Life of Marvin Gaye* (New York: Da Capo Press, 1985), 148–152.

2. On the social visions embedded in expressive culture, see Clyde Woods, *Development Arrested: The Blues and Plantation Power in the Mississippi Delta* (New York: Verso, 1998), 25–39.

3. This chapter's analysis benefits a great deal from the original and generative study of the League of Revolutionary Black Workers and social struggles in Detroit in this period by Dan Georgakas and Marvin Surkin, *Detroit: I Do Mind Dying*. See *Finally Got the News*, directed by Stewart Bird, Rene Lichtman, and Peter Gessner, produced in association with the League of Revolutionary Black Workers (Detroit: Black Star Productions, 1970). On the significance of events of 1967 and 1968 for Black freedom and socialist movements, see Martin Glaberman, "Black Cats, White Cats, Wildcats: Autoworkers in Detroit," *Radical America* 9, no. 1 (January–February 1975): 28; George P. Rawick, *Listening to Revolt: The Selected Writings of George P. Rawick*, ed. David Roediger (Chicago: Charles H. Kerr Publishing, 2010), 76–82; Vincent Harding, *The Other American Revolution* (Los Angeles and Atlanta: Center for Afro-American Studies University of California, Los Angeles, and Institute of the Black World, 1980), 189–200; James A. Geschwender, *Class, Race, and Worker Insurgency: The League of Revolutionary Black Workers* (New York: Cambridge University Press, 1977), 71–82; Peter Linebaugh and Bruno Ramirez, "Crisis in the Auto Sector," in *Midnight Oil: Work, Energy, War 1973–1992*, ed. Midnight Notes Collective (New York: Autonomedia, 1992), 149–68; Grace Lee Boggs, *Living for Change*, 143–89; Manning Marable, *Race, Reform and Rebellion: The Second Reconstruction in Black America* (Jackson: University of Mississippi Press, 2007), 102–3; Thomas J. Sugrue, *The Origins of the Urban Crisis: Race and Inequality in Postwar Detroit* (Princeton, NJ: Princeton University Press, 1996), 259; Heather Ann Thompson, *Whose Detroit? Politics, Labor, and Race in a Modern American City* (Ithaca, NY: Cornell University Press, 2001), 1–4, 71–127. On the meaning of the events for the civil rights movement in Motown, see Suzanne E. Smith, *Dancing in the Street: Motown*

and the Cultural Politics of Detroit (Cambridge, MA: Harvard University Press, 1999), 181–208.

4. Kieran Taylor, "American Petrograd: Detroit and the League of Revolutionary Black Workers," in *Rebel Rank and File: Labor Militancy and Revolt from Below During the Long 1970s,* ed. Aaron Brenner, Robert Brenner, and Cal Winslow (New York: Verso, 2010), 327; Nikhil Pal Singh, *Black Is a Country: Race and the Unfinished Struggle for Democracy* (Cambridge, MA: Harvard University Press, 2004), 109.

5. Stuart Hall et al., *Policing the Crisis: Mugging, the State, and Law and Order* (London: MacMillan, 1978), 241; Neil Smith, foreword to Henri Levebre, *The Urban Revolution* (Minneapolis: University of Minnesota Press, 2003), vii; Ruth Wilson Gilmore, *Golden Gulag: Prisons, Surplus, Crisis, and Opposition in Globalizing California* (Berkeley: University of California Press, 2007), 26. For an exploration of the crisis of Fordism in Detroit, see *Detroit: Ruin of a City,* directed by Michael Chanan and George Steinmetz (Bristol Docs, 2005).

6. James A. Geschwender, *Class, Race, and Worker Insurgency* 87–102.

7. Manning Marable, foreword to *Detroit: I Do Mind Dying,* ix–x. On the study group with Martin Glaberman and League members, see Martin Glaberman, "Workers Have to Deal with Their Own Reality and That Transforms Them" (1997), https://www.marxists.org/archive/glaberman/1997/xx/workersreality.htm; the oral history interview with Dan Georgakas in Robert H. Mast, *Detroit Lives* (Philadelphia: Temple University Press, 1994), 290; David Roediger, "A White Intellectual Among Thinking Black Intellectuals," in *Listening to Revolt,* xliii. Rawick became friends with John Watson during their activism in CORE; see "Paul Buhle Interviews George Rawick," Oral History of the American Left, Tamiment Institute of Bobst Library, New York University. See also Cedric Johnson, *Revolutionaries to Race Leaders: Black Power and the Making of African American Politics* (Minneapolis: University of Minnesota Press, 2007), 16.

8. Manning Marable, foreword to *Detroit: I Do Mind Dying,* ix. This methodological approach indebted to Robin D. G. Kelley, *Hammer and Hoe: Alabama Communists During the Great Depression* (Chapel Hill: University of North Carolina Press, 1990). For a genealogy of the concept of self-activity, see for example C. L. R. James, *Notes on Dialectics: Hegel-Marx-Lenin* (1948; reprint, London: Allison and Busby, 1980); George Rawick, "Working-Class Self-Activity," *Radical America* 3, no. 2 (1969): 23–31; Don Fitz and David Roediger, eds., *Within the Shell of the Old: Essays on Workers Self-Organization, A Salute to George Rawick* (Chicago: Charles H. Kerr Publishing Company, 1990); Robin D. G. Kelley, *Race Rebels: Culture, Politics, and the Black Working Class* (New York: The New Press, 1994); David Roediger, *Towards the Abolition of Whiteness* (1994; reprint, New York: Verso, 2000); Peter Linebaugh and Marcus Rediker, *The Many-Headed Hydra: Sailors, Slaves, Commoners, and the Hidden History of the Revolutionary Atlantic* (Boston: Beacon Press, 2000).

9. Paula J. Massood, *Black City Cinema: African American Urban Experiences in Film* (Philadelphia: Temple University Press, 2003), 81–101; Bulletin, "Detroit: The July Days," *Speak Out* 13 (Detroit: Facing Reality Publishing

Committee, July 1967); Luke Tripp, "Drum: Vanguard of the Black Revolution," *South End*, January 23, 1969, http://libcom.org/library/drum-vanguard-black-revolution; Martin Glaberman, *Punching Out and Other Writings* (Chicago: Charles H. Kerr Press, 2002), 106. See Robin D. G. Kelley, *Hammer and Hoe*, 92–116; George Lipsitz, *A Life in the Struggle: Ivory Perry and the Culture of Opposition* (Philadelphia: Temple University Press, 1995), 227–47; Manning Marable, *Race, Reform and Rebellion*, 114; Brent Hayes Edwards, "The 'Autonomy' of Black Radicalism," *Social Text* 19, no. 2 (Summer 2001): 1–13; Daniel Widener, *Black Arts West: Culture and Struggle in Postwar Los Angeles* (Durham, NC: Duke University Press, 2010), 6.

10. George Lipsitz, *Rainbow at Midnight: Labor and Culture in the 1940s* (1981; reprint, Urbana and Chicago: University of Illinois Press, 1994), 20, 99–154; Cal Winslow, "Rebellion from Below," in *Rebel Rank and File*, 4.

11. W. E. B. Du Bois, *Black Reconstruction in America: An Essay Toward a History of the Part Which Black Folk Played in the Attempt to Reconstruct Democracy in America, 1860–1880* (1935; reprint, New York: The Free Press, 1962), 727; Peter Linebaugh, introduction to *George Rawick, 1930–1990* (Jamaica Plain, MA: Midnight Notes, 1990); Peter Linebaugh and Bruno Ramirez, "Crisis in the Auto Sector," 149–68; David Roediger, *Towards the Abolition of Whiteness*, 66; Cedric J. Robinson, *Forgeries of Memory and Meaning: Blacks and the Regimes of Race in American Theatre and Film Before World War II* (Chapel Hill: University of North Carolina Press, 2007), xv; Manning Marable, *Race, Reform and Rebellion*, 113–14.

12. C. L. R. James, "The Role of the Black Scholar," public lecture at the Institute of the Black World, Atlanta, June 18, 1971, cassette.

13. Anthony Bogues, "Working Outside Criticism: Thinking Beyond Limits," *boundary 2* 3, no. 1 (2005): 78.

14. Antonio Gramsci, *Selections from the Prison Notebooks* (New York: International Publishers, 1971), 377; Raymond Williams, *Marxism and Literature* (Oxford: Oxford University Press, 1977), 38; Stuart Hall, "Signification, Representation, Ideology: Althusser and the Post-Structuralist Debates," *Critical Studies in Mass Communication* 2, no. 2 (June 1985): 91–114; Ernesto Laclau, *Politics and Ideology in Marxist Theory* (New York: Verso, 1977), 173; Stan Weir, *Singlejack Solidarity* (Minneapolis: University of Minnesota Press, 2004), 330; Neil Smith, *The New Urban Frontier: Gentrification and the Revanchist City* (New York: Routledge, 1996), 211.

15. Thomas J. Sugrue, *The Origins of the Urban Crisis*, 17.

16. Antonio Gramsci, *Selections from the Prison Notebooks*, 279; Martin Glaberman, *Punching Out and Other Writings*, 104; Martin Glaberman, *"Be His Payment High or Low": The American Working Class of the Sixties* (1966; reprint, Detroit: Bewick Editions, 1975). For an influential analysis of the culture of American Fordism, see Michael Denning, *The Cultural Front: The Laboring of American Culture in the Twentieth Century* (New York: Verso, 1996), 28.

17. Thomas J. Sugrue, *The Origins of the Urban Crisis*, 17, 19; Robin D. G. Kelley, *Hammer and Hoe*, 1; Michael Denning, *The Cultural Front*, 27–35; David Harvey, *The New Imperialism* (New York: Oxford University Press,

2003), 48, 76; George Lipsitz, *Rainbow at Midnight,* 234–35; Cedric J. Robinson, *Forgeries of Memory and Meaning,* 201.

18. David Roediger, *How Race Survived U.S. History* (New York: Verso, 2008), 104; Robert Korstad and Nelson Lichenstein, "Opportunities Found and Lost: Labor, Radicals, and Civil Rights," *Journal of American History* 75, no. 3 (1988): 787.

19. Robin D.G. Kelley, "Building Bridges: The Challenge of Organized Labor in Communities of Color," *New Labor Forum* (1999): 50, 51. See Michael Denning, *The Cultural Front,* 24.

20. George Lipsitz, *Rainbow at Midnight,* 183, 184, 187, 190.

21. Bill Fletcher Jr. and Fernando Gapasin, *Solidarity Divided: The Crisis in Organized Labor and a New Path Toward Social Justice* (Berkeley: University of California Press, 2009), 26–29.

22. Robert Korstad and Nelson Lichenstein, "Opportunities Found and Lost," 807, 808.

23. Robin D.G. Kelley, "Building Bridges," 50.

24. Bobby M. Wilson, *America's Johannesburg: Industrialization and Racial Transformation in Birmingham* (Lanham, MD: Rowman and Littlefield, 2000), 1; George Lipsitz, *The Possessive Investment in Whiteness: How White People Profit from Identity Politics* (Philadelphia: Temple University Press, 2006), 98–99; David Roediger, *Working Toward Whiteness: How America's Immigrants Became White* (Cambridge, MA: Basic Books, 2005), 224.

25. Thomas J. Sugrue, *The Origins of the Urban Crisis,* 209–30, 261. On trap economics, see Clyde Woods, "Les Misérables of New Orleans: Trap Economics and the Asset Stripping Blues, Part 1," *American Quarterly* 61, no. 3 (2009): 769–96. On segregation, see Jacqueline Jones, *The Dispossessed: America's Underclasses from the Civil War to the Present* (New York: Basic Books, 1992), 261. For an analysis of the deadly consequences of capital's speed-ups at the point of production, see JoAnn Wypijewski, "Pounding Out a DRUM Beat," *New Left Review* 1, no. 234 (1999): 142; David Roediger and Elizabeth Esch, *The Production of Difference: Race and the Management of Labor in U.S. History* (New York: Oxford University Press, 2012), 207.

26. "An Interview with Ken Cockrel and Mike Hamlin of the League of Revolutionary Black Workers," *Leviathan* 2, no. 2 (June 1970); Kieran Taylor, "American Petrograd," 314.

27. Mike Hamlin, foreword to *Rebel Rank and File,* vii–viii.

28. Karl Marx, *Capital: A Critique of Political Economy,* trans. Ben Fowkes (New York: Penguin Books, 1976), 640–48; Peter Linebaugh, "Karl Marx, the Theft of the Wood, and Working-Class Composition: A Contribution to the Current Debate," *Crime and Social Justice* 6 (Fall–Winter 1976): 5.

29. John Watson quoted in "Black Editor: An Interview," *Radical America* 2, no. 4 (July–August 1968): 37; Dan Georgakas and Marvin Surkin, *Detroit,* 35; JoAnn Wypijewski, "Pounding Out a DRUM Beat," 142; Robert Brenner, "The Political Economy of Rank-and-File Rebellion," in *Rebel Rank and File,* 37; Robin D.G. Kelley, *Race Rebels,* 78.

30. Dan Georgakas and Marvin Surkin, *Detroit,* 107–8. On the cultural politics of pleasure and leisure in public spaces and musical cultures, see Robin

D.G. Kelley, *Race Rebels*, 35–53; Suzanne E. Smith, *Dancing in the Street*, 192–93.

31. Suzanne E. Smith, *Dancing in the Street*, 192; Otto Kerner et al., *Report of the National Advisory Commission on Civil Disorders* (New York: Bantam Books, 1968), 85–86.

32. Robin D.G. Kelley, *Race Rebels*, 89; Thomas J. Sugrue, *The Origins of the Urban Crisis*, 259.

33. Dan Georgakas and Marvin Surkin, *Detroit*, 155; George Rudé, *The Crowd in History: A Study of Popular Disturbances in France and England, 1730–1848* (London: Lawrence and Wishart, 1981).

34. "An American Tragedy, 1967 Detroit," *Newsweek*, August 7, 1967, 20; "Detroit Is Swept by Rioting and Fires; Romney Calls in Guard; 700 Arrested: Negroes in Detroit Defy Curfew and Loot Wide Area," *New York Times*, July 24, 1967; Heather Ann Thompson, *Whose Detroit?*, 72–73. On the escalation of state violence despite the clear absence of corresponding violence in the streets, see Albert Bergeson, "Race Riots of 1967: An Analysis of Police Violence in Detroit and Newark," *Journal of Black Studies* 12, no. 3 (March 1982): 261. On the struggle over the meaning of the events, see Martin Glaberman, *Punching Out and Other Writings*, 106; Manning Marable, *Race, Reform and Rebellion*, 102–3; "LBJ's Ideas on How to Stop Riots in the Nation's Cities," *U.S. News & World Report*, August 7, 1967; Ranajit Guha, *Elementary Aspects of Peasant Insurgency in Colonial India* (Durham, NC: Duke University Press, 1999), 16–17; Jack O'Dell, *Climbin' Jacob's Ladder: The Black Freedom Movement Writings of Jack O'Dell*, ed. Nikhil Pal Singh (Berkeley: University of California Press, 2010), 183–84.

35. Ranajit Guha, *Elementary Aspects of Peasant Insurgency in Colonial India*, 333; Naomi Murakawa, "The Origins of the Carceral Crisis: Racial Order as 'Law and Order' in Postwar American Politics," in *Race and American Political Development*, ed. Joseph Lowndes, Julie Novkov, and Dorian T. Warren (New York: Routledge, 2008), 253.

36. Stuart Hall, *The Hard Road to Renewal: Thatcherism and the Crisis of the Left* (New York: Verso, 1988), 154; Angela Y. Davis, "Race and Criminalization: Black Americans and the Punishment Industry," in *The Angela Y. Davis Reader*, ed. Joy James (Malden, MA: Blackwell, 1998), 74–95; Don Mitchell, "State Intervention in Landscape Production: The Wheatland Riot and the California Commission of Immigration and Housing," *Antipode* 25, no. 2 (1993): 91–113; Ruth Wilson Gilmore and Craig Gilmore, "Restating the Obvious," in *Indefensible Space: The Architecture of the National Security State*, ed. Michael Sorkin (New York: Routledge, 2007), 144–45; David Harvey, *The New Imperialism* (New York: Oxford University Press, 2003), 89–90; Pamela Oliver, "Repression and Crime Control: Why Social Movement Scholars Should Pay Attention to Mass Incarceration as a Form of Repression," *Mobilization: The International Quarterly* 13, no. 1 (2008): 1–24; Cedric J. Robinson, *Forgeries of Memory and Meaning*, xii; Jimmie L. Reeves and Richard Campbell, *Cracked Coverage: Television News, the Anti-Cocaine Crusade, and the Reagan Legacy* (Durham, NC: Duke University Press, 1994), 76.

37. W. W. Rostow quoted in Tracy Tullis, "A Vietnam at Home: Policing the Ghettoes in the Counter-Insurgency Era" (PhD diss., New York University,

1999), 24. On the impact of counterinsurgency strategy on the policing of urban rebellion, see Paul Gilroy, "The Myth of Black Criminality," in *Law, Order and the Authoritarian State,* ed. Phil Scraton (Philadelphia: Open University Press, 1987), 107–20; Martha K. Huggins, *Political Policing: The United States and Latin America* (Durham, NC: Duke University Press, 1998), 99–100.

38. "An American Tragedy, 1967 Detroit," *Newsweek,* August 7, 1967.

39. "Riot Control: Hold the Street and Seize 'The High Ground,'" *Time,* August 4, 1967.

40. Hazel V. Carby, *Cultures in Babylon: Black Britain and African America* (New York: Verso, 1999), 23, 24, 28. In part eight of the first volume of *Capital,* Karl Marx argues that the use of force exercises "the greatest part" in the accumulation of capital. He observes that "in most cases under the *force of circumstances*" expropriation created new conditions for the poor, who in turn were criminalized based on the conceit that "it was entirely within their powers to go on working under the old conditions which in fact no longer existed." Karl Marx, *Capital,* vol. 1, 874, 875, 889, 896.

41. General Gordon Baker, interview with the author, August 20, 2009. On the ways in which Black workers have transformed segregated spaces into places of struggle, see Earl Lewis, *In Their Own Interests: Race, Class, and Power in Twentieth-Century Norfolk, Virginia* (Berkeley: University of California Press, 1991), 91–92; Robin D. G. Kelley, *Race Rebels,* 45; George Lipsitz, *The Possessive Investment in Whiteness,* 243; David Roediger, *How Race Survived U.S. History,* 82–98.

42. Peter Linebaugh, "Karl Marx, the Theft of the Wood, and Working-Class Composition," 5; Suzanne E. Smith, *Dancing in the Street,* 296 note 25.

43. General Gordon Baker, interview with the author, August 20, 2009; George P. Rawick, *Listening to Revolt,* 81.

44. Quoted in Kieran Taylor, "American Petrograd," 317.

45. General Gordon Baker, interview with the author, August 20, 2009.

46. George P. Rawick, *Listening to Revolt,* 133.

47. Martin Glaberman, "The Dodge Revolutionary Union Movement," *International Socialism* 36 (April–May 1969), http://www.marxists.org/archive/glaberman/1969/04/drum.htm; David Roediger, "Where Do Great Ideas Come From? The Life and Work of George Rawick," in *Listening to Revolt,* xxxv; Friedrich Engels, introduction to Karl Marx, *The Civil War in France* (New York: International Publishers, 1993), 15. This analysis of the situation has been shaped by George Lipsitz, "The Struggle for Hegemony," *Journal of American History* 75, no. 1 (June 1998): 148. For a highly suggestive interpretation of the politics and culture of the Paris Commune, see Kristin Ross, *The Emergence of Social Space: Rimbaud and the Paris Commune* (1988; reprint, New York: Verso, 2008).

48. Ruth Wilson Gilmore, *Golden Gulag,* 185.

49. Bulletin, "The Meaning of Watts," *Speak Out* 3 (Detroit: Facing Reality Publishing Committee, January 1966). On the global significance of the uprisings for antiracist, feminist, and socialist movements, see Selma James, *Sex, Race, Class* (1975; reprint, London: Housewives in Dialogue, 1986), 8.

50. Anthony M. Platt, *The Politics of Riot Commissions* (New York: MacMillan Company, 1971); Institute for the Study of Labor and Economic Crisis,

The Iron Fist and the Velvet Glove: An Analysis of U.S. Police (1975; reprint, Berkeley: Crime and Social Justice Associates, 1982), 126–31; Robert M. Fogelson and Robert B. Hill, "Who Riots? A Study of Participation in the 1967 Riots," in *Racial Violence in the United States,* ed. Allen Grimshaw (Chicago: Aldine Publishing Company, 1969), 316; Daniel P. Moynihan, *The Negro Family: The Case for National Action* (Washington, DC: Office of Policy Planning and Research, United States Department of Labor, March 1965); Daniel Patrick Moynihan quoted in "An American Tragedy, 1967 Detroit," *Newsweek,* 32.

51. Frank Donner, *Protectors of Privilege: Red Squads and Policing in Urban America* (Berkeley: University of California Press, 1990), 385 note 1.

52. On the "exhaustion of consent," see Stuart Hall et al., *Policing the Crisis,* 218–72. For an analysis of the Kerner Commission, see Peniel E. Joseph, *Waiting 'Til the Midnight Hour: A Narrative History of Black Power in America* (New York: Holt Paperbacks, 2006), 189; Andrew Kopkind, "White on Black: The Riot Commission and the Rhetoric," in *The Politics of Riot Commissions,* 379, 380–81.

53. Ibid., 379; Naomi Murakawa, *The First Civil Right: How Liberals Built Prison America* (New York: Oxford University Press, 2014), 40; Otto Kerner et al., *Report of the National Advisory Commission on Civil Disorders,* 1; Thomas J. Sugrue, *The Origins of the Urban Crisis,* 360 note 1.

54. Otto Kerner et al., *Report of the National Advisory Commission on Civil Disorders,* 10–15; David Roediger, *Towards the Abolition of Whiteness,* 121; Robin D. G. Kelley, *Yo' Mama's Disfunktional! Fighting the Culture Wars in Urban America* (Boston: Beacon Press, 1997), 91; Daniel P. Moynihan, *The Negro Family;* Laura Briggs, *Reproducing Empire: Race, Sex, Science, and Imperialism in Puerto Rico* (Berkeley and Los Angeles: University of California Press, 2002), 164; Rosa Linda Fregoso, *meXicana Encounters: The Making of Social Identities in the Borderlands* (Berkeley and Los Angeles: University of California Press, 2003), 4, 5, 12.

55. Naomi Murakawa, *The First Civil Right,* 76.

56. Otto Kerner et al., *Report of the National Advisory Commission on Civil Disorders,* 487, 21.

57. Frank Donner, *The Age of Surveillance: The Aims and Methods of America's Political Intelligence System* (New York: Vintage Books, 1981), 283; Andrew Kopkind, "White on Black: The Riot Commission and the Rhetoric," in *The Politics of Riot Commissions,* 379–81; Richard Slotkin, *Gunfighter Nation: The Myth of the Frontier in Twentieth-Century America* (Norman: University of Oklahoma Press, 1998), 534–77.

58. Michael K. Honey, *Going Down Jericho Road: The Memphis Strike, Martin Luther King's Last Campaign* (New York: W.W. Norton, 2007), 173–90.

59. King quoted in Vincent Harding, *The Other American Revolution,* 198; Suzanne E. Smith, *Dancing in the Street,* 209–20; Vincent Harding, *The Other American Revolution,* 200.

60. Nikhil Pal Singh, "The Black Panthers and the Underdeveloped Country of the Left," in *The Black Panther Party Reconsidered,* ed. Charles Jones (Baltimore: Black Classic Press, 1998), 84–87; Ruth Wilson Gilmore, *Golden*

Gulag, 24–26; Walter Rodney, *The Groundings with My Brothers* (1969; reprint, London: Bogle-L'Ouverture Publications, 1996); Robin D. G. Kelley, "'Slangin' Rocks . . . Palestinian Style,' Dispatches from the Occupied Zones of North America," in *Police Brutality,* ed. Jill Nelson (New York: W. W. Norton and Company, 2000), 39; Paco Ignacio Taibo II, *'68* (New York: Seven Stories Press, 2004); George Katsiaficas, *The Imagination of the New Left: A Global Analysis of 1968* (Cambridge, MA: South End Press, 1987), xiii; David Roediger, *Towards the Abolition of Whiteness,* 66.

61. Suzanne E. Smith, *Dancing in the Street,* 4–5, 220; Muhammad Ahmad, *We Will Return in the Whirlwind: Black Radical Organizations, 1960–1975* (Chicago: Charles H. Kerr Publishing Company, 2007); Grace Lee Boggs, *Living for Change,* 158; Frank Donner, *Protectors of Privilege,* 291, 293, 297.

62. Vijay Prashad, "Second-Hand Dreams," *Social Analysis* 49, no. 2 (2005): 192; Ruth Wilson Gilmore, *Golden Gulag,* 29, 79. On struggles for moral authority at the point of production, see George Lipsitz, *Rainbow at Midnight,* 253–78; Martin Glaberman, *Punching Out and Other Writings,* 104–7.

63. Robin D. G. Kelley, *Freedom Dreams: The Black Radical Imagination* (New York: Beacon Press, 2002), 75; Stuart Hall, *The Hard Road to Renewal,* 177–95.

64. George P. Rawick, *Listening to Revolt,* 76–92.

65. Dan Georgakas and Marvin Surkin, *Detroit,* 115; Robin D. G. Kelley, *Freedom Dreams;* Peter Linebaugh, *The London Hanged: Crime and Civil Society in the Eighteenth Century* (2003; reprint, New York: Verso, 2006). This analysis of the cultural history of social movements and film as class criticism follows the lead of Daniel Widener, *Black Arts West,* 252.

66. Fred Moten, *In the Break: The Aesthetics of the Black Radical Tradition* (Minneapolis: University of Minnesota Press, 2003), 215. On the history of this encounter, see Cedric J. Robinson, *Black Marxism: The Making of the Black Radical Tradition* (1983; reprint, Chapel Hill: University of North Carolina Press, 2000), and Robin D. G. Kelley, *Hammer and Hoe.*

67. David Harvey, *Rebel Cities: From the Right to the City to the Urban Revolution* (New York: Verso, 2012), 37–38, 53–54.

68. Quoted in Dan Georgakas and Marvin Surkin, *Detroit,* 116–17.

69. See also Werner Bonefeld, "Monetarism and Crisis," in *Global Capital, National State and the Politics of Money,* ed. Werner Bonefeld and John Holloway (London: MacMillan, 1995), 22.

70. *Finally Got the News.*

71. Gaye Theresa Johnson, "Spatial Entitlement: Race, Displacement, and Reclamation in Post-War Los Angeles," in *Black and Brown Los Angeles: A Contemporary Reader,* ed. Josh Kun and Laura Pulido (Los Angeles: University of California Press, 2013), 324.

72. *Finally Got the News;* Jared Sexton, "The Ruse of Engagement: Black Masculinity and the Cinema of Policing," *American Quarterly* 61, no. 1 (2009): 39–63; Stuart Hall et al., *Policing the Crisis;* Robin D. G. Kelley, *Race Rebels;* Ruth Wilson Gilmore, *Golden Gulag;* George Lipsitz, *The Possessive Investment in Whiteness,* 98–99; David Harvey, *Spaces of Global Capitalism: Towards a Theory of Uneven Geographical Development* (New York: Verso,

2006), 59, 26, 49; Ruth Wilson and Craig Gilmore, "Restating the Obvious," 144. For a suggestive analysis of the League's critique of spaces of capitalism, see Fred Moten, *In the Break*, 224.

73. Ruth Wilson Gilmore, "In the Shadow of the Shadow State," in *The Revolution Will Not Be Funded: Beyond the Non-Profit Industrial Complex*, ed. Incite! Women of Color Against Violence (Cambridge, MA: South End Press, 2007), 44; Michel Foucault, *Security, Territory, Population: Lectures at the Collège de France, 1977–78*, ed. Michel Senellart, trans. Graham Burchell (New York: Palgrave MacMillan, 2007); Stuart Hall et al., *Policing the Crisis*, 19, 242, 222; Christian Parenti, *Lockdown America: Police and Prisons in the Age of Crisis* (New York: Verso, 2000).

74. Mike Davis, *City of Quartz: Excavating the Future in Los Angeles* (1990; reprint, New York: Verso, 2006), 223–316, 263 note 39; Robin D. G. Kelley, "Slangin' Rocks . . . Palestinian Style," 40–43, Cedric J. Robinson, *Black Movements in America* (New York: Routledge, 1997), 151–52; Christian Parenti, *Lockdown America*, 17–18, 112, 133, 159–60, 167; Tracy Tullis, "A Vietnam at Home," 14; Philip S. Foner, *U.S. Labor and the Vietnam War* (New York: International Publishers, 1989); Nicos Poulantzas, *State, Power, Socialism* (London: Verso, 1980), 203–47; Stuart Hall, *The Hard Road to Renewal*, 123–60.

75. Dan Georgakas and Marvin Surkin, *Detroit*, 203; Barbara Ransby, "The Black Poor and the Politics of Expendability," in *A New Introduction to Poverty: The Role of Race, Power, and Politics*, ed. Louis Kushnick and James Jennings (New York: New York University Press, 1999), 321–30.

76. Dan Georgakas and Marvin Surkin, *Detroit*, 207; Cedric J. Robinson, *The Terms of Order: Political Science and the Myth of Leadership* (Albany: State University of New York Press, 1980); Mazher Ali et al., *State of the Dream 2011: Austerity for Whom?* (Boston: United for a Fair Economy, 2011); Heather Ann Thompson, *Whose Detroit?*, 21–22, 38–41, 46–47, 75–79; Ranajit Guha, *Elementary Aspects of Peasant Insurgency in Colonial India*.

77. Fredric Jameson, "Cognitive Mapping," in *Marxism and the Interpretation of Culture*, ed. Cary Nelson and Lawrence Grossberg (Urbana and Chicago: University of Illinois Press, 1988), 351–52; Robert H. Mast, *Detroit Lives*, 1–2; Robert Brenner, "Political Economy of Rank-and-File Rebellion," in *Rebel Rank and File*, 38; Marc Mauer, *Race to Incarcerate* (New York: The New Press, 2006); Pew Center on the States, *One in 31: The Long Reach of American Corrections* (Washington, DC: Pew Charitable Trusts, March 2009), 9.

78. Amy Kaplan, "Homeland Insecurities: Reflections on Language and Space," *Radical History Review* 85 (Winter 2003): 82–93; Amy Kaplan, "Violent Belongings and the Question of Empire Today: Presidential Address, American Studies Association, October 17, 2003," *American Quarterly* 56, no. 1 (March 2004): 1–18.

CHAPTER 3: THE SOUND BEFORE THE FURY

1. Phil Scraton, "Protests and 'Riots' in the Violent Institution," in *The Violence of Incarceration*, ed. Phil Scraton and Jude McCulloch (New York:

Routledge, 2009), 63; Angela Y. Davis in *Eyes on the Prize: A Nation of Law?* (Blackside Productions, 1987) and Angela Y. Davis, *Are Prisons Obsolete?* (New York: Seven Stories Press, 2003), 17–18; Nikhil Pal Singh, *Black Is a Country: Race and the Unfinished Struggle for Democracy* (Cambridge, MA: Harvard University Press, 2004), 203, and Nikhil Pal Singh, "The Black Panthers and the 'Undeveloped Country of the Left,'" in *The Black Panther Party Reconsidered,* ed. Charles E. Jones (Baltimore: Black Classic Press, 1998), 57–105.

2. "The Attica Liberation Faction Manifesto of Demands and Anti-Depression Platform," in Sam Melville, *Letters from Attica* (New York: Morrow, 1972), 175; *New Yorker* quoted in Jessica Mitford, *Kind and Usual Punishment* (New York: Alfred A. Knopf, 1973), 13.

3. Ranajit Guha, "The Prose of Counter-Insurgency," in *Selected Subaltern Studies,* ed. Ranajit Guha and Gayatri Chakravorty Spivak (New York: Oxford University Press, 1988), 45–86; Russell G. Oswald quote is from his *Attica: My Story* (New York: Doubleday and Company, 1972), 24. On Marxist theory and the role of inherent ideologies in social protest, see George Rudé, *Ideology and Popular Protest* (New York: Pantheon Books, 1980), 29, 30, 33. See also Robert Weiss, "Attica: The 'Bitter Lessons' Forgotten?" *Social Justice* 18, no. 3 (Fall 1991): 3; Rebecca N. Hill, *Men, Mobs, and Law: Anti-Lynching and Labor Defense in U.S. Radical History* (Durham, NC: Duke University Press, 2009), 267.

4. Jessica Mitford, *Kind and Usual Punishment,* 233. See Alan Eladio Gómez, "'Nuestras Vidas Corren Casi Paralelas': Chicanos, *Independistas,* and the Prison Rebellions in Leavenworth, 1969–1972," *Latino Studies* 6 (2008): 65; Dylan Rodríguez, *Forced Passages: Imprisoned Radical Intellectuals and the U.S. Prison Regime* (Minneapolis: University of Minnesota Press, 2006), 41–74; Inmates of Attica Prison, "The Five Demands," in Tom Wicker, *A Time to Die* (New York: Quadrangle/New York Times Book Co., 1975), 315–16; *Fighting Back! Attica Memorial Book* (Buffalo, NY: Attica Brothers Legal Defense, 1974).

5. New York State Commission on Attica, *Attica: The Official Report of the New York State Special Commission on Attica* (New York: Bantam Books, 1972); Michael E. Deutsch, Dennis Cunningham, and Elizabeth Fink, "Twenty Years Later—Attica Civil Rights Case Finally Cleared for Trial," *Social Justice* 18, no. 3 (Fall 1991): 13; Elizabeth Fink quoted in the documentary *Safety Orange* (2001), directed by James Davis and Juliana Fredman. On the impact of counterinsurgency theory on Rockefeller's response to Attica, see Micol Siegel, "William Bratton in the Other L.A.," in *Without Fear . . . Claiming Safe Communities Without Sacrificing Ourselves* (Los Angeles: Southern California Library, 2007), 55. On the ways in which the event was perceived as a crisis of authority by state officials, see Russell G. Oswald, *Attica,* vi–vii, and Rockefeller quoted in Bert Useem and Peter Kimball, *States of Siege: U.S. Prison Riots, 1971–1986* (New York: Oxford University Press, 1989), 37.

6. Bert Useem and Peter Kimball, *States of Siege,* 11; New York State Commission on Attica, *Attica.* See for example Linda Charlton, "Deaths Decried; Critics Disagree," *New York Times,* September 14, 1971; William E. Farrell,

"Governor Defends Order to Quell Attica Uprising," *New York Times,* September 16, 1971.

7. Edward C. Burks, "Prison Officers Here Ask Stiffer Penalties for Inmates Who Riot," *New York Times,* September 14, 1971; NBC Evening News, September 13, 1971, http://tvnews.vanderbilt.edu/program.pl?ID=459837; Dennis Cunningham, interview with the author, September 17, 2009; Angela Y. Davis, *Abolition Democracy: Beyond Empire, Prisons, and Torture* (New York: Seven Stories Press, 2005), 42–43, 45–46, 86–87; Nikhil Pal Singh, *Black Is a Country,* 5; Stuart Hall, "Notes on Deconstructing 'the Popular,' " in *People's History and Socialist Theory,* ed. Raphael Samuel (London: Routledge and Kegan Paul Ltd., 1981), 227–40.

8. Marie Gottschalk, *The Prison and the Gallows: The Politics of Mass Incarceration in America* (Cambridge: Cambridge University Press, 2006), 179; Louis Kushnick, "Responding to Urban Crisis," in *A New Introduction to Poverty: The Role of Race, Power, and Politics,* ed. James Jennings and Louis Kushnick (New York: New York University Press, 1999), 156–63; Stuart Hall et al., *Policing the Crisis: Mugging, the State, and Law and Order* (London: MacMillan Press, 1978), 278.

9. On racism and state violence in the period, see George Jackson, *Soledad Brother: The Prison Letters of George Jackson* (1970; reprint, New York: Coward-McCann, 1994); Angela Y. Davis, eds., *If They Come in the Morning: Voices of Resistance* (New York: Third Press, 1971); Angela Y. Davis, *Abolition Democracy,* 110; Robert Justin Goldstein, *Political Repression in Modern America: From 1870 to the Present* (New York: Schenkman Publishing, 1978), 429; Scott Christianson, *With Liberty for Some: 500 Years of Imprisonment in America* (Boston: Northeastern University Press, 1998), 272; Joy James, "Erasing the Spectacle of Racialized State Violence," in *Resisting State Violence: Radicalism, Gender, and Race in U.S. Culture* (Minneapolis: University of Minnesota Press, 1998), 24; Christian Parenti, *Lockdown America: Police and Prisons in the Age of Crisis* (1999; reprint, New York: Verso, 2000); Ruth Wilson Gilmore, "Globalisation and U.S. Prison Growth: From Military Keynesianism to Post-Keynesian Militarism," *Race and Class* 40 (1999): 171, 175–77.

10. This emphasis on the insurgent consciousness is inspired by Ranajit Guha, *Elementary Aspects of Peasant Insurgency in Colonial India* (Durham, NC: Duke University Press, 1999), 4, and Ranajit Guha, "The Prose of Counter-Insurgency," 45–86. It also follows the lead of the following works: Centre for Contemporary Cultural Studies, ed., *The Empire Strikes Back: Race and Racism in 70s Britain* (London: Hutchinson/Centre for Contemporary Cultural Studies, University of Birmingham, 1982); Stuart Hall et al., *Policing the Crisis,* 221; Ruth Wilson Gilmore, "Terror Austerity Race Gender Excess Theatre," in *Reading Rodney King/Reading Urban Uprising,* ed. Robert Gooding-Williams (New York: Routledge, 1993), 23–37; Joy James, ed., *Warfare in the American Homeland: Policing and Prison in a Penal Democracy* (Durham, NC: Duke University Press, 2007), 19; Robin D. G. Kelley, *Hammer and Hoe: Alabama Communists During the Great Depression* (Chapel Hill: University of North Carolina Press, 1990), 99.

11. Stuart Hall et al., *Policing the Crisis,* 22; Paul Gilroy and Joe Simm, "Law, Order and the State of the Left," *Capital and Class* 25 (1985): 15–55; Martha Biondi, *To Stand and Fight: The Struggle for Civil Rights in Postwar New York City* (Cambridge, MA: Harvard University Press, 2003), 285–86; David Harvey, *A Brief History of Neoliberalism* (New York: Oxford University Press, 2005), 48; Marie Gottschalk, *The Prison and the Gallows,* 196; David Harvey, *The New Imperialism* (New York: Oxford University Press, 2005), 183–212; H. Bruce Franklin, "The American Prison and the Normalization of Torture," Historians Against the War, http://www.historiansagainstwar.org /resources/torture/brucefranklin.html; Angela Y. Davis, *Abolition Democracy,* 124; Laleh Khalili, *Time in the Shadows: Confinement in Counterinsurgencies* (Stanford, CA: Stanford University Press, 2013), 5. On the role of the criminalization of dissent in the buildup of contemporary regimes of mass imprisonment, see Avery Gordon, "The U.S. Military Prison: The Normalcy of Exceptional Brutality," in *The Violence of Incarceration,* 174.

12. Edward Said, *Covering Islam: How the Media and Experts Determine How We See the Rest of the World* (New York: Vintage Books, 1997). See for example Randy James, "Prison Riots," *Time,* August 11, 2009.

13. Editorial, "The Nation: War at Attica: Was There No Other Way?" *Time,* September 27, 1971.

14. Bettina Aptheker, *The Morning Breaks: The Trial of Angela Davis* (1975; reprint, New York: Cornell University Press, 1999), 49–50.

15. Claude McKay, *A Long Way from Home* (1937; reprint, New York: Harcourt Brace Jovanovich, 1970), 31, 227; Paul Ortiz, *Emancipation Betrayed: The Hidden History of Black Organizing and White Violence in Florida from Reconstruction to the Bloody Election of 1920* (Berkeley: University of California Press, 2005), 128–70.

16. Philip S. Foner, *American Socialism and Black Americans: From the Age of Jackson to World War II* (Westport, CT: Greenwood Press, 1977), 288–90, 291; Brent Hayes Edwards, "The 'Autonomy' of Black Radicalism," *Social Text* 19, no. 2 (Summer 2001): 2; Gary Edward Holcomb, *Code Name Sasha: Queer Black Marxism and the Harlem Renaissance* (Gainesville: University Press of Florida, 2007), 8; Claude McKay, *A Long Way from Home,* 31.

17. William J. Maxwell, *New Negro, Old Left: African-American Writing and Communism Between the Wars* (New York: Columbia University Press, 1999), 72–73.

18. Cedric J. Robinson, *Black Marxism: The Making of the Black Radical Tradition* (1983; reprint, Chapel Hill: University of North Carolina Press, 2000), 221; William J. Maxwell, *New Negro, Old Left,* 75, 90; Gary Edward Holcomb, *Code Name Sasha,* 8–9; Robin D.G. Kelley, *Freedom Dreams: The Black Radical Imagination* (Boston: Beacon Press, 2002), 47–48; Fred Moten, *In the Break: The Aesthetics of the Black Radical Tradition* (London: University of Minnesota Press, 2003); Brent Hayes Edwards, *The Practice of Diaspora: Literature, Translation, and the Rise of Black Internationalism* (Cambridge, MA: Harvard University Press, 2003), 299, 303, 382 note 167.

19. That is not to say that audiences took a passive approach to interpreting the text. Certainly when readers perceive the meaning of a text, they actively

engage in a struggle over meaning. See M.M. Bakhtin, *Speech Genres and Other Late Essays* (Austin: University of Texas Press, 1986), 68. On collective memory, see George Lipsitz, *A Life in the Struggle: Ivory Perry and the Culture of Opposition* (Philadelphia: Temple University Press, 1995); Jordan T. Camp, "Black Radicalism, Marxism, and Collective Memory: An Interview with Robin D.G. Kelley," *American Quarterly* 65, no. 1 (2013): 215–30; Macarena Gomez-Barris, *Where Memory Dwells: Culture and State Violence in Chile* (Berkeley: University of California Press, 2009), 6–12, 81. On the "poetry of revolt," see David Roediger, *History Against Misery* (Chicago: Charles H. Kerr, 2006), 114.

20. George Jackson, *Soledad Brother: The Prison Letters of George Jackson* (Chicago: Lawrence Hill Books, 1994); Dan Berger, *Captive Nation: Black Prison Organizing in the Civil Rights Era* (Chapel Hill: University of North Carolina Press, 2014), 91–138; Walter Rodney, "George Jackson: Black Revolutionary" (November 1971), http://historyisaweapon.com/defcon1/rodney jackson.html; Michel Foucault, Catherine Von Bulow, and Daniel Defert, "The Masked Assassination," in *Warfare in the American Homeland: Policing and Prison in a Penal Democracy*, ed. Joy James (Durham, NC: Duke University Press, 2007), 138; Cedric J. Robinson, *Black Movements in America* (New York: Routledge, 1997), 152; Joy James, "American 'Prison Notebooks,'" *Race and Class* 45, no. 3 (2004): 35–37.

21. Frank "Big Black" Smith quoted in Rebecca N. Hill, *Men, Mobs, and Law,* 309. See also *Attica: Roots of Resistance,* directed by Ashley Hunt (Corrections Documentary Project, 2001).

22. For an elaboration of the concept of a "spatial event" and the revolutionary transformation of space, see Kristin Ross, *The Emergence of Social Space: Rimbaud and the Paris Commune* (1988; reprint, New York: Verso, 2008), 4.

23. Angela Y. Davis, *Abolition Democracy*, 22; Jessica Mitford, *Kind and Usual Punishment*, 249. On "preventative counterrevolution" see Herbert Marcuse, *Counterrevolution and Revolt* (Boston: Beacon Press, 1967), 1–2, and Angela Y. Davis and Bettina Aptheker, "Preface," *If They Come in the Morning*, xiv.

24. Angela Y. Davis, "Lessons: From Attica to Soledad," in *If They Come in the Morning*, 45, 46, 51; Kristin Ross, *The Emergence of Social Space*, 4.

25. Christopher Hill, *The World Turned Upside Down* (1972; reprint, London: Penguin Books, 1991); Nikhil Pal Singh, "The Black Panthers and the 'Undeveloped Country of the Left,'" 57–105; Rebecca N. Hill, *Men, Mobs, and Law,* 309; Angela Y. Davis, "Lessons: From Attica to Soledad," 45; Angela Y. Davis quoted in *Prisons on Fire: George Jackson, Attica, and Black Liberation* (Freedom Archives, CD, 2002).

26. Attica Defense Committee, *Voices from Inside: 7 Interviews with Attica Prisoners* (New York: National Lawyers Guild, 1972).

27. Stuart Hall et al., *Policing the Crisis,* 348–62; Alan Eladio Gómez, "'Nuestras Vidas Corren Casi Paralelas,'" 66; Flip Crawley quoted in *Attica* (1973), directed by Cynthia Firestone.

28. Stuart Hall, "Gramsci and Us," *Marxism Today* (June 1987): 16. Flip Crawley quoted in Tom Wicker, *A Time to Die,* 96–97, and the film *Attica*

(1974), directed by Cynthia Firestone; James C. Scott, *Domination and the Arts of Resistance* (New Haven, CT: Yale University, 1990), 202–27; Daniel Widener, *Black Arts West: Culture and Struggle in Postwar Los Angeles* (Durham, NC: Duke University Press, 2010), 252; Rebecca N. Hill, *Men, Mobs, and Law,* 269; Louis Althusser, *Lenin and Philosophy and Other Essays* (New York: Monthly Review Press, 1971), 15–22, 86.

29. Bert Useem and Peter Kimball, *States of Siege,* 37; Michael E. Deutsch, Dennis Cunningham, and Elizabeth Fink, "Twenty Years Later—Attica Civil Rights Case Finally Cleared for Trial," 13.

30. Tom Wicker, *A Time to Die,* 318; "Rockefeller Bars a Visit to Attica," *New York Times,* September 13, 1971.

31. Heather Thompson, "Rethinking Political Transformation in Postwar America: The Attica Prison Uprising of 1971, Liberalism, and the Rise of the Right," presented at a session organized by the Center for the Study of Work, Labor, and Democracy, University of California, Santa Barbara, February 6, 2009; Bert Useem and Peter Kimball, *States of Siege,* 4.

32. Robert B. McKay et al., *Attica: The Official Report of the New York State Special Commission on Attica* (New York: Bantam Books, 1972), 104–5.

33. Ibid., 113.

34. Jamie Peck, *Constructions of Neoliberal Reason* (New York: Oxford University Press, 2010), 137, 143; Naomi Murakawa, "Origins of the Carceral Crisis: Racial Order as 'Law and Order' in Postwar American Politics," in *Race and American Political Development,* ed. Joseph Lowndes, Julie Novkov, and Dorian T. Warren (New York: Routledge, 2008), 235, 237.

35. Neil Smith, *The New Urban Frontier: Gentrification and the Revanchist City* (New York: Routledge, 1996), 222, and Neil Smith, "Revanchist Planet," *The Urban Reinventors* 3, no. 9 (2009): 13–14. On the ways in which the restructuring of New York in the 1970s provided a model for Reaganism in the 1980s, see William K. Tabb, "The Urban Fiscal Crisis and the Rebirth of Conservatism," in *Civil Rights Since 1787: A Reader on the Black Struggle,* ed. Jonathan Birnbaum and Clarence Taylor (New York: New York University Press, 2000), 753.

36. Manning Marable, *Race, Reform, and Rebellion: The Second Reconstruction and Beyond in Black America, 1945–2006* (1984; reprint, Jackson: University of Mississippi Press, 2007), 128; Mike Davis, "Hell Factories in the Field: A Prison Industrial Complex," *The Nation,* February 20, 1995, 229–34; Christian Parenti, *Lockdown America,* 167, 214–15. On the restructuring of the state form as a political response to neoliberal capitalism, see Ruth Wilson Gilmore, "Globalisation and U.S. Prison Growth," 174.

37. David Harvey, *A Brief History of Neoliberalism,* 45.

38. Neil Smith, "Giuliani Time: The Revanchist 1990s," *Social Text* 16, no. 4 (Winter 1998): 14; H. Bruce Franklin, "The American Prison in the Culture Wars," presented at the Modern Language Association Convention, Washington, DC, 2000, http://andromeda.rutgers.edu/~hbf/priscult.html; David Harvey, *A Brief History of Neoliberalism,* 46, 48; William K. Tabb, "The Urban Fiscal Crisis and the Rebirth of Conservatism," 756.

39. Jamie Peck, *Constructions of Neoliberal Reason,* 140.

40. Jessica Mitford, *Kind and Usual Punishment*, 188–89.

41. Robert McKay et al., *Attica: The Official Report of the New York State Special Commission on Attica*, 467.

42. "Excerpts from the Message by Governor Rockefeller on the State of the State," *New York Times*, January 4, 1973.

43. Eric Schlosser, "The Prison-Industrial Complex," *Atlantic Monthly* (December 1998), http://www.theatlantic.com/magazine/archive/1998/12/the-prison-industrial-complex/4669/; Scott Christianson, *With Liberty for Some*, 273; Julilly Kohler-Hausmann, "'The Attila the Hun Law': New York's Rockefeller Drug Laws and the Making of a Punitive State," *Journal of Social History* 44, no. 1 (Fall 2010): 88; Bert Useem and Peter Kimball, *States of Siege*, 82; Phil Scraton, "Protests and 'Riots' in the Violent Institution," 82; Richard D. Vogel, "Capitalism and Incarceration Revisited," *Monthly Review* 55, no. 4 (September 2003): 38–55.

44. "Michel Foucault on Attica: An Interview," *Telos* 19 (Spring 1974): 156; Michel Foucault, *Discipline and Punish: The Birth of the Prison* (New York: Vintage Books, 1977), 31; "Michel Foucault on Attica," 161. On the "insurrection of subjugated knowledges" see Michel Foucault, *Society Must Be Defended: Lectures at the Collége de France, 1975–76*, trans. David Macey (New York: Picador, 2003), 7, 8; Michel Foucault, "Useless to Revolt?," in *Power: Essential Works of Michel Foucault 1954–1984*, volume 3, ed. James D. Faubion (New York: Free Press, 2000), 449–50; Michel Foucault, *Society Must Be Defended*, 8.

45. Vicky Munro-Bjorklund, "Popular Cultural Images of Criminals and Prisoners Since Attica," *Social Justice* 18, no. 3 (Fall 1991): 48–70; John M. Sloop, *The Cultural Prison: Discourse, Prisoners, and Punishment* (Tuscaloosa: University of Alabama Press, 1996), 145; Kelly Lytle Hernández, Khalil Gibran Muhammad, and Heather Ann Thompson, "Introduction: Constructing the Carceral State," *Journal of American History* 102, no. 1 (June 2015): 21.

46. Robin D. G. Kelley, *Freedom Dreams*, 187; David Roediger, *History Against Misery*, 57. See also D. H. Melhem, "Interview with Jayne Cortez," *MELUS* 21, no. 1 (Spring 1996): 71–79; Yolanda Williams Page, "Jayne Cortez," in *Encyclopedia of African American Women Writers* (Westport, CT: Greenwood Press, 2007), 121–26; Robin D. G. Kelley and Franklin Rosemont, *Black, Brown, and Beige: Surrealist Writings from Africa and the Diaspora* (Austin: University of Texas Press, 2009); Penelope Rosemont, ed., *Surrealist Women: An International Anthology* (Austin: University of Texas Press, 1998), 358.

47. Vincent Harding, Robin D. G. Kelley, and Earl Lewis, *We Changed the World: African Americans, 1945–1970* (New York: Oxford University Press, 1997), 175; Fred Ho, *Wicked Theory, Naked Practice: A Fred Ho Reader*, ed. Diane Fujino (Minneapolis: University of Minnesota, 2009), 141; Stuart Hall, *The Hard Road to Renewal: Thatcherism and the Crisis of the Left* (New York: Verso, 1988), 177–95; Archie Shepp, *Attica Blues* (Verve, 1972); Robin D. G. Kelley, "Dig They Freedom: Meditations on History and the Black Avant-Garde," *Lenox Avenue: A Journal of Interarts Inquiry* 3 (1997): 16, 18; James Smethurst, *The Black Arts Movement: Literary Nationalism in the 1960s and*

1970s (Chapel Hill: University of North Carolina Press, 2005), 142; Robin D.G. Kelley, *Freedom Dreams, 192*; Paul Garon, conversation with the author, August 12, 2009.

48. Alan Eladio Gómez, "Resisting Living Death at Marion Federal Penitentiary, 1972," *Radical History Review* 96 (Fall 2006): 59–60, 65; Alan Eladio Gómez, "'Nuestras Vidas Corren Casi Paralelas,'" 64–96; Marc Mauer, *The Lessons of Marion, the Failure of a Maximum Security Prison: A History and Analysis, with Voices of Prisoners* (1985; reprint, Philadelphia: American Friends Service Committee, 1993), 8–9.

49. Raúl Salinas quoted in Alan Eladio Gómez, "Troubadour of Justice: An Interview with raúlsalinas," *Latino Studies* 6 (2008): 182–83.

50. Alan Eladio Gómez, "Resisting Living Death at Marion Federal Penitentiary, 1972," 58–86. This analysis of the events draws on archival materials on the Marion control unit prisons from the Freedom Archives in San Francisco as well as primary sources gathered by the Committee to End the Marion Lockdown (CEML) that formed in Chicago during the 1980s and 1990s to abolish the use of the control units. On the ideological legitimation of the super-maximum regime, see for example the response of A.M. Rosenthal, "On My Mind; In the Marion Prison," *New York Times,* August 23, 1988, A21, to criticisms of the human-rights abuses, the holding of political prisoners, and torture tactics deployed at Marion in the name of security articulated in Ivan Rakhmanin, "America, Too, Has Its Prisoners of Conscience," *New York Times,* August 23, 1988.

51. Michael Isikoff, "Marion Prison: Hard Time for Hardened Criminals," *Washington Post,* May 28, 1991; John Clark quoted in "Prisoners: Rights and Wrongs," *The '90s* television program, WTTW Chicago Public Media, January 1, 1991, http://mediaburn.org/Video-Priview.128.0.html?uid=5127.

52. *20/20*, ABC News, March 18, 1988.

53. "Protestors Confront Federal Prison Chief," *Chicago Tribune,* November 12, 1988, http://articles.chicagotribune.com/1988-11-12/news/8802150633_1_federal-prison-michael-quinlan-inmates; *20/20*, ABC, March 18, 1988; Marc Mauer, *The Lessons of Marion,* 5, 6; "Human Rights Group Faults Super Security Prisons," *Washington Post,* November 14, 1991; Alan Eladio Gómez, "Resisting Living Death at Marion Federal Penitentiary, 1972," 59.

54. Christian Parenti, *Lockdown America, 167*; Alan Eladio Gómez, "Resisting Living Death at Marion Federal Penitentiary, 1972," 58–59.

55. Paul W. Keve, *Prisons and the American Conscience: A History of U.S. Federal Corrections* (Carbondale: Southern Illinois University, 1991), 186–87; Ruth Wilson Gilmore, *Golden Gulag: Prisons, Surplus, Crisis, and Opposition in Globalizing California* (Berkeley: University of California Press, 2007), 128–80.

56. Ralph Aron quoted in Alan Eladio Gómez, "Resisting Living Death at Marion Federal Penitentiary, 1972," 61; Michael E. Deutsch and Jan Susler, "Political Prisoners in the United States: The Hidden Reality," *Social Justice* 18, no. 3 (1991): 92–106; Cisco Lassiter, "RoboPrison," *Mother Jones* (September–October 1990): 55; Committee to End the Marion Lockdown, *Can't Jail the Spirit: Political Prisoners in the U.S.* (Chicago: Editorial El Coquí Publishers, 1992), 36–38, 83–84; Leonard Peltier, *Prison Writings: My Life Is My Sun*

Dance, ed. Harvey Arden (New York: St. Martin's Press, 1999), 164; Allen Feldman, *Formations of Violence: The Narrative of the Body and Terror in Northern Ireland* (Chicago: University of Chicago Press, 1991), 219.

57. Leonard Peltier, "Statement to Commemorate the 1981 Irish Hunger Strike," August 15, 2006, https://www.liberationnews.org/06–08–15-leonard -peltiers-statement-to-c-html/; Committee to End the Marion Lockdown, "From Alcatraz to Marion to Florence—Control Unit Prisons in the United States" (1992), http://people.umass.edu/~kastor/ceml_articles/cu_in_us.html; Cisco Lassiter, "RoboPrison," 52–61.

58. Marc Mauer, *The Lessons of Marion,* 5; Committee to End the Marion Lockdown, "From Alcatraz to Marion to Florence"; Marion Prisoners' Rights Project, "Response to Report and Recommendations of Breed and Ward Report to the Judiciary Committee on Marion Prison," in *Marion Penitentiary—1985: Oversight Hearing Before the Subcommittee on Courts, Civil Liberties, and the Administration of Justice of the Committee on the Judiciary, House of Representatives, Ninety-Ninth Congress, First Session, on Marion Penitentiary—1985,* June 26, 1985, 99.

59. David Matas, *Allegations of Ill-Treatment in Marion Prison, Illinois, USA* (London: Amnesty International, 1987), 7; Committee to End the Marion Lockdown, "From Alcatraz to Marion to Florence"; Marion Prisoners' Rights Project, "Response to Report," 100; Tom Gibbons, "Human Rights Group Rips Marion Prison," *Chicago Sun-Times,* May 31, 1987, 30.

60. Marc Mauer, *The Lessons of Marion,* 5.

61. Marion Prisoners' Rights Project, "Response to Report," 104.

62. Office of the United Nations High Commissioner for Human Rights, "Convention Against Torture and Other Cruel, Inhuman or Degrading Treatment or Punishment," December 10, 1984, http://www.ohchr.org/EN/ProfessionalInterest/Pages/CAT.aspx.

63. Human Rights Watch, *Prison Conditions in the United States* (New York and Washington, DC: Human Rights Watch Report, 1991), https://www.hrw .org/sites/default/files/reports/US91N.pdf.

64. David A. Ward, *Alcatraz: The Gangster Years* (Berkeley: University of California Press, 2009), 464.

65. David A. Ward and Thomas G. Werlich, "Alcatraz and Marion: Evaluating Supermaximum Custody," *Punishment and Society* 5 (2003): 56–57.

66. David Matas, *Allegations of Ill-Treatment in Marion Prison,* 1–14; Colin Dayan, "Due Process and Lethal Confinement," *South Atlantic Quarterly* 107, no. 3 (Summer 2008): 496.

67. David A. Ward and Norman A. Carlson, "Super-Maximum Custody Prisons in the United States: Why Successful Regimes Remain Controversial," paper delivered at the University of Leicester, England, April 9, 1994; Colin Dayan, "Due Process and Lethal Confinement," 496.

68. Stuart Hall et al., *Policing the Crisis,* 18, 23; Colin Dayan, "Due Process and Lethal Confinement," 485–507; Avery Gordon, "The U.S. Military Prison," 166–86; Hazel Carby, "US/UK's Special Relationship: The Culture of Torture in Abu Ghraib and Lynching Photographs," *Journal of Contemporary African Art* (Fall 2006): 60–71.

69. John M. Sloop, *The Cultural Prison*, 142, 143, 151, 152.

70. Angela Y. Davis, "From the Convict Lease System to the Super-Max Prison," in *States of Confinement: Policing, Detention, and Prisons*, ed. Joy James (New York: St. Marin's Press, 2000), 71–73; Michel Foucault, *Discipline and Punish*, 209; Peter Linebaugh, *The London Hanged: Crime and Civil Society in the Eighteenth Century* (2003; reprint, New York: Verso, 2006), 371–73; Alessandro De Giorgi, *Re-Thinking the Political Economy of Punishment: Perspectives on Post-Fordism and Penal Politics* (Burlington, VT: Ashgate, 2006).

71. For the archive of Mumia Abu-Jamal's radio essays, see the Prison Radio website: http://prisonradio.org/media/audio/Mumia. Following a ten-year moratorium, the death penalty was reinstated in the United States in 1977. See Peter Linebaugh, *The London Hanged*, xvii. On Abu-Jamal's prison writing, see H. Bruce Franklin, ed., *Prison Writing in 20th-Century America* (New York: Penguin Books, 1998), 350.

72. Rebecca N. Hill, *Men, Mobs, and Law*, 20; David Roediger, "Mumia Time or Sweeney Time?," in *Colored White: Transcending the Racial Past* (Berkeley: University of California, 2002), 203–10; Robin D. G. Kelley, foreword to Angela Y. Davis, *The Meaning of Freedom* (San Francisco: City Lights Press, 2012), 9; Dipannita Basu and Sidney J. Lemelle, introduction to *The Vinyl Ain't Final*, ed. Dipannita Basu and Sidney J. Lemelle (London: Pluto Press, 2006), 7; Robin D. G. Kelley, "Some Thoughts on the BRC, the 'Post-Civil Rights Era,' and the History of Black Radicalism," June 20, 1998, http://www.hartford-hwp.com/archives/45a/226.html; Angela Y. Davis, foreword to Mumia Abu-Jamal, *Jailhouse Lawyers: Prisoners Defending Prisoners v. the U.S.A.* (San Francisco: City Lights Books, 2009), 13–19.

73. Mumia Abu-Jamal, *Live from Death Row* (New York: Addison-Wesley Publishing Company, 1995), 90; Atul Gawande, "Hellhole: The United States Holds Tens of Thousands of Inmates in Long-Term Solitary Confinement. Is This Torture?" *The New Yorker*, March 20, 2009; Joy James, *Resisting State Violence: Radicalism, Gender, and Race in U.S. Culture* (Minneapolis: University of Minnesota Press, 1996), 35; Jimmie L. Reeves and Richard Campbell, *Cracked Coverage: Television News, the Anti-Cocaine Crusade, and the Reagan Legacy* (Durham, NC: Duke University Press, 1994), 73, 75; John M. Sloop, *The Cultural Prison*, 90–184.

74. Mumia Abu-Jamal, "Another Reagan, Another America," Prison Radio, June 6, 2004, http://archive.prisonradio.org/maj/maj_6_6_04regan.html; H. Bruce Franklin, ed., *Prison Writing in 20th-Century America* 15; Marie Gottschalk, *The Prison and the Gallows*, 195.

75. Frank Donner, *The Age of Surveillance: The Aims and Methods of America's Political Intelligence System* (New York: Vintage Books, 1981); Christian Parenti, *Lockdown America*, 9; Louis Althusser, *Lenin and Philosophy and Other Essays*, 174. The racist repudiation of civil rights advances in the period is well documented in Manning Marable, *How Capitalism Underdeveloped Black America* (1983; reprint, Cambridge, MA: South End Press, 2000), 242.

76. Nikhil Pal Singh, "Racial Formation in an Age of Permanent War," in *Racial Formation in the Twenty-First Century*, ed. Daniel Martinez HoSang,

Oneka LaBennett, and Laura Pulido (Berkeley: University of California Press, 2012), 280.

77. Anne Braden speech in the film *Anne Braden: Southern Patriot* (2012), directed by Anne Lewis and Mimi Pickering. On the ways in which the rhetoric of Reaganism impacted the interplay of racial and class formation during this conjuncture, see George Lipsitz, *The Possessive Investment in Whiteness: How White People Profit from Identity Politics* (Philadelphia: Temple University Press, 2006), 73.

78. Ronald Reagan quoted in Vijay Prashad, *Keeping Up with the Dow Joneses: Debt, Prisons, Workfare* (Boston: Sound End Press, 2003), xvi.

79. Stuart Hall, *The Hard Road to Renewal*, 138–46; George Lipsitz, *The Possessive Investment in Whiteness*, 78.

80. Christian Parenti, *Lockdown America*, 47; Michael Rogin, *Ronald Reagan, the Movie, and Other Episodes of Political Demonology* (Berkeley: University of California Press, 1987), 77; Joy James, "Erasing the Spectacle of Racialized State Violence," 37; Scott Christianson, *With Liberty for Some*, 297.

81. Scott Christianson, *With Liberty for Some*, 283; Manning Marable, *Race, Reform, and Rebellion*, 193.

82. Marc Mauer, *The Lessons of Marion*, 1, 14, and Marc Mauer, *Race to Incarcerate* (New York: The New Press, 2006).

83. Manning Marable, *How Capitalism Underdeveloped Black America*, 127; Scott Christianson, *With Liberty for Some*, 283; Erica Thompson and Jan Susler, "Supermax Prisons: High-Tech Dungeons and Modern-Day Torture," in *Criminal Injustice*, ed. Elihu Rosenblatt (Cambridge, MA: South End Press, 1996), 303–7; Atul Gawande, "Hellhole"; Daniel P. Mears and Jamie Watson, "Towards a Fair and Balanced Assessment of Supermax Prisons," *Justice Quarterly* 23, no. 2 (June 2006): 232.

84. Mike Davis, "Hell Factories in the Field: A Prison Industrial Complex," *The Nation*, February 20, 1995, 229–34.

85. Jonathan Simon, "Rise of the Carceral State," *Social Research* 74, no. 2 (2007): 494.

86. Department of Corrections, "California Prisoners and Parolees 1993 and 1994," Sacramento, 1996, http://www.cdcr.ca.gov/Reports_Research /Offender_Information_Services_Branch/Annual/CalPris/CALPRISd1994.pdf; Ruth Wilson Gilmore, *Golden Gulag*, 26; Alan Eladio Gómez, "Resisting Living Death at Marion Federal Penitentiary, 1972," 58–86.

87. Craig Haney, "Mental Health Issues in Long-Term Solitary and 'Supermax' Confinement," *Crime and Delinquency* 49, no. 1 (January 2003): 124–56.

88. Craig Haney quoted in Cisco Lassiter, "RoboPrison"; Michelle Brown, "Setting the Conditions for Abu Ghraib: The Prison Nation Abroad," *American Quarterly* 57, no. 3 (2005): 973–97; Neil Smith, "Contours of a Spatialized Politics: Homeless Vehicles and the Production of Geographical Scale," *Social Text* 33 (1992): 58.

89. Mumia Abu-Jamal, *Live from Death Row*, 90; Colin Dayan, "The Least Worst Place," *London Review of Books*, August 2, 2007.

90. Neil Smith, *The Endgame of Globalization* (New York: Routledge, 2005), ix, and Neil Smith, "Revanchist Planet," 11–12.

91. Colin Dayan, "Due Process and Lethal Confinement," 487, 496, 499, 501.

92. Hazel Carby, "US/UK's Special Relationship," 66.

93. David H. Hackworth, "This Was No Riot, It Was a Revolt," *Newsweek*, May 25, 1992.

CHAPTER 4: READING THE WRITING ON THE WALL

1. Ruth Wilson Gilmore, "Terror Austerity Race Gender Excess Theatre," in *Reading Rodney King/Reading Urban Uprising*, ed. Robert Gooding-Williams (New York: Routledge, 1993), 24; Robin D. G. Kelley, "Straight from the Underground," *The Nation*, June 8, 1992, 793–96; Johnny Otis, *Upside Your Head! Rhythm and Blues on Central Avenue* (Middletown, CT: Wesleyan University Press, 1993), 148–52; Gerald Horne, *Fire This Time* (New York: Da Capo Press, 1997), 355–64.

2. Warren Christopher et al., *Report of the Independent Commission on the Los Angeles Police Department* (Los Angeles: Independent Commission of the Los Angeles Police Department, 1991), xii; Daryl Gates quoted in Shelby Coffey, ed., *Understanding the Riots: Los Angeles Before and After the Rodney King Case* (Los Angeles: Los Angeles Times, 1992), 39.

3. Cindi Katz and Neil Smith, "L.A. Intifada: An Interview with Mike Davis," *Social Text* 33 (1992): 20.

4. Chuck D interview with *MTV Week in Rock*, May 1992.

5. Shelby Coffey, ed., *Understanding the Riots*, 37; Cindi Katz and Neil Smith, "L.A. Intifada," 20; Robin D. G. Kelley, "Straight from the Underground," 793; Robin D. G. Kelley, *Race Rebels: Culture, Politics, and the Black Working Class* (New York: The New Press, 1994), 207.

6. For a description of the motley crew that protested in downtown Los Angeles after the verdict, see Ruben Martínez, "Riot Scenes," in *Inside the L.A. Riots: What Really Happened—and Why It Will Happen Again*, ed. Don Hazen (Los Angeles: Institute for Alternative Journalism, 1992): 31; Edward W. Soja, *Postmetropolis: Critical Studies of Regions and Cities* (Malden, MA: Blackwell Publishers, 2000), 379 note 16. For Walter Benjamin's historical and materialist intervention, see his "Theses on the Philosophy of History," in *Illuminations: Essays and Reflections*, ed. Hannah Arendt (New York: Schocken Books, 1968), 257.

7. United Nations Human Settlement Programme, *The Challenge of Slums: Global Report on Human Settlements* (London: Earthscan Publications, 2003), 214; Peter Linebaugh, *The London Hanged: Crime and Civil Society in the Eighteenth Century* (2003; reprint, New York: Verso, 2006), 443. For an exploration of the debated meaning of the urban uprisings—or "riots"—in postwar U.S. history, see Heather Ann Thompson, "Understanding Rioting in Postwar America," *Journal of Urban History* 26, no. 3 (March 2000): 391–402.

8. Mike Davis, *Ecology of Fear: Los Angeles and the Imagination of Disaster* (New York: Metropolitan Books, 1998), 373–74; Edward W. Soja, *Postmetropolis*, 143; Ruth Wilson Gilmore, *Golden Gulag: Prisons, Surplus, Crisis, and Opposition in Globalizing California* (Berkeley: University of California

Press, 2007), 50; Richard Walker, "California Rages Against the Dying of the Light," *New Left Review*, no. 209 (1995): 43; Mike Davis, "In L.A., Burning All Illusions," *The Nation*, June 1, 1992, 743–46; Gerald Horne, *Fire This Time*, 355–64; ; Robin D. G. Kelley, "Straight From the Underground," 796.

9. Vijay Prashad, *Everybody Was Kung Fu Fighting: Afro-Asian Connections and the Myth of Cultural Purity* (Minneapolis: University of Minnesota Press, 2001), 104.

10. Eric Tang, "A Gulf Unites Us: The Vietnamese Americans of Black New Orleans East," *American Quarterly* 63, no. 1 (2011): 140.

11. American Civil Liberties Union of Southern California (ACLU/SC), *Civil Liberties in Crisis: Los Angeles During the Emergency* (June 23, 1992).

12. George Bush, address to the nation on the civil disturbances in Los Angeles, May 1, 1992, http://www.presidency.ucsb.edu/ws/index.php?pid=20910; Daniel Widener, "Another City Is Possible: Interethnic Organizing in Contemporary Los Angeles," *Race/Ethnicity: Multidisciplinary Global Perspectives* 1, no. 2 (Spring 2008): 190; Giorgio Agamben, *State of Exception*, trans. Kevin Attell (Chicago: University of Chicago Press, 2005). For an example of the discourse of mob rule and its attendant visual representations, see Shelby Coffey, ed., *Understanding the Riots*, 61. On the depictions of mass protests as mob behavior to justify repression, see David Harvey, *Spaces of Global Capitalism: Towards a Theory of Uneven Geographical Development* (New York: Verso, 2006), 27; Martha Huggins, *Political Policing: The United States and Latin America* (Durham, NC: Duke University Press, 1998), 2–3.

13. Shelby Coffey, ed., *Understanding the Riots*, 45, 56, 61, 63, 65, 67, 68, 72, 75; Paul Gilroy, *"There Ain't No Black in the Union Jack": The Cultural Politics of Race and Nation* (Chicago: University of Chicago Press, 1991), 108. On the militarization of Southern California, see Mike Davis, *Ecology of Fear*, 361; Gerald Horne, *Fire This Time*, 356.

14. Ruth Gilmore, *Golden Gulag*, 7; California Department of Corrections, *California Prisoners and Parolees*, 2000, http://www.cdcr.ca.gov/Reports_Research/Offender_Information_Services_Branch/Annual/CalPris/CAL-PRISd2000.pdf; Neil Smith, *The New Urban Frontier: Gentrification and the Revanchist City* (New York: Routledge, 1996), 211; Cedric J. Robinson, "Race, Capitalism, and Antidemocracy," in *Reading Rodney King/Reading Urban Uprising*, 77; Janet L. Abu-Lughod, *Race, Space, and Riots in Chicago, New York, and Los Angeles* (New York: Oxford University Press, 2007), 285, 286; Stuart Hall et al., *Policing the Crisis: Mugging, the State, and Law and Order* (London: MacMillan Press, 1978), 304–5.

15. Janet L. Abu-Lughod, *Race, Space, and Riots in Chicago, New York, and Los Angeles*, 291, 292.

16. Mike Davis, "The Embers of April 1992," *Los Angeles Review of Books*, April 30, 2012, https://lareviewofbooks.org/essay/the-embers-of-april-1992; Mike Davis, *Ecology of Fear*, 364; George Lipsitz, "We Know What Time It Is: Race, Class, and Youth Culture in the Nineties," in *Microphone Fiends: Youth Music & Youth Culture*, ed. Andrew Ross and Tricia Rose (New York: Routledge, 1994), 17–28; Hazel V. Carby, *Cultures in Babylon: Black Britain and African America* (New York: Verso, 1999), 100–103; Edward W. Soja,

Postmetropolis, 398; Cindi Katz, "Childhood as Spectacle: Relays of Anxiety and the Reconfiguration of the Child," *Cultural Geographies* 15 (2008): 5–17.

17. Robin D. G. Kelley, *Race Rebels,* 183–227; Paul Gilroy, "One Nation Under a Groove: The Cultural Politics of 'Race' and Racism in Britain," in *Anatomy of Racism,* ed. David Theo Goldberg (Minneapolis: University of Minnesota Press, 1990), 265; Daniel Widener, *Black Arts West: Culture and Struggle in Postwar Los Angeles* (Durham, NC: Duke University Press, 2010), 250–82; Victor Viesca, "Battle of Los Angeles," *American Quarterly* 56, no. 3 (September 2004): 720; Verta Taylor, "Social Movement Continuity: The Women's Movement in Abeyance, " *American Sociological Review* 54 (1989): 761–75; George Lipsitz, "We Know What Time It Is," 17–28; Robin D. G. Kelley, "'Slangin' Rocks . . . Palestinian Style,' Dispatches from the Occupied Zones of North America," in *Police Brutality,* ed. Jill Nelson (New York: W. W. Norton and Company, 2000); 50; Mike Davis, *Dead Cities* (New York: The New Press, 2002), 232; Jason Hackworth, *The Neoliberal City: Governance, Ideology, and Development in American Urbanism* (Ithaca, NY: Cornell University Press, 2007).

18. David H. Hackworth, "This Was No Riot, It Was a Revolt," *Newsweek,* May 25, 1992; U.S. Army and Marine Corps, *Counter-Insurgency Field Manual: U.S. Army Field Manual No. 3–24* (Chicago: University of Chicago Press, 2007), xxiii.

19. "Uprising and Repression in L.A.: An Interview with Mike Davis by the *CovertAction Information Bulletin,*" in *Reading Rodney King / Reading Urban Uprising,* 150.

20. Ranajit Guha, *Elementary Aspects of Peasant Insurgency in Colonial India* (Durham, NC: Duke University Press, 1999), 16–17.

21. Mike Davis, *City of Quartz: Excavating the Future in Los Angeles* (New York: Verso, 2006), 223–24. The concept of the "carceral city" was introduced in Michel Foucault, *Discipline and Punish: The Birth of the Prison* (New York: Vintage Books, 1977), 307. For the broader political and economic shifts underpinning the restructuring of urban space in this period, see Neil Smith, *The New Urban Frontier,* 211, 213–14, 220, 222.

22. Daniel Martinez HoSang, *Racial Propositions: Ballot Initiatives and the Making of Postwar California* (Berkeley: University of California Press, 2010), 265.

23. Richard Walker, "California Rages Against the Dying of the Light," 43; Gilda Haas, *Plant Closures: Myths, Realities and Responses* (Boston: South End Press, 1985), 12; Mike Davis, *City of Quartz,* vi, 267–316; Robin D. G. Kelley, *Race Rebels,* 202.

24. William I. Robinson, *Promoting Polyarchy: Globalization, U.S. Intervention, and Hegemony* (New York: Cambridge University Press, 1996); Greg Grandin, *Empire's Workshop: Latin America, the United States, and the Rise of the New Imperialism* (New York: Metropolitan Books, 2006), 8, 122–23, 143; Michael Rogin, *Ronald Reagan, the Movie, and Other Episodes of Political Demonology* (Berkeley: University of California Press, 1987).

25. Mike Davis, "Who Killed Los Angeles? Part Two: The Verdict Is Given," *New Left Review* 1, no. 199 (1993): 47 note 35; Timothy J. Dunn, "Border

Militarization via Drug and Immigration Enforcement: Human Rights Implications," *Social Justice* 28, no. 2 (2001): 7–30; Gaye Theresa Johnson, "A Sifting of Centuries: Afro-Chicano Interaction and Popular Musical Culture in California, 1960–2000," in *Decolonial Voices: Chicana and Chicano Cultural Studies in the 21st Century,* ed. Arturo J. Aldama and Naomi H. Quiñonez (Bloomington: Indiana University Press, 2002), 320–23; David Harvey, *Spaces of Global Capitalism,* 59, 26, 49.

26. Melvin L. Oliver et al., "Anatomy of a Rebellion: A Political-Economic Analysis," in *Reading Rodney King / Reading Urban Uprising,* 122; Mike Davis, *City of Quartz,* 272, 267–316; Robin D. G. Kelley, *Race Rebels,* 202, and Robin D. G. Kelley, "'Slangin' Rocks . . . Palestinian Style,'" 46.

27. Ruth Wilson Gilmore, *Golden Gulag,* 28, 50; Neil Smith, "Revanchist Planet," *The Urban Reinventors* 3, no. 9 (2009): 16; Mike Davis, *Ecology of Fear,* 372; Maxine Waters, "Testimony Before the Senate Banking Committee," in *Inside the L.A. Riots,* 26; Gerald Horne, *Fire This Time,* 361; David R. Roediger, *How Race Survived U.S. History: From Settlement and Slavery to the Obama Phenomenon* (New York: Verso, 2008), x–xvi, 169–230.

28. Mike Davis, *Ecology of Fear,* 373; Vijay Prashad, *Keeping Up with the Dow Joneses: Debt, Prisons, Workfare* (Cambridge, MA: South End Press, 2003), xv; Gary Blasi and the UCLA School of Law Fact Investigation Clinic, *Policing Our Way Out of Homelessness? The First Year of the Safer Cities Initiative on Skid Row* (Los Angeles: UCLA and USC Center for Sustainable Cities, September 24, 2007), 5, 10; The Labor/Community Strategy Center, *Reconstructing Los Angeles from the Bottom Up: A Long-Term Strategy for Workers, Low-Income People, and People of Color to Create an Alternative Vision of Urban Development* (Los Angeles: Labor/Community Strategy Center, 1993): 31–32.

29. Ruth Wilson Gilmore, *Golden Gulag,* 204; "Uprising and Repression in L.A.: An Interview with Mike Davis," 144; Robin D. G. Kelley, *Race Rebels,* 78.

30. Ruben Martínez, "Riot Scenes," 32; Cynthia Hamilton, "The Making of an American Bantustan," in *Inside the L.A. Riots,* 20; Edward W. Soja, *Postmetropolis,* 379, 387.

31. Ruth Wilson Gilmore, *Golden Gulag,* 72; Rebecca N. Hill, *Men, Mobs, and Law: Anti-Lynching and Labor Defense in U.S. Radical History* (Durham, NC: Duke University Press, 2009), 7; Neil Smith, "Contours of a Spatialized Politics: Homeless Vehicles and the Production of Geographical Scale," *Social Text* 33 (1992): 54–81; The Labor/Community Strategy Center, *Reconstructing Los Angeles from the Bottom Up,* 5.

32. ACLU/SC, *Civil Liberties in Crisis,* v–vi. James H. Johnson, Cloyzelle K. Jones, Walter C. Farrell Jr., and Melvin L. Oliver, "The Los Angeles Rebellion: A Retrospective View," *Economic Development Quarterly* 6, no. 4 (1992): 357.

33. Sylvester Monroe, "The Struggle Over Who Will Rebuild L.A.," *Time,* July 13, 1992, http://www.time.com/time/magazine/article/0,9171,976003,00.html.

34. The Labor/Community Strategy Center, *Reconstructing Los Angeles from the Bottom Up,* 46; Robin D. G. Kelley, *Yo' Mama's Disfunktional! Fighting the Culture Wars in Urban America* (Boston: Beacon Press, 1997), 150.

35. Manning Marable, *Race, Reform, and Rebellion: The Second Reconstruction and Beyond in Black America, 1945–2006* (1984; reprint, Jackson: University of Mississippi Press, 2007), 225; Christian Parenti, *Lockdown America: Police and Prisons in the Age of Crisis* (1999; reprint, New York: Verso, 2000), 142; Marc Mauer, *Race to Incarcerate* (New York: The New Press, 2006), 78; Neil Smith, "Giuliani Time: The Revanchist 1990s," *Social Text* 57 (Winter 1998): 11.

36. Matthew Frye Jacobson, "Where We Stand: U.S. Empire at Street Level and in the Archive," *American Quarterly* 65, no. 2 (2013): 280–83; Susan George, "How to Win the War of Ideas: Lessons from the Gramscian Right," *Dissent* (Summer 1997): 49; Henry A. Giroux, "Mis/Education and Zero Tolerance: Disposable Youth and the Politics of Domestic Militarization," *boundary 2* 28, no. 3 (2001): 63.

37. Miguel Pickard, "In the Crossfire: Mesoamerican Migrants Journey North," americaspolicy.org, March 18, 2005; David Manuel Hernández, "Pursuant to Deportation: Latinos and Immigrant Detention," *Latino Studies* 6 (2008): 41; Christina Jose Kampfner, "Las Mujeres Olvidadas: Women in Mexican Prisons," in *Global Lockdown: Race, Gender and the Prison-Industrial Complex,* ed. Julia Sudbury (New York: Routledge, 2005), 127–36; Juanita Díaz-Cotto, "Latinas and the War on Drugs in the United States, Latin America, and Europe," in *Global Lockdown,* 141–43.

38. Bill Clinton quoted in Barbara Vobejda, "Clinton Signs Welfare Bill Amid Division," *Washington Post,* August 23, 1996, https://www.washingtonpost.com/wp-srv/politics/special/welfare/stories/wf082396.htm; Manning Marable, *Race, Reform, and Rebellion,* 225.

39. Richard Walker, "California Rages Against the Dying of the Light," 45, 49, 60, 72; Manning Marable, *Race, Reform, and Rebellion,* 221; George Lipsitz, "'Home Is Where the Hatred Is': Work, Music, and the Transnational Economy," in *The Chicana/o Cultural Studies Reader,* ed. Angie Chabram-Dernersesian (New York: Routledge, 2006), 301.

40. The Labor/Community Strategy Center, *Reconstructing Los Angeles from the Bottom Up,* 46, 42; Robin D. G. Kelley, *Yo' Mama's Disfunktional!,* 150. In using the concept of polyculturalism I am drawing on the following works: Robin D. G. Kelley, "Polycultural Me," *Colorlines* 2, no. 1 (September–October 1999); Vijay Prashad, *Everybody Was Kung Fu Fighting,* xi, 65–69; Victor Hugo Viesca, "Native Guns and Stray Bullets: Cultural Activism and Filipino American Rap Music in Post-Riot Los Angeles," *Amerasia Journal* 38, no. 1 (2012): 116, 119–22. On spatial justice, see Edward W. Soja, *Seeking Spatial Justice* (Minneapolis: University of Minnesota Press, 2010).

41. June Jordan, "Burning All Illusions Tonight," in *Inside the L.A. Riots,* 77–78; Bob Marley and the Wailers, "Burnin' and Lootin'," *Burnin'* (Tuff Gong/Island, 1973). This analysis follows the lead of Peter Linebaugh, "All the Atlantic Mountains Shook," *Labour/Le Traveailleur* 10 (Autumn 1982): 87–121; Peter Linebaugh and Marcus Rediker, *The Many-Headed Hydra: Sailors, Slaves, Commoners, and the Hidden History of the Revolutionary Atlantic* (Boston: Beacon Press, 2001); Paul Gilroy, *Darker Than Blue: On the Moral Economies of Black Atlantic Culture* (Cambridge, MA: Harvard University Press, 2010), 106.

42. On 1973 as a critical turning point in the history of capitalism, see David Harvey, *The Condition of Postmodernity: An Enquiry Into the Origins of Cultural Change* (Cambridge, MA: Blackwell, 1989), 140. For original and generative analysis of the crisis of hegemony in the Atlantic world, see Stuart Hall, *The Hard Road to Renewal: Thatcherism and the Crisis of the Left* (New York: Verso, 1988), 2; Mike Davis, *City of Quartz*, 224; Paul Gilroy, "One Nation Under a Groove: The Cultural Politics of 'Race' and Racism in Britain," in *Anatomy of Racism*, 278; Horace Campbell, *Rasta and Resistance: From Marcus Garvey to Walter Rodney* (Trenton, NJ: Africa World Press, 1987), 140.

43. Paul Gilroy, "Steppin' Out of Babylon: Race, Class, and Autonomy," in *The Empire Strikes Back: Race and Racism in 70s Britain,* ed. University of Birmingham Centre for Contemporary Cultural Studies (London: Centre for Contemporary Cultural Studies, Routledge, 1982), 293–94; George Lipsitz, *Dangerous Crossroads: Popular Music, Postmodernism and the Poetics of Place* (New York: Verso, 1994). On the politics embedded in the music produced by Bob Marley and the Wailers, and particularly the influence of Walter Rodney's lectures on Marxist theory in the "grounding" sessions with Rastafarians, see Horace Campbell, *Rasta and Resistance,* 136; Walter Rodney, *The Groundings with My Brothers* (1969; reprint, London: Bogle-L'Ouverture Publications, 1990), 61, 64. On the ways in which Marley became the voice of the Third World political project, see Vijay Prashad, *The Darker Nations: A People's History of the Third World* (New York: The New Press, 200), 228. On reggae's depiction the dialectics of change, see Paul Gilroy, *"There Ain't No Black in the Union Jack,"* 72–113. For an exploration of Marley's role as a prophetic social critic and why his insurgent poetics continued to resonate across the planet well into the twenty-first century, see Anthony Bogues, *Black Heretics, Black Prophets: Radical Political Intellectuals* (New York: Routledge, 2003), chapter 7.

44. Paul Gilroy, *The Black Atlantic: Modernity and Double Consciousness* (Cambridge, MA: Harvard University Press); Paul Gilroy, *Darker Than Blue,* 106, 107; June Jordan, "Burning All Illusions Tonight," 77.

45. Cedric J. Robinson, "Race, Capitalism, and Antidemocracy," 73–81; Daniel Widener, "Another City Is Possible," 190; Victor Hugo Viesca, "Native Guns and Stray Bullets,"139 note 23; Vijay Prashad, *Everybody Was Kung Fu Fighting,* 103.

46. June Jordan, "Burning All Illusions Tonight," 78; Melvin L. Oliver et al., "Anatomy of a Rebellion," 118. My analysis of the expressive culture of the revolt has benefited a great deal from Paul Gilroy, "Police and Thieves," in *The Empire Strikes Back,* 145. On struggles for dignity, see John Holloway, "Dignity's Revolt," in *Zapatista! Reinventing Revolution in Mexico,* ed. John Holloway and Eloína Peláez (London: Pluto Press, 1998), 159–98; Manuel Callahan, ed., "Zapatismo as Political and Cultural Practice," *Humboldt Journal of Social Relations* 29, no. 1 (Spring 2005); Alan Goméz, "From Below and to the Left: Re-Imagining Chicano/a Movements Through the Circulation of Third World Struggles, 1970–1979" (PhD diss., University of Texas at Austin, 2006); Luis Alvarez, *The Power of the Zoot: Youth Culture and Resistance During World War II* (Berkeley: University of California Press, 2008), 8.

47. Robin D. G. Kelley, "Straight from the Underground," 796; Mike Davis, *Dead Cities*, 227–37.

48. Martín Espada, *Zapata's Disciple* (Cambridge, MA: South End Press, 1998), 100, 93, 91.

49. Robin D. G. Kelley, "Straight from the Underground," 796; George Lipsitz, "Con Safos: Can Cultural Studies Read the Writing on the Wall," in *The Chicana/o Cultural Studies Reader*, 47–60.

50. Raul Villa, *Barrio-Logos: Space and Place in Urban Chicano Literature and Culture* (Austin: University of Texas, 2000); José Ramírez, interview with the author, February 10, 2011; Victor Viesca, "Battle of Los Angeles," 727; George Lipsitz, *Footsteps in the Dark: The Hidden Histories of Popular Music* (Minneapolis: University of Minnesota Press, 2007), 61–63, 69, 72, 76; Mike Davis, *Dead Cities*, 228.

51. George Lipsitz, *Footsteps in the Dark*, 61–63, 69, 72, 76; José Ramírez, interview with the author, February 10, 2011.

52. Luis Alvarez, "From Zoot Suits to Hip Hop: Towards a Relational Chicana/o Studies," *Latino Studies* 5 (2007): 67; Victor Viesca, "Battle of Los Angeles," 734; Gaye Theresa Johnson, "A Sifting of Centuries," 320–23; Daniel Widener, "Another City Is Possible," 189–219.

53. John Berger, *Ways of Seeing* (London: Penguin Books, 1972); David Manuel Hernández, "Pursuant to Deportation: Latinos and Immigrant Detention," *Latino Studies* 6 (2008): 35–63; Walter Benjamin, "Theses on the Philosophy of History," 224, 260; George Lipsitz, "The Possessive Investment in Whiteness: Racialized Social Democracy and the 'White' Problem in American Studies," *American Quarterly* 47, no. 3 (September 1995): 369–87; Daniel Widener, *Black Arts West*, 250–82.

54. The Chicago Surrealist Group, "Three Days That Shook the New World Order," *Race Traitor* 2 (Summer 1993): 1–17; Walter Benjamin, *The Arcades Project* (Cambridge, MA: Harvard University Press, 1999), 473.

55. Michael Denning, *The Cultural Front: The Laboring of American Culture in the Twentieth Century* (New York: Verso, 1998); Gaye Theresa Johnson, *Spaces of Conflict, Sounds of Solidarity: Music, Race, and Spatial Entitlement in Los Angeles* (Berkeley: University of California Press, 2013), 180–88; Josh Kun, *Audiotopia: Music, Race, and America* (Berkeley: University of California Press, 2005), 219–25; Victor Viesca, "Battle of Los Angeles," 724; Daniel Widener, "Another City Is Possible," 191, 205. On the potential for counterhegemonic alliances in expressive culture, see George Lipsitz, "Cruising Around the Historical Bloc: Postmodernism and Popular Music in East Los Angeles," *Cultural Critique* 5 (1986–87): 165.

56. Russell Rodríguez, "Agustín Lira and Alma & Quetzal: Cantos de mi Cantón (Songs from My Home) Chicano Music from California," American Folklife Center at the Library of Congress, September 14, 2011, http://www.loc.gov/folklife/events/HomegrownArchives/2011flyers/AlmaAndQuetzalFlyer.html; Russell Rodríguez, liner notes to Quetzal's album *Imaginaries* (Smithsonian Folkways Recordings, 2011).

57. Chris Barton, "Rage Against the Machine's Fiery Legacy," *Los Angeles Times*, November 26, 2012, http://articles.latimes.com/2012/nov/26/entertainment

/la-et-ms-rage-against-machine-notebook-20121127; Zach de la Rocha quoted in "The 100 Best Debut Albums of All Time," *Rolling Stone,* http://www.rollingstone .com/music/lists/the-100-greatest-debut-albums-of-all-time-20130322/rage-against-the-machine-19691231.

58. Matthew Duersten, "Ozomatli's Map of Your World," *Los Angeles Magazine,* June 26, 2014, http://www.lamag.com/culturefiles/ozomatlis-map -of-your-world/; Raul Campos interview with Ozomatli, *Which Way, L.A.?,* KCRW 89.9 FM, Santa Monica, California, April 29, 1992, http://blogs.kcrw .com/whichwayla/2012/04/ozomatlis-la-rebellion-playlist.

59. Victor Viesca, "Battle of Los Angeles," 725–26, 730; Daniel Widener, "Another City Is Possible," 205.

60. David Roediger, *Towards the Abolition of Whiteness* (New York: Verso, 1994), 17; Vijay Prashad, *Everybody Was Kung Fu Fighting,* 69.

61. June Jordan, "Burning All Illusions Tonight," 78; Vijay Prashad, *Everybody Was Kung Fu Fighting,* 69; Paul Ortiz, "The Battle of New Orleans," in *Hurricane Katrina: Response and Responsibilities,* ed. John Brown Childs (Santa Cruz, CA: New Pacific Press, 2008), 4.

62. Karl Marx, *The Eighteenth Brumaire of Louis Bonaparte* (1963; reprint, New York: International Publishers, 2004), 118; Nicholas De Genova, "The 'War on Terror' as Racial Crisis: Homeland Security, Obama, and Racial (Trans)Formations," *Racial Formation in the Twenty-First Century,* ed. Daniel Martinez HoSang, Oneka LaBennett, and Laura Pulido (Berkeley: University of California Press, 2012), 246.

CHAPTER 5: WHAT'S GOING ON?

1. Clyde Woods, "Do You Know What It Means to Miss New Orleans? Katrina, Trap Economics, and the Rebirth of the Blues," *American Quarterly* 57, no. 4 (2005): 1005–18; Neil Smith, "There's No Such Thing as a Natural Disaster," in *Understanding Katrina: Perspectives from the Social Sciences* (Social Science Research Council, June 11, 2006), http://understandingkatrina .ssrc.org/Smith/; George Lipsitz, *How Racism Takes Place* (Philadelphia: Temple University Press, 2011), 211; David Theo Goldberg, *The Threat of Race: Reflections on Racial Neoliberalism* (Malden, MA: Blackwell, 2009), 89–91; Stephen Graham, *Cities Under Siege: The New Military Urbanism* (New York: Verso, 2010), 25; Kathleen Tierney, Christine Bevc, and Erica Kuligowski, "Metaphors Matter: Disaster Myths, Media Frames, and Their Consequences in Hurricane Katrina," *Annals of the American Academy* 604 (March 2006): 61; D'Ann R. Penner and Keith C. Ferdinand, eds., *Overcoming Katrina: African American Voices from the Crescent City and Beyond* (New York: Palgrave MacMillan, 2009), xvii.

2. See for example Joseph B. Treaster and Kate Zernike, "Hurricane Katrina Slams Into Gulf Coast; Dozens Are Dead," *New York Times,* August 30, 2005, http://www.nytimes.com/2005/08/30/national/30storm.html; Joseph B. Treaster and N.R. Kleinfield, "New Orleans Is Now Off Limits; Pentagon Joins in Relief Effort," *New York Times,* August 31, 2005, http://www.nytimes.com/2005/08/31 /national/nationalspecial/31storm.html; D'Ann R. Penner and Keith C. Ferdinand,

eds., *Overcoming Katrina*, xvi; George Lipsitz, "Learning from New Orleans: The Social Warrant of Hostile Privatism and Competitive Consumer Citizenship," *Cultural Anthropology* 21, no. 3 (2006): 454; "Troops Told to 'Shoot to Kill,'" ABC News, September 2, 2005, http://www.abc.net.au/news/2005-09-02/troops-told-shoot-to-kill-in-new-orleans/2094678.

3. Wendy Cheng and Michelle Commander, "Language Matters: Hurricane Katrina and Media Responsibility," in *Hurricane Katrina: Response and Responsibilities,* ed. John Brown Childs (Santa Cruz, CA: New Pacific Press, 2008), 93; Clyde Woods, "'Sittin' on Top of the World': The Challenges of Blues and Hip Hop Geography," in *Black Geographies and the Politics of Place,* ed. Katherine McKittrick and Clyde Woods (Cambridge, MA: South End Press, 2007), 47–48; Paul Gilroy, *"There Ain't No Black in the Union Jack":* *The Cultural Politics of Race and Nation* (Chicago: University of Chicago Press, 1991); Michel Foucault, *Society Must Be Defended: Lectures at the Collège de France, 1975–76,* trans. David Macey (New York: Picador, 2003), 56; Amy Kaplan, "Homeland Insecurities: Reflections on Language and Space," *Radical History Review* 85 (Winter 2003): 88; David McNally, *Global Slump: The Economics and Politics of Crisis and Resistance* (Oakland, CA: PM Press, 2011), 138–40.

4. Stephen Graham, *Cities Under Siege,* 23, xvi, xvii; Kathleen Tierney, Christine Bevc, and Erica Kuligowski, "Metaphors Matter," 72.

5. Clyde Woods, "Les Misérables of New Orleans: Trap Economics and the Asset Stripping Blues, Part 1," *American Quarterly* 61, no. 3 (2009): 775, and Clyde Woods, "Katrina's World: Blues, Bourbon, and the Return to the Source," *American Quarterly* 61, no. 3 (September 2009): 444; National Prison Project of the American Civil Liberties Union, "Abandoned and Abused: Prisoners in the Wake of Hurricane Katrina," *Race and Class* 49, no. 1 (2007): 83.

6. Lydia Pelot-Hobbs, "Louisiana Lockdown," in *Unfathomable City: A New Orleans Atlas,* ed. Rebecca Solnit and Rebecca Snedeker (Berkeley: University of California Press, 2013), 55, 58; Justice Policy Institute, "Louisiana Leads the Nation and the World in Lock Up Prison and Jails: Expensive—Not Keeping Communities Safer," http://criticalresistance.net/katrina/louisiana-leads.html; Jordan Flaherty, "Imprisoned in New Orleans," *Colorlines* 32, March 21, 2006, http://www.colorlines.com/articles/imprisoned-new-orleans; Spatial Information Design Lab, *Justice Reinvestment New Orleans* (New York: Columbia University Graduate School of Architecture, Planning and Preservation, February 2009), 16, 17.

7. Angela Y. Davis, "Race and Criminalization: Black Americans and the Punishment Industry," in *The Angela Y. Davis Reader,* ed. Joy James (Malden, MA: Blackwell, 1998), 66; Aaron Kinney, "'Looting' or 'Finding'?" Salon.com, September 1, 2005, http://www.salon.com/2005/09/02/photo_controversy/.

8. Human Rights Watch, "New Orleans: Prisoners Abandoned to Floodwaters," September 22, 2005, https://www.hrw.org/news/2005/09/21/new-orleans-prisoners-abandoned-floodwaters; Gwen Filosa, "ACLU Sues Over Arrest," *Times-Picayune,* January 27, 2007; "At the Train Station, New Orleans' Newest Jail Is Open for Business," Komo TV, September 6, 2005, http://www.komonews.com/news/archive/4163081.html; Marina Sideris and the Criti-

cal Resistance Amnesty Working Group, "Amnesty for Prisoners of Katrina: A Special Report," Critical Resistance New Orleans, December 2007; Allen Feldman, *Formations of Violence: The Narrative of the Body and Political Terror in Northern Ireland* (Chicago: University of Chicago Press, 1991), 109; Ruth Wilson Gilmore, *Golden Gulag: Prisons, Surplus, Crisis, and Opposition in Globalizing California* (Berkeley: University of California Press, 2007), 25; "Angela Davis Speaks Out on Prisons and Human Rights Abuses in the Aftermath of Hurricane Katrina," DemocracyNow.org, December 28, 2006. For a visual representation of the abolitionist struggle to gain amnesty for "Prisoners of Katrina," see the film *I Won't Drown on That Levee and You Ain't Gonna' Break My Back,* directed by Ashley Hunt (Corrections Documentary Project, 2006).

9. Susan Willis, *Specifying: Black Women Writing the American Experience* (Madison: University of Wisconsin, 1987), 15–16, 25; Clyde Woods, "Do You Know What It Means to Miss New Orleans?," 1005; Bessie Smith, "Back Water Blues" (Columbia, 1927); Richard Wright, *Uncle Tom's Children* (New York: Harper and Brothers, 1940); Ruth Wilson Gilmore, "Scholar-Activists in the Mix," *Progress in Human Geography* 29, no. 2 (2005): 177–82; Joy James, "Political Literacy and Voice," in *What Lies Beneath: Katrina, Race, and the State of the Nation,* ed. South End Press Collective (Cambridge, MA: South End Press, 2007), 158, 159, 164; Hazel V. Carby, *Cultures in Babylon: Black Britain and African America* (New York: Verso, 1999), 9.

10. The Dirty Dozen Brass Band, *What's Going On* (Shout Factory, 2006); E. Ethelbert Miller, "An Interview with Kalamu ya Salaam" *Foreign Policy in Focus,* May 15, 2007, http://www.fpif.org/articles/interview_with_kalamu_ya _salaam; Suzanne E. Smith, *Dancing in the Street: Motown and the Cultural Politics of Detroit* (Cambridge, MA: Harvard University Press, 1999), 237.

11. David Ritz, *Divided Soul: The Life of Marvin Gaye* (New York: Da Capo Press, 1985), 152; Suzanne E. Smith, *Dancing in the Street,* 16, 237–39. For a comparative analysis of urban uprisings, see Janet L. Abu-Lughod, *Race, Space, and Riots in Chicago, New York, and Los Angeles* (New York: Oxford University Press, 2007).

12. Paul Gilroy, *"There Ain't No Black in the Union Jack,"* 171–87; David Harvey, *Rebel Cities: From the Right to the City to the Urban Revolution* (New York: Verso, 2012).

13. Robin D. G. Kelley, *Race Rebels: Culture, Politics, and the Black Working Class* (New York: New Press, 1994), 207; Rebecca N. Hill, *Men, Mobs, and Law: Anti-Lynching and Labor Defense in U.S. Radical History* (Durham, NC: Duke University Press, 2009), 3; Charles Tilly, *Contentious Performances* (New York: Cambridge University Press, 2008); Neil Smith, "Urban Politics, Urban Security," lecture delivered at Harvard Graduate School, Cambridge, MA, September 29, 2010; Hazel V. Carby, *Cultures in Babylon,* 36.

14. David Roediger, *The Wages of Whiteness: Race and the Making of the American Working Class* (1991; reprint, New York: Verso, 2007), 15.

15. Ruth Wilson Gilmore, "Race, Prisons, and War: Scenes from the History of U.S. Violence," *Socialist Register* 45 (2009): 73–87; Avery F. Gordon, "Abu Ghraib: Imprisonment and the War on Terror," *Race and Class* 48, no. 1 (2006): 52.

16. Walter Benjamin, "Theses on the Philosophy of History," in *Illuminations: Essays and Reflections,* ed. Hannah Arendt (New York: Schocken Books, 1968), 255, 262; George Lipsitz, *The Possessive Investment in Whiteness: How White People Profit from Identity Politics* (Philadelphia: Temple University Press, 2006), 1–2.

17. Kim Lacy Rogers, *Righteous Lives: Narratives of the New Orleans Civil Rights Movement* (New York: New York University Press, 1993); Neil Smith, "Revanchist Planet," *The Urban Reinventors* 3, no. 9 (2009): 3–18; Cedric J. Robinson, *Black Marxism: The Making of the Black Radical Tradition* (1983; reprint, Chapel Hill: University of North Carolina Press, 2000), 308; Ruth Wilson Gilmore, "Eleven Theses," presented at the symposium "Cedric Robinson's Radical Thought: Toward Critical Social Theories and Practice," University of California, Santa Barbara, November 5–7, 2004.

18. Robin D. G. Kelley, *Freedom Dreams: The Black Radical Imagination* (Boston: Beacon Press, 2002), 9–12, 184–94; Ruth Wilson Gilmore, "Fatal Couplings of Power and Difference: Notes on Racism and Geography," *Professional Geographer* 54, no. 1 (2002): 15–24; Robin D. G. Kelley, foreword to *Pedagogy, Policy, and the Privatized City: Stories of Dispossession and Defiance from New Orleans,* ed. Kristen L. Buras with Jim Randels, Kalamu Ya Salaam, and Students at the Center (New York: Teachers College Press, 2010), xi–xiv; Mike Davis and Daniel Bertrand Monk, introduction to *Evil Paradises: Dreamworlds of Neoliberalism,* ed. Mike Davis and Daniel Bertrand Monk (New York: The New Press, 2007), x.

19. Cedric Johnson, introduction to *The Neoliberal Deluge: Hurricane Katrina, Late Capitalism, and the Remaking of New Orleans,* ed. Cedric Johnson (Minneapolis: University of Minnesota Press, 2011), xviii; Mike Davis, *The Ecology of Fear: Los Angeles and the Imagination of Disaster* (New York: Metropolitan Books, 1998), 371; Cindi Katz, "Bad Elements: Katrina and the Soured Landscape of Social Reproduction," *Gender, Place and Culture* 15, no. 1 (February 2008): 15–29; Barbara Ransby, "Katrina, Black Women, and the Deadly Discourse of Black Poverty in America," *Du Bois Review* 3, no. 1 (2006): 216.

20. Julia Sudbury, ed., *Global Lockdown: Race, Gender and the Prison-Industrial Complex* (New York: Routledge, 2005); Vijay Prashad, "Second-Hand Dreams," *Social Analysis* 49, no. 2 (Summer 2005): 192.

21. See U.S. Census Bureau, "State and County Quickfacts," http://quickfacts.census.gov/qfd/states/22/2255000.html. For a sense of the mood at NBC's studios about the media drama, see *Nightly News with Brian Williams,* NBC, September 16, 2005, http://www.msnbc.msn.com/id/9314188/#050916.

22. Jared Sexton, "The Obscurity of Black Suffering," in *What Lies Beneath,* 120–32; Manning Marable, *Race, Reform, and Rebellion: The Second Reconstruction and Beyond in Black America, 1945–2006* (1984; reprint, Jackson: University of Mississippi Press, 2007), 252.

23. "New Orleans Braces for Monster Hurricane," CNN, August 29, 2005, http://www.cnn.com/2005/WEATHER/08/28/hurricane.katrina/; Sunni Patterson, interview with the author, March 11, 2009; Daisy Hernández, "The Future of the Ninth Ward," *Colorlines* 32 (Spring 2006).

24. Herman Gray, "Where the Natural and the Social Meet," in *Hurricane Katrina: Response and Responsibilities*, 89.

25. Manuel Roig-Franzia and Spencer Hsu, "Many Evacuated, but Thousands Still Waiting: White House Shifts Blame to State and Local Officials," *Washington Post,* September 4, 2005, http://www.washingtonpost.com/wp-dyn /content/article/2005/09/03/AR2005090301680_pf.html.

26. Joseph R. Chenelly, "Troops Begin Combat Operations in New Orleans to Fight 'Insurgents,'" *Army Times,* September 4, 2005; "Troops Told to 'Shoot to Kill,'" ABC News; Manuel Roig-Franzia and Spencer Hsu, "Many Evacuated, but Thousands Still Waiting"; Scott McClellan, "Press Briefing," White House Office of the Press Secretary, September 1, 2005.

27. Felicity Barringer and Maria Newman, "Troops Bring Food, Water, and Promise of Order to New Orleans," *New York Times,* September 2, 2005.

28. Amy Kaplan, "Violent Belongings and the Question of Empire Today: Presidential Address, American Studies Association, October 17, 2003," *American Quarterly* 56, no. 1 (March 2004): 5; Amy Kaplan, *The Anarchy of Empire in the Making of U.S. Culture* (Cambridge, MA: Harvard University Press, 2002), 1; George Lipsitz, "Learning from New Orleans: The Social Warrant of Hostile Privatism and Competitive Consumer Citizenship," *Cultural Anthropology* 21, no. 3 (2006): 454; Michel Foucault, *Security, Territory, Population: Lectures at the Collège de France, 1977–78,* ed. Michel Senellart, trans. Graham Burchell (New York: Palgrave MacMillan, 2007), 44–49.

29. George Lipsitz, *American Studies in a Moment of Danger* (Minneapolis: University of Minnesota Press, 2001), 57–88; Cedric J. Robinson, *Black Movements in America* (New York: Routledge, 1997), 151–52; Kim Lacy Rogers, *Righteous Lives,* 191; Cedric Johnson, introduction to *The Neoliberal Deluge,* xxvii–xxviii.

30. "New Orleans Fights to Stop Looting," CBS News, August 21, 2005, http://www.cbsnews.com/stories/2005/08/31/katrina/main808193.shtml; "The Militarization of New Orleans: Jeremy Scahill Reports from Louisiana," DemocracyNow.org, September 16, 2005; Marina Sideris and the Critical Resistance Amnesty Working Group, "Amnesty for Prisoners of Katrina."

31. Raúl Zibechi, "The Militarization of the World's Urban Peripheries," *Americas Policy Program,* February 9, 2007, http://www.cipamericas.org /archives/835; Jeremy Scahill, "In the Black(water)," *The Nation,* May 22, 2006, http://www.thenation.com/article/blackwater/; Jeremy Scahill, "Blackwater Down," *The Nation,* September 21, 2005, http://www.thenation.com /article/blackwater-down/. "Crisis Profiteering: Dick Cheney, Halliburton, and Hurricane Katrina," DemocracyNow.org, September 9, 2005; George Lipsitz, "Change the Focus and Reverse the Hypnosis: Learning from New Orleans," presented at the symposium "The Color of Disaster: Race, Class, and Hurricane Katrina," University of California, Santa Barbara, October 15, 2005.

32. Ruth Wilson Gilmore, "Race, Prisons, and War," 73–87; Mike Davis, "The Predators of New Orleans," *Le Monde Diplomatique,* October 2005, http://mondediplo.com/2005/10/02katrina.

33. Nicole Gelinas, "New Orleans Still Drowning in Crime," *Dallas Morning News,* May 13, 2007, http://www.manhattan-institute.org/html/miarticle .htm?id=3945.

34. Nicole Gelinas, "What New Orleans Needs Now: Law, Sweet Law," *New York Post*, August 28, 2007, http://nypost.com/2007/08/28/what-new-orleans-needs-now/; Nicole Gelinas, "New Orleans Owes W," *New York Post*, August 30, 2012, http://nypost.com/2012/08/30/new-orleans-owes-w/.

35. Stephen Graham, *Cities Under Siege*, 25; Jamie Peck, *Constructions of Neoliberal Reason* (New York: Oxford University Press, 2010), 137, 143.

36. Mike Davis, "Gentrifying Disaster," *Mother Jones* (October 2005), http://motherjones.com/politics/2005/10/gentrifying-disaster; Cindi Katz, "Bad Elements," 21, 22.

37. Mike Davis, "Gentrifying Disaster"; Rachel E. Luft with Shana Griffin, "A Status Report on Housing in New Orleans After Katrina: An Intersectional Analysis," in *Katrina and the Women of New Orleans*, ed. Beth Willinger (New Orleans: Newcomb College Center for Research on Women, Tulane University, December 2008), 50–53; Naomi Klein, "Purging the Poor," *The Nation*, September 22, 2005; "Thousands of New Orleans Public Housing Units to Be Destroyed and Low-Income Remain Displaced," DemocracyNow.org, June 20, 2006; "The Privatization of New Orleans: Curtis Muhammad on Tycoons, Trump, and Gulf Coast Oil," DemocracyNow.org, September 4, 2007; "Fight to Reopen New Orleans Public Housing 'Horrible Slow and Tragic,'" DemocracyNow.org, September 4, 2007; Naomi Klein, *The Shock Doctrine: The Rise of Disaster Capitalism* (New York: Picador, 2007), 513–34; Community Labor United quoted in Jordan Flaherty, *Floodlines: Community and Resistance from Katrina to the Jena Six* (Chicago: Haymarket Books, 2010), 48.

38. Mike Davis, "Who Is Killing New Orleans?" *The Nation*, March 23, 2006, http://www.thenation.com/article/who-killing-new-orleans; Gary Rivlin, "A Mogul Who Would Rebuild New Orleans," *New York Times,* September 29, 2005, http://www.nytimes.com/2005/09/29/business/a-mogul-who-would-rebuild-new-orleans.html; Neil Smith, "Revanchist Planet," 17.

39. Clyde Woods, "Les Misérables of New Orleans," 780; William I. Robinson, "*Aqui Estamos y no Nos Vamos!*: Global Capital and Immigrant Rights," *Race and Class* 48, no. 2 (2006): 87; Saket Soni, "Organizing the Future of Work?" Labor and Worklife Program, Harvard Law School, February 14, 2013, http://www.law.harvard.edu/programs/lwp/wurf_lectures/2013soniwurf.pdf.

40. Laura Carlsen, "Militarizing Mexico: The New War on Drugs," *Foreign Policy in Focus*, July 12, 2007; Curtis Marez, *Drug Wars: The Political Economy of Narcotics* (Minneapolis: University of Minnesota Press, 2004); Timothy J. Dunn, "Border Militarization via Drug and Immigration Enforcement: Human Rights Implications," *Social Justice* 28, no. 2 (2001): 7–30.

41. "President Bush Participates in Joint Press Availability with President Calderón of Mexico and Prime Minister Harper of Canada," Office of the Press Secretary, April 22, 2008, http://georgewbush-whitehouse.archives.gov/news/releases/2008/04/20080422-5.html.

42. Alan Eladio Gómez, "From Below and to the Left: Re-Imagining the Chicano Movement Through the Circulation of Third World Struggles, 1970–1979" (PhD diss., University of Texas at Austin, 2006); Laura Carlsen, "Plan Mexico," *Foreign Policy in Focus,* October 30, 2007; Manning Marable, "Globalization and Racialization," *ZNet*, August 13, 2004, https://zcomm.org

/znetarticle/globalization-and-racialization-by-manning-marable/; David Roediger, *History Against Misery* (Chicago: Charles H. Kerr, 2006), ix.

43. JJ Sutherland, "National Guard Still Patrols New Orleans," National Public Radio, July 15, 2008, http://www.npr.org/templates/story/story.php?storyId=92563043; National Prison Project of the American Civil Liberties Union, "Abandoned and Abused," 84.

44. Dan Barry, "Three Years After Hurricane, the Backup Is a Fixture," *New York Times,* August 25, 2008, http://www.nytimes.com/2008/08/25/us/25land .html; Rosa Linda Fregoso, *meXicana Encounters: The Making of Social Identities in the Borderlands* (Berkeley: University of California Press, 2003), 4, 5, 12.

45. For the historical context shaping these events, see Manning Marable, *Race, Reform, and Rebellion,* 251; Alisa Bierria, Shana Griffin, Mayaba Liebenthal, and Incite! Women of Color Against Violence and Racism, "To Render Ourselves Visible: Women of Color Organizing and Hurricane Katrina," in *What Lies Beneath,* 32; Henry A. Giroux, *Stormy Weather: Katrina and the Politics of Disposability* (Boulder, CO: Paradigm, 2006), 3–11, 23–31.

46. Sunni Patterson, "We Know This Place," *American Quarterly* 61, no. 3 (September 2009): 719–21; Sunni Patterson, interview with the author, March 11, 2009; Robin D. G. Kelley, *Freedom Dreams,* 9; Marcus Rediker, *The Slave Ship: A Human History* (New York: Penguin, 2007).

47. Sunni Patterson, interview with the author, March 11, 2009.

48. George Lipsitz, "Abolition Democracy and Global Justice," *Comparative American Studies* 2, no. 3 (2004): 271–86.

49. Jordan Flaherty, *Floodlines,* 48–49; Eric Mann, *Katrina's Legacy: White Racism and Black Reconstruction in New Orleans and the Gulf Coast* (Los Angeles: Frontlines Press, 2006), 61–152; Adolph Reed, "Malcolm Suber: Good for New Orleans," *The Nation,* October 29, 2007, http://www.thenation .com/article/malcolm-suber-good-new-orleans; Rachel E. Luft, "Community Organizing in the Katrina Diaspora: Race, Gender, and the Case of the People's Hurricane Relief Fund," in *Displaced: Life in the Katrina Diaspora* (Austin: University of Texas Press, 2012), 233–55; Clyde Woods, introduction to "An Evening with Sunni Patterson," Department of Black Studies, University of California, Santa Barbara, November 15, 2007.

50. Paul Ortiz, "The New Battle for New Orleans," in *Hurricane Katrina: Response and Responsibilities,* 5.

51. Moon-Ho Jung, *Coolies and Cane: Race, Labor, and Sugar in the Age of Emancipation* (Baltimore: Johns Hopkins University Press, 2006), 41; C. L. R. James, *The Black Jacobins: Toussaint L'Ouverture and the San Domingo Revolution* (1938; reprint, New York: Vintage Books, 1989).

52. Cedric J. Robinson, *Forgeries of Memory and Meaning: Blacks and the Regimes of Race in American Theatre and Film Before World War II* (Chapel Hill: University of North Carolina Press, 2007), xvii; Sunni Patterson, "We Know This Place."

53. Kathleen McKittrick and Clyde Woods, "No One Knows the Mysteries at the Bottom of the Ocean," in *Black Geographies and the Politics of Place,* 2.

54. Sunni Patterson, "We Know This Place."

55. Gaye Theresa Johnson, "Spatial Entitlement: Race, Displacement, and Reclamation in Post-War Los Angeles," in *Black and Brown Los Angeles: A Contemporary Reader,* ed. Josh Kun and Laura Pulido (Los Angeles: University of California Press, 2013).

56. Sunni Patterson, "We Made It," from the album *Porch Prophesies* (New Orleans, 2006).

57. Orissa Arend, *Showdown in Desire: The Black Panthers Take a Stand in New Orleans* (Fayetteville: University of Arkansas Press, 2009); Ruth Wilson Gilmore, *Golden Gulag,* 28.

58. Sunni Patterson, "We Made It."

59. Avery Gordon, *Ghostly Matters: Haunting and the Sociological Imagination* (Minneapolis: University of Minnesota Press, 2008), 200, 137–90; Sunni Patterson, "We Made It."

60. Kalamu ya Salaam, "We Stand by Our Students," in *Pedagogy, Policy, and the Privatized City,* 65.

61. Kalamu ya Salaam, "Below the Water Line," in *What Lies Beneath,* xvii–xviii.

62. "The Privatization of New Orleans: Curtis Muhammad on Tycoons, Trump, and Gulf Coast Oil," DemocracyNow.org, September 4, 2007.

63. Charles M. Payne, *I've Got the Light of Freedom: The Organizing Tradition and the Mississippi Freedom Struggle* (Berkeley: University of California Press, 1995), 67–68; Vincent Harding, *There Is a River: The Black Struggle for Freedom in America* (San Francisco: Harcourt Brace and Company, 1981), xii, xiii; Kim Lacy Rogers, *Righteous Lives,* 110–89.

64. Benjamin Holtzman, "An Interview with Robin D. G. Kelley," *In the Middle of a Whirlwind* (2008), http://inthemiddleofthewhirlwind.wordpress .com/an-interview-with-robin-dg-kelley/; Amnesty International, "The Right to Return: Rebuilding the Gulf Through the Framework of International Human Rights," http://www.amnestyusa.org/sites/default/files/pdfs/therighttoreturn.pdf; Paul Ortiz, "The New Battle for New Orleans," 5.

65. Clyde Woods, "The Politics of Reproductive Violence: An Interview with Shana Griffin," *American Quarterly* 61, no. 3 (2009): 591; Ruth Wilson Gilmore, *Golden Gulag,* 245, 248.

66. See C. L. R. James, *The Future in the Present* (London: Allison and Busby, 1977); Clyde Woods, *Development Arrested: The Blues and Plantation Power in the Mississippi Delta* (New York: Verso, 1998), 140.

67. Sunni Patterson, "We Know This Place."

CHAPTER 6: SHUT 'EM DOWN

1. Steve Diaz, "Operation Freedom and Freedom Now!," *Community Connection,* January–February 2012, http://cangress.wordpress.com/tag/community-connection/; Ernest Hardy, "Public Enemy Puts Spotlight on Skid Row," *Los Angeles Times,* January 17, 2012.

2. Gary Blasi and the UCLA School of Law Fact Investigation Clinic, *Policing Our Way Out of Homelessness? The First Year of the Safer Cities Initiative on Skid Row* (Los Angeles: UCLA and USC Center for Sustainable Cities,

September 24, 2007); Christina Heatherton, ed., *Downtown Blues: A Skid Row Reader* (Los Angeles: Los Angeles Community Action Network, 2011); Jordan T. Camp and Christina Heatherton, *Freedom Now! Struggles for the Human Right to Housing in L.A. and Beyond* (Los Angeles: Freedom Now Books, 2012); Nicholas Dahmann with the Los Angeles Community Action Network, "Los Angeles: I Do Mind Dying, Recent Reflections on Urban Revolution in Skid Row," *Los Angeles Public Interest Law Journal* 2 (2009–10): 210–19.

3. Mike Davis, *A Planet of Slums* (New York: Verso, 2006), 36; Neil Smith, "New Globalism, New Urbanism: Gentrification as Global Urban Strategy," *Antipode* 34, no. 3 (2002): 427–50; Craig Willse, "Neo-Liberal Biopolitics and the Invention of Chronic Homelessness," *Economy and Society* 39, no. 2 (2010): 155–56.

4. Clyde Woods, "'Sitting on Top of the World': The Challenges of Blues and Hip Hop Geography," in *Black Geographies and the Politics of Place*, ed. Katherine McKittrick and Clyde Woods (Cambridge, MA: South End, 2007), 49; Clyde Woods, "Traps, Skid Row, and Katrina," in *Downtown Blues*, 51; Clyde Woods, "The Challenges of Blues and Hip Hop Historiography," *Kalfou* 1, no. 1 (2010): 33–34; Stuart Hall, *The Hard Road to Renewal: Thatcherism and the Crisis of the Left* (New York: Verso, 1988), 96; Robin D.G. Kelley, *Race Rebels: Culture, Politics, and the Black Working Class* (New York: The New Press, 1994), 207.

5. Clyde Woods, "Do You Know What It Means to Miss New Orleans? Katrina, Trap Economics, and the Rebirth of the Blues," *American Quarterly* 57, no. 4 (2005): 1005; George Lipsitz, "The Struggle for Hegemony," *Journal of American History* 75, no. 1 (1988): 146–50.

6. George Lipsitz, *Footsteps in the Dark: The Hidden Histories of Popular Music* (Minneapolis: University of Minnesota Press, 2007), 108; Mike Davis, *A Planet of Slums*, 36; Clyde Woods, "Les Misérables of New Orleans: Trap Economics and the Asset Stripping Blues, Part 1," *American Quarterly* 61, no. 3 (2009): 769–96; Christina Heatherton, ed., *Downtown Blues*, 4–6; David Harvey, *The New Imperialism* (New York: Oxford University Press, 2003), 137–82; Robin D.G. Kelley, *Yo' Mama's Disfunktional! Fighting the Culture Wars in Urban America* (Boston: Beacon Press, 1997), 8; Stuart Hall, "Gramsci's Relevance for the Study of Race and Ethnicity," *Journal of Communications Inquiry* 10, no. 5 (1986): 24.

7. Neil Smith, "Giuliani Time: The Revanchist 1990s," *Social Text* 57 (Winter 1998): 1–20.

8. Ruth Wilson Gilmore and Christina Heatherton, "Fixing Broken Windows Without Batons," in *Freedom Now!*, 1. See Gari Blasi and Forrest Stuart, "Has the Safer Cities Initiative in Skid Row Reduced Serious Crime?" (Los Angeles: UCLA Law School, September 15, 2008), http://wraphome.org/downloads/safer_cities.pdf; Fred Moten, "The Meaning of 'Broken Windows,'" talk presented at Eso Won Books, Los Angeles, June 23, 2005; Manhattan Institute, "Why Cities Matter," YouTube.com, March 21, 2014; Gary Blasi and the UCLA School of Law Fact Investigation Clinic, *Policing Our Way Out of Homelessness?*, 23; Alex S. Vitale, "The Safer Cities Initiative and the Removal of the Homeless: Reducing Crime or Promoting Gentrification on Los Angeles's Skid Row?" *American Society of Criminology* 9, no. 4 (2010): 867–73.

9. Edward W. Soja, *Seeking Spatial Justice* (Minneapolis: University of Minnesota Press, 2010), 131–132;

10. Robert D. Bullard and Charles Lee, "Introduction: Racism and American Apartheid," in *Residential Apartheid: The American Legacy*, ed. Robert D. Bullard et al. (Los Angeles: Center for Afro-American Studies Publications, UCLA, 1994), 7.

11. Stuart Hall and Doreen Massey, "Interpreting the Crisis," *Soundings: A Journal of Politics and Culture* 44 (Spring 2010): 57–71; Stuart Hall, "The Neoliberal Revolution," *Soundings: A Journal of Politics and Culture* 48 (Summer 2011): 10; Cindi Katz, "Vagabond Capitalism and the Necessity of Social Reproduction," *Antipode* 33, no. 4 (2001): 724; Vijay Prashad, "Second-Hand Dreams," *Social Analysis* 49, no. 2 (2005): 191–98.

12. Cindi Katz, "Childhood as Spectacle: Relays of Anxiety and the Reconfiguration of the Child," *Cultural Geographies* 15 (2008): 15–17; Stuart Hall and Doreen Massey, "Interpreting the Crisis," 58.

13. Nikhil Pal Singh, "The Afterlife of Fascism," *South Atlantic Quarterly* 105, no. 1 (Winter 2006): 71–93; Avery F. Gordon, "The U.S. Military Prison: The Normalcy of Exceptional Brutality," in *The Violence of Incarceration*, ed. Phil Scraton and Jude McCulloch (New York: Routledge, 2009), 174; Stephen Graham, *Cities Under Siege: The New Military Urbanism* (New York: Verso, 2010), 94; Daniel Martinez HoSang, *Racial Propositions: Ballot Initiatives and the Making of Postwar California* (Berkeley: University of California Press, 2010), 20–23.

14. See Daniel Widener, *Black Arts West: Culture and Struggle in Postwar Los Angeles* (Durham, NC: Duke University Press, 2010), 11; Gaye Theresa Johnson, "A Sifting of Centuries: Afro-Chicano Interaction and Popular Musical Culture in California, 1960–2000," in *Decolonial Voices: Chicana and Chicano Cultural Studies in the 21st Century*, ed. Arturo J. Aldama and Naomi H. Quiñonez (Bloomington: Indiana University Press, 2002), 320–23.

15. Cedric J. Robinson, *Black Marxism: The Making of the Black Radical Tradition* (1983; reprint, Chapel Hill: University of North Carolina Press, 2000); Neil Brenner, Jamie Peck, and Nik Theodore, "After Neoliberalization?" *Globalizations* 7, no. 3 (2010): 327–45; George Lipsitz, "Learning from Los Angeles: Another One Rides the Bus," *American Quarterly* 56, no. 3 (2004): 511–29.

16. Paula Chakravartty and John D. H. Downing, "Media, Technology, and the Global Financial Crisis," *International Journal of Communication* 4 (2010): 693–95; George Lipsitz, *Time Passages: Collective Memory and American Popular Culture* (1990; reprint, Minneapolis: University of Minnesota Press, 2006), 5; Gary A. Dymski, "Racial Exclusion and the Political Economy of the Subprime Crisis," *Historical Materialism* 17 (2009): 149–79; David Harvey, *The Enigma of Capital and the Crises of Capitalism* (New York: Oxford, 2010), 1.

17. Amaad Rivera et al., *The Silent Depression: State of the Dream 2009* (Boston: United for a Fair Economy, 2009); David McNally, *Global Slump: The Economics and Politics of Crisis and Resistance* (Oakland, CA: PM Press, 2010), 125–26; Amaad Rivera et al., *Foreclosed: State of the Dream 2008* (Boston: United for a Fair Economy, 2008), v. See also Rakesh Kochhar, Richard Fry, and

Paul Taylor, "Wealth Gaps Rise to Record Highs Between Whites, Blacks, Hispanics," Pew Research Center, July 26, 2011, http://www.pewsocialtrends.org/2011/07/26/wealth-gaps-rise-to-record-highs-between-whites-blacks-hispanics/.

18. David Harvey, "The Enigma of Capital and the Crisis This Time," paper presented at the American Sociological Association Meeting, Atlanta, August 16, 2010, http://davidharvey.org/2010/08/the-enigma-of-capital-and-the-crisis-this-time/; Ashok Bardhan and Richard Walker, "California, Pivot of the Great Recession," Working Paper Series no. 203-10 (Berkeley: Institute for Research on Labor and Employment, University of California, March 2010), http://metrostudies.berkeley.edu/pubs/reports/Walker_93.pdf.

19. Richard Walker, "Golden State Adrift," *New Left Review* 66 (2010): 6–9; David R. Roediger, *How Race Survived U.S. History: From Settlement and Slavery to the Obama Phenomenon* (New York: Verso, 2008), 229; National Coalition for the Homeless, "Foreclosure to Homelessness: The Forgotten Victims of the Subprime Crisis," June 2009, http://www.nationalhomeless.org/factsheets/foreclosure.html.

20. George Lipsitz, *How Racism Takes Place* (Philadelphia: Temple University Press, 2011), 20.

21. Mike Davis, *Ecology of Fear: Los Angeles and the Imagination of Disaster* (New York: Metropolitan Books, 1998), 362; Jacob S. Rugh and Douglas S. Massey, "Racial Segregation and the American Foreclosure Crisis," *American Sociological Review* 75, no. 5 (2010): 629, 634; Jordan T. Camp, "Housing Is a Human Right: California's Forty-Years Struggle, an Interview with Daniel Martinez HoSang," in *Freedom Now!*, 94; Laura Pulido, "Rethinking Environmental Racism: White Privilege and Urban Development in Southern California," *Annals of the Association of American Geographers* 90, no. 1 (2000): 561; George Lipsitz, *How Racism Takes Place*, 9.

22. Howard Husock, "Housing Goals We Can't Afford," *New York Times*, December 10, 2008.

23. James D. Sidaway, "Subprime Crisis: American Crisis or Human Crisis?" *Environment and Planning D: Society and Space* 26 (2008): 195–98.

24. Neil Smith, *The New Urban Frontier: Gentrification and the Revanchist City* (New York: Routledge, 1996); Jamie Peck, "Liberating the City: Between New York and New Orleans," *Urban Geography* 27, no. 8 (2006): 68.

25. Neil Smith, "Urban Politics, Urban Security," paper presented at Harvard Graduate School, Cambridge, MA, September 29, 2010; Don Mitchell, *The Right to the City: Social Justice and the Fight for Public Space* (New York: Guilford, 2003), 15–16; David R. Roediger, *How Race Survived U.S. History*, 229.

26. Denise Ferreira da Silva, "No-Bodies: Law, Raciality, and Violence," *Griffith Law Review* 18, no. 2 (2009): 224–27; Paula Chakravartty and Denise Ferreira da Silva, "Accumulation, Dispossession, and Debt: The Racial Logic of Global Capitalism," *American Quarterly* 64, no. 3 (2012): 380. See also David Theo Goldberg, *The Threat of Race Reflections on Racial Neoliberalism* (Malden, MA: Blackwell, 2009), 80–91; Jordan T. Camp and Christina Heatherton, "The Housing Question: An Interview with Mike Davis," in *Freedom Now!*,

85; Stuart Hall, *The Hard Road to Renewal*, 188; Daniel Martinez HoSang, *Racial Propositions*, 264; Stuart Hall et al., *Policing the Crisis: Mugging, the State, and Law and Order* (London: MacMillan, 1978), 217; Ruth Wilson Gilmore and Craig Gilmore, "Restating the Obvious," in *Indefensible Space: The Architecture of the National Security State*, ed. Michael Sorkin (New York: Routledge, 2007), 144.

27. Karl Marx, *Capital: A Critique of Political Economy*, trans. Ben Fowkes (New York: Penguin Books, 1976), 640–48; Peter Linebaugh, "Karl Marx, the Theft of the Wood, and Working-Class Composition: A Contribution to the Current Debate," *Crime and Social Justice* 6 (Fall–Winter 1976): 5; Ruth Wilson Gilmore, *Golden Gulag: Prisons, Surplus, Crisis, and Opposition in Globalizing California* (Berkeley: University of California Press, 2007), 77, 64; Don Mitchell, *The Right to the City*, 128–29; Neil Smith, "New Globalism, New Urbanism," 433.

28. Craig Willse, "Neo-Liberal Biopolitics and the Invention of Chronic Homelessness," 164; Jeremy Németh, "Security in Public Space: An Empirical Assessment of Three U.S. Cities," *Environment and Planning A* 42 (2010): 2487–507.

29. David Wagner and Pete White, "Why the Silence? Homelessness and Race," in *Freedom Now!*, 43–44; Marie Gottschalk, "It's Not Just the Drug War," *Jacobin*, March 5, 2015, https://www.jacobinmag.com/2015/03/mass-incarceration-war-on-drugs/. On the ways that dominant racial ideologies have obscured the multiraciality of poverty, see Cedric J. Robinson, "Race, Capitalism, and Antidemocracy," in *Reading Rodney King/Reading Urban Uprising*, ed. Robert Gooding-Williams (New York: Routledge, 1993), 77; Cedric J. Robinson, *Forgeries of Memory and Meaning: Blacks and the Regimes of Race in American Theatre and Film Before World War II* (Chapel Hill: University of North Carolina Press, 2007), 276; Jodi Melamed, *Represent and Destroy: Rationalizing Violence in the New Racial Capitalism* (Minneapolis: University of Minnesota Press, 2011), 38.

30. Avery F. Gordon, "The U.S. Military Prison," 174; Ashley Dawson and Malini Johar Schueller, eds., *Exceptional State: Contemporary U.S. Culture and the New Imperialism* (Durham, NC: Duke University Press, 2007), 16; Gerald Horne, *Fire This Time* (New York: Da Capo, 1997), 41; Nikhil Pal Singh, "'Learn Your Horn': Jack O'Dell and the Long Civil Rights Movement," introduction to Jack O'Dell, *Climbin' Jacob's Ladder: The Black Freedom Movement Writings of Jack O'Dell*, ed. Nikhil Pal Singh (Berkeley: University of California Press, 2010), 57.

31. Michael Anderson et al., eds., *Without Housing: Decades of Federal Housing Cutbacks, Massive Homelessness, and Policy Failures* (San Francisco: Western Regional Advocacy Project, 2010); Jordan T. Camp and Christina Heatherton, "Housing Question," in *Freedom Now!*, 83; Laura Pulido, "Rethinking Environmental Racism," 561.

32. Gilda Haas and Allan David Heskin, *Community Struggles in Los Angeles* (Los Angeles: UCLA School of Architecture and Urban Planning, 1981), 13–19; Mike Davis, *City of Quartz: Excavating the Future in Los Angeles* (1990; reprint, New York: Verso, 2006), 232.

33. Christina Heatherton and Yusef Omowale, "Skid Row in Transition: An Interview with Gary Blasi," in *Downtown Blues*, 36; The Labor/Community Strategy Center, *Reconstructing Los Angeles from the Bottom Up* (Los Angeles: Labor/Community Strategy Center, 1993), 31–32; Gary Blasi and the UCLA School of Law Fact Investigation Clinic, *Policing Our Way Out of Homelessness?*, 1–9; Richard Walker, "Golden State Adrift," 5; Mike Davis, *City of Quartz,* 234.

34. David Wagner and Pete White, "Why the Silence?," 45; Neil Smith, "New Globalism, New Urbanism," 442; David Harvey, "The Right to the City," *New Left Review* 53 (2008): 34–35; Daniel Martinez HoSang, "The Economics of the New Brutality," *Colorlines,* December 10, 1999, http://www .colorlines.com/articles/economics-new-brutality; Ellen Reese, Geoffrey Deverteuil, and Leanne Thach, "'Weak-Center' Gentrification and the Contradictions of Containment," *International Journal of Urban and Regional Research* 34, no. 2 (2010): 311. For an elaboration of the transitions on Skid Row, see the interview with Gary Blasi by Christina Heatherton and Yusef Omowale, "Skid Row in Transition," 38–40.

35. Charlie Beck, William J. Bratton, and George L. Kelling, "Who Will Police the Criminologists? The Dangers of Politicized Social Science," *City Journal* 21, no. 2 (Spring 2011). On the failures of the broken-windows policing approach on both empirical and theoretical grounds, see the systematic analyses by Bernard E. Harcourt, *Illusion of Order: The False Promise of Broken Windows Policing* (Cambridge, MA: Harvard University Press, 2001); Don Mitchell, *The Right to the City,* 195–222.

36. Neil Smith, *The New Urban Frontier,* 220, 222; Neil Smith, "Giuliani Time," 10; Richard Winton, "LAPD Adds 10 Cameras to Curb Skid Row Crime," *Los Angeles Times,* September 15, 2006, http://articles.latimes. com/2006/sep/15/local/me-cameras15; George Lipsitz, "Learning from Los Angeles: Producing Anarchy in the Name of Order," in *Freedom Now!,* 33–40; Daniel Martinez HoSang, "The Economics of the New Brutality"; Alex S. Vitale, "The Safer Cities Initiative and the Removal of the Homeless," 870–71.

37. Deborah Burton, statement at the United Nations Universal Periodic Review, in *Freedom Now!*; Doudou Diène, *Report of the Special Rapporteur on Contemporary Forms of Racism, Racial Discrimination, Xenophobia and Related Intolerance* (Geneva: Human Rights Council, April 2009), 20; *Universal Declaration of Human Rights* (Geneva: United Nations Department of Public Information, 1948); Rhonda Y. Williams, "'We Refuse': Privatization, Housing, and Human Rights," in *Freedom Now!,* 15. On the politics of scale, see Neil Smith, "Contours of a Spatialized Politics: Homeless Vehicles and the Production of Geographical Scale," *Social Text* 33 (1992): 54–81; Bobby Wilson, "Scale Politics of the Civil Rights Movement," paper presented at the Association of American Geographers, New York, February 2012. On the stakes in feminist struggles for the social wage, see Cindi Katz, "Vagabond Capitalism and the Necessity of Social Reproduction," 709–28. For a critique of the human rights paradigm, see Randall Williams, *The Divided World: Human Rights and Its Violence* (Minneapolis: University of Minnesota Press, 2010).

38. Daniel Fischlin, Ajay Heble, and George Lipsitz, *The Fierce Urgency of Now: Improvisation, Rights, and the Ethics of Cocreation* (Durham, NC: Duke

University Press, 2013), 42; Clyde Woods, "Life After Death," *Professional Geographer* 54, no. 1 (2002): 64; Mike Davis, *Prisoners of the American Dream* (New York: Verso, 1986), 310; Robin D. G. Kelley, *Yo' Mama's Disfunktional!*, 155; Clyde Woods, *Development Drowned and Reborn: The Blues and Bourbon Restorations in Post-Katrina New Orleans*, ed. Laura Pulido and Jordan T. Camp (Athens: University of Georgia Press, forthcoming); Jordan T. Camp and Christina Heatherton, "Asset Stripping and Broken Windows Policing on L.A.'s Skid Row: An Interview with Becky Dennison and Pete White," in *Policing the Planet: Why the Policing Crisis Led to Black Lives Matter*, eds. Jordan T. Camp and Christina Heatherton (New York: Verso, 2016).

39. *Community Connection*, September–October 2011, https://cangress. files.wordpress.com/2011/10/cc42-final-small-for-web.pdf; Don Mitchell, *The Right to the City*, 21; Robin D. G. Kelley, "Ground Zero," in *Downtown Blues*, 13, 15; Jordan T. Camp and Christina Heatherton, "Asset Stripping and Broken Windows Policing on L.A.'s Skid Row," in *Policing the Planet*.

40. Raquel Rolnik, *Report of the Special Rapporteur on Adequate Housing as a Component of the Right to an Adequate Standard of Living, and on the Right to Non-Discrimination in This Context* (Geneva: Human Rights Council, February 12, 2010), 8.

41. Don Mitchell, "Homelessness, American Style," in *Downtown Blues*, 42; Mazher Ali et al., *State of the Dream 2011: Austerity for Whom?* (Boston: United for a Fair Economy, 2011); Michael Anderson et al., eds., *Without Housing*, 6, 42; George Lipsitz, "Policing Place and Taxing Time on Skid Row," in *Policing the Planet*.

42. Paul Boden, "Didn't Work Then, Won't Work Now," HuffingtonPost. com, January 31, 2013; Clyde Woods, "Traps, Skid Row, and Katrina"; Christina Heatherton, ed., *Downtown Blues*, 55; Jack O'Dell, *Climbin' Jacob's Ladder*, 113–16, 263–93; George Lipsitz, "Learning from Los Angeles: Another One Rides the Bus," 511–29; Daniel Widener, "Another City Is Possible: Interethnic Organizing in Contemporary Los Angeles," *Race/Ethnicity: Multidisciplinary Global Perspectives* 1, no. 2 (2008): 189–219; Jacquelyn Dowd Hall, "The Long Civil Rights Movement and the Political Uses of the Past," *Journal of American History* 91, no. 4 (2005): 1261.

EPILOGUE

1. James Baldwin, *The Evidence of Things Not Seen* (New York: Henry Holt and Company, 1985); Avery F. Gordon, *Ghostly Matters: Haunting and the Sociological Imagination* (Minneapolis: University of Minnesota Press, 2008), 195; Karl Marx, *The Eighteenth Brumaire of Louis Bonaparte* (1963; reprint, New York: International Publishers, 2004), 18.

2. James Baldwin and Margaret Mead, *A Rap on Race* (New York: J. B. Lippincott Company, 1971), 201.

3. Robin D. G. Kelley, *Freedom Dreams: The Black Radical Imagination* (Boston: Beacon Press, 2002), 9–12; Stuart Hall, "Gramsci's Relevance for the Study of Race and Ethnicity," *Journal of Communications Inquiry* 10 (1986):

15, 27; Manning Marable, *How Capitalism Underdeveloped Black America* (1983; reprint, Cambridge, MA: South End Press, 2000), 16, 231–53.

4. Jordan T. Camp and Christina Heatherton, *Freedom Now! Struggles for the Human Right to Housing in Los Angeles and Beyond* (Los Angeles: Freedom Now Books, 2012); James Kilgore, *Understanding Mass Incarceration: A People's Guide to the Key Civil Rights Struggle of Our Time* (New York: The New Press, 2015), 234.

5. Angela Y. Davis, "James and Esther Jackson: Connecting the Past to the Present," *American Communist History* 7, no. 2 (2008): 272; Angela Y. Davis, *Abolition Democracy: Beyond Empire, Prisons, and Torture* (New York: Seven Stories Press, 2005), 103.

6. Angela Y. Davis, "James and Esther Jackson," 272; Angela Y. Davis, *Abolition Democracy*, 95–96. See also George Lipsitz, "Abolition Democracy and Global Justice," *Comparative American Studies* 2, no. 3 (2004): 271–86.

7. Angela Y. Davis, "Policing the Crisis Today," Stuart Hall International Conference: Conversations, Projects, and Legacy, Goldsmiths University, London, November 28, 2014; Stuart Jeffries, "There Is an Unbroken Line of Police Violence in the U.S. That Takes Us All the Way Back to the Days of Slavery: A Conversation with Activist Angela Davis," *The Guardian*, December 14, 2014, http://www.theguardian.com/global/2014/dec/14/angela-davis-there-is-an-unbroken-line-of-police-violence-in-the-us-that-takes-us-all-the-way-back-to-the-days-of-slavery; Stuart Hall, Chas Critcher, Tony Jefferson, John Clarke, and Brian Roberts, *Policing the Crisis: Mugging, the State, and Law and Order* (London: Palgrave MacMillan, 2013); Ruth Wilson Gilmore and Craig Gilmore, "Beyond Bratton," in *Policing the Planet: Why the Policing Crisis Led to Black Lives Matter*, ed. Jordan T. Camp and Christina Heatherton (New York: Verso, 2016); Don Mitchell, Kafui Attoh, and Lynn A. Staeheli, "'Broken Windows Is Not the Panacea': Common Sense, Good Sense, and Police Accountability in American Cities," in *Policing the Planet*.

8. Robin D.G. Kelley, "Why We Won't Wait," Counterpunch.org, November 25, 2014; Vijay Prashad, "Now, Ferguson," *Frontline*, December 26, 2014, http://www.frontline.in/worldaffairs/nowferguson/article6672415.ece; Barbara Ransby, "Ella Taught Me: Shattering the Myth of the Leaderless Movement," Colorlines.com, June 12, 2015, https://www.colorlines.com/articles/ella-taught-me-shattering-myth-leaderless-movement; Keeanga-Yamahtta Taylor, "Organizing Fergusons," *Jacobin* (November 2014), https://www.jacobinmag.com/2014/11/organizing-fergusons/; Marie Gottschalk, *Caught: The Prison State and the Lockdown of American Politics* (Princeton, NJ: Princeton University Press, 2014), 260.

9. Doreen Massey, "The Political Struggle Ahead," *Soundings* 44 (Spring 2010): 15; "Editorial," *Soundings* 44 (Spring 2010): 5; Stuart Hall and Doreen Massey, "Interpreting the Crisis," *Soundings* 44 (Spring 2010): 58; David Theo Goldberg, *The Threat of Race: Reflections on Racial Neoliberalism* (Malden, MA: Wiley-Blackwell, 2009), 80.

10. Martha Biondi, *To Stand and Fight: The Struggle for Civil Rights in Postwar New York City* (Cambridge, MA: Harvard University Press, 2003), 285; Robin D.G. Kelley, "John Brown's Body: Abolition Democracy and Permanent War," Toni Morrison Lectures, Center for African American Studies,

Princeton University, April 13, 2015; Mahmood Mamdani, *Good Muslim, Bad Muslim: America, the Cold War, and the Roots of Terror* (New York: Doubleday, 2004), 95, 124; Clyde Woods, "'Sittin' on Top of the World': The Challenges of Blues and Hip Hop Geography," in *Black Geographies and the Politics of Place,* ed. Katherine McKittrick and Clyde Woods (Cambridge, MA: South End Press, 2007), 47–48; Vijay Prashad, "This Ends Badly: Race and Capitalism," in *Policing the Planet*; Stuart Hall et al., *Policing the Crisis*, 332–33.

11. Stuart Hall, "The Problem of Ideology—Marxism Without Guarantees," *Journal of Communication Inquiry* (1986): 43; George Lipsitz, "The Struggle for Hegemony," *Journal of American History* 75, no. 1 (June 1988): 146–50; Daniel Widener, *Black Arts West: Culture and Struggle in Postwar Los Angeles* (Durham, NC: Duke University Press, 2010), 8, 225; Stuart Hall et al., *Policing the Crisis,* 332–33.

12. Paul Gilroy, "Civilisationism, Securitocracy and Racial Resignation," Johannesburg Workshop in Theory and Criticism Salon 1 (2009), http://www.jwtc.org.za/the_salon/volume_1/paul_gilroy.htm; Nikhil Singh, "Cold War Redux: On the 'New Totalitarianism,'" *Radical History Review* 85 (Winter 2003): 171–81.

13. Paul Ortiz, "The Anatomy of a Rebellion," *Against the Current* (January–February 2000), solidarity-us.org; Penny M. Von Eschen, *Race Against Empire: Black Americans and Anticolonialism, 1937–1957* (Ithaca, NY: Cornell University Press, 1997); Nikhil Pal Singh, *Black Is a Country: Race and the Unfinished Struggle for Democracy* (Cambridge, MA: Harvard University Press, 2005).

14. Stuart Hall and Martin Jacques, eds., *The Politics of Thatcherism* (London: Lawrence and Wishart, 1983), 11; James Kilgore, *Understanding Mass Incarceration,* 228–34.

15. Stuart Hall, "Gramsci's Relevance for the Study of Race and Ethnicity," 15, 27; Antonio Gramsci, *Selections from the Prison Notebooks* (New York: International Publishers, 1971), 178.

16. Cyril Neville, "Brand New Blues," from the album *Brand New Blues* (M. C. Records, 2009).

17. On the ways in which neoliberalism has persisted despite popular mystifications declaring the "end of neoliberalism," see Neil Smith, *Uneven Development: Nature, Capital, and the Production of Space* (1984; reprint, Athens: University of Georgia Press, 2008), 240; Doreen Massey, "The Political Struggle Ahead," 16–17; David Theo Goldberg, *The Threat of Race,* 89.

18. Cyril Neville, "Cheatin' and Lyin'," from the album *Brand New Blues*.

19. Christina Heatherton, ed., *Downtown Blues: A Skid Row Reader* (Los Angeles: Freedom Now Books, 2011); Gillian Hart, "D/developments After the Meltdown," *Antipode* 41, no. S1 (2010): 125–26; Paul Gilroy, *Darker Than Blue: On the Moral Economies of Black Atlantic Culture* (Cambridge, MA: Harvard University Press, 2010), 7, 13, 176.

20. Alicia Garza, "A Herstory of the Black Lives Matter Movement," TheFeministWire.com, October 7, 2014; Alicia Garza and Patrisse Cullors-Brignac, "Celebrating MLK Day: Reclaiming Our Movement Legacy," Huffin-

gtonPost.com, January 18, 2015; Robin D.G. Kelley, "Why We Won't Wait," Counterpunch.org, November 25, 2014; Manning Marable, "The Third Reconstruction: Black Nationalism and Race in a Revolutionary America," *Social Text* 4 (Autumn 1981): 3–27; Walda Katz-Fishman and Jerome Scott, "The South and the Black Radical Tradition: Then and Now," *Critical Sociology* 28, nos. 1–2 (2002): 169–99; Paul Ortiz, "The Battle of New Orleans," in *Hurricane Katrina: Response and Responsibilities,* ed. John Brown Childs (Santa Cruz, CA: New Pacific Press, 2008), 5.

21. George Lipsitz, *How Racism Takes Place* (Philadelphia: Temple University Press, 2011), 17; Robin D.G. Kelley, *Yo' Mama's Disfunktional! Fighting the Culture Wars in Urban America* (Boston: Beacon Press, 1997), 125–58.

22. Robin D.G. Kelley, "Thug Nation: On State Violence and Disposability," in *Policing the Planet*; Barbara Ransby, "The Class Politics of Black Lives Matter," *Dissent* 62, no. 4 (Fall 2015): 31–34.

23. Christina Heatherton, "#BlackLivesMatter and Global Visions of Abolition: An Interview with Patrisse Cullors," in *Policing the Planet*.

24. George Lipsitz, "From Plessy to Ferguson," *Cultural Critique* 90 (Spring 2015): 135.

25. Mike Davis, *Prisoners of the American Dream* (New York: Verso, 1986), 299, 310; Vijay Prashad, "This Ends Badly: Race and Capitalism," in *Policing the Planet*.

26. Tony Jefferson, "Exploring the Continuing Relevance of Policing the Crisis," *City* 18, no. 2 (2014): 157; Stuart Hall and Martin Jacques, eds., *The Politics of Thatcherism*, 9–12, 21–23; Stuart Hall, *The Hard Road to Renewal: Thatcherism and the Crisis of The Left* (London: Verso, 1988), 195, 183.

27. Mike Davis, *Prisoners of the American Dream*, 310.

28. Gillian Hart, "D/developments After the Meltdown" 136–37; Robin D.G. Kelley, *Yo' Mama's Disfunktional!*, 155; George P. Rawick, *From Sundown to Sunup: The Making of the Black Community* (Westport, CT: Greenwood Publishing, 1972), 159; Stuart Hall, *The Hard Road to Renewal*, 183; Stuart Hall, "The Kilburn Manifesto: Our Challenge to the Neoliberal Victory," *The Guardian*, April 24, 2013, http://www.theguardian.com/commentisfree/2013/apr/24/kilburn-manifesto-challenge-neoliberal-victory.

Bibliography

PRIMARY SOURCES

COLLECTIONS OF PAPERS

Berkeley

    Bancroft Library, University of California at Berkeley

Social Protest Collection

Detroit

    Walter P. Reuther Library of Labor and Urban Affairs, Wayne State University

Martin and Jessie Glaberman Collection
Detroit Revolutionary Movements Collection
Ken and Sheila Cockrel Collection

Los Angeles

    Southern California Library for Social Studies and Research

1992 Uprising Collection
Civil Rights Congress Collection

    UCLA Film and Television Archive

News and Public Affairs Collection

Pacifica Radio News Archive

New York

Tamiment Institute Archive, Bobst Library, New York University
James E. Jackson and Esther Cooper Jackson Collection
National Lawyers Guild Records
Newspapers Collection
Printed Ephemera Collection
Radical Pamphlet Collection

New York Public Library

Schomburg Center for Research in Black Culture
Angela Davis Legal Defense Collection
Louis E. Burnham Newspaper Collection
W. E. B. Du Bois Papers
Paul Robeson Papers
Civil Rights Congress Records
National Alliance Against Racism and Political Repression Records

Palo Alto, California

Department of Special Collections and University Archives, Stanford
University Libraries
Dr. Huey P. Newton Foundation Inc. Collection
Black Panther Party Records

San Francisco

Freedom Archives
Committee to End the Marion Lockdown Collection
Freedom Is a Constant Struggle Collection
Political Prisoners Collection

ORAL HISTORIES AND INTERVIEWS

"Black Editor: An Interview [with John Watson]." *Radical America* 2, no. 4 (July–August, 1968): 30–38.

Boggs, Grace Lee. Interview by Dan Georgakas. March 28, 1983. Oral History of the American Left Collection, Tamiment Library, New York University.

Boggs, James. Interview by Dan Georgakas. March 29, 1983. Oral History of the American Left Collection, Tamiment Library, New York University.

Camp, Jordan T. "Black Radicalism, Marxism, and Collective Memory: An Interview with Robin D. G. Kelley." *American Quarterly* 65, no. 1 (2013): 215–30.

CovertAction Information Bulletin. "Uprising and Repression in L.A.: An Interview with Mike Davis." In *Reading Rodney King/Reading Urban Uprising*, 142–54. Edited by Robert Gooding-Williams. New York: Routledge, 1993.

Fighting Back! Attica Memorial Book. Buffalo, New York: Attica Brothers Legal Defense, 1974. Printed Ephemera Collection on Organizations, Tamiment Library, New York University.

Glaberman, Martin. Interview by Dan Georgakas. March 29, 1983. Oral History of the American Left Collection, Tamiment Library, New York University.

Gómez, Alan Eladio. "Troubadour of Justice: An Interview with raúlsalinas." *Latino Studies* 6 (2008): 182–83.

Gordon, Avery F. "Globalism and the Prison Industrial Complex: An Interview with Angela Davis." *Race and Class* 40, nos. 2–3 (1999): 145–57.

Hall, Stuart, and Les Back. "In Conversation: At Home and Not at Home." *Cultural Studies* 23, no. 4 (July 2009): 658–87.

Holtzman, Benjamin. "An Interview with Robin D. G. Kelley." *In the Middle of a Whirlwind.* 2008. http://inthemiddleofthewhirlwind.wordpress.com/an-interview-with-robin-dg-kelley/.

"An Interview with Ken Cockrel and Mike Hamlin of the League of Revolutionary Black Workers." *Leviathan* 2, no. 2 (June 1970). Detroit Revolutionary Movements Collection, Walter P. Reuther Library of Labor and Urban Affairs, Wayne State University, Detroit.

Jhally, Sut. Interview with Stuart Hall. London, August 30, 2012. http://www.mediaed.org/stuarthall/.

Katz, Cindi, and Neil Smith. "L.A. Intifada: An Interview with Mike Davis." *Social Text* 33 (1992): 19–33.

Mast, Robert H. *Detroit Lives.* Philadelphia: Temple University Press, 1994.

Melhem, D. H. "Interview with Jayne Cortez." *MELUS* 21, no. 1, "Poetry and Poetics" (Spring 1996): 71–79.

Miller, E. Ethelbert. "An Interview with Kalamu ya Salaam." *Foreign Policy in Focus.* May 15, 2007. http://www.fpif.org/articles/interview_with_kalamu_ya_salaam.

Morse, Chuck. "Capitalism, Marxism, and the Black Radical Tradition: An Interview with Cedric Robinson." *Perspectives on Anarchist Theory* (Spring 1999). http://flag.blackened.net/ias/5robinsoninterview.htm.

Rawick, George P. Interview by Paul Buhle. October 4, 1984. Oral History of the American Left Collection, Tamiment Library, New York University.

Rubin, Rachel. "'We Don't Have Much Time': An Interview with Raúl Salinas." In *Radicalism in the South Since Reconstruction*, 227–37. Edited by Chris Green, Rachel Rubin, and James Smethurst. New York: Palgrave MacMillan, 2006.

Schwartz, Bill. "Living with Difference: An Interview with Stuart Hall." *Soundings* 37 (2007): 148–58.

Simon, John K. "Michel Foucault on Attica: An Interview." *Telos* 19 (Spring 1974): 154–61.

Voices from Inside: 7 Interviews with Attica Prisoners (April 1972). National Lawyers Guild Records, Tamiment Library, New York University.

Weir, Stan. Interview by Paul Buhle. October 22, 1982. Oral History of the American Left Collection, Tamiment Library, New York University.

Woods, Clyde "The Politics of Reproductive Violence: An Interview with Shana Griffin." *American Quarterly* 61, no. 3 (2009): 583–91.

ORAL HISTORY INTERVIEWS WITH THE AUTHOR

Baker, General Gordon. Detroit. August 20, 2009.

Cunningham, Dennis. San Francisco. September 17, 2009.

Deutsch, Michael. Chicago. August 12, 2009.

Fink, Elizabeth. San Francisco. September 15, 2009.

Garon, Paul. Chicago. August 13, 2009.

Jackson, Esther Cooper. Brooklyn. October 12, 2012.

Kurshan, Nancy. Chicago. August 11, 2009.

O'Dell, Jack. Vancouver. November 24, 2012.

Patterson, Sunni. Telephone interview. March 11, 2009.

Ramírez, José. Los Angeles. February 10, 2011.

Rosemont, Penelope. Chicago. August 13, 2009.

Scott, Jerome. Atlanta. February 17, 2011.

Whitman, Steve. Chicago. August 11, 2009.

GOVERNMENT DOCUMENTS

Bush, George. "Address to the Nation on the Civil Disturbances in Los Angeles, California." May 1, 1992. http://www.presidency.ucsb.edu/ws/index.php?pid=20910.

California Department of Corrections. *California Prisoners: Summary Statistics of Felon Prisoners and Parolees.* Sacramento, 1969.

———. *California Prisoners and Parolees, 1993 and 1994.* Sacramento, 1996.

———. *California Prisoners and Parolees, 2000.* Sacramento, 2000.

Christopher, Warren, et al. *Report of the Independent Commission on the Los Angeles Police Department.* Los Angeles: Independent Commission of the Los Angeles Police Department, 1991.

Glaze, Lauren E., and Danielle Kaeble. "Correctional Populations in the United States, 2013." *Bureau of Justice Statistics,* December 19, 2014.

Johnson, Lyndon. "Statement on Watts Riots." 1965. http://www.historycentral.com/documents/LBJwatts.html.

Kerner, Otto, et al. *Report of the National Advisory Commission on Civil Disorders.* New York: Bantam Books, 1968.

Langan, Patrick A. "Race of Prisoners Admitted to State and Federal Institutions, 1926–86." *Bureau of Justice Statistics.* Washington, DC: U.S. Department of Justice, May 1991.

McKay, Robert B., et al. *Attica: The Official Report of the New York State Special Commission on Attica.* New York: Bantam Books, 1972.

Moynihan, Daniel P. *The Negro Family: The Case for National Action.* Washington, DC: Office of Policy Planning and Research, United States Department of Labor, March 1965.

U.S. Army and Marine Corps. *Counter-Insurgency Field Manual: U.S. Army Field Manual No. 3–24*. Chicago: University of Chicago Press, 2007.

U.S. Census Bureau. "State and County Quick Facts: New Orleans, Louisiana." http://quickfacts.census.gov/qfd/states/22/2255000.html.

U.S. Congress. *Marion Penitentiary—1985: Oversight Hearing Before the Subcommittee on Courts, Civil Liberties, and the Administration of Justice of the Committee on the Judiciary, House of Representatives, Ninety-Ninth Congress, First Session, on Marion Penitentiary—1985*. June 26, 1985.

U.S. Office of the Press Secretary. "President Bush Participates in Joint Press Availability with President Calderón of Mexico and Prime Minister Harper of Canada." April 22, 2008. http://georgewbush-whitehouse.archives.gov /news/releases/2008/04/20080422–5.html.

———. "Press Briefing by Scott McClellan." September 1, 2005.

NEWSPAPERS, CONTEMPORARY MAGAZINES,
RADIO, AND TELEVISION NEWS

ABC News
Army Times
Atlantic Monthly
Attica News
CBS News
Chicago Sun-Times
Chicago Tribune
City Journal (New York)
CNN
Colorlines
Community Connection
Counterpunch.org
Daily Worker
Daily World
Dallas Morning News
Democracy Now!
Detroit Free Press
Feminist Wire
Foreign Policy in Focus
Freedom
Freedomways
Frontline
The Guardian
Harper's
Huffington Post
Inner City Voice (Detroit)
Jacobin
KOMO TV (Seattle)
Le Monde Diplomatique
London Review of Books
Los Angeles Magazine

Los Angeles Times
Mother Jones
The Nation
NBC News
Newsweek
New Yorker
New York Post
New York Times
National Public Radio
Political Affairs
Prisonradio.org
Rolling Stone
Salon
South End (Wayne State University)
Speak Out (Detroit)
Time
Times-Picayune (New Orleans)
USA Today
U.S. News & World Report
Washington Post
WTTW Chicago Public Media
ZNet

SECONDARY SOURCES
Books, Articles, and Published Proceedings
Abu-Jamal, Mumia. *Live from Death Row*. New York: Addison-Wesley Publishing Company, 1995.
Abu-Lughod, Janet L. *Race, Space, and Riots in Chicago, New York, and Los Angeles*. New York: Oxford University Press, 2007.
Agamben, Giorgio. *State of Exception*. Translated by Kevin Attell. Chicago: University of Chicago Press, 2005.
Ahmad, Muhammad. *We Will Return in the Whirlwind: Black Radical Organizations, 1960–1975*. Chicago: Charles H. Kerr Publishing, 2007.
Alexander, Michelle. *The New Jim Crow: Mass Incarceration in the Age of Colorblindness*. New York: The New Press, 2010.
Ali, Mazher, et al. *State of the Dream 2011: Austerity for Whom?* Boston: United for a Fair Economy, 2011.
Althusser, Louis. *For Marx*. New York: Verso, 2005.
———. *Lenin and Philosophy and Other Essays*. New York: Monthly Review Press, 1971.
Alvarez, Luis. "From Zoot Suits to Hip Hop: Towards a Relational Chicana/o Studies." *Latino Studies* 5 (2007): 53–75.
———. *The Power of the Zoot: Youth Culture and Resistance During World War II*. Berkeley: University of California Press, 2008.
American Civil Liberties Union of Southern California. *Civil Liberties in Crisis: Los Angeles During the Emergency*. Los Angeles: ACLU, June 23, 1992.

Anderson, Michael, et al., eds. *Without Housing: Decades of Federal Housing Cutbacks, Massive Homelessness, and Policy Failures.* San Francisco: Western Regional Advocacy Project, 2010.

Aptheker, Bettina. *The Morning Breaks: The Trial of Angela Davis.* New York: Cornell University Press, 1999.

Arend, Orissa. *Showdown in Desire: The Black Panthers Take a Stand in New Orleans.* Fayetteville: University of Arkansas Press, 2009.

Arrighi, Giovanni. *Adam Smith in Beijing: Lineages of the Twenty-First Century.* New York: Verso, 2007.

———. *The Long Twentieth Century: Money, Power, and the Origins of Our Times.* New York: Verso, 2010.

Arrighi, Giovanni, Terence K. Hopkins, and Immanuel Wallerstein. *Antisystemic Movements.* London and New York: Verso, 1989.

Ash, Amin, ed. *Post-Fordism: A Reader.* Malden, MA: Blackwell, 1994.

Bakhtin, M. M. *Speech Genres and Other Late Essays.* Austin: University of Texas Press, 1986.

Baldwin, James. *The Evidence of Things Not Seen.* New York: Henry Holt and Company, 1985.

———. *The Fire Next Time.* New York: Dial Press, 1963.

———. *No Name in the Street.* New York: Random House, 1972.

———. *The Price of the Ticket: Collected Nonfiction 1948–1945.* New York: St. Martin's Press, 1985.

Baldwin, James, and Margaret Mead. *A Rap on Race.* New York: J. B. Lippincott, 1971.

Bardhan, Ashok, and Richard Walker. "California, Pivot of the Great Recession." *Working Paper Series no. 203–210.* Berkeley: Institute for Research on Labor and Employment, University of California, Berkeley, March 2010.

Basu, Dipannita, and Sidney J. Lemelle, eds. *The Vinyl Ain't Final.* London: Pluto Press, 2006.

Benjamin, Walter. *The Arcades Project.* Cambridge, MA: Harvard University Press, 1999.

———. "Theses on the Philosophy of History." In *Illuminations: Essays and Reflections*, 253–64. Edited by Hannah Arendt. New York: Schocken Books, 1968.

Berger, Dan. *Captive Nation: Black Prison Organizing in the Civil Rights Era.* Chapel Hill: University of North Carolina Press, 2014.

Berger, John. *Ways of Seeing.* London: Penguin Books, 1972.

Bergeson, Albert. "Race Riots of 1967: An Analysis of Police Violence in Detroit and Newark." *Journal of Black Studies* 12, no. 3 (March 1982): 261–74.

Bierria, Alisa, Shana Griffin, Mayaba Liebenthal, and Incite! Women of Color Against Violence and Racism. "To Render Ourselves Visible: Women of Color Organizing and Hurricane Katrina." In *What Lies Beneath: Katrina, Race, and the State of the Nation*, 31–47. Edited by South End Press Collective. Cambridge, MA: South End Press, 2007.

Biondi, Martha. *To Stand and Fight: The Struggle for Civil Rights in Postwar New York City.* Cambridge, MA: Harvard University Press, 2003.

Birnbaum, Jonathan, and Clarence Taylor, eds. *Civil Rights Since 1787: A Reader on the Black Struggle.* New York: New York University Press, 2000.

Blackstock, Nelson, ed. *Cointelpro: The FBI's Secret War on Political Freedom.* New York: Pathfinder Press, 1988.

Blasi, Gary, and the UCLA School of Law Fact Investigation Clinic. *Policing Our Way Out of Homelessness? The First Year of the Safer Cities Initiative on Skid Row.* Los Angeles: UCLA and USC Center for Sustainable Cities, September 24, 2007.

Blasi, Gari, and Forrest Stuart. *Has the Safer Cities Initiative in Skid Row Reduced Serious Crime?* Los Angeles: UCLA Law School, September 15, 2008.

Boggs, Grace Lee. *Living for Change: An Autobiography.* Minneapolis: University of Minnesota Press, 1998.

Bogues, Anthony. *Black Heretics, Black Prophets: Radical Political Intellectuals.* New York: Routledge, 2003.

———. "Working Outside Criticism: Thinking Beyond Limits." *boundary 2* 32, no. 1 (2005): 71–93.

Bond, Julian. Foreword to *If They Come in the Morning: Voices of Resistance.* Edited by Angela Y. Davis. New York: Signet, 1971.

Bonefeld, Werner. "Monetarism and Crisis." In *Global Capital, National State and the Politics of Money*, 35–68. Edited by Werner Bonefeld and John Holloway. London: MacMillan, 1995.

Brenner, Neil, Jamie Peck, and Nik Theodore. "After Neoliberalization?" *Globalizations* 7, no. 3 (2010): 327–45.

Brenner, Robert. "The Political Economy of Rank-and-File Rebellion." In *Rebel Rank and File: Labor Militancy and Revolt from Below During the Long 1970s*, 37–74. Edited by Aaron Brenner, Robert Brenner, and Cal Winslow. New York: Verso, 2010.

Briggs, Laura. *Reproducing Empire: Race, Sex, Science, and Imperialism in Puerto Rico.* Berkeley and Los Angeles: University of California Press, 2002.

Brown, Michelle. "Setting the Conditions for Abu Ghraib: The Prison Nation Abroad." *American Quarterly* 57, no. 3 (2005): 973–97.

Buff, Rachel. "The Deportation Terror." *American Quarterly* 60, no. 3 (September 2008): 523–51.

Bullard, Robert D., and Charles Lee. "Introduction: Racism and American Apartheid." In *Residential Apartheid: The American Legacy.* Edited by Robert D. Bullard et al. Los Angeles: Center for Afro-American Studies Publications, 1994.

Bush, Rod. *We Are Not What We Seem: Black Nationalism and Class Struggle in the American Century.* New York: New York University Press, 2000.

Callahan, Manuel, ed. "Zapatismo as Political and Cultural Practice." Special issue of *Humboldt Journal of Social Relations* 29, no. 1 (Spring 2005).

Camp, Jordan T., and Christina Heatherton. *Freedom Now! Struggles for the Human Right to Housing in Los Angeles and Beyond.* Los Angeles: Freedom Now Books, 2012.

———. *Policing the Planet: Why the Policing Crisis Led to Black Lives Matter.* New York: Verso, 2016.

Campbell, Horace. *Rasta and Resistance: From Marcus Garvey to Walter Rodney*. Trenton, NJ: Africa World Press, 1987.

Carby, Hazel V. *Cultures in Babylon: Black Britain and African America*. New York: Verso, 1999.

———. "US/UK's Special Relationship: The Culture of Torture in Abu Ghraib and Lynching Photographs." *Journal of Contemporary African Art* 20 (Fall 2006): 60–71.

Centre for Contemporary Cultural Studies, eds. *The Empire Strikes Back: Race and Racism in 70s Britain*. London: Hutchinson/Centre for Contemporary Cultural Studies, University of Birmingham, 1982.

Césaire, Aimé. "Poetry and Knowledge." In *Refusal of the Shadow: Surrealism and the Caribbean*, 134–46. Edited and translated by Michael Richardson and Krzysztof Fijalkowski. London: Verso, 1996.

Chakravartty, Paula, and John D. H. Downing, "Media, Technology, and the Global Financial Crisis." *International Journal of Communication* 4 (2010): 693–95.

Chakravartty, Paula, and Denise Ferreira da Silva. "Accumulation, Dispossession, and Debt: The Racial Logic of Global Capitalism." *American Quarterly* 64, no. 3 (2012): 361–85.

Cheng, Wendy, and Michelle Commander. "Language Matters: Hurricane Katrina and Media Responsibility." In *Hurricane Katrina: Response and Responsibilities*, 92–94. Edited by John Brown Childs. Santa Cruz, CA: New Pacific Press, 2008.

Chicago Surrealist Group. "Three Days That Shook the New World Order." *Race Traitor* 2 (Summer 1993): 1–17.

Christianson, Scott. *With Liberty for Some: 500 Years of Imprisonment in America*. Boston: Northeastern University Press, 1998.

Churchill, Ward, and Jim Vander Wall. *Agents of Repression: The FBI's Secret Wars Against the Black Panther Party and the American Indian Movement*. Boston: South End Press, 1990.

Civil Rights Congress. *We Charge Genocide: The Historic Petition to the United Nations for Relief from a Crime of the United States Government Against the Negro People*. New York: International Publishers, 1971.

Clarke, John. "Still Policing the Crisis?" *Crime, Media, Culture* 41, no. 1 (2008): 123–29.

Coffey, Shelby, ed. *Understanding the Riots: Los Angeles Before and After the Rodney King Case*. Los Angeles: Los Angeles Times, July 1992.

Cohen, Stanley. *Folk Devils and Moral Panics*. New York: Routledge, 2002.

Committee to End the Marion Lockdown. *Can't Jail the Spirit: Political Prisoners in the U.S.* Chicago: Editorial El Coquí, 1992.

Crenshaw, Kimberlé, and Gary Peller. "Reel Time/Real Justice." In *Reading Rodney King/ Reading Urban Uprising*, 56–70. Edited by Robert Gooding-Williams. New York: Routledge, 1993.

Dahmann, Nicholas, with the Los Angeles Community Action Network. "Los Angeles: I Do Mind Dying, Recent Reflections on Urban Revolution in Skid Row." *Los Angeles Public Interest Law Journal* 2 (2009–10): 210–19.

da Silva, Denise Ferreira. "No-Bodies: Law, Raciality, and Violence." *Griffith Law Review* 18, no. 2 (2009): 224–27.

Davis, Angela Y. *Abolition Democracy: Beyond Empire, Prisons, and Torture.* New York: Seven Stories Press, 2005.

———. *Are Prisons Obsolete?* New York: Seven Stories Press, 2003.

———. Foreword to Mumia Abu-Jamal, *Jailhouse Lawyers: Prisoners Defending Prisoners v. the U.S.A.* San Francisco: City Lights Books, 2009.

———. "From the Convict Lease System to the Super-Max Prison." In *States of Confinement: Policing, Detention, and Prisons,* 60–74. Edited by Joy James. New York: St. Martin's Press, 2000.

———. "James and Esther Jackson: Connecting the Past to the Present." *American Communist History* 7, no. 2 (2008): 271–76.

———. "Lessons: From Attica to Soledad." In *If They Come in the Morning,* 44–47. Edited by Angela Y. Davis. New York: Signet, 1971.

———. *The Meaning of Freedom.* San Francisco: City Lights Press, 2012.

———. "Race and Criminalization: Black Americans and the Punishment Industry." In *The Angela Y. Davis Reader,* 74–95. Edited by Joy James. Malden, MA: Blackwell, 1998.

Davis, Angela Y., ed. *If They Come in the Morning: Voices of Resistance.* New York: Signet, 1971.

Davis, Mike. *City of Quartz: Excavating the Future in Los Angeles.* New York: Verso, 2006.

———. *Dead Cities.* New York: The New Press, 2002.

———. *Ecology of Fear: Los Angeles and the Imagination of Disaster.* New York: Metropolitan Books, 1998.

———. *A Planet of Slums.* New York: Verso, 2006.

———. *Prisoners of the American Dream.* New York: Verso, 1986.

———. "Who Killed Los Angeles? Part Two: The Verdict Is Given." *New Left Review* 1, no. 199 (1993): 29–54.

Davis, Mike, and Daniel Bertrand Monk, eds. *Evil Paradises: Dreamworlds of Neoliberalism.* New York: The New Press, 2007.

Dawson, Ashley, and Malini Johar Schueller, eds. *Exceptional State: Contemporary U.S. Culture and the New Imperialism.* Durham, NC: Duke University Press, 2007.

Dayan, Colin. "Due Process and Lethal Confinement." *South Atlantic Quarterly* 107, no. 3 (Summer 2008): 485–507.

De Genova, Nicholas. "The 'War on Terror' as Racial Crisis: Homeland Security, Obama, and Racial (Trans)Formations." In *Racial Formation in the Twenty-First Century,* 246–75. Edited by Daniel Martinez HoSang, Oneka LaBennet, and Laura Pulido. Berkeley: University of California Press, 2012.

De Giorgi, Alessandro. *Re-Thinking the Political Economy of Punishment: Perspectives on Post-Fordism and Penal Politics.* Burlington, VT: Ashgate, 2006.

Denning, Michael. *The Cultural Front: The Laboring of American Culture in the Twentieth Century.* New York: Verso, 1996.

———. *Culture in the Age of Three Worlds.* New York: Verso, 2005.

———. "Wageless Life." *New Left Review* 66 (November–December 2010): 79–97.

Deutsch, Michael E., Dennis Cunningham, and Elizabeth Fink. "Twenty Years Later—Attica Civil Rights Case Finally Cleared for Trial." *Social Justice* 18, no. 3 (Fall 1991): 13–25.

Deutsch, Michael E., and Jan Susler. "Political Prisoners in the United States: The Hidden Reality." *Social Justice* 18, no. 3 (1991): 92–106.

Díaz-Cotto, Juanita. "Latinas and the War on Drugs in the United States, Latin America, and Europe." In *Global Lockdown: Race, Gender, and the Prison-Industrial Complex*, 137–53. Edited by Julia Sudbury. New York: Routledge, 2005.

Diène, Doudou. *Report Submitted by the Special Rapporteur on Contemporary Forms of Racism, Racial Discrimination, Xenophobia And Related Intolerance*. Geneva: Human Rights Council, April 2009.

Domanick, Joe. *To Protect and Serve: The LAPD's Century of War in the City of Dreams*. New York: Pocket Books, 1994.

Donald, James, and Stuart Hall, eds. *Politics and Ideology*. Philadelphia: Open University Press, 1986.

Donner, Frank. *The Age of Surveillance: The Aims and Methods of America's Political Intelligence System*. New York: Vintage Books, 1981.

———. *Protectors of Privilege: Red Squads and Policing in Urban America*. Berkeley: University of California Press, 1990.

Du Bois, W. E. B. *Autobiography of W. E. B. Du Bois: A Soliloquy on Viewing My Life from the Last Decade of Its First Century*. New York: International Publishers, 1968.

———. *Black Reconstruction in America: An Essay Toward a History of the Part Which Black Folk Played in the Attempt to Reconstruct Democracy in America, 1860–1880*. New York: The Free Press, 1992.

Duggan, Lisa. *The Twilight of Equality? Neoliberalism, Cultural Politics, and the Attack on Democracy*. Boston: Beacon, 2003.

Dunn, Timothy J. "Border Militarization via Drug and Immigration Enforcement: Human Rights Implications." *Social Justice* 28, no. 2 (2001): 7–30.

Dymski, Gary A. "Racial Exclusion and the Political Economy of the Subprime Crisis." *Historical Materialism* 17 (2009): 149–79.

Edwards, Brent Hayes. "The 'Autonomy' of Black Radicalism." *Social Text* 19, no. 2 (Summer 2001): 1–13.

———. *The Practice of Diaspora: Literature, Translation, and the Rise of Black Internationalism*. Cambridge, MA: Harvard University Press, 2003.

Engels, Friedrich. *The Housing Question*. Moscow: Progress Publishers, 1979.

Espada, Martín. *Zapata's Disciple*. Cambridge, MA: South End Press, 1998.

Feldman, Allen. *Formations of Violence: The Narrative of the Body and Terror in Northern Ireland*. Chicago: University of Chicago Press, 1991.

Ferguson, Roderick. *Aberrations in Black: Toward a Queer of Color Critique*. Minneapolis: University of Minnesota Press, 2004.

Fischlin, Daniel, Ajay Heble, and George Lipsitz. *The Fierce Urgency of Now: Improvisation, Rights, and the Ethics of Cocreation*. Durham, NC: Duke University Press, 2013.

Fitz, Don, and David Roediger, eds. *Within the Shell of the Old: Essays on Workers Self-Organization, A Salute to George Rawick*. Chicago: Charles H. Kerr Publishing Company, 1990.

Flaherty, Jordan. *Floodlines: Community and Resistance from Katrina to the Jena Six*. Chicago: Haymarket Books, 2010.

Fletcher Jr., Bill, and Fernando Gapasin. *Solidarity Divided: The Crisis in Organized Labor and a New Path Toward Social Justice*. Berkeley: University of California Press, 2009.

Fogelson, Robert M., and Robert B. Hill. "Who Riots? A Study in of Participation in the 1967 Riots." In *Racial Violence in the United States*, 313–16. Edited by Allen Grimshaw. Chicago: Aldine Publishing Company, 1969.

Foner, Philip S. *American Socialism and Black Americans: From the Age of Jackson to World War II*. Westport, CT: Greenwood Press, 1977.

Foner, Philip S., ed. *Paul Robeson Speaks*. New York: Citadel Press, 1978.

Foucault, Michel. *Discipline and Punish: The Birth of the Prison*. New York: Vintage Books, 1977.

———. *Power: Essential Works of Michel Foucault 1954–1984*, volume 3. Edited by James D. Faubion. New York: The Free Press, 2000.

———. *Security, Territory, Population: Lectures at the Collège de France, 1977–78*. Edited by Michel Senellart. Translated by Graham Burchell. New York: Palgrave MacMillan, 2007.

———. *Society Must Be Defended: Lectures at the Collège de France, 1975–76*. Translated by David Macey. New York: Picador, 2003.

Foucault, Michel, Catharine von Bülow, and Daniel Defert. "The Masked Assassination." In *Warfare in the American Homeland: Policing and Prisons in a Penal Democracy*, 140–60. Edited by Joy James. Durham, NC: Duke University Press, 2007.

Franklin, H. Bruce, ed. *Prison Writing in 20th-Century America*. New York: Penguin Books, 1998.

Freedomways, ed. *Paul Robeson: The Great Forerunner*. New York: International Publishers, 1998.

Freer, Regina. "L.A. Race Woman: Charlotta Bass and the Complexities of Black Political Development in Los Angeles." *American Quarterly* 56, no. 3 (2004): 607–32.

Fregoso, Rosa Linda. *meXicana Encounters: The Making of Social Identities in the Borderlands*. Berkeley: University of California Press, 2003.

Garrow, David J. *Bearing the Cross: Martin Luther King Jr. and the Southern Christian Leadership Conference*. New York: HarperCollins, 1986.

———. *The FBI and Martin Luther King Jr.: From Solo to Memphis*. New York: W. W. Norton & Company, 1981.

Georgakas, Dan, and Marvin Surkin. *Detroit: I Do Mind Dying*. Cambridge, MA: South End Press, 1998.

George, Susan. "How to Win the War of Ideas: Lessons from the Gramscian Right." *Dissent* (Summer 1997): 47–53.

Geschwender, James A. *Class, Race, and Worker Insurgency: The League of Revolutionary Black Workers*. New York: Cambridge University Press, 1977.

Gilmore, Ruth Wilson. "Fatal Couplings of Power and Difference: Notes on Racism and Geography." *Professional Geographer* 54, no. 1 (2002): 15–24.

———. "Globalisation and U.S. Prison Growth: From Military Keynesianism to Post-Keynesianism Militarism." *Race and Class* 40, nos. 2–3 (October 1998–March 1999): 171–88.

———. *Golden Gulag: Prisons, Surplus, Crisis, and Opposition in Globalizing California.* Berkeley: University of California Press, 2007.

———. "In the Shadow of the Shadow State." In *The Revolution Will Not Be Funded: Beyond the Non-Profit Industrial Complex.* Edited by Incite! Women of Color Against Violence. Cambridge, MA: South End Press, 2007.

———. "Race, Prisons, and War: Scenes from the History of U.S. Violence." *Socialist Register* 45 (2009): 73–87.

———. "Scholar-Activists in the Mix." *Progress in Human Geography* 29, no. 2 (2005): 177–82.

———. "Terror Austerity Race Gender Excess Theatre." In *Reading Rodney King/Reading Urban Uprising*, 23–37. Edited by Robert Gooding-Williams. New York: Routledge, 1993.

Gilmore, Ruth Wilson, and Craig Gilmore. "Beyond Bratton." In *Policing the Planet: Why the Policing Crisis Led to Black Lives Matter.* Edited by Jordan T. Camp and Christina Heatherton. New York: Verso, 2016.

———. "Restating the Obvious." In *Indefensible Space: The Architecture of the National Security State*, 141–61. Edited by Michael Sorkin. New York: Routledge, 2007.

Gilroy, Paul. *The Black Atlantic: Modernity and Double Consciousness.* Cambridge, MA: Harvard University Press, 1993.

———. "Civilisationism, Securitocracy and Racial Resignation." *Johannesburg Workshop in Theory and Criticism Salon* 1 (2009). http://www.jwtc.org.za/the_salon/volume_1/paul_gilroy.htm.

———. *Darker Than Blue: On the Moral Economies of Black Atlantic Culture.* Cambridge, MA: Harvard University Press, 2010.

———. "The Myth of Black Criminality." In *Law, Order and the Authoritarian State*, 107–20. Edited by Phil Scraton. Philadelphia: Open University Press, 1987.

———. "One Nation Under A Groove: The Cultural Politics of 'Race' and Racism in Britain." In *Anatomy of Racism*, 263–82. Edited by David Theo Goldberg. Minneapolis: University of Minnesota Press, 1990.

———. "Police and Thieves." In *The Empire Strikes Back: Race and Racism in 70s Britain*, 143–82. Edited by the Centre for Contemporary Cultural Studies. London: Hutchinson/Centre for Contemporary Cultural Studies, University of Birmingham, 1982.

———. "Steppin' Out of Babylon: Race, Class, and Autonomy." In *The Empire Strikes Back: Race and Racism in 70s Britain*, 276–34. Edited by the Centre for Contemporary Cultural Studies. London: Hutchinson/Centre for Contemporary Cultural Studies, University of Birmingham, 1982.

———. *"There Ain't No Black in the Union Jack": The Cultural Politics of Race and Nation.* Chicago: University of Chicago Press, 1991.

Gilroy, Paul, and Joe Simm. "Law, Order and the State of the Left." *Capital and Class* 25 (1985): 15–55.

Giroux, Henry A. "Mis/Education and Zero Tolerance: Disposable Youth and the Politics of Domestic Militarization." *boundary 2* 28, no. 3 (2001): 61–94.

———. *Stormy Weather: Katrina and the Politics of Disposability.* Boulder, CO: Paradigm, 2006.

Glaberman, Martin. *"Be His Payment High or Low": The American Working Class of the Sixties.* Detroit: Bewick Editions, 1975.

———. "Black Cats, White Cats, Wildcats: Autoworkers in Detroit." *Radical America* 9, no. 1 (January–February 1975): 25–29.

———. "The Dodge Revolutionary Union Movement." *International Socialism* 36 (April–May 1969). http://www.marxists.org/archive/glaberman/1969/04/drum.htm.

———. *Punching Out and Other Writings.* Edited by Staughton Lynd. Chicago: Charles H. Kerr Press, 2002.

———. "Workers Have to Deal with Their Own Reality and That Transforms Them." 1997. https://www.marxists.org.

Goldberg, David Theo. *The Threat of Race: Reflections on Racial Neoliberalism.* Malden, MA: Blackwell, 2009.

Goldstein, Alyosha. *Poverty in Common: The Politics of Community Action During the American Century.* Durham, NC: Duke University Press, 2012.

Goldstein, Robert Justin. *Political Repression in Modern America: From 1870 to the Present.* New York: Schenkman Publishing, 1978.

Gómez, Alan Eladio. "'Nuestras Vidas Corren Casi Paralelas': Chicanos, Independistas, and the Prison Rebellions in Leavenworth, 1969–1972." *Latino Studies* 6 (2008): 64–96.

———. "Resisting Living Death at Marion Federal Penitentiary, 1972." *Radical History Review* 96 (Fall 2006): 58–86.

Gomez-Barris, Macarena. *Where Memory Dwells: Culture and State Violence in Chile.* Berkeley: University of California Press, 2009.

Gordon, Avery F. "Abu Ghraib: Imprisonment and the War on Terror." *Race and Class* 48 (2006): 42–59.

———. "The Black Radical Tradition and the Academy: The Future of Radical Scholarship." *Race and Class* 47, no. 2 (2005): 82–87.

———. *Ghostly Matters: Haunting and the Sociological Imagination.* Minneapolis: University of Minnesota Press, 2008.

———. "The U.S. Military Prison: The Normalcy of Exceptional Brutality." In *The Violence of Incarceration*, 166–86. Edited by Phil Scraton and Jude McCulloch. New York: Routledge, 2009.

Gore, Dayo F. *Radicalism at the Crossroads: African American Women Activists in the Cold War.* New York: New York University Press, 2011.

Gottschalk, Marie. *Caught: The Prison State and the Lockdown of American Politics.* Princeton, NJ: Princeton University Press, 2014.

———. *The Prison and the Gallows: The Politics of Mass Incarceration in America.* New York: Cambridge University Press, 2006.

Graham, Stephen. *Cities Under Siege: The New Military Urbanism*. New York: Verso, 2010.

Gramsci, Antonio. *Selections from the Prison Notebooks*. New York: International Publishers, 1971.

Grandin, Greg. *Empire's Workshop: Latin America, the United States, and the Rise of the New Imperialism*. New York: Metropolitan Books, 2006.

Gray, Herman. "Where the Natural and the Social Meet." In *Hurricane Katrina: Response and Responsibilities*, 87–91. Edited by John Brown Childs. Santa Cruz, CA: New Pacific Press, 2008.

Guha, Ranajit. *Elementary Aspects of Peasant Insurgency in Colonial India*. Durham, NC: Duke University Press, 1999.

———. "The Prose of Counter-Insurgency." In *Selected Subaltern Studies*, 45–86. Edited by Ranajit Guha and Gayatri Chakravorty Spivak. New York: Oxford University Press, 1988.

Haas, Gilda. *Plant Closures: Myths, Realities and Responses*. Boston: South End Press, 1985.

Haas, Gilda, and Allan David Heskin. *Community Struggles in Los Angeles*. Los Angeles: UCLA School of Architecture and Urban Planning, 1981.

Hackworth, Jason. *The Neoliberal City: Governance, Ideology, and Development in American Urbanism*. Ithaca, NY: Cornell University Press, 2007.

Hall, Jacquelyn Dowd. "The Long Civil Rights Movement and the Political Uses of the Past." *Journal of American History* 91, no. 4 (March 2005): 1233–63.

Hall, Stuart. "Cultural Studies and Its Theoretical Legacies." In *Cultural Studies*, 277–86. Edited by Lawrence Grossberg, Cary Nelson, and Paul Treichler. New York: Routledge, 1992.

———. "Encoding/Decoding." In *Culture, Media, Language*, 128–38. Edited by Stuart Hall, Dorothy Hobson, Andrew Lowe, and Paul Willis. New York: Routledge, 1996.

———. "Gramsci and Us." *Marxism Today* (June 1987): 16–21.

———. "Gramsci's Relevance for the Study of Race and Ethnicity." *Journal of Communications Inquiry* 10 (1986): 5–27.

———. "Great Moving Right Show." *Marxism Today* (1979): 14–20.

———. *The Hard Road to Renewal: Thatcherism and the Crisis of the Left*. New York: Verso, 1988.

———. "The Neoliberal Revolution." *Soundings: A Journal of Politics and Culture* 48 (Summer 2011): 9–27.

———. "Notes on Deconstructing 'the Popular.'" In *People's History and Socialist Theory*, 227–40. Edited by Raphael Samuel. London: Routledge and Kegan Paul Ltd., 1981.

———. "The Problem of Ideology: Marxism Without Guarantees." *Journal of Communications Inquiry* 10, no. 28 (1986): 28–44.

———. "Race, Articulation and Societies Structured in Dominance." In *Sociological Theories: Race and Colonialism*, 305–45. Paris: UNESCO, 1980.

———. "Re-Thinking the 'Base-and-Superstructure' Metaphor." In *Class, Hegemony, and Party*, 43–72. Edited by Jon Bloomfield. London: Lawrence and Wishart, 1977.

———. "Signification, Representation, Ideology: Althusser and the Post-Structuralist Debates." *Critical Studies in Mass Communication* 2, no. 2 (June 1985): 91–114.

———. "Variants of Liberalism." In *Politics and Ideology*, 34–69. Edited by James Donald and Stuart Hall. Philadelphia: Open University Press, 1986.

Hall, Stuart, and Les Back. "In Conversation: At Home and Not at Home." *Cultural Studies* 23, no. 4 (July 2009): 658–88.

Hall, Stuart, Chas Critcher, Tony Jefferson, John Clarke, and Brian Roberts. *Policing the Crisis: Mugging, the State, and Law and Order*. New York: Palgrave MacMillan, 2013.

Hall, Stuart, and Martin Jacques, eds. *The Politics of Thatcherism*. London: Lawrence and Wishart, 1983.

Hall, Stuart, and Doreen Massey. "Interpreting the Crisis." *Soundings: A Journal of Politics and Culture* 44 (Spring 2010): 57–71.

Hamilton, Cynthia. "The Making of an American Bantustan." In *Inside the L.A. Riots: What Really Happened—and Why It Will Happen Again*, 19–20. Edited by Don Hazen. Los Angeles: Institute for Alternative Journalism, 1992.

Hamlin, Mike. Foreword to. *Rebel Rank and File: Labor Militancy and Revolt from Below During the Long 1970s*, vii–viii. Edited by Aaron Brenner, Robert Brenner, and Cal Winslow. New York: Verso, 2010.

Haney, Craig. "Mental Health Issues in Long-Term Solitary and 'Supermax' Confinement." *Crime and Delinquency* 49, no. 1 (January 2003): 124–56.

Haney-López, Ian F. "Post-Racial Racism: Racial Stratification and Mass Incarceration in the Age of Obama." *California Law Review* 98, no. 3 (2010): 1023–73.

Harcourt, Bernard E. *Illusion of Order: The False Promise of Broken Windows Policing*. Cambridge, MA: Harvard University Press, 2001.

Harding, Vincent. Introduction to Martin Luther King Jr., *Where Do We Go from Here: Chaos or Community?* Boston: Beacon, 2010.

———. *The Other American Revolution*. Los Angeles: Center for Afro-American Studies, University of California, 1980.

———. *There Is a River: The Black Struggle for Freedom in America*. San Francisco: Harcourt Brace and Company, 1981.

Harding, Vincent, Robin D. G. Kelley, and Earl Lewis. *We Changed the World: African Americans, 1945–1970*. New York: Oxford University Press, 1997.

Hardt, Michael, and Antonio Negri. *Empire*. Cambridge, MA: Harvard University Press, 2000.

Hart, Gillian. "D/developments After the Meltdown." *Antipode* 41, no. S1 (2010): 117–41.

———. *Disabling Globalization: Places of Power in Post-Apartheid South Africa*. Berkeley: University of California Press, 2002.

———. "Gramsci, Geography, and the Languages of Populism." In *Gramsci: Space, Nature, Politics*. Edited by Michael Ekers, Gillian Hart, Stefan Kipler, and Alex Loftus. Malden, MA: Wiley-Blackwell, 2013.

———. *Rethinking the South African Crisis: Nationalism, Populism, and Hegemony*. Athens: University of Georgia Press, 2014.

———. *Reworking Apartheid Legacies: Global Competition, Gender and Social Wages in South Africa, 1980–2000*. Geneva: United Nations Research Institute for Social Development, 2002.

Harvey, David. *A Brief History of Neoliberalism*. New York: Oxford University Press, 2005.

———. *The Condition of Postmodernity: An Enquiry Into the Origins of Cultural Change*. Cambridge, MA: Basil Blackwell, 1989.

———. *The Enigma of Capital and the Crises of Capitalism*. New York: Oxford, 2010.

———. *The New Imperialism*. New York: Oxford University Press, 2003.

———. *Rebel Cities: From the Right to the City to the Urban Revolution*. New York: Verso, 2012.

———. "The Right to the City." *New Left Review* 53 (2008): 23–40.

———. *Spaces of Global Capitalism: Towards a Theory of Uneven Geographical Development*. New York: Verso, 2006.

Heatherton, Christina, ed. *Downtown Blues: A Skid Row Reader*. Los Angeles: Los Angeles Community Action Network, 2011.

———. "Relief and Revolution: Southern California Struggles Against Unemployment, 1930–1933." In *Rising Tides of Color: Race, State Violence, and Radical Movements Across the Pacific*, 159–87. Edited by Moon-Ho Jung. Seattle: University of Washington Press, 2014.

Hebdige, Dick. *Subculture: The Meaning of Style*. New York: Routledge, 1989.

Hernández, David Manuel. "Pursuant to Deportation: Latinos and Immigrant Detention." *Latino Studies* 6 (2008): 35–63.

Hernández, Kelly Lytle, Khalil Gibran Muhammad, and Heather Ann Thompson. "Introduction: Constructing the Carceral State." *Journal of American History* 102, no. 1 (June 2015): 21.

Hill, Christopher. *The World Turned Upside Down*. London: Penguin Books, 1991.

Hill, Rebecca. "Fosterites and Feminists, or 1950s Ultra-Leftists and the Invention of AmeriKKKa." *New Left Review* 1, no. 228 (1998): 67–90.

———. *Men, Mobs, and Law: Anti-Lynching and Labor Defense in U.S. Radical History*. Durham, NC: Duke University Press, 2009.

Hinton, Elizabeth. "'A War Within Our Own Boundaries': Lyndon Johnson's Great Society and the Rise of the Carceral State." *Journal of American History* 102, no. 1 (June 2015): 100–112.

Ho, Fred. *Wicked Theory, Naked Practice: A Fred Ho Reader*. Edited by Diane Fujino. Minneapolis: University of Minnesota, 2009.

Holcomb, Gary Edward. *Code Name Sasha: Queer Black Marxism and the Harlem Renaissance*. Gainesville: University Press of Florida, 2007.

Holloway, John. "Dignity's Revolt." In *Zapatista! Reinventing Revolution in Mexico*, 159–98. Edited by John Holloway and Eloína Peláez. London: Pluto Press, 1998.

Honey, Michael K. *Going Down Jericho Road: The Memphis Strike, Martin Luther King's Last Campaign*. New York: W. W. Norton, 2007.

Horne, Gerald. *Black and Red: W. E. B. Du Bois and the Afro-American Response to the Cold War, 1944–1963*. Albany: State University of New York, 1986.

———. *Black Revolutionary: William Patterson and the Globalization of the African American Freedom Struggle.* Champaign: University of Illinois Press, 2013.

———. "Civil Rights Congress." In *Encyclopedia of the American Left,* 134–35. Edited by Mari Jo Buhle, Paul Buhle, and Dan Georgakas. New York: Oxford University Press, 1988.

———. *A Communist Front? The Civil Rights Congress, 1946–1956.* Rutherford, NJ: Fairleigh Dickinson University Press, 1988.

———. *Fire This Time: The Watts Uprising and the 1960s.* New York: Da Capo Press, 1997.

HoSang, Daniel Martinez. *Racial Propositions: Ballot Initiatives and the Making of Postwar California.* Berkeley: University of California Press, 2010.

HoSang, Daniel Martinez, Oneka LaBennet, and Laura Pulido, eds. *Racial Formation in the Twenty-First Century.* Berkeley: University of California Press, 2012.

Huggins, Martha K. *Political Policing: The United States and Latin America.* Durham, NC: Duke University Press, 1998.

Inmates of Attica Prison. "The Five Demands." In Tom Wicker, *A Time to Die,* 315–16. New York: Quadrangle/New York Times Book Co., 1975.

Institute for the Study of Labor and Economic Crisis. *The Iron Fist and the Velvet Glove: An Analysis of U.S. Police.* Berkeley: Crime and Social Justice Associates, 1982.

Jackson, George. *Soledad Brother: The Prison Letters of George Jackson.* New York: Coward-McCann 1994.

Jacobson, Matthew Frye. "Where We Stand: U.S. Empire at Street Level and in the Archive." *American Quarterly* 65, no. 2 (2013): 265–90.

James, C. L. R. *The Black Jacobins: Toussaint L'Ouverture and the San Domingo Revolution.* New York: Vintage Books, 1989.

———. *The Future in the Present.* London: Allison and Busby, 1977.

———. *Notes on Dialectics: Hegel–Marx-Lenin.* London: Allison and Busby, 1980.

James, Joy. "American 'Prison Notebooks.'" *Race and Class* 45, no. 3 (2004): 35–37.

———. "Political Literacy and Voice." In *What Lies Beneath: Katrina, Race, and the State of the Nation,* 157–66. Edited by South End Press Collective. Cambridge, MA: South End Press, 2007.

———. *Resisting State Violence: Radicalism, Gender, and Race in U.S. Culture.* Minneapolis: University of Minnesota Press, 1996.

James, Joy, ed. *Warfare in the American Homeland: Policing and Prison in a Penal Democracy.* Durham, NC: Duke University Press, 2007.

James, Selma. *Sex, Race, Class.* London: Housewives in Dialogue, 1986.

Jameson, Fredric. "Cognitive Mapping." In *Marxism and the Interpretation of Culture,* 347–57. Edited by Cary Nelson and Lawrence Grossberg. Urbana and Chicago: University of Illinois Press, 1988.

Jefferson, Tony. "Exploring the Continuing Relevance of Policing the Crisis." *City* 18, no. 2 (2014): 152–59.

Johnson, Cedric. Introduction to *The Neoliberal Deluge: Hurricane Katrina, Late Capitalism, and the Remaking of New Orleans,* xvii–xliii. Edited by Cedric Johnson. Minneapolis: University of Minnesota Press, 2011.

———. *Revolutionaries to Race Leaders: Black Power and the Making of African American Politics.* Minneapolis: University of Minnesota Press, 2007.

Johnson, Gaye Theresa. "A Sifting of Centuries: Afro-Chicano Interaction and Popular Musical Culture in California, 1960–2000." In *Decolonial Voices: Chicana and Chicano Cultural Studies in the 21st Century,* 316–29. Edited by Arturo J. Aldama and Naomi H. Quiñonez. Bloomington: Indiana University Press, 2002.

———. *Spaces of Conflict, Sounds of Solidarity: Music, Race, and Spatial Entitlement in Los Angeles.* Berkeley: University of California Press, 2013.

———. "Spatial Entitlement: Race, Displacement, and Reclamation in Post-War Los Angeles." In *Black and Brown Los Angeles: Beyond Conflict and Coalition,* 316–40. Edited by Josh Kun and Laura Pulido. Los Angeles: University of California Press, 2014.

Johnson, James H., Cloyzelle K. Jones, Walter C. Farrell Jr., and Melvin L. Oliver. "The Los Angeles Rebellion: A Retrospective View." *Economic Development Quarterly* 6, no. 4 (1992): 356–72.

Jones, Jacqueline. *The Dispossessed: America's Underclasses from the Civil War to the Present.* New York: Basic Books, 1992.

Jordan, June. "Burning All Illusions Tonight." In *Inside the L.A. Riots: What Really Happened—and Why it Will Happen Again,* 77–78. Edited by Don Hazen. Los Angeles: Institute for Alternative Journalism, 1992.

Joseph, Peniel E. *Waiting 'Til the Midnight Hour: A Narrative History of Black Power.* New York: Owl Books, 2006.

Jung, Moon-Ho. *Coolies and Cane: Race, Labor, and Sugar in the Age of Emancipation.* Baltimore: Johns Hopkins University Press, 2006.

———. "Seditious Subjects: Race, State Violence, and the U.S. Empire." *Journal of Asian American Studies* 14, no. 2 (June 2011): 221–47.

Jung, Moon-Kie, and Yaejoon Kwon. "Theorizing the U.S. Racial State: Sociology Since Racial Formation." *Sociology Compass* 7, no. 11 (2013): 927–40.

Kampfner, Christina Jose. "Las Mujeres Olvidadas: Women in Mexican Prisons." In *Global Lockdown: Race, Gender, and the Prison-Industrial Complex,* 127–36. Edited by Julia Sudbury. New York: Routledge, 2005.

Kaplan, Amy. *The Anarchy of Empire in the Making of U.S. Culture.* Cambridge, MA: Harvard University Press, 2002.

———. "Homeland Insecurities: Reflections on Language and Space." *Radical History Review* 85 (Winter 2003): 82–93.

———. "Violent Belongings and the Question of Empire Today: Presidential Address, American Studies Association, October 17, 2003." *American Quarterly* 56, no. 1 (March 2004): 1–18.

Katsiaficas, George. *The Imagination of the New Left: A Global Analysis of 1968.* Cambridge, MA: South End Press, 1987.

Katz, Cindi. "Bad Elements: Katrina and the Soured Landscape of Social Reproduction." *Gender, Place and Culture* 15, no. 1 (February 2008): 15–29.

———. "Childhood as Spectacle: Relays of Anxiety and the Reconfiguration of the Child." *Cultural Geographies* 15 (2008): 5–17.

———. "Vagabond Capitalism and the Necessity of Social Reproduction." *Antipode* 33, no. 4 (2001): 709–28.

Katz-Fishman, Walda, and Jerome Scott. "The South and the Black Radical Tradition: Then and Now." *Critical Sociology* 28, nos. 1–2 (2002): 169–99.

Kelley, Robin D. G. "Building Bridges: The Challenge of Organized Labor in Communities of Color." *New Labor Forum* (Fall–Winter 1999): 42–58.

———. "'Comrades, Praise Gawd for Lenin and Them!': Ideology and Culture Among Black Communists in Alabama, 1930–1935." *Science and Society* 52, no. 1 (Spring 1988): 59–82.

———. "Dig They Freedom: Meditations on History and the Black Avant-Garde." *Lenox Avenue: A Journal of Interarts Inquiry* 3 (1997): 13–27.

———. Foreword to Kristen L. Buras with Jim Randels, Kalamu ya Salaam, and Students at the Center, eds. *Pedagogy, Policy, and the Privatized City: Stories of Dispossession and Defiance from New Orleans.* New York: Teachers College Press, 2010.

———. *Freedom Dreams: The Black Radical Imagination.* New York: Beacon Press, 2002.

———. *Hammer and Hoe: Alabama Communists During the Great Depression.* Chapel Hill: University of North Carolina Press, 1990.

———. *Into the Fire: African Americans Since 1970.* New York: Oxford University Press, 1996.

———. Foreword to Angela Y. Davis, *The Meaning of Freedom.* San Francisco: City Lights Press, 2012.

———. *Race Rebels: Culture, Politics, and the Black Working Class.* New York: New Press, 1994.

———. "'Slangin' Rocks . . . Palestinian Style,' Dispatches from the Occupied Zones of North America." In *Police Brutality*, 21–59. Edited by Jill Nelson. New York: W. W. Norton and Company, 2000.

———. "Thug Nation: On State Violence and Disposability." In *Policing the Planet: Why the Policing Crisis Led to Black Lives Matter.* Edited by Jordan T. Camp and Christina Heatherton. New York: Verso, 2016.

———. *Yo' Mama's Disfunktional! Fighting the Culture Wars in Urban America.* Boston: Beacon Press, 1997.

Kelley, Robin D. G., and Franklin Rosemont. *Black, Brown, and Beige: Surrealist Writings from Africa and the Diaspora.* Austin: University of Texas Press, 2009.

Keve, Paul W. *Prisons and the American Conscience: A History of U.S. Federal Corrections.* Carbondale: Southern Illinois University, 1991.

Khalili, Laleh. *Time in the Shadows: Confinement in Counterinsurgencies.* Stanford, CA: Stanford University Press, 2013.

Kilgore, James. *Understanding Mass Incarceration: A People's Guide to the Key Civil Rights Struggle of Our Time.* New York: The New Press, 2015.

King Jr., Martin Luther. *"All Labor Has Dignity."* Edited and introduced by Michael Honey. Boston: Beacon Press, 2012.

———. "Honoring Dr. Du Bois, No. 2, 1968." In *Freedomways Reader: Prophets in Their Own Country*. Edited by Esther Cooper Jackson. Boulder, CO: Westview Press, 2000.

———. *Trumpet of Conscience*. Boston, Beacon Press, 2010.

———. *A Testament of Hope: The Essential Writings and Speeches of Martin Luther King*. New York: HarperCollins, 1986.

———. *Where Do We Go from Here: Chaos or Community?* Boston: Beacon Press, 2010.

Klein, Naomi. *The Shock Doctrine: The Rise of Disaster Capitalism*. New York: Picador, 2007.

Kohler-Hausmann, Julilly. "'The Attila the Hun Law': New York's Rockefeller Drug Laws and the Making of a Punitive State." *Journal of Social History* 44, no. 1 (Fall 2010): 71–95.

Kopkind, Andrew. "White on Black: The Riot Commission and the Rhetoric." In *The Politics of Riot Commissions*. Edited by Anthony M. Platt. New York: MacMillan Company, 1971.

Korstad, Robert, and Nelson Lichenstein. "Opportunities Found and Lost: Labor, Radicals, and Civil Rights." *Journal of American History* 75, no. 3 (1988): 786–811.

Kun, Josh. *Audiotopia: Music, Race, and America*. Berkeley: University of California Press, 2005.

Kushnick, Louis. "Responding to Urban Crisis." In *A New Introduction to Poverty: The Role of Race, Power, and Politics*, 156–63. Edited by James Jennings and Louis Kushnick. New York: New York University Press, 1999.

Labor/Community Strategy Center. *Reconstructing Los Angeles from the Bottom Up: A Long-Term Strategy for Workers, Low-Income People, and People of Color to Create an Alternative Vision of Urban Development*. Los Angeles: Labor/Community Strategy Center Report, 1993.

Laclau, Ernesto. *Politics and Ideology in Marxist Theory*. New York: Verso, 1977.

Lefebvre, Henri. *The Production of Space*. Malden, MA: Blackwell, 1991.

Lewis, David Levering. *W. E. B. Du Bois: The Fight for Equality and the American Century*. New York: Henry Holt and Company, 2000.

Lewis, Earl. *In Their Own Interests: Race, Class, and Power in Twentieth-Century Norfolk, Virginia*. Berkeley: University of California Press, 1991.

Linebaugh, Peter. "All the Atlantic Mountains Shook." *Labour/Le Traveailleur* 10 (Autumn 1982): 87–121.

———. Introduction to *George Rawick, 1930–1990*. Jamaica Plain, MA: Midnight Notes, 1990.

———. "Karl Marx, the Theft of the Wood, and Working-Class Composition: A Contribution to the Current Debate." *Crime and Social Justice* 6 (Fall–Winter 1976): 5–16.

———. *The London Hanged: Crime and Civil Society in the Eighteenth Century*. New York: Verso, 2006.

Linebaugh, Peter, and Bruno Ramirez. "Crisis in the Auto Sector." In *Midnight Oil: Work, Energy, War 1973–1992*. Edited by the Midnight Notes Collective. New York: Autonomedia, 1992.

Linebaugh, Peter, and Marcus Rediker. *The Many-Headed Hydra: Sailors, Slaves, Commoners, and the Hidden History of the Revolutionary Atlantic.* Boston: Beacon Press, 2001.

Lipsitz, George. "Abolition Democracy and Global Justice." *Comparative American Studies* 2, no. 3 (2004): 271–86.

———. *American Studies in a Moment of Danger.* Minneapolis: University of Minnesota Press, 2001.

———. "Con Safos: Can Cultural Studies Read the Writing on the Wall." In *The Chicana/o Cultural Studies Reader,* 47–69. Edited by Angie Chabram-Dernersesian. New York: Routledge, 2006.

———. "Cruising Around the Historical Bloc: Postmodernism and Popular Music in East Los Angeles." *Cultural Critique* 5 (1986–87): 157–77.

———. *Dangerous Crossroads: Popular Music, Postmodernism and the Poetics of Place.* New York: Verso, 1994.

———. *Footsteps in the Dark: The Hidden Histories of Popular Music.* Minneapolis: University of Minnesota Press, 2007.

———. Foreword to Johnny Otis, *Listen to the Lambs.* Minneapolis: University of Minnesota Press, 2009.

———. "'Home Is Where the Hatred Is': Work, Music, and the Transnational Economy." In *The Chicana/o Cultural Studies Reader,* 299–313. Edited by Angie Chabram-Dernersesian. New York: Routledge, 2006.

———. *How Racism Takes Place.* Philadelphia: Temple University Press, 2011.

———. "In an Avalanche Every Snowflake Pleads Not Guilty: The Collateral Consequences of Mass Incarceration and Impediments to Women's Fair Housing Rights." *UCLA Law Review* 59, no. 6 (2012): 1746–809.

———. "Learning from Los Angeles: Another One Rides the Bus." *American Quarterly* 56, no. 3 (2004): 511–29.

———. "Learning from Los Angeles: Producing Anarchy in the Name of Order." In *Freedom Now! Struggles for the Human Right to Housing in Los Angeles and Beyond,* 33–40. Edited by Jordan T. Camp and Christina Heatherton. Los Angeles: Freedom Now Books, 2012.

———. "Learning from New Orleans: The Social Warrant of Hostile Privatism and Competitive Consumer Citizenship." *Cultural Anthropology* 21, no. 3 (2006): 451–68.

———. *A Life in the Struggle: Ivory Perry and the Culture of Opposition.* Philadelphia: Temple University Press, 1998.

———. "Policing Place and Taxing Time on Skid Row." In *Policing the Planet: Why the Policing Crisis Led to Black Lives Matter.* Edited by Jordan T. Camp and Christina Heatherton. New York: Verso, 2016.

———. *The Possessive Investment in Whiteness: How White People Profit from Identity Politics.* Philadelphia: Temple University Press, 2006.

———. "The Possessive Investment in Whiteness: Racialized Social Democracy and the 'White' Problem in American Studies." *American Quarterly* 47, no. 3 (September 1995): 369–87.

———. *Rainbow at Midnight: Labor and Culture in the 1940s.* Urbana and Chicago: University of Illinois Press, 1994.

———. "The Struggle for Hegemony." *Journal of American History* 75, no. 1 (June 1988): 146–50.

———. *Time Passages: Collective Memory and American Popular Culture.* Minneapolis: University of Minnesota Press, 2006.

———. "We Know What Time It Is: Race, Class, and Youth Culture in the Nineties." In *Microphone Fiends: Youth Music & Youth Culture,* 17–28. Edited by Andrew Ross and Tricia Rose. New York: Routledge, 1994.

Lott, Eric. *Love and Theft: Blackface Minstrelsy and the American Working Class.* New York: Oxford University Press, 1993.

Lubiano, Wahneema, ed. *The House That Race Built.* New York: Vintage Books, 1998.

Luft, Rachel E. "Community Organizing in the Katrina Diaspora: Race, Gender, and the Case of the People's Hurricane Relief Fund." In *Displaced: Life in the Katrina Diaspora,* 233–55. Edited by Lynn Weber and Lori Peek. Austin: University of Texas Press, 2012.

Luft, Rachel E., with Shana Griffin. "A Status Report on Housing in New Orleans after Katrina: An Intersectional Analysis." In *Katrina and the Women of New Orleans,* 50–53. Edited by Beth Willinger. Newcomb College Center for Research on Women, December 2008.

Mamdani, Mahmood. *Good Muslim, Bad Muslim: America, the Cold War, and the Roots of Terror.* New York: Doubleday, 2004.

Mann, Eric. *Katrina's Legacy: White Racism and Black Reconstruction in New Orleans and the Gulf Coast.* Los Angeles: Frontlines Press, 2006.

Mantler, Gordon K. *Power to the Poor: Black-Brown Coalition and the Fight for Economic Justice, 1960–1974.* Chapel Hill: University of North Carolina Press, 2013.

Marable, Manning. Foreword to Dan Georgakas and Marvin Surkin, *Detroit: I Do Mind Dying,* ix–xi. Cambridge, MA: South End Press, 1998.

———. "Globalization and Racialization." *ZNet,* August 14, 2004. https://zcomm.org/znetarticle/globalization-and-racialization-by-manning-marable/.

———. *How Capitalism Underdeveloped Black America.* Cambridge, MA: South End Press, 2000.

———. *Race, Reform, and Rebellion: The Second Reconstruction and Beyond in Black America, 1945–2006.* Jackson: University of Mississippi Press, 2007.

———. "The Third Reconstruction: Black Nationalism and Race in a Revolutionary America." *Social Text* 4 (Autumn 1981): 3–27.

Marcuse, Herbert. *Counterrevolution and Revolt.* Boston: Beacon Press, 1967.

Marez, Curtis. *Drug Wars: The Political Economy of Narcotics.* Minneapolis: University of Minnesota Press, 2004.

Martinez, Ruben. "Riot Scenes." In *Inside the L.A. Riots: What Really Happened—and Why It Will Happen Again,* 30–34. Edited by Don Hazen. Los Angeles: Institute for Alternative Journalism, 1992.

Marx, Karl. *Capital: A Critique of Political Economy.* Translated by Ben Fowkes. New York: Penguin Books, 1976.

———. *The Civil War in France: The Paris Commune.* New York: International Publishers, 1988.

———. "Contribution to the Critique of Hegel's *Philosophy of Right*: Introduction." In *The Marx-Engels Reader*, 53–65. Edited by Robert C. Tucker. New York: W. W. Norton, 1978.

———. *The Eighteenth Brumaire of Louis Bonaparte*. New York: International Publishers, 2004.

———. "From Population, Crime and Pauperism." *New York Tribune*, 1859. http://www.marxists.org/archive/marx/works/1859/09/16.htm.

Massey, Doreen. "The Political Struggle Ahead." *Soundings: A Journal of Politics and Culture* 44 (Spring 2010): 6–18.

Massood, Paula J. *Black City Cinema: African American Urban Experiences in Film*. Philadelphia: Temple University Press, 2003.

Matas, David. *Allegations of Ill-Treatment in Marion Prison, Illinois, USA*. London: Amnesty International, 1987.

Mauer, Marc. *The Lessons of Marion, the Failure of a Maximum Security Prison: A History and Analysis, with Voices of Prisoners*. Philadelphia: American Friends Service Committee, 1993.

———. *Race to Incarcerate*. New York: The New Press, 2006.

Maxwell, William J. *New Negro, Old Left: African-American Writing and Communism Between the Wars*. New York: Columbia University Press, 1999.

McDuffie, Eric S. "Black and Red: Black Liberation, the Cold War, and the Horne Thesis." *Journal of African American History* 96, no. 2 (2011): 236–47.

McGirr, Lisa. *Suburban Warriors: The Origins of the New American Right*. Princeton, NJ: Princeton University Press, 2001.

McKay, Claude. *A Long Way from Home*. New York: Harcourt Brace Jovanovich, 1970.

McKittrick, Kathleen, and Clyde Woods. "No One Knows the Mysteries at the Bottom of the Ocean." In *Black Geographies and the Politics of Place*, 46–81. Edited by Katherine McKittrick and Clyde Woods. Cambridge, MA: South End Press, 2007.

McNally, David. *Global Slump: The Economics and Politics of Crisis and Resistance*. Oakland, CA: PM Press, 2010.

Mears, Daniel P., and Jamie Watson. "Towards a Fair and Balanced Assessment of Supermax Prisons." *Justice Quarterly* 23, no. 2 (June 2006): 232–70.

Melamed, Jodi. *Represent and Destroy: Rationalizing Violence in the New Racial Capitalism*. Minneapolis: University of Minnesota Press, 2011.

———. "W. E. B. Du Bois's UnAmerican End." *African American Review* 40, no. 3 (Fall 2006): 533–50.

Melville, Sam. *Letters from Attica*. New York: Morrow, 1972.

Mitchell, Don. "Homelessness, American Style." In *Downtown Blues: A Skid Row Reader*, 42–49. Edited by Christina Heatherton. Los Angeles: Los Angeles Community Action Network, 2011.

———. *The Right to the City: Social Justice and the Fight for Public Space*. New York: Guilford, 2003.

———. "State Intervention in Landscape Production: The Wheatland Riot and the California Commission of Immigration and Housing." *Antipode* 25, no. 2 (1993): 91–113.

Mitchell, Don, Kafui Attoh, and Lynn A. Staeheli. "Broken Windows Is Not the Panacea: Common Sense, Good Sense, and Police Accountability in American Cities." In *Policing the Planet: Why the Policing Crisis Led to Black Lives Matter*. Edited by Jordan T. Camp and Christina Heatherton. New York: Verso, 2016.

Mitford, Jessica. *A Fine Old Conflict*. New York: Vintage Books, 1978.

———. *Kind and Usual Punishment*. New York: Alfred A. Knopf, 1973.

Moten, Fred. *In the Break: The Aesthetics of the Black Radical Tradition*. Minneapolis: University of Minnesota Press, 2003.

Muhammad, Khalil Gibran. *The Condemnation of Blackness: Race, Crime, and the Making of Modern Urban America*. Cambridge, MA: Harvard University Press, 2010.

Munro, John. "Continuities in the Freedom Movement: Jack O'Dell in the Early Cold War." In *Jack O'Dell: The Fierce Urgency of Now*, 3–11. New York: Center for the Study of Working Class Life, 2005.

———. "Imperial Anticommunism and the African American Freedom Movement in the Early Cold War." *History Workshop Journal* 79, no. 1 (2015): 52–75.

Munro-Bjorklund, Vicky. "Popular Cultural Images of Criminals and Prisoners Since Attica." *Social Justice* 18, no. 3 (Fall 1991): 48–70.

Murakawa, Naomi. *The First Civil Right: How Liberals Built Prison America*. New York: Oxford University Press, 2014.

———. "The Origins of the Carceral Crisis: Racial Order as 'Law and Order' in Postwar American Politics." In *Race and American Political Development*, 234–55. Edited by Joseph Lowndes, Julie Novkov, and Dorian T. Warren. New York: Routledge, 2008.

Murch, Donna. "Crack in Los Angeles: Crisis, Militarization, and the Black Response to the Late Twentieth Century War on Drugs." *Journal of American History* 102, no. 1 (June 2015): 162–73.

National Prison Project of the American Civil Liberties Union. "Abandoned and Abused: Prisoners in the Wake of Hurricane Katrina." *Race and Class* 49, no. 1 (2007): 81–92.

Németh, Jeremy. "Security in Public Space: An Empirical Assessment of Three U.S. Cities." *Environment and Planning A* 42 (2010): 2487–507.

Newton, Huey P. *War Against the Panthers: A Study of Repression in America*. New York: Harlem River Press, 2000.

O'Connor, James. *The Fiscal Crisis of the State*. New York: St. Martin's Press, 1973.

O'Dell, Jack. *Climbin' Jacob's Ladder: The Black Freedom Movement Writings of Jack O'Dell*. Edited by Nikhil Pal Singh. Berkeley: University of California Press, 2010.

Oliver, Melvin L., James H. Johnson Jr., and Walter C. Farrell Jr. "Anatomy of a Rebellion: A Political-Economic Analysis." In *Reading Rodney King/Reading Urban Uprising*, 117–41. Edited by Robert Gooding-William. New York: Routledge, 1993.

Oliver, Pamela. "Repression and Crime Control: Why Social Movement Scholars Should Pay Attention to Mass Incarceration as a Form of Repression." *Mobilization: The International Quarterly* 13, no. 1 (2008): 1–24.

Omi, Michael, and Howard Winant. *Racial Formation in the United States: From the 1960s to the 1990s.* New York: Routledge, 1994.

Ortiz, Paul. "The Anatomy of a Rebellion." *Against the Current* (January–February 2000). http://www.solidarity-us.org.

———. "The Battle of New Orleans." In *Hurricane Katrina: Response and Responsibilities*, 1–6. Edited by John Brown Childs. Santa Cruz, CA: New Pacific Press, 2008.

———. *Emancipation Betrayed: The Hidden History of Black Organizing and White Violence in Florida from Reconstruction to the Bloody Election of 1920.* Berkeley: University of California Press, 2005.

Oswald, Russel G. *Attica: My Story.* New York: Doubleday and Company, 1972.

Otis, Johnny. *Listen to the Lambs.* Minneapolis: University of Minnesota Press, 2009.

———. *Upside Your Head! Rhythm and Blues on Central Avenue.* Middletown, CT: Wesleyan University Press, 1993.

Page, Yolanda Williams. "Jayne Cortez." In *Encyclopedia of African American Women Writers*, 121–26. Westport, CT: Greenwood Press, 2007.

Parenti, Christian. *Lockdown America: Police and Prisons in the Age of Crisis.* New York: Verso, 2000.

Parson, Don. *Making a Better World: Public Housing, the Red Scare, and the Direction of Modern Los Angeles.* Minneapolis: University of Minnesota Press, 2005.

Patterson, Sunni. "We Know This Place." *American Quarterly* 61, no. 3 (September 2009): 719–21.

Patterson, William L. *The Man Who Cried Genocide: An Autobiography.* New York: International Publishers, 1971.

Payne, Charles M. *I've Got the Light of Freedom: The Organizing Tradition and the Mississippi Freedom Struggle.* Berkeley: University of California Press, 1995.

Peck, Jamie. *Constructions of Neoliberal Reason.* New York: Oxford University Press, 2010.

———. "Liberating the City: Between New York and New Orleans." *Urban Geography* 27, no. 8 (2006): 681–713.

Pelot-Hobbs, Lydia. "Louisiana Lockdown." In *Unfathomable City: A New Orleans Atlas*, 55–61. Edited by Rebecca Solnit and Rebecca Snedeker. Berkeley: University of California Press, 2013.

Peltier, Leonard. *Prison Writings: My Life Is My Sun Dance.* Edited by Harvey Arden. New York: St. Martin's Press, 1999.

Penner, D'Ann R., and Keith C. Ferdinand, eds. *Overcoming Katrina: African American Voices from the Crescent City and Beyond.* New York: Palgrave MacMillan, 2009.

Pew Center on the States. *One in 31: The Long Reach of American Corrections.* Washington, DC: Pew Charitable Trusts, March 2009.

Pickard, Miguel. "In the Crossfire: Mesoamerican Migrants Journey North." americaspolicy.org. March 18, 2005.

Piven, Frances Fox, and Richard A. Cloward. *Poor People's Movements: Why They Succeed, How They Fail.* New York: Vintage Books, 1979.

Platt, Anthony M. *The Politics of Riot Commissions*. New York: MacMillan, 1971.

Porter, Eric. *The Problem of the Future World: W. E. B. Du Bois and the Race Concept at Midcentury*. Durham, NC: Duke University Press, 2010.

Poulantzas, Nicos. *The Poulantzas Reader: Marxism, Law, and the State*. New York: Verso, 2008.

———. *State, Power, Socialism*. New York, Verso, 2001.

Prashad, Vijay. *The Darker Nations: A People's History of the Third World*. New York: The New Press, 2007.

———. *Everybody Was Kung Fu Fighting: Afro-Asian Connections and the Myth of Cultural Purity*. Minneapolis: University of Minnesota Press, 2001.

———. *Keeping Up with the Dow Joneses: Debt, Prisons, Workfare*. Cambridge, MA: South End Press, 2003.

———. "Second-Hand Dreams." *Social Analysis* 49, no. 2 (2005): 191–98.

———. "This Ends Badly: Race and Capitalism." In *Policing the Planet: Why the Policing Crisis Led to Black Lives Matter*. Edited by Jordan T. Camp and Christina Heatherton. New York: Verso, 2016.

Pulido, Laura. "Rethinking Environmental Racism: White Privilege and Urban Development in Southern California." *Annals of the Association of American Geographers* 90, no. 1 (2000): 12–40.

Ransby, Barbara. "The Black Poor and the Politics of Expendability." In *A New Introduction to Poverty: The Role of Race, Power, and Politics*, 321–30. Edited by Louis Kushnick and James Jennings. New York: New York University Press, 1999.

———. "The Class Politics of Black Lives Matter." *Dissent* 62, no. 4 (Fall 2015): 31–34.

———. *Ella Baker and the Black Freedom Movement: A Radical Democratic Vision*. Chapel Hill: University of North Carolina Press, 2003.

———. "Katrina, Black Women, and the Deadly Discourse of Black Poverty in America," *Du Bois* Review 3, no. 1 (2006): 215–22.

Rawick, George P. *From Sundown to Sunup: The Making of the Black Community*. Westport, CT: Greenwood Publishing, 1972.

———. *Listening to Revolt: The Selected Writings of George P. Rawick*. Edited by David Roediger. Chicago: Charles H. Kerr Publishing, 2010.

———. "Working-Class Self-Activity." *Radical America* 3, no. 2 (1969): 23–31.

Rediker, Marcus. *The Slave Ship: A Human History*. New York: Penguin, 2007.

Redmond, Shana L. *Anthem: Movement Cultures and the Sound of Solidarity in the African Diaspora*. New York: New York University Press, 2014.

Reed Jr., Adolph. "Marx, Race, and Neoliberalism." *New Labor Forum* 22, no. 1 (2013): 49–57.

Reese, Ellen, Geoffrey Deverteuil, and Leanne Thach. "'Weak-Center' Gentrification and the Contradictions of Containment: Deconcentrating Poverty in Downtown Los Angeles." *International Journal of Urban and Regional Research* 34, no. 2 (2010): 310–27.

Reeves, Jimmie L., and Richard Campbell. *Cracked Coverage: Television News, the Anti-Cocaine Crusade, and the Reagan Legacy*. Durham, NC: Duke University Press, 1994.

Rickford, Russell. "'Socialism from Below': A Black Scholar's Marxist Genealogy." *Souls: A Critical Journal of Black Politics, Culture, and Society* 13, no. 4 (2011): 371–92.

Ritz, David. *Divided Soul: The Life of Marvin Gaye.* New York: Da Capo Press, 1985.

Rivera, Amaad, et al. *Foreclosed: State of the Dream 2008.* Boston: United for a Fair Economy, 2008.

———. *The Silent Depression: State of the Dream 2009.* Boston: United for a Fair Economy, 2009.

Robinson, Cedric J. *Black Marxism: The Making of the Black Radical Tradition.* Chapel Hill: University of North Carolina Press, 2000.

———. *Black Movements in America.* New York: Routledge, 1997.

———. *Forgeries of Memory and Meaning: Blacks and the Regimes of Race in American Theatre and Film before World War II.* Chapel Hill: University of North Carolina Press, 2007.

———. "Race, Capitalism, and Antidemocracy." In *Reading Rodney King / Reading Urban Uprising*, 73–81. Edited by Robert Gooding-Williams. New York: Routledge, 1993.

———. *The Terms of Order: Political Science and the Myth of Leadership.* Albany: State University of New York Press, 1980.

Robinson, William I. "*Aqui Estamos y no Nos Vamos!*: Global Capital and Immigrant Rights." *Race and Class* 48, no. 2 (2006): 77–91.

———. *Promoting Polyarchy: Globalization, U.S. Intervention, and Hegemony.* New York: Cambridge University Press, 1996.

———. *A Theory of Global Capitalism: Production, Class, and State in a Transnational World.* Baltimore: Johns Hopkins University Press, 2004.

Rocksborough-Smith, Ian. "'Filling the Gap': Intergenerational Black Radicalism and the Popular Front Ideals of *Freedomways* Magazine's Early Years (1961–1965)." *Afro-Americans in New York Life and History* 31, no. 1 (January 2007): 7–42.

Rodney, Walter. "George Jackson: Black Revolutionary." November 1971. http://historyisaweapon.com/defcon1/rodneyjackson.html.

———. *The Groundings with My Brothers.* London: Bogle-L'Ouverture Publications, 1996.

———. *How Europe Underdeveloped Africa.* Washington, DC: Howard University, 1982.

Rodríguez, Dylan. *Forced Passages: Imprisoned Radical Intellectuals and the U.S. Prison Regime.* Minneapolis: University of Minnesota Press, 2006.

Rodríguez, Russell C. "Agustín Lira and Alma & Quetzal: Cantos de mi Cantón (Songs from My Home) Chicano Music from California." American Folklife Center at the Library of Congress. September 14, 2011. http://www.loc.gov/folklife/events/HomegrownArchives/2011flyers/AlmaAndQuetzal-Flyer.html.

Roediger, David R. "Accounting for the Wages of Whiteness: U.S. Marxism and the Critical History of Race." In *Wages of Whiteness and Racist Symbolic Capital*, 9–36. Edited by Wulf D. Hund, Jeremy Krikler, and David Roediger. Berlin: Lit Verlag, 2010.

——. *Colored White: Transcending the Racial Past.* Berkeley: University of California, 2002.

——. *History Against Misery.* Chicago: Charles H. Kerr, 2006.

——. *How Race Survived U.S. History.* New York: Verso, 2008.

——. *Towards the Abolition of Whiteness.* New York: Verso, 2000.

——. *The Wages of Whiteness: Race and the Making of the American Working Class.* New York: Verso, 2007.

——. "Where Do Great Ideas Come From? The Life and Work of George Rawick." In George P. Rawick, *Listening to Revolt: The Selected Writings of George P. Rawick,* vii–li. Edited by David Roediger. Chicago: Charles H. Kerr Publishing, 2010.

——. *Working Toward Whiteness: How America's Immigrants Became White.* Cambridge, MA: Basic Books, 2005.

Roediger, David R., and Elizabeth D. Esch. *The Production of Difference: Race and the Management of Labor in U.S. History.* New York: Oxford University Press, 2012.

Rogers, Kim Lacy. *Righteous Lives: Narratives of the New Orleans Civil Rights Movement.* New York: New York University Press, 1993.

Rogin, Michael. *Ronald Reagan, the Movie, and Other Episodes of Political Demonology.* Berkeley: University of California Press, 1987.

Rolnik, Raquel. *Report of the Special Rapporteur on Adequate Housing as a Component of the Right to an Adequate Standard of Living, and on the Right to Non-Discrimination in This Context.* Geneva: Human Rights Council, February 12, 2010.

Rose, Tricia. *Black Noise: Rap Music and Black Culture in Contemporary America.* Hanover, NH: Wesleyan University Press, 1994.

Rosemont, Penelope, ed. *Surrealist Women: An International Anthology.* Austin: University of Texas Press, 1998.

Ross, Kristin. *The Emergence of Social Space: Rimbaud and the Paris Commune.* New York: Verso, 2008.

Rudé, George. *The Crowd in History: A Study of Popular Disturbances in France and England, 1730–1848.* London: Lawrence and Wishart, 1981.

——. *Ideology and Popular Protest.* New York: Pantheon Books, 1980.

Rugh, Jacob S., and Douglas S. Massey. "Racial Segregation and the American Foreclosure Crisis." *American Sociological Review* 75, no. 5 (2010): 629–51.

Said, Edward. *Covering Islam: How the Media and Experts Determine How We See the Rest of the World.* New York: Vintage Books, 1997.

Saul, John S., and Stephen Gelb. *The Crisis in South Africa: Class Defense, Class Revolution.* New York: Monthly Review Press, 1981.

Saxton, Alexander. *The Rise and Fall of the White Republic: Class Politics and Mass Culture in Nineteenth Century America.* New York: Verso, 2003.

Schrecker, Ellen. "Immigration and Internal Security: Political Deportations During the McCarthy Era." *Science and Society* 60, no. 4 (Winter 1996–97): 393–426.

Scott, James C. *Domination and the Arts of Resistance.* New Haven, CT: Yale University, 1990.

Scraton, Phil, and Jude McCulloch, *The Violence of Incarceration*. New York: Routledge, 2009.

Sexton, Jared. "The Obscurity of Black Suffering." In *What Lies Beneath: Katrina, Race, and the State of the Nation*, 120–32. Edited by South End Press Collective. Cambridge, MA: South End Press, 2007.

———. "The Ruse of Engagement: Black Masculinity and the Cinema of Policing." *American Quarterly* 61, no. 1 (2009): 39–63.

Sidaway, James D. "Subprime Crisis: American Crisis or Human Crisis?" *Environment and Planning D: Society and Space* 26 (2008): 195–98.

Sideris, Marina, and the Critical Resistance Amnesty Working Group. "Amnesty for Prisoners of Katrina: A Special Report." Critical Resistance New Orleans. December 2007.

Sides, Josh. *L.A. City Limits: African American Los Angeles from the Great Depression to the Present*. Berkeley: University of California Press, 2003.

———. "'You Understand My Condition': The Civil Rights Congress in the Los Angeles African-American Community, 1946–1952." *Pacific Historical Review* 67, no. 2 (1998): 233–57.

Siegel, Micol. "William Bratton in the Other L.A." In *Without Fear . . . Claiming Safe Communities Without Sacrificing Ourselves*, 54–62. Los Angeles: Southern California Library, 2007.

Simon, Jonathan. "Rise of the Carceral State." *Social Research* 74, no. 2 (2007): 471–508.

Singh, Nikhil Pal. "The Afterlife of Fascism." *South Atlantic Quarterly* 105, no. 1 (Winter 2006): 71–93.

———. *Black Is a Country: Race and the Unfinished Struggle for Democracy*. Cambridge, MA: Harvard University Press, 2004.

———. "The Black Panthers and the 'Undeveloped Country of the Left.'" In *The Black Panther Party Reconsidered*, 57–105. Edited by Charles E. Jones. Baltimore: Black Classic Press, 1998.

———. "Cold War Redux: On the 'New Totalitarianism.'" *Radical History Review* 85 (Winter 2003): 171–81.

———. "'Learn Your Horn': Jack O'Dell and the Long Civil Rights Movement." Introduction to *Climbin' Jacob's Ladder: The Black Freedom Movement Writings of Jack O'Dell*, 1–68. Edited by Nikhil Pal Singh. Berkeley: University of California Press, 2010.

———. "Racial Formation in an Age of Permanent War." In *Racial Formation in the Twenty-First Century*, 276–301. Edited by Daniel Martinez HoSang, Oneka LaBennet, and Laura Pulido. Berkeley: University of California Press, 2012.

Sivanandan, Ambalavaner. *Communities of Resistance: Writings on Black Struggles for Socialism*. New York: Verso, 1990.

———. *A Different Hunger: Writings on Black Resistance*. London: Pluto Press, 1991.

Sklair, Leslie. *Globalization: Capitalism and Its Alternatives*. New York: Oxford University Press, 2002.

Sloop, John M. *The Cultural Prison: Discourse, Prisoners, and Punishment*. Tuscaloosa: University of Alabama Press, 1996.

Slotkin, Richard. *Gunfighter Nation: The Myth of the Frontier in Twentieth-Century America*. Norman: University of Oklahoma Press, 1998.

Smethurst, James. *The Black Arts Movement: Literary Nationalism in the 1960s and 1970s*. Chapel Hill: University of North Carolina Press, 2005.

Smith, Neil. *American Empire: Roosevelt's Geographer and the Prelude to Globalization*. Berkeley: University of California Press, 2003.

———. "Contours of a Spatialized Politics: Homeless Vehicles and the Production of Geographical Scale." *Social Text* 33 (1992): 54–81.

———. *The Endgame of Globalization*. New York: Routledge, 2005.

———. Foreword to Henri Levebre, *The Urban Revolution*, vii–xxiii. Minneapolis: University of Minnesota Press, 2003.

———. "Giuliani Time: The Revanchist 1990s." *Social Text* 16, no. 4 (Winter 1998): 1–20.

———. "New Globalism, New Urbanism: Gentrification as Global Urban Strategy." *Antipode* 34, no. 3 (2002): 427–50.

———. *The New Urban Frontier: Gentrification and the Revanchist City*. New York: Routledge, 1996.

———. "Revanchist Planet." *The Urban Reinventors* 3, no. 9 (2009): 3–18.

———. "There's No Such Thing as a Natural Disaster." In *Understanding Katrina: Perspectives from the Social Sciences*. Social Science Research Council. June 11, 2006. http://katrinaresearchhub.ssrc.org/there2019s-no-such-thing-as-a-natural-disaster/resource_view.

———. *Uneven Development: Nature, Capital, and the Production of Space*. Athens: University of Georgia Press, 2008.

Smith, Neil, and Deborah Cowen. "Martial Law in the Streets of Toronto: G20 Security and State Violence." *Human Geography* 3, no. 3 (2010): 29–46.

Smith, Suzanne E. *Dancing in the Street: Motown and the Cultural Politics of Detroit*. Cambridge, MA: Harvard University Press, 1999.

Soja, Edward W. "Poles Apart: Urban Restructuring in New York and Los Angeles." In *Dual City: Restructuring New York*, 361–75. Edited by Jon H. Mollenkopf and Manuel Castells. New York: Russell Sage Foundation, 1991.

———. *Postmetropolis: Critical Studies of Regions and Cities*. Malden, MA: Blackwell, 2000.

———. *Seeking Spatial Justice*. Minneapolis: University of Minnesota Press, 2010.

Soja, Edward W., Rebecca Morales, and Goetz Wolff. "Urban Restructuring: An Analysis of Social and Spatial Change in Los Angeles." *Economic Geography* 59, no. 2 (April 1983): 195–230.

Solomos, John, Bob Findlay, Simon Jones, and Paul Gilroy. "The Organic Crisis of British Capitalism and Race: The Experience of the Seventies." In *The Empire Strikes Back: Race and Racism in 70s Britain*, 9–46. Edited by the Centre for Contemporary Cultural Studies. London: Hutchinson/Centre for Contemporary Cultural Studies, University of Birmingham, 1982.

Spatial Information Design Lab. *Justice Reinvestment New Orleans*. New York: Columbia University Graduate School of Architecture, Planning and Preservation, February 2009.

Sudbury, Julia, ed. *Global Lockdown: Race, Gender and the Prison-Industrial Complex*. New York: Routledge, 2005.

Sullivan, Tim, Maz Ali, Carlos Perez de Alejo, Brian Miller, and Nicole Márin Baena. *A Long Way From Home: Housing, Asset Policy and the Racial Wealth Divide*. Boston: United for a Fair Economy, 2013.

Sugrue, Thomas J. *The Origins of Urban Crisis: Race and Inequality in Postwar Detroit* Princeton, NJ: Princeton University Press, 1996.

Tabb, William K. "The Urban Fiscal Crisis and the Rebirth of Conservatism." In *Civil Rights Since 1787: A Reader on the Black Struggle*, 753–58. Edited by Jonathan Birnbaum and Clarence Taylor. New York: New York University Press, 2000.

Taibo II, Paco Ignacio. *'68*. New York: Seven Stories Press, 2004.

Takagi, Paul. "A Garrison State in 'Democratic' Society." *Social Justice* 40, nos. 1–2 (2014): 118–30.

Tang, Eric. "A Gulf Unites Us: The Vietnamese Americans of Black New Orleans East." *American Quarterly* 63, no. 1 (2011): 117–49.

Taylor, Kieran. "American Petrograd: Detroit and the League of Revolutionary Black Workers." In *Rebel Rank and File: Labor Militancy and Revolt from Below During the Long 1970s*, 311–44. Edited by Aaron Brenner, Robert Brenner, and Cal Winslow. New York: Verso, 2010.

Taylor, Verta. "Social Movement Continuity: The Women's Movement in Abeyance." *American Sociological Review* 54 (1989): 761–75.

Thompson, Erica, and Jan Susler. "Supermax Prisons: High-Tech Dungeons and Modern-Day Torture." In *Criminal Injustice: Confronting the Prison Crisis*, 303–7. Edited by Elihu Rosenblatt. Cambridge, MA: South End Press, 1996.

Thompson, Heather Ann. "Understanding Rioting in Postwar America." *Journal of Urban History* 26, no. 3 (March 2000): 391–402.

———. *Whose Detroit? Politics, Labor, and Race in a Modern American City*. Ithaca, NY: Cornell University Press, 2001.

———. "Why Mass Incarceration Matters: Rethinking Crisis, Decline, and Transformation in Postwar American History." *Journal of American History* 97, no. 3 (2010): 703–34.

Tierney, Kathleen, Christine Bevc, and Erica Kuligowski. "Metaphors Matter: Disaster Myths, Media Frames, and Their Consequences in Hurricane Katrina." *Annals of the American Academy* 604, no. 1 (March 2006): 57–81.

Tilly, Charles. *Contentious Performances*. New York: Cambridge University Press, 2008.

United Nations. *Universal Declaration of Human Rights*. Geneva: United Nations Department of Public Information, 1948.

United Nations Human Settlement Programme. *The Challenge of Slums: Global Report on Human Settlements*. London: Earthscan Publications, 2003.

Useem, Bert, and Peter Kimball, *States of Siege: U.S. Prison Riots, 1971–1986*. New York: Oxford University Press, 1991.

Viesca, Victor. "The Battle of Los Angeles: The Cultural Politics of Chicana/o Music in the Greater Eastside." *American Quarterly* 56, no. 3 (September 2004): 719–39.

————. "Native Guns and Stray Bullets: Cultural Activism and Filipino American Rap Music in Post-Riot Los Angeles." *Amerasia Journal* 38, no. 1 (2012): 113–42.

Villa, Raul Homero. *Barrio-Logos: Space and Place in Urban Chicano Literature and Culture.* Austin: University of Texas, 2000.

Vitale, Alex S. "The Safer Cities Initiative and the Removal of the Homeless: Reducing Crime or Promoting Gentrification on Los Angeles's Skid Row?" *American Society of Criminology* 9, no. 4 (2010): 867–73.

Vogel, Richard D. "Capitalism and Incarceration Revisited." *Monthly Review* 55, no. 4 (September 2003): 38–55.

Von Eschen, Penny M. *Race Against Empire: Black Americans and Anticolonialism.* Ithaca, NY: Cornell University Press, 1997.

Wacquant, Loïc. "Deadly Symbiosis: When Ghetto and Prison Meet and Mesh." *Punishment & Society* 3, no. 1 (2001): 95–134.

————. "From Slavery to Mass Incarceration: Rethinking the Race Question in the U.S." *New Left Review* 13 (January–February 2002): 41–60.

————. *Punishing the Poor: The Neoliberal Government of Social Insecurity.* Durham, NC: Duke University Press, 2009.

Wagner, David, and Pete White. "Why the Silence? Homelessness and Race." In *Freedom Now! Struggles for the Human Right to Housing in Los Angeles and Beyond*, 42–48. Edited by Jordan T. Camp and Christina Heatherton. Los Angeles: Freedom Now Books, 2012.

Walker, Richard. "California Rages Against the Dying of the Light." *New Left Review*, no. 209 (1995): 42–74.

————. "Golden State Adrift." *New Left Review*, no. 66 (2010): 5–30.

Walmsley, Roy. *World Prison Population List.* London: Kings College, International Centre for Prison Studies, 2007. http://www.prisonstudies.org/research-publications?shs_term_node_tid_depth=27.

Ward, David A. *Alcatraz: The Gangster Years.* Berkeley: University of California Press, 2009.

Ward, David A., and Thomas G. Werlich. "Alcatraz and Marion: Evaluating Supermaximum Custody." *Punishment and Society* 5 (2003): 53–75.

Washington, Mary Helen. "Alice Childress, Lorraine Hansberry, and Claudia Jones: Black Women Write the Popular Front." In *Left of the Color Line: Race, Radicalism, and Twentieth-Century Literature of the United States*, 183–204. Edited by Bill V. Mullen and James Smethurst. Chapel Hill: University of North Carolina Press, 2003.

————. *The Other Blacklist: The African American Literary and Cultural Left of the 1950s.* New York: Columbia University Press, 2014.

Waters, Maxine. "Testimony Before the Senate Banking Committee." In *Inside the L.A. Riots: What Really Happened—and Why It Will Happen Again*, 26. Edited by Don Hazen. Los Angeles: Institute for Alternative Journalism, 1992.

Weir, Stan. *Singlejack Solidarity.* Minneapolis: University of Minnesota Press, 2004.

Weiss, Robert. "Attica: The 'Bitter Lessons' Forgotten?" *Social Justice* 18, no. 3 (Fall 1991): 1–12.

West, Cornel, ed. *The Radical King.* Boston: Beacon Press, 2015.

Wicker, Tom. *A Time to Die.* New York: Quadrangle/New York Times Book Co., 1975.

Widener, Daniel. "Another City Is Possible: Interethnic Organizing in Contemporary Los Angeles." *Race/Ethnicity: Multidisciplinary Global Perspectives* 1, no. 2 (2008): 189–219.

———. *Black Arts West: Culture and Struggle in Postwar Los Angeles.* Durham, NC: Duke University Press, 2010.

Williams, Randall. *The Divided World: Human Rights and Its Violence.* Minneapolis: University of Minnesota Press, 2010.

Williams, Raymond. *Marxism and Literature.* Oxford: Oxford University Press, 1977.

Williams, Rhonda Y. "'We Refuse': Privatization, Housing, and Human Rights." In *Freedom Now! Struggles for the Human Right to Housing in Los Angeles and Beyond.* Edited by Jordan T. Camp and Christina Heatherton. Los Angeles: Freedom Now Books, 2012.

Willis, Susan. *Specifying: Black Women Writing the American Experience.* Madison: University of Wisconsin, 1987.

Willse, Craig. "Neo-Liberal Biopolitics and the Invention of Chronic Homelessness." *Economy and Society* 39, no. 2 (2010): 155–84.

Wilson, Bobby M. *America's Johannesburg: Industrialization and Racial Transformation in Birmingham.* Lanham, MD: Rowman and Littlefield, 2000.

Winslow, Cal. "Overview: The Rebellion from Below, 1965–1981." In *Rebel Rank and File: Labor Militancy and Revolt from Below During the Long 1970s,* 1–35. Edited by Aaron Brenner, Robert Brenner, and Cal Winslow. New York: Verso, 2010.

Wolpe, Harold. *Race, Class, and the Apartheid State.* Trenton, NJ: Africa World Press, 1990.

Woods, Clyde. "The Challenges of Blues and Hip Hop Historiography." *Kalfou* 1, no. 1 (2010): 33–54.

———. *Development Arrested: The Blues and Plantation Power in the Mississippi Delta.* New York: Verso, 1998.

———. *Development Drowned and Reborn: The Blues and Bourbon Restorations in Post-Katrina New Orleans.* Edited by Laura Pulido and Jordan T. Camp. Athens: University of Georgia Press, forthcoming.

———. "Do You Know What It Means to Miss New Orleans? Katrina, Trap Economics, and the Rebirth of the Blues." *American Quarterly* 57, no. 4 (2005): 1005–18.

———. "Katrina's World: Blues, Bourbon, and the Return to the Source." *American Quarterly* 61, no. 3 (September 2009): 427–53.

———. "Les Misérables of New Orleans: Trap Economics and the Asset Stripping Blues, Part 1." *American Quarterly* 61, no. 3 (2009): 769–96.

———. "Life After Death." *Professional Geographer* 54, no. 1 (2002): 62–66.

———. "'Sittin' on Top of the World': The Challenges of Blues and Hip Hop Geography." In *Black Geographies and the Politics of Place,* 46–81. Edited by Katherine McKittrick and Clyde Woods. Cambridge, MA: South End Press, 2007.

———. "Traps, Skid Row, and Katrina." In *Downtown Blues: A Skid Row Reader*, 50–55. Edited by Christina Heatherton. Los Angeles: Los Angeles Community Action Network, 2011.

Woods, Clyde, ed. *In the Wake of Hurricane Katrina: New Paradigms and Social Visions*. Baltimore, MD: Johns Hopkins University Press, 2010.

Wright, Richard. *Uncle Tom's Children*. New York: Harper and Brothers, 1940.

Wypijewski, JoAnn. "Pounding Out a DRUM Beat." *New Left Review* 1, no. 234 (1999): 141–59.

ya Salaam, Kalamu. "Below the Water Line." In *What Lies Beneath: Katrina, Race, and the State of the Nation*, ix–xviii. Edited by South End Press Collective. Cambridge, MA: South End Press, 2007.

———. "We Stand by Our Students." In *Pedagogy, Policy, and the Privatized City: Stories of Dispossession and Defiance from New Orleans*, 65–72. Edited by Kristen L. Buras with Jim Randels, Kalamu ya Salaam, and Students at the Center. New York: Teachers College Press, 2010.

Yee, Min S. *The Melancholy History of Soledad Prison*. New York: Harper's Magazine Press, 1973.

Zibechi, Raúl. "The Militarization of the World's Urban Peripheries." *Americas Policy Program*. February 9, 2007. http://americas.irc-online.org/am/4954.

Dissertations, Papers, and Unpublished Sources

Davis, Angela Y. "Policing the Crisis Today." Keynote lecture presented at the Stuart Hall International Conference: Conversations, Projects, and Legacy, Goldsmiths University, London, November 28, 2014.

Franklin, H. Bruce. "The American Prison in the Culture Wars." Paper presented at the Modern Language Association Convention, Washington, DC, 2000. http://andromeda.rutgers.edu/~hbf/priscult.html.

Gilmore, Ruth Wilson. "Eleven Theses." Presented at the symposium Cedric Robinson's Radical Thought: Toward Critical Social Theories and Practice, University of California, Santa Barbara, November 5–7, 2004.

Gómez, Alan Eladio. "From Below and to the Left: Re-Imagining the Chicano Movement Through the Circulation of Third World Struggles, 1970–1979." PhD diss., University of Texas at Austin, 2006.

Harvey, David. "The Enigma of Capital and the Crisis This Time." Paper presented at the American Sociological Association Meetings, Atlanta, August 16, 2010.

James, C.L.R. "The Role of the Black Scholar." Public lecture presented at the Institute of the Black World, Atlanta, June 18, 1971, cassette.

Kelley, Robin D.G. "Labor Against Empire, at Home and Abroad." Keynote address, Race and Labor Matters, CUNY Graduate Center, December 5, 2003. http://arts.muohio.edu/cce/papers/labor_v_empire.pdf.

———. "John Brown's Body: Abolition Democracy and Permanent War." Toni Morrison Lectures, Center for African American Studies, Princeton University, April 13, 2015.

King Jr., Martin Luther. "The Crisis in America's Cities: An Analysis of Social Disorder and a Plan of Action Against Poverty, Discrimination, and Racism in Urban America." Lecture delivered at the Southern Christina Leadership Conference, Atlanta, August 15, 1967. http://www.thekingcenter.org /archive/document/crisis-americas-cities#.

Lipsitz, George. "Change the Focus and Reverse the Hypnosis: Learning from New Orleans." Lecture presented at the symposium Color of Disaster: Race, Class, and Hurricane Katrina, University of California, Santa Barbara, October 15, 2005.

Moten, Fred. "The Meaning of 'Broken Windows.'" Talk presented at Eso Won Books, Los Angeles, June 23, 2005.

Munro, John. "The Anticolonial Front: Cold War Imperialism and the Struggle Against Global White Supremacy, 1945–1960." PhD diss., University of California, Santa Barbara, 2009.

Smith, Neil. "Urban Politics, Urban Security." Lecture delivered at Harvard Graduate School, Cambridge, Massachusetts, September 29, 2010.

Soni, Saket. "Organizing the Future of Work?" Lecture presented at the Labor and Worklife Program, Harvard Law School, February 14, 2013. http:// www.law.harvard.edu/programs/lwp/wurf_lectures/2013soniwurf.pdf

Thompson, Heather. "Rethinking Political Transformation in Postwar America: The Attica Prison Uprising of 1971, Liberalism, and the Rise of the Right." Lecture presented at the Center for the Study of Work, Labor, and Democracy, University of California, Santa Barbara, February 6, 2009.

Tullis, Tracy. "A Vietnam at Home: Policing the Ghettoes in the Counter-Insurgency Era." PhD diss., New York University, 1999.

Ward, David A., and Norman A. Carlson. "Super-Maximum Custody Prisons in the United States: Why Successful Regimes Remain Controversial." Paper delivered at the University of Leicester, England, April 9, 1994.

Wilson, Bobby. "Scale Politics of the Civil Rights Movement." Paper presented at the Association of American Geographers, New York, February 2012.

Woods, Clyde A. Introduction to a lecture and poetry reading by Sunni Patterson, Department of Black Studies, University of California, Santa Barbara, November 15, 2007.

DISCOGRAPHY

The Dirty Dozen Brass Band, *What's Going On?* Shout Factory, 2006.

Gaye, Marvin. *What's Going On?* Motown Records, 1971.

Marley, Bob, and the Wailers, *Burnin'.* Tuff Gong/Island, 1973.

Neville, Cyril. *Brand New Blues.* M.C. Records, 2009.

Ozomatli, *Ozomatli.* Almo Sounds, 1998.

Patterson, Sunni. *Porch Prophesies.* New Orleans, 2006.

———. *Words of Power.* New Orleans. 2005.

Shepp, Archie. *Attica Blues.* Verve, 1972.

Smith, Bessie. "Back Water Blues." Columbia, 1927.

Quetzal, *Imaginaries.* Smithsonian Folkways Recordings, 2011.

Rage Against the Machine, *Rage Against the Machine.* Epic, 1992.

FILMOGRAPHY

Bird, Stewart, Rene Lichtman, and Peter Gessner in Association with the League of Revolutionary Black Workers. *Finally Got the News*, 1970.

Chanan, Michael, and George Steinmetz. *Detroit: Ruin of a City*, 2005.

Cousino, Nicole. *Concrete and Sunshine*, 2002.

Firestone, Cynthia. *Attica*, 1974.

Grant, Joanne. *Fundi: The Story of Ella Baker*, 1981.

Hampton, Henry. *Eyes on the Prize*, 1987.

Hunt, Ashley. *Attica: Roots of Resistance*, 2001.

———. *I Won't Drown on that Levee and You Ain't Gonna' Break My Back*, 2006.

James, Davis, and Juliana Fredman. *Safety Orange*, 2001.

Lewis, Anne, and Mimi Pickering. *Anne Braden: Southern Patriot*, 2012.

Massiah, Louis. *W. E. B. Du Bois: A Biography in Four Voices*, 1995.

Index

Page numbers in italics refer to figures.

Abu-Jamal, Mumia, 92–93, *96*
African Blood Brotherhood, 74
agricultural workers, 31–32, 48–49
Alcatraz Federal Penitentiary (California), 87–88, 90
Alexander, Michelle, 8
Ali, Bilal, 141
Althusser, Louis, 68
Amnesty International, 89
Angola State Penitentiary (Louisiana), 117–18
anticommunism, 22, 26, 28, 31–33, 36, 49–50, 148–49
apartheid, 3, 94, 162–63n36. *See also* spatial apartheid
Aptheker, Bettina, 76
Aron, Ralph, 88
Attica (documentary), 70, *84*
Attica prison uprising (1971), 4, 13, 19, 67, 152; Attica Liberation Faction, 78; "Attica Manifesto," 68, 69; Bloody Monday (September 13, 1971), 70–71; and cultural production, 73–86; and legitimating state violence, 72, 79–80, 84; media coverage of, 73–74; and neoliberalism, 72–73, 79–82, 91–94; revolt, 69–70

Baker, General Gordon, 45, 54–55, 61

Baldwin, James, 3, 6, 11–13, 23, 40–42, 68, 146–47; *Fire Next Time, The,* 12; with King, *36; No Name in the Street,* 1–2, 12, 40, 146
Ballard, Florence, 52
Bambara, Toni Cade, 24
Barkley, Elliot James L.D., 68–69; in *Attica* documentary, 70
Barry, Dan, 126
Bass, Charlotta, 29–30, 35
Beck, Charlie, 142
Benjamin, Walter, 99, 119
Black Panther Party, 41–42, 75–79, 93, 130
Black Power movement, 7, 36, 38, 54
#BlackLivesMatter, 148, 151–52
Blackwater, 123
Blanco, Kathleen, 116
Blasi, Gary, 141
Blyden, Herbert X., 78
Boden, Paul, 145
Boggs, Grace Lee, 45
Boggs, James, 45
Braden, Anne, 94
Bradley, Tom, 98, 100, 106
Bratton, William, 136, 142
Briseño, Theodore, 99
broken windows policing, 136, 142, 151
Brown, Michael (FEMA director), 121

Brown, Michael (Ferguson shooting victim), 148
Brown v. Board of Education, 7
Burnham, Margaret, 76
Burton, Deborah, 143
Bush, George W., 98, 100–101, 106, 117, 121–23, 125
Butler, Peter, 78

Cain, Burl, 118
Calderón, Felipe, 125
Canizaro, Joseph, 124
capitalism, 27, 43–50, 53–56, 61–64, 69, 76, 80, 92, 104–106, 114, 119, 122, 144, 147–48; capitalist restructuring, 4–5, 11, 16–17, 53, 100, 104, 107, 114, 158n11; global capitalism, 3, 10, 64, 66, 72, 135, 137, 155–56n2; Jim Crow capitalism, 2–3, 5–6, 9–10, 22, 25, 29, 31, 129, 155–56n2; racial capitalism, 2, 9–10, 16–17, 22–25, 28, 33, 36–37, 42, 43, 61, 64, 124–25, 129, 138, 140–41, 151, 155–56n2, 158n11
carceral state, 3–18, 146–49; and abandoned communities, 130; and anticipatory criminalization, 126; and Attica prison uprising, 73, 82–83; and the carceral city, 58, 65, 101–108, 122–23; carceral Keynesianism, 81; and Chilean coup (1973), 72; Cold War roots of, 8–9, 22–23, 27–42, 148–49; expansion of, 3, 81–85, 88, 94, 147; and Kerner Commission, 58; and neoliberal turn, 5, 15–17, 66, 72, 81–82, 93, 122, 137; and racialization, 4, 15, 116–17, 148; and racism, 9–13, 65, 81–83, 85, 92; and Second Reconstruction, 22–27, 39–40, 42; and super-maximum-security prison system, 73, 86, 90–97; and Vietnam War, 42
Carlson, Norman, 90
Castle, Oretha, 132
Chaney, James, 93
Chenille, Joseph, 121–22
Chilean coup (1973), 19, 72, 81, 197n42
Christianson, Scott, 94
Christopher, Warren, 98
Chuck D, 99, 118, 134; at Operation Skid Row music festival, *135*
City University of New York (CUNY), 82
Civil Rights Act (1964), 39
Civil Rights Congress (CRC), 27–31
civil rights movement, 5–12, 22; civil rights activists, 13, 25, 32–33, 40, 93–94, 132,

142; "collapse" of, 6–7, 38; and Congress of Industrial Organizations, 48; and counterinsurgent ideology, 47, 50–53, 72, 90, 96; and Detroit rebellion, 47–53; and labor, 22–23, 113, 151; and neoliberalism, 81, 93–94; "post-civil rights era," 7–8, 147; and revanchism, 82, 93; and U.S. cities, 35–40; and Watts uprising, 23, 32–35, 38, 41. *See also* long civil rights movement; Second Reconstruction
Clark, John, 87
Clark, Ramsey, 52
Clarke, John, 14, 44, 147
class struggle, 2, 5, 13, 17, 24–25, 43–51, 61–63, 66, 76, 80–83, 102–110, 118, 149, 156n5, 163n37
Clinton, William Jefferson, 106–107
Clutchette, John, 76
Cockrel, Kenneth, 45, 62–63
Cold War: and anticommunism, 28, 31–33, 36, 49–50, 149; and carceral state, 8–9, 22–23, 27–42, 148–49; and criminalization, 11, 13, 15, 42, 84, 103–108; and countersubversive ideology, 11, 13, 31–33, 50, 58, 152; and incarceration rates, 22–23; and neoliberalism, 8, 16, 148; and racial liberalism, 7–9, 15, 31, 33, 38–40, 49–51, 56–58, 148; and Reaganism, 93–94; and security, 8–9, 12–13, 18–19, 23, 27, 31–33, 35, 38–41, 49–50, 53, 56–58
color-blind discourse, 5, 8, 11, 16, 104, 137, 139–40
common sense, 6, 9–10, 16–20, 38, 61–62, 90, 120, 146–47, 151–52, 159–60n17, 161n27; carceral, 90, 92–93, 105–106; defined, 16; and poverty, 57–58; and prison unrest, 78, 81, 82, 85–86; and race, 28, 45, 100; and Reaganism, 93; and security narrative, 122; and social wage, 133; and super-maximum-security prisons, 90; and torture, 96; and urban militarization, 35
Communist Party, 28, 31, 34, 41, 74, 76. *See also* anticommunism
Congress of Racial Equality (CORE), 41, 45, 51
Congress of Industrial Organizations (CIO), 25, 28, 30, 48–49, 62–63
conjuncture, 20, 42, 78; and Black freedom movement, 2, 74; and consent and coercion, 27; conjunctural analysis, 14–16, 137–38, 141, 147–52;

conjunctural interventionist work, 47; 17–19, 47, 62, 65–67, 78, 85, 91–92, 102, 130

Cortez, Jayne: "National Security," 83–85

counterinsurgency, 4–6, 9–13, 15–19; and Attica prison uprising, 71–73, 76–80; and Black freedom movement, 41–42; "carceral counterinsurgency," 1, 159–60n17; and civil rights movement, 47, 50–53, 72, 90, 96; definition of counterinsurgency missions, 103; and Detroit rebellion, 47–48, 52–56, 61–67; insurgency dialectic, 6, 15, 23, 62–63, 103; and Kerner Commission, 58; and long civil rights movement, 9–10, 18–19; and Los Angeles uprising, 104–108; and mass criminalization, 11, 17, 84; and mass incarceration, 96; and prison reform, 90–92; and revanchism, 12, 72, 79–83; and security discourse, 82–97; urban counterinsurgency, 103–104; and Vietnam War, 38

Counter-Insurgency Field Manual (U.S. Army and Marine Corps), 103

countersubversive ideology, 11, 13, 31–33, 38, 49–50, 58

Crawley, Flip, 78

criminalization, 15, 117–20; anticipatory, 126; and countersubversive ideology, 11, 42, 84, 103–108; and crisis management, 101, 117–18; and Detroit rebellion, 52, 55–56; Du Bois on, 27; of dissent, 45, 49; and gentrification, 141–42; legitimating, 64–66; and Los Angeles, 28–29; and neoliberalism, 4, 6, 10, 113; and policy, 141; and Red Scare, 31; and revanchism, 10; of worker self-activity, 61; of working class sectors, 78, 81–82, 86, 107–108, 113; See also mass criminalization

Critcher, Chas, 14, 44, 147

Cullors, Patrisse, 151–52

cultural production, 11–12, 32, 46–47, 61, 67; and Detroit rebellion, 59–67; and Hurricane Katrina, 126–33; and Los Angeles uprising, 108–115; and prison uprisings, 73–78, 83–85. See also expressive culture

Davis, Angela Y., 11, 13, 76–78, 91–92, 147; Abolition Democracy, 12; If They Come in the Morning, 76–77; "Policing the Crisis Today" address, 147–48; portrait of, 77

Davis, Mike, 103–104

Dayan, Colin, 96–97

de la Rocha, Zach, 113–14. See also Rage Against the Machine

death row, 92–93

Detroit, Michigan, 94, 104, 118; and Black freedom movement, 43–44; and Civil Rights Congress (CRC), 28–31; and DRUM, 19, 44–45, 54, 59, 61; labor strikes, 13 (see also Detroit rebellion). See also League of Revolutionary Black Workers

Detroit rebellion (1967), 4, 19, 44–46, 151, 152; and Black freedom movement, 43–44; and Cold War racial liberalism, 56–58; and cultural production, 59–67; and Fordism, 47–52; inciting incident, 52; Johnson's response to, 51–53, 56–57, 101; revolt, 52–56

Deukmejian, George, 95–96

dialiectics of insurgency and counterinsurgency, 6, 15, 23, 62–63, 103, 155–56n2

Dirksen, Everett, 87

Dirty Dozen Brass Band, 118–20

Dodge Revolutionary Union Movement (DRUM), 19, 44–45, 54, 59, 61

Donner, Frank, 56–58

Drumgo, Fleeta, 76

Du, Soon Ja, 99

Du Bois, W. E. B., 11, 23–26, 26, 27, 29–31, 46–47, 148; "Behold the Land" address, 25; Black Reconstruction in America, 24–25, 62, 147; one hundredth birthday celebration, 35–36, 36

Dunayevskaya, Raya, 45

Dunbar, Walter, 71

Edland, John, 71

Egyptian Lover, 134

Eldon Avenue Revolutionary Movement, 45

Espada, Martín, 102, 110

Eve, Arthur O., 79

expressive culture, 2, 5, 12, 24, 52, 102, 108, 113, 132, 156–57n5, 197n46; and Black freedom movement, 29, 42, 63, 146; and conjunctural analysis, 148; and Hurricane Katrina, 127, 129; and Marxist theory, 18, 45, 74, 85; and metaleptic definitions of events, 11–12, 163n37; and moral economy, 109; and social visions, 12, 43–44, 128, 144–45, 150, 173n2; and urban social movements, 118–19. See also cultural production; poetry of social movements

Fast, Howard, 25
FBI, 33, 58, 94, 98; COINTELPRO, 41
Federal Bureau of Prisons, 86–90, 94
Federal Emergency Management Agency
    (FEMA), 121
Ferguson uprising, 147–48, 151–52
Finally Got the News (film), 44, 46, 62–67
finance capitalists, 95, 139
financial crisis of 2008, 20, 147
Firestone, Cinda, 70, 84
Flores, Quetzal, 113. *See also* Quetzal
Ford, Gerald, 81
Ford, Henry, 47–48. *See also* Fordism
Ford Revolutionary Union Movement, 45.
    See also League of Revolutionary Black
    Workers
Fordism, 9, 47–51, 62–63
Foucault, Michel, 83–84
Fourteenth Amendment, 97, 127, 128
free trade, 107, 125
Freedom Summer, 93
Freestyle Fellowship, 134
Frye, Marquette, 21. *See also* Watts
    insurrection (1965)

Gates, Daryl, 41, 98–99, 104
Gaye, Marvin: *What's Going On?* 43, 116,
    118–20
Gelinas, Nicole, 123
gentrification, 20, 120, 124, 137, 142–43,
    145
Georgakas, Dan, 52, 65
Gilmore, Ruth Wilson, 10, 101
Giuliani, Rudolph, 136
Glaberman, Martin, 45, 48, 55
global capitalism, 3, 10, 64, 66, 72, 135,
    137, 155–56n2
globalization, 10, 96, 104, 113, 119
Goodman, Andrew, 93
González, Martha 113
Gordy, Berry, 52
Gottschalk, Marie, 7, 8
Graham, Shirley, 26
Gramsci, Antonio, 13–16, 47, 76, 149;
    Prison Notebooks, 1, 2, 13–14
Great Depression, 24–25, 28, 34, 42, 66,
    99, 135
Griffin, Shana, 133

Hackworth, David H., 97, 102–103
Hall, Stuart, 2, 14–16, 20, 44, 72, 135,
    147–48, 149–50, 152–53; at Trafalgar
    Square, *149*
Halliburton, 123–24

Hamilton, Cynthia, 105
Hamlin, Mike, 45, 47, 51, 62
"Hands Up, Don't Shoot," 148
Haney, Craig, 96
Harding, Vincent, 40, 59
Harlins, Latasha, 99
Harper, Stephen, 125
Harris, William "Beaver," 85
Harvey, David, 11, 81
hegemony, 8, 10, 27, 38, 67, 103;
    counterhegemony, 17, 113, 151; crisis
    of, 2–4, 11, 13–15, 18–19, 43–45, 49,
    52–53, 55, 58, 72–73, 80, 108, 148,
    155–56n2
hip-hop, 99, 134–35
Holliday, George, 98
homelessness, 3, 16, 19–20, 105–106, 120,
    135, 142–45, 150–51
Hoover, J. Edgar, 33, 58
Horne, Gerald, 33
housing, 32, 40, 50, 55, 62, 105, 120, 124,
    129; in Los Angeles, 34–35, 105,
    134–45; in New Orleans, 120, 124, 129;
    public housing, 32, 105, 120, 124, 129,
    137, 141, 144, 147
Huggins, Ericka, 76
hunger strikes, 76, 88
Hunton, Alphaeus, 30, 35–36
Hurricane Katrina, 4, 19, 150–51; context
    and circumstances, 116–26; and cultural
    production, 126–33; media coverage,
    120–23; and militarization, 119,
    122–24, 126, 130; and People's
    Hurricane Relief Fund (PHRF), 129
Husock, Howard, 138, 139

ideology, 13. 30, 36, 39, 42, 58, 68, 148,
    153; and broken windows policing,
    136–37; and capitalism, 5–6, 8–9, 11,
    44–45, 58; and the carceral city,
    102–106, 109; and conjunctural
    analysis, 14; and criminalization of
    dissent, 13, 15; and cultural production,
    19, 84–85, 119; and "hearts and minds"
    battle, 6, 16; and mass criminalization,
    5–6, 142; and neoliberal security
    regimes, 16–17, 23, 64, 67, 90–92,
    122–23, 126, 140–43; and organized
    labor, 49–50; and politics of significa-
    tion, 2, 18, 84, 119; and prison
    uprisings, 73, 78, 84; of privatization,
    106, 120, 124, 137; and racism, 2, 4,
    23, 28, 64, 82, 109, 122, 136–37; and
    segregation, 49; and social welfare

reform, 107; and torture, 90–91, 96; of whiteness, 33, 50, 122. *See also* neoliberalism; revanchism
Ingram, James, 79
Insurrection Act (1807), 52, 101, 117, 121
insurrection of poetic knowledges, 17–18, 165n60. *See also* poetry of social movements
International Monetary Fund, 104

Jackson, Alphonso, 124
Jackson, Esther Cooper, 25, 35
Jackson, George, 75–77, 85; memorial service program for, 75
James, C. L. R., 31, 45, 47, 129
jazz, 85
Jefferson, Tony, 14, 44, 147, 152
Jim Crow era and policies, 1–3, 5–6, 8–10, 22–29, 39–40, 48, 53, 129, 132, 155–56n2
John Birch Society, 33
Johnson, Lyndon B., 38, 51, 52–53, 56–57, 101
Johnson-Forest Tendency, 45
Jones, Clarence, 79
Jones, Claudia, 31, 148
Jones, Gary, 121–22
Jones-El, Carl, 78
Jordan, June, 11, 102, 108–109, 114
Jung, Moon-Ho, 129

Kaplan, Amy, 122
Katrina. *See* Hurricane Katrina
Katz, Cindi, 124
Kelling, George, 136, 142
Kent State shootings, 72
Kerner, Otto, 57
Kerner Commission, 19, 45, 57–59, 80
Keve, Paul W., 85, 87
Keynesianism, 81
Kid Frost, 134
King, Martin Luther, Jr., 11, 32, 35–36, 134, 149; assassination of, 40, 59, 60; with Baldwin, 36; and Watts, 21–22, 34; *Where Do We Go from Here: Chaos or Community?* 38–40
King, Rodney, 97, 98–99, 109
Ku Klux Klan, 27, 38, 93
Kunstler, William, 79, 85

LaVette, Bettye, 118–19
League of Revolutionary Black Workers, 13, 19, 44–45, 54; *Finally Got the News,* 44, 46, 62–67; *Inner City Voice,* 46, 60, 61, 66
Leavenworth federal penitentiary (Kansas), 86, 88; Special Operations Response Team, 88–89
Letten, Jim, 122
Lombard, Rudy, 132
long civil rights movement, 2, 5–7, 9–12, 15, 18–20, 138, 143–51, 156n3; and Cold War countersubversion, 27–32; and counterinsurgency, 9–10, 18–19, 159n16; and crisis of legitimacy, 5–6; and Detroit rebellion, 51; and evolving skill, 2, 6; and Los Angeles uprising, 99; and neoliberalism, 81, 107; and Watts insurrection, 23, 35, 40. *See also* civil rights movement
Los Angeles, California. *See* Los Angeles uprising (1992); Skid Row (Los Angeles); Watts insurrection (1965)
Los Angeles Community Action Network (LA CAN), 134, 143–45; *Community Connection* (newspaper), 144
Los Angeles Police Department (LAPD), 28–29, 33–34, 41, 97, 98–99, 101, 109, 136, 142, 145
Los Angeles uprising (1992), 4, 19; context of, 99–102; and cultural production, 108–115; inciting incident, 98–99; and LAPD, 98–99, 101, 109; as Low Intensity Conflict (LIC), 102–103; media coverage, 101, 103; and race and class struggle, 102–108; and Rebuild L.A. coalition, 106
Los Lobos, 113
Lott, Frank, 78

Malcolm X, 34, 73, 78, 130–31
Manhattan Institute, 136, 139–40, 142
Marable, Manning, 34
Marion federal penitentiary (Illinois), 4, 85–92, 95–96, 188n50; Marion Prisoners' Rights Project, 89
"Marionization" of prisons, 92–93
Marley, Bob, 108–109
Marx, Karl, 18, 45, 55, 62, 146, 178n40
Marxism, 19, 24, 45, 51, 63, 69, 74–78, 85, 148
mass criminalization: and crisis management, 55, 101, 118, 138; and counterinsurgent ideology, 11, 17, 84; and gentrification, 141–42; and homelessness, 141–42; and Hurricane Katrina, 118; legitimating, 6, 10, 19, 66, 151;

mass criminalization *(continued)*
and long civil rights movement, 15, 147;
and neoliberalism, 4–6, 10, 147; and
revanchism, 10, 82; and urban design,
103–104. *See also* criminalization
mass incarceration, 104–105, 112–14,
118–20, 127, 130, 132, 149–53; and
counterinsurgent ideology, 96; in
homelessness, 20, 134–45; legitimating,
9, 16; and Jim Crow, 8; origins of, 8;
and racism, 8; and revanchism, 10; and
super-max prisons, 73
McCarthyism, 31, 47
McKay, Claude, 73–75
McKay, Robert, 80
McKay Commission, 80
Medusa, 134
Mendenhall, Jim, 110
metaleptic definitions of events, 11–12
Milson, Mary, 52
Mitford, Jessica, 30, 31, 82
Moore, Howard, 76
moral panic, 10, 15, 49, 54, 71–72, 82,
106, 111, 119–20, 126, 142, 148,
164n48
Morello, Tom, 113. *See also* Rage Against
the Machine
Moten, Fred, 136
Moynihan, Daniel Patrick, 56
Moynihan Report, 45, 58
Murakawa, Naomi, 7
Murray, Melissa, 121–22
music: *banda,* 111; blues, 118–19, 150–51;
Chuck D, 99, 118, 134; Dirty Dozen
Brass Band, 118–20; Gaye, Marvin, 43,
116, 118–20; hip-hop, 99, 134–35; jazz,
85; Marley, Bob, 108–109; Neville,
Cyril, 150–51; Operation Skid Row
music festival, 134–36; Ozomatli, 102,
113–14; Quetzal, 102, 113; Rage
Against the Machine, 102, 113–14; *son
jarocho,* 113
Myrdal, Gunnar, 57

Nagin, Ray, 121, 124
Nation of Islam (NOI), 33–34, 41
National Association for the Advancement
of Colored People (NAACP), 29, 41, 45,
51
national security state: and Black radical
activists, 31, 41; and countersubversive
ideology, 11, 13, 31–33, 38, 49–50, 58;
and domestic enemies, 117, 122, 130;
King on, 38–39; and long civil rights
movement, 15; and racism, 23, 27; and
Reaganism, 94. *See also* carceral state;
counterinsurgency
neoliberal racial and security regimes, 5–6,
9, 17, 120, 132–33, 158n12; defined, 4;
and prison expansion, 5; and Reaganism, 73, 93. *See also* national security
state; racial regimes
neoliberalism: and civil rights movement,
81, 93–94, 107; and criminalization, 4,
6, 10, 113; economic restructuring, 5,
93–95, 119, 147; "end of," 150,
214n17; globalization, 10, 96, 104, 113,
119; and mass criminalization, 4–6, 10,
147; neoliberal turn, 5, 15–17, 66, 72,
81–82, 93, 122, 137; origins of, 72; and
prison uprising, 72–73, 79–82, 91–94;
racial capitalism, 2, 9–10, 16–17,
22–25, 28, 33, 36–37, 42, 43, 61, 64,
124–25, 129, 138, 140–41, 151,
155–56n2, 158n11
Neville, Cyril: *Brand New Blues,* 150–51
New Orleans, Louisiana. *See* Hurricane
Katrina
New York City, 19, 28, 78, 81
New York state, neoliberalization of 72–73,
79–82, 91–94, 186n35. *See also* Attica
prison uprising (1971)
Newton, Huey P., 41, 76
Nixon, Richard, 8, 32, 68, 72
Noble, Donald, 78
North American Free Trade Agreement
(NAFTA), 107

O'Dell, Jack, 34–35
Oliver, Pamela, 7
Operation Hammer (Los Angeles), 104
Orleans Parish Prison, 117, 121
Ortiz, Juan "Fi," 79
Oswald, Russell, 69, 71, 79, 82
Ozomatli, 102, 113–14

Paris, Jose "G.I.," 79
Parker, William, 33
Patterson, Sunni, 127–31, 133; cover of
Porch Prophesies, 128; "We Know This
Place," 127–29; "We Made It," 130–31
Patterson, William L., 27–30, 35; with Paul
Robeson, 30
Peace Information Center, 26
Peck, Jamie, 81
Pelican Bay State Prison (California),
95–96
Peltier, Leonard, 85, 88

Personal Responsibility and Work Opportunity Act (1996), 107

poetry: of Cortez, Jayne, 83–85; of McKay, Claude, 73–75; of Patterson, Sunni, 127–33

poetry of social movements, 11, 17–18, 23, 119–20, 133, 146–47; and Detroit rebellion, 59–67; and Hurricane Katrina, 126–33; and Los Angeles uprising, 108–115; and prison uprisings, 73–78, 83–85. *See also* Baldwin, James; Davis, Angela Y.; Du Bois, W. E. B.; Jordan, June; King, Martin Luther, Jr.; music; poetry; Robeson, Paul

policing, 2, 7–9, 22, 28; aggressive policing, 1, 9, 34, 42, 134, 104, 142; authoritarian policing, 33, 142–43; Baldwin on, 1–2; broken windows policing, 136, 142, 151; expansion of, 10, 15–16, 19, 56, 66, 81, 93, 104–107; militarized policing, 9–11, 17, 35, 106–107, 117, 126, 130, 144; "Policing the Crisis Today" address (Davis), 147–48; police violence, 7, 12, 17, 21–22, 27–29, 31, 41, 45, 51–52, 59, 61, 89, 98–99, 114, 118, 151–52; and racism, 98, 104–105, 147–49; of racialized space, 29–30, 102, 139; and revanchism, 125, 136, 142; SWAT teams, 41; urban policing, 20, 34, 41–42, 50, 53–54, 98, 103–106, 123, 126, 135–37, 142–43. *See also* Los Angeles Police Department (LAPD)

Policing the Crisis: Mugging, the State, and Law and Order (Hall, Critcher, Jefferson, Clarke, Roberts), 14–15, 44, 147–48, 152

polyculturalism, 108, 110–11, 113–14, 152, 196n40

Poulantzas, Nicos, 92

poverty, 1, 3, 7–8, 16–20, 24, 32–35, 66, 82, 93–94, 101–107, 135–36, 139–42, 149–50, 152, 210n29; and Black freedom movement, 39–40; and capitalist restructuring, 16; criminalization of, 120, 141; "culture of poverty," 56–58; demonization of, 103; and economic crises, 66, 150; feminization of, 113, 120; and Hurricane Katrina, 118, 121–22, 125, 130, 132–33; and police repression, 50; and politics of scale, 136; Poor People's Campaign, 40, 59; and racism, 22–23, 35; and Reagan, 40; and social wage, 152; and spatial apartheid, 139; and subprime mortgage crisis, 138–40

Powell, Laurence, 99

Prashad, Vijay, 100

prison expansion, 3–5, 10, 13, 16, 27, 91, 94–96, 101, 105–107, 114, 147

prison reform, 90

prison uprisings, 13, 78, 80, 86, 151. *See also* Attica prison uprising (1971)

privatization, 106, 120, 124, 137

Public Enemy, 99, 134–35; "Shut 'Em Down," 134–36; *See also* Chuck D

public transportation, 34–35, 39

Pulido, Laura, 141

Quetzal, 102, 113

racial regimes, 4–6, 12, 23–25, 133, 141, 144. *See also* Jim Crow era and policies; neoliberal racial and security regimes

racialization, 4–5, 7–8, 10, 15, 20, 22–23, 29, 64–66, 119–20, 122–23, 133, 135, 137–39, 142, 152; and carceral state, 4, 15, 116–17, 148; and crisis management, 38, 42, 58, 100–103, 116–17; and poverty, 28, 101, 113; state violence, 71, 80–81, 84, 94

racism, 2, 4–6, 8–13, 19–20, 22–24, 97–102, 108–10, 118, 131–32, 137; antiracism, 5, 10, 13, 24–25, 30–32, 44, 49, 51, 56, 61, 101–102, 111, 114, 118, 129, 144, 150–53; and capitalism, 44–46, 50–51, 54; and carceral state, 9–13, 65, 81–83, 85, 92; and Cold War countersubversion, 28–31, 33, 35, 50; and color-blind discourse, 5, 8, 11, 16, 104, 137, 139–40; and prisons, 75–76, 80–82, 92; and revanchism, 12–13; and state violence, 71–72, 97, 98–99; and urban uprisings, 57, 59, 61, 64–66; and U.S. cities, 35–36, 38–39

Rage Against the Machine, 102, 113–14

Rainey, Ma, 118

Ramírez, José, 102, 111–13; *Prisoners, 112; Quebradita en Sur Central, 111–12, 112*

Randels, Jim, 131–32

Ransby, Barbara, 120

Rawick, George, 45, 55

Reagan, Ronald, 19, 23, 32, 40–41, 68, 93–94, 141; and Black Panther Party, 41, 93; Reagan era, 8, 103; Reaganism, 19, 73, 93–94, 107, 186n35, 191n77

Reconstruction, 12, 117; and rise of Jim Crow, 24–25; *See also* Second Reconstruction

Red Scare, 22, 26, 31, 148–49. *See also* anticommunism
Reuther, Walter, 49–50
revanchism, 16, 20, 40, 120, 133, 150–51, 159–60n17; and counterinsurgency, 72, 79–83; and crisis management, 12–13, 20, 85, 136, 140; defined, 9–10; and policing, 125, 136, 142; and racism, 12–13; and Reaganism, 41, 92–97; and war on terror, 96; and welfare reform, 107. *See also* common sense
Rivera, Diego, 63
Roberts, Brian, 14, 44, 147
Robeson, Paul, 11, 25, 29–31, 35, 148–49; presentation of "We Charge Genocide" petition, 30
Rockefeller, Nelson, 71–72, 79, 81–84
Rodney, Walter, 59
Rodríguez, Russell, 113
Rolnik, Raquel, 145
Romney, George, 52
Ross, Diana, 52
Rostow, W. W., 53

Safer Cities Initiative (SCI), 136, 142, 144
Salinas, Raúl, 86
Sands, Bobby, 88
Schell, Jonathan, 69
Schwerner, Michael, 93
Shepp, Archie: *Attica Blues*, 85
Seale, Bobby, 41, 73, 79
Second Reconstruction, 2, 22, 23–25, 39–40, 42, 48, 62, 66, 86, 120, 156n4. *See also* Civil Rights Movement
Skid Row (Los Angeles), 4, 105; and homelessness, 20, 140–43, 151; Operation Skid Row music festival, 134–36
Sloop, John, 91
Smith, Bessie, 118
Smith, Frank "Big Black," 76
Smith, Jerome, 132
Smith, Neil, 9, 81–82
social wage, 32, 38–39, 61, 66, 129, 133; advocacy, 20, 25–26, 59, 61, 144–45, 149–53; defined, 4, 18; and Keynesian economics, 81; and neoliberal public policy, 4, 8, 10, 13, 18, 82, 93–94, 107, 119, 120, 137, 159n14; and Reaganism, 93–94
socialist movements, 13, 22, 25, 29–33, 41–42, 45–47, 56, 61–63, 74–77, 147, 152–53

social visions, 12, 31, 43–44, 70, 81, 128, 144–45, 150, 173n2
Soledad prison, 75–76
solitary confinement, 86, 91, 95–97
Soni, Saket, 125
South End (Wayne State University campus paper), 46, 61
Southern Christian Leadership Conference (SCLC), 41
spatial apartheid, 139
Special Weapons and Tactics (SWAT), 41
Stokes, Ronald, 34
Student Non-Violent Coordinating Committee, 45
Suber, Malcolm, 126, 129
subprime mortgage crisis, 138–39, 145
super-maximum-security prison system, 19, 73, 86, 90–97
Surkin, Marvin, 52, 65
Sutherland, JJ, 126

Taft-Hartley Act (1947), 49
Tang, Eric, 100
Temptations, 118
Till, Emmett, 131
torture, 86, 89–91, 96–97
Trotsky, Leon, 74, 78
Truman, Harry, 31, 49

Ueberroth, Peter, 106
United Auto Workers (UAW), 45, 49–50, 61
United Nations, 30–31, 89, 143, 145
urban restructuring, 9, 41, 65, 97, 103–104, 106, 115, 119, 133, 186n35, 194n21

Vietnam War, 1, 35, 37, 38, 41–43, 52–54, 59, 63, 65, 72, 85, 118
Villaraigosa, Antonio, 136
Violent Crime Control and Law Enforcement Act (1994), 106–107
Vitale, Alex, 143
Voting Rights Act (1965), 21, 39

Wacquant, Loïc, 6–7
Wagner, David, 140
Ward, David, 90–91
Watson, John, 43–45, 46, 51, 61–64
Watts insurrection (1965), 3–4, 12, 18–19, 53–54, 140, 150, 151, 152; and Black freedom movement, 32–35; inciting incident, 21; Johnson's statement on, 38; and King, 21–22, 34; and Reagan, 23, 32, 40–4; and unemployment, 34; and Vietnam War, 35, 37, 38, 41–43

Wayne State University, 44, 45–46, 61
welfare programs, 8, 107, 122–23;
    "warfare-welfare," 168n16
Werlich, Thomas, 90–91
Western Regional Advocacy Project
    (WRAP), 144–45
White, Pete, 140, 144
Wicker, Tom, 57, 79
Widener, Daniel, 114
Williams, Rhonda, 143
Wilson, Pete, 100, 106, 107

Wind, Timothy, 99
Winton, Richard, 143
Wonder, Stevie, 118
Woods, Clyde, 118, 124, 133
Wright, Richard, 118

ya Salaam, Kalamu, 131–32
Yee, Min S., 23
Yo-Yo, 134

Zapatista uprising, 113

AMERICAN CROSSROADS

Edited by Earl Lewis, George Lipsitz, George Sánchez, Dana Takagi, Laura Briggs, and Nikhil Pal Singh

1. *Border Matters: Remapping American Cultural Studies*, by José David Saldívar

2. *The White Scourge: Mexicans, Blacks, and Poor Whites in Texas Cotton Culture*, by Neil Foley

3. *Indians in the Making: Ethnic Relations and Indian Identities around Puget Sound*, by Alexandra Harmon

4. *Aztlán and Viet Nam: Chicano and Chicana Experiences of the War*, edited by George Mariscal

5. *Immigration and the Political Economy of Home: West Indian Brooklyn and American Indian Minneapolis, 1945–1992*, by Rachel Buff

6. *Epic Encounters: Culture, Media, and U.S. Interests in the Middle East since 1945*, by Melani McAlister

7. *Contagious Divides: Epidemics and Race in San Francisco's Chinatown*, by Nayan Shah

8. *Japanese American Celebration and Conflict: A History of Ethnic Identity and Festival, 1934–1990*, by Lon Kurashige

9. *American Sensations: Class, Empire, and the Production of Popular Culture*, by Shelley Streeby

10. *Colored White: Transcending the Racial Past*, by David R. Roediger

11. *Reproducing Empire: Race, Sex, Science, and U.S. Imperialism in Puerto Rico*, by Laura Briggs

12. *meXicana Encounters: The Making of Social Identities on the Borderlands*, by Rosa Linda Fregoso

13. *Popular Culture in the Age of White Flight: Fear and Fantasy in Suburban Los Angeles*, by Eric Avila

14. *Ties That Bind: The Story of an Afro-Cherokee Family in Slavery and Freedom*, by Tiya Miles

15. *Cultural Moves: African Americans and the Politics of Representation*, by Herman S. Gray

16. *Emancipation Betrayed: The Hidden History of Black Organizing and White Violence in Florida from Reconstruction to the Bloody Election of 1920*, by Paul Ortiz

17. *Eugenic Nation: Faults and Frontiers of Better Breeding in Modern America*, by Alexandra Stern

18. *Audiotopia: Music, Race, and America*, by Josh Kun

19. *Black, Brown, Yellow, and Left: Radical Activism in Los Angeles*, by Laura Pulido

20. *Fit to Be Citizens? Public Health and Race in Los Angeles, 1879–1939*, by Natalia Molina

21. *Golden Gulag: Prisons, Surplus, Crisis, and Opposition in Globalizing California*, by Ruth Wilson Gilmore

22. *Proud to Be an Okie: Cultural Politics, Country Music, and Migration to Southern California*, by Peter La Chapelle

23. *Playing America's Game: Baseball, Latinos, and the Color Line*, by Adrian Burgos, Jr.

24. *The Power of the Zoot: Youth Culture and Resistance during World War II*, by Luis Alvarez

25. *Guantánamo: A Working-Class History between Empire and Revolution*, by Jana K. Lipman

26. *Between Arab and White: Race and Ethnicity in the Early Syrian-American Diaspora*, by Sarah M. A. Gualtieri

27. *Mean Streets: Chicago Youths and the Everyday Struggle for Empowerment in the Multiracial City, 1908–1969*, by Andrew J. Diamond

28. *In Sight of America: Photography and the Development of U.S. Immigration Policy*, by Anna Pegler-Gordon

29. *Migra! A History of the U.S. Border Patrol*, by Kelly Lytle Hernández

30. *Racial Propositions: Ballot Initiatives and the Making of Postwar California*, by Daniel Martinez HoSang

31. *Stranger Intimacy: Contesting Race, Sexuality, and the Law in the North American West*, by Nayan Shah

32. *The Nicest Kids in Town:* American Bandstand, *Rock 'n' Roll, and the Struggle for Civil Rights in 1950s Philadelphia*, by Matthew F. Delmont

33. *Jack Johnson, Rebel Sojourner: Boxing in the Shadow of the Global Color Line*, by Theresa Rundstedler

34. *Pacific Connections: The Making of the US-Canadian Borderlands*, by Kornel Chang

35. *States of Delinquency: Race and Science in the Making of California's Juvenile Justice System*, by Miroslava Chávez-García

36. *Spaces of Conflict, Sounds of Solidarity: Music, Race, and Spatial Entitlement in Los Angeles*, by Gaye Theresa Johnson

37. *Covert Capital: Landscapes of Denial and the Making of U.S. Empire in the Suburbs of Northern Virginia*, by Andrew Friedman

38. *How Race Is Made in America: Immigration, Citizenship, and the Historical Power of Racial Scripts*, by Natalia Molina

39. *We Sell Drugs: The Alchemy of US Empire*, by Suzanna Reiss

40. *Abrazando el Espíritu: Bracero Families Confront the US-Mexico Border*, by Ana Elizabeth Rosas

41. *Houston Bound: Culture and Color in a Jim Crow City*, by Tyina L. Steptoe

42. *Why Busing Failed: Race, Media, and the National Resistance to School Desegregation*, by Matthew F. Delmont

43. *Incarcerating the Crisis: Freedom Struggles and the Rise of the Neoliberal State*, by Jordan T. Camp